The Taxation of Fees for Technical Services on the Basis of Article 12A UN Model Convention

Series on International Taxation

VOLUME 86

Series Editors

Introduction & Contents

The Series on International Taxation deals with a wide variety of topics in the global tax arena. The authors include many of the field's leading experts as well as talented newcomers. Their expert views and incisive commentary have proven highly useful to practitioners and academics alike.

Objective

The volumes published in this series are aimed at offering high-quality analytical information and practical solutions to international tax practitioners.

Readership

Practitioners, academics and policy makers in international tax law.

Frequency of Publication

2-3 new volumes published each year.

The titles published in this series are listed at the end of this volume.

The Taxation of Fees for Technical Services on the Basis of Article 12A UN Model Convention

David Orzechowski-Zölzer

Wolters Kluwer

About the Author

Dr David Orzechowski-Zölzer, BSc (WU) works in the field of international taxation at the Ministry of Finance of Austria. He is responsible for tax treaty negotiations and represents Austria in several OECD and EU working parties. David is also a former teaching and research associate of the Institute for Austrian and International Tax Law of Vienna University of Economics and Business (WU). Moreover, he completed an internship at the United Nations, Financing for Development Office, Tax Cooperation Unit in New York. In addition to giving various lectures in Austria and abroad, David Orzechowski-Zölzer has published a variety of papers and articles on national, European, and international tax law.

Preface

The inclusion of Article 12A to the UN Model 2017 has led to a significant change to the policy question of how to allocate taxing rights over fees for technical services under a bilateral tax treaty. Until this change, model tax treaty rules as enshrined in the UN Model allowed for source taxation of business services only if a company established a permanent establishment or a fixed base in the source state. African countries, however, started to include provisions on the taxation of fees for technical services, as broadly defined in Article 12A(3) UN Model, as early as the 1970s in their respective bilateral tax treaties. In addition, several Asian and South American countries negotiated the inclusion of a provision for fees for technical services already before Article 12A was introduced to the UN Model.

As state practice on the taxation of fees for technical services has been highly heterogeneous since the 1970s, the UN Tax Committee intended to increase tax certainty through the inclusion of an article on the taxation of fees for technical services as a basis for tax treaty negotiations. In this respect, non-OECD members increasingly make use of Article 12A UN Model as a basis for tax treaty negotiations. This is reflected in the rising number of tax treaties concluded with a provision similar to Article 12A UN Model. In addition, the UN Tax Committee discusses the consideration of an option for a more multilateralized form of implementing Article 12A to the tax treaty network of UN Member States as this article may be potentially relevant to taxing the digitalized and globalized economy. Therefore, it is of utmost importance to provide tax lawyers, persons working in academia, tax officials and students with guiding literature on the interpretation of Article 12A UN Model.

The objective of this publication is to contribute to the current academic discourse on Article 12A UN Model and examine the definition of the scope of technical services in comparison to ordinary (non technical) services and the differentiation between Article 12A and the other allocation rules of the UN Model. In this respect, the author also analyses whether the term 'technical' is sufficiently defined in the Commentaries to the UN Model or whether it shall be ascribed a different meaning to increase legal certainty for tax administrations and taxpayers.

The author textually analyses the provisions of Article 12A UN Model in the context of their historical evolution, object and purpose and the systematic context in which Article 12A UN Model is embedded. The focus lies on the interpretation of the concept of technical services by examining the historical evolution of Article 12 OECD and UN Models. The historical evolution of the definition of these services in tax treaty practice will be discussed in the context of an objective of inclusion of a provision on fees for technical services to the UN Model. In this regard, especially tax treaties of selected African countries shall be examined as these countries were the earliest adopters of the concept of fees for technical services into their tax treaty network. This is often overlooked within the academic debate that primarily focuses on the fees for technical services provisions included in tax treaties concluded by India. The book also provides an overview of already existing literature and jurisprudence published on the topic of fees for technical services, e.g., on country practices in Brazil or India; jurisprudence from different countries; and historical documents of international organizations.

Acknowledgements

Research on the topic of the book began during my employment as a teaching and research associate at the Institute for Austrian and International Tax Law at WU Vienna. During my time as a teaching and research associate, I was provided several opportunities to gain knowledge in the field of international taxation and more concretely to deepen my knowledge of the relevance of the UN Model in the field of international taxation. In this respect, I would like to thank Mr *Michael Lennard* for giving me the possibility to complete an internship at the Financing for Development Office in NYC in 2017 and entrusting me with drafting a Secretariat Paper on 'The taxation of fees for technical, managerial and consultancy services in the digital economy with respect to art 12A of the 2017 UN Model' and subsequently presenting the paper at the fifteenth session of the UN Tax Committee in Geneva.

My deepest gratitude goes to Prof. *Michael Lang* and Prof. *Karoline Spies* who supervised my PhD thesis and consistently provided invaluable support, both intellectually and personally, during this long journey.

I would also like to thank my (former) colleagues and friends for their everlasting support in whatever manner. Thank you, Mrs *Christina Grassl*, Ms *Rita Julien*, Mr *Martin Reiter*, Mrs *Laura Weiss-Turcan*, Mr *Pedro Schoueri*, Ms *Selina Siller*, Mr *Jan Szczepanski*, Ms *Stephanie Zolles*, and last but not least Mrs *Viktoria Wöhrer* who gave me the idea on writing a PhD thesis on Article 12A UN Model. The publication has also been made possible because of your support.

I would like to express my love and a very special thank you to my parents and my wife. You are my anchor in a stormy sea.

Finally, to my dearest daughter who at the time of publication should have seen the light of this world: I cannot wait to finally hold you in my arms and to spend the rest of my life with you!

CHAPTER 1

Introduction

A BACKGROUND

Article 12A of the United Nations Model Double Taxation Convention (UN Model)[1] on the taxation of fees for technical services was introduced to the UN Model in the sixteenth session of the Committee of Experts on International Cooperation in Tax Matters (UN Tax Committee) in May 2018 in New York. Provisions on the taxation of fees for technical services, as broadly defined in Article 12A(3) UN Model, were already found in tax treaties concluded by African countries as early as the 1970s. In addition, several Asian and South American countries commonly negotiated the inclusion of a provision of fees for technical services much earlier than when Article 12A was introduced to the UN Model. One of the goals with its introduction was to increase legal certainty for the treatment of fees for technical and other similar services under the UN Model for both taxpayers and tax authorities. Provisions on the taxation of these fees have become increasingly popular among developing countries, and the number of treaties including such clauses is expected to increase despite the plausible negotiation resistance from some treaty partners.

Article 12A UN Model grants a taxing right for fees for technical services to the residence state of the recipient of the fees. However, such fees may also be taxed in the state in which they arise (source state). According to Article 12A(5) UN Model, fees for these types of services arise in the residence state of the payer of the fees. However, if the payer is not a resident of a contracting state, the fees will still be deemed to arise in a contracting state if they are borne by a PE or fixed base situated therein. The place of performance is not decisive for the definition of the source state which means that fees for technical services might also arise if services are performed in a third state, e.g., through means of distance communication. This is a change of paradigm for the

1. References to the UN Model relate to its most recent updated version of 2021 if not otherwise indicated.

allocation of taxing rights for active business income as, prior to the inclusion of Article 12A to the UN Model 2017, granting taxing rights to the source state was made conditional solely upon the existence of a PE or a fixed base therein.

B STATE OF THE FIELD

The taxation of cross-border services with respect to developing countries was already intensively discussed in international tax literature even before the introduction of Article 12A to the UN Model 2017. A monograph written by *Fernando Souza de Man* and titled 'Taxation of Services in Treaties between Developed and Developing Countries' was published in 2016. It focuses on legal and economic theories supporting residence and source taxation. The author provides an overview of the historical documents concerning the model conventions that were drafted by the League of Nations, the OECD, and the United Nations. With the objective to more effectively grasp the perspective of developing countries, the author also analysed the respective situations of Brazil and India with reference to the taxation of services based on domestic legislation and their tax treaty practices.

In another publication titled 'Taxing Cross-Border Services: Current Worldwide Practices and the Need for Change',[2] the connecting factors used in the OECD and UN Models for the allocation of taxing rights with respect to cross-border services are examined. In addition, the author determines whether the connecting factors to allocate taxing rights are acceptable to both tax administrations and taxpayers in the context of economic allegiance and limiting base erosion. The publication also analyses to what extent the connecting factors are adopted in the OECD and UN Models. This is followed by establishing a comprehensive study of provisions ascertained in existing double taxation conventions for a selected number of states.

Research has also been conducted by *Wijnen/de Goede/Alessi*[3] who – at the request of the UN Tax Committee – examined provisions on the taxation of services in more than 1,500 tax treaties concluded between 1 April 1997 and 1 January 2011. The authors deduced that examined provisions covering the taxation of fees for technical services can basically be distinguished between 'included services' – provisions[4] within the respective royalty's article of the DTC – and an autonomous provision on the taxation of fees for technical services.[5]

2. Angharad Miller, *Taxing Cross-Border Services: Current Worldwide Practices and the Need for Change* vol. 37 (IBFD 2015).
3. Wim Wijnen, Jan de Goede & Andrea Alessi, *The Treatment of Services in Tax Treaties*, 66 BIT 27-38 (2012) DOI: 10.59403/2wm7nvs.
4. Wijnen, de Goede & Alessi, *supra* n. 3, at 32: The authors emphasized the similarities of the examined provisions with Article 12 (royalties and fees for included services) of the DTC India-USA (1989).
5. Committee of Experts on International Cooperation in Tax Matters, *The taxation of fees for technical, managerial and consultancy services in the digital economy with respect to Art 12A of the 2017 UN Model*, E/C.18/2017/CRP.23, https://financing.desa.un.org/sites/default/files/2023-03/15STM_CRP23_Technical-Services.pdf (accessed 6 January 2024), at para. 25; *see also* David Orzechowski, *Die abkommensrechtliche Relevanz von Art 12A UN-MA 2017*, ÖStZ 638, 640 (2019).

The academic debate on the change in the allocation of taxing rights for technical services as defined by Article 12A UN Model is occurring more frequently. The first attempts were made to compare the concept of technical services in literature[6] with already existing concepts of the UN Model. As Article 12A UN Model will be increasingly important as the basis for treaty negotiations in the future, further examination of the interpretation and differentiation is needed of this recently introduced distributive rule in comparison to other distributive rules. The objective of this publication is to contribute to the current academic discourse on Article 12A UN Model and examine the definition of the scope of technical services in comparison to ordinary (non-technical) services and the differentiation between Article 12A and other allocation rules of the UN Model. The focus lies on the interpretation of the concept of technical services by examining the historical evolution of Article 12 OECD and UN Models. The historical evolution of the definition of these services in tax treaty practice will be discussed in the context of an objective of inclusion of a provision on fees for them to the UN Model. In this regard, especially tax treaties of selected African countries shall be examined as these countries were the earliest adopters of the concept of fees for technical services into their tax treaty network. This is often overlooked within the academic debate that primarily focuses on the fees for technical services provisions included in tax treaties concluded by India.

C PROBLEM FORMULATION, RESEARCH QUESTION AND METHODOLOGY

Article 12A UN Model leads to a significant change in the allocation of taxing rights of income from technical, managerial, and consultancy services. Until the inclusion of Article 12A to the UN Model 2017, rules of tax treaty law written down in the UN Model only allowed for source taxation of business services if a company established a permanent establishment or a fixed base in the source state. The UN Model establishes – in this respect – high (time) thresholds that must be met for a permanent establishment to exist in the source state. Article 12A UN Model, however, neither requires a certain threshold nor a physical nexus to the source state. In this regard, Article 12A is very similar to Article 12 UN Model as both of them principally refer to the residence state of the payer as the state in which the fees or payments arise.[7] The definition of the source state is not the only similarity of Articles 12 and 12A UN Model. Although technical services are generally excluded from the scope of Article 12 of the OECD and

6. Brian J. Arnold, *The Taxation of Income from Services under Tax Treaties: Cleaning Up the Mess*, 65 BIT 59-68 (2011); Andrés Báez Moreno, *The Taxation of Technical Services under the United Nations Model Double Taxation Convention: A Rushed – Yet Appropriate – Proposal for (Developing) Countries?*, 7 WTJ 267-328 (2015) DOI: 10.59403/3r66pf1; Franziska Sixdorf & Sebastian Leitsch, *Taxation of Technical Services under the New Article 12A of the UN Model – Improved Taxation or a Step in the Wrong Direction*, 57 ET 234-242 (2017) DOI: 10.59403/dj51tg; Monique T. Malan, *New Article 12A of the UN Model Regarding Fees for Technical Services: Ahead of Its Time or a Step Too Far?*, 73 BIT 58-68 (2019) DOI: 10.59403/249c1x8.
7. *See also* Article 12(5) and Article 12A(5) UN Model for further explanations.

UN Models,[8] several countries are of the opinion that the phrase 'information concerning industrial, commercial or scientific experience'[9] also encompasses certain technical services. Other countries tax 'fees for technical services' by extending the scope of Article 12 to services that are ancillary and subsidiary to the application or enjoyment of a right, property, or information for which a royalty payment is received. This also occurs if the services make technical knowledge, experience, skill, know-how, or processes available;[10] or if they consist of the development and transfer of a technical plan or technical design.[11] Besides the inclusion of technical services in the scope of Articles 7 and 12, some states consider that technical services might also fall within the scope of Article 14[12] or 21[13] of the UN Model.

In this respect, the research question arises:

> Can the concept of 'technical services' be differentiated from ordinary (non-technical) services covered by other allocation rules of the UN Model?

This element of the research is based on an examination of possible interpretations. The process of interpretation needs to take into account the ordinary meaning of the terms, the context in which they are embedded, the object and purpose of their inclusion, and the historical developments.

The intention of this publication is to textually analyse the provisions of Article 12A UN Model in the context of its historical evolution and its object and purpose.

The aims of the inclusion of a provision on the taxation of fees for technical services are manifold. The uncertainty on the treatment of the fees was one of the reasons why the UN Tax Committee has dealt with issues on the taxation of income from technical, managerial, consultancy, and other similar services within the UN

8. *See*, however, para. 11.6 of the Commentary on Article 12 OECD Model 2017 and its reproduction in para. 12 of the Commentary on Article 12 UN Model 2017: The Commentaries to the OECD Model allow for taxation of technical services that are of an ancillary and unimportant nature to the supply of know-how. These services are often referred to as 'technical assistance'.
9. *See* Article 12(3) UN Model 2021.
10. So-called make-available clauses. The inclusion of such clauses in tax treaties can be seen as a non-acceptance of the more restrictive changes to the OECD Model 1977 in which, in comparison to its preceding version of 1963, payments for know-how and technical assistance (show-how) were no longer included: Adolfo M. Jiménez, *Article 12 OECD/UN Models: Definition of Royalties and 'Overlapping' between Articles 7, 12 and 13*, in: Guglielmo Maisto (ed.), *Taxation of Intellectual Property under Domestic Law, EU Law and Tax Treaties* vol. 16, at 132 et seq. (IBFD 2018).
11. *See also* the proposed alternative ('fees for included services') of the inclusion of Article 12A of the UN Model 2017 in the Commentary to Article 12 UN Model 2017: Committee of Experts on International Cooperation in Tax Matters, *Proposed addition to the Commentary on Article 12: Fees for Included Services*, E/C.18/2016/CRP.1 Annex 3, https://www.un.org/esa/ffd/wp-content/uploads/2016/10/12STM_CRP1_Services.pdf (accessed 6 January 2024), at 2 et seq.
12. *See, e.g.*, Sergio A. Rocha, *Brazil's Treaty Policy*, 71 BIT 333, 338 (2017) DOI: 10.59403/1ye6yy1, with further references.
13. *See* with reference to the approach taken by the Brazil tax authorities before 2014: Leonardo Freitas de Moraes e Castro & Alexandre Luiz Moraes do Rêgo Monteiro, *Qualification of Services under Double Tax Treaties in Brazil: Open Issues after Iberdrola Case*, 45 Intertax 54, 54 et seq. (2017) DOI: 10.54648/taxi2017005.

Model since 2008.[14] Other purposes for the inclusion of Article 12A to the UN Model 2017 that must be examined are base erosion through the deductibility of expenses in relation to the provision of technical services (base-erosion principle), the substantial economic involvement of service providers in a state without a PE or fixed base,[15] and the unequal tax treatment of resident and non-resident service providers.[16]

The use of the term 'technical' in the description of Article 12A 'Fees for technical services' in contrast to 'service fees' stems from the fact that, from a historical perspective, these types of fees are closely connected to those that are related to the provision of intellectual property.[17] Therefore, one of the keystones of research shall be the historical perspective of Article 12A with respect to the evolution of Article 12 OECD and UN Models. Additionally, an analysis will be performed of the tax treaties of selected developing African countries[18] which shall supplement already existing work on this issue, e.g., by *Wijnen/de Goede/Alessi*.[19] That work examines provisions on the taxation of services in more than 1,500 tax treaties concluded between 1 April 1997 and 1 January 2011 at the request of the UN Tax Committee. Another is *Miller* in which a survey of treaty practices is conducted including approximately 2,500 tax treaties in force as of August 2012.[20]

The publication will also provide an overview of already existing literature and jurisprudence published on the topic of fees for technical services, e.g., on country practices in Brazil[21] or India;[22] jurisprudence from different countries;[23] and historical documents of international organizations.

14. *See, e.g.*, Committee of Experts on International Cooperation in Tax Matters, *Report on the fifth session*, E/C.18/2009/6 (SUPP), https://financing.desa.un.org/sites/default/files/2023-03/N1021312_0.pdf (accessed 6 January 2024), 7.
15. The BEPS Action 1 Final Report 'Addressing the Tax Challenges of the Digital Economy' (2015) by the OECD did not recommend a withholding tax on services that are rendered by means of remote communication channels but did recognize that states are free to include such provisions in their respective tax treaties as a safeguard against Base Erosion and Profit Shifting; *see, e.g.*, para. 2 of the Commentary on Article 12A UN Model 2021.
16. *See, e.g.*, para. 11 of the Commentary on Article 12A UN Model 2021.
17. *See* Miller, *supra* n. 2, at 253.
18. Provisions on the taxation of fees for technical services as broadly defined in Article 12A(3) UN Model are already found in tax treaties concluded by African countries as of the early 1970s; *see, e.g.*, Article 14 DTC Denmark-Kenya (1972) or Article 14 DTC Kenya-Norway (1972): Both Articles refer to 'Management or professional fees', which per definition also cover fees for technical services as defined in Article 12A(3) UN Model ('...any services of a managerial, technical,...or consultancy nature.').
19. Wijnen, de Goede & Alessi, *supra* n. 3, at 27.
20. *See* Miller, *supra* n. 2, at 131 et seq.
21. *See, e.g.*, Freitas de Moraes e Castro & Moraes do Rego Monteiro, *supra* n. 13, at 54; Rocha, *supra* n. 12, at 333.
22. *See, e.g.*, Sanjay Sanghvi & Ritu Shaktawat, *Taxation of Fees for Technical Services and Royalties*, 18 APTB 452-459 (2012) DOI: 10.59403/16qnc5m; Manoj K. Singh, *Conflict of Source versus Residence-Based Taxation in India with Reference to Fees for Technical Service*, 44 Intertax 525-537 (2016) DOI: 10.54648/taxi2016042.
23. *See, e.g.*, ITAT Mumbai, *Mark & Spencer Reliance India v. Department of Income Tax*, I.T.A. No. 905/M/2012 (4 September 2013); Federal Court of Australia, *Tech Mahindra Ltd. v. Australian Tax Office*, FCA 1082 (7 October 2015); Tribunal Regional Federal da 3ª Região, *Euroclear Bank N.V. v. Fazenda Nacional*, Appeal No. 0015571-05.2012.4.03.6100 / SP (19 May 2016).

CHAPTER 2

Theoretical Background on the Interpretation of Tax Treaties and the UN Model

A INTRODUCTION

Most legal systems adhere to a dualist approach which results in the view that national and international law are two separate and independent legal systems.[24] When following this approach, treaties must be interpreted independently from national law as treaty law is intrinsically its own legal system.[25] However, as tax treaties do not constitute new taxing rights, treaty law provisions are clearly linked to the national law of the contracting states. It may appear that tax treaty provisions may be interpreted differently by the contracting states due to dissimilar tax systems and their definitions of a certain type of income or a term; this could plausibly lead to double taxation or non-taxation. Such a result would be contrary to the object and purpose of a tax treaty and should therefore be avoided. Hence, tax treaties shall be interpreted on the basis of common rules and – as much as possible – independently from the domestic law of the contracting states. This leads to the primacy of treaty autonomous interpretation, i.e., an interpretation that is independent of national concepts and terminologies.[26]

Rules regarding treaty interpretation of treaties concluded between states are found in Articles 31-33 Vienna Convention on the Law of Treaties (VCLT). They generally include accepted principles constituting a component of international customary law and are therefore also applicable to treaties concluded by states that have

24. Matthias Herdegen, *Völkerrecht*, 173 et seq. (17th ed., Beck 2018).
25. Christiane Anger & Thorsten Wagemann, *Zweifelsfragen bei der Auslegung von Doppelbesteuerungsabkommen*, 17 IStR 611, 611 (2014).
26. Oliver Dörr & Kirsten Schmalenbach, *Vienna Convention on the Law of Treaties – A Commentary*, Article 31, m.no. 31 (Springer 2012).

not ratified the VCLT.[27] According to Article 2(1)(a) VCLT, treaties are international agreements concluded between states in written form that are independent of their designation. Therefore, those concluded between states in written form are within the scope of the definition of Article 2(1)(a) VCLT and, as a result, are governed by the rules of interpretation of Articles 31-33 VCLT. The final objective of the rules of interpretation is to ascertain the 'true meaning' of a treaty by using elements originating from an objective and a subjective approach to interpretation.[28]

This chapter will provide an overview of the relevance of the UN Model on tax treaty interpretation in the context of the rules of treaty interpretation enshrined in Articles 31-33 VCLT. For this purpose, recourse will also be made to literature on interpretative aspects referring to the Commentaries to the OECD Model as the UN Model adopts – in most parts – the provisions of the OECD Model and its corresponding commentaries, and both the OECD and the UN Model are similarly employed by states as a template for tax treaty negotiations.

B THE UN MODEL AND ITS RELEVANCE FOR THE TAX TREATY NETWORK

i The UN Model as Template for Tax Treaty Negotiations

Although the OECD is an assertive leader in the field of elimination of double taxation in the context of international cross-border business, the UN Model's influence as a template for tax treaty negotiations has increased in recent years. This is especially true for tax treaties concluded between developed and developing countries as, from the perspective of developing countries, imbalanced income flows between states are not taken into account in the OECD Model.[29] In particular, developing countries often seek to preserve greater sovereignty of source taxing rights in order to foster economic development.[30]

States often refer to the provisions of the UN Model as a basis for tax treaty negotiations.[31] The interpretation of the articles of the UN Model is established by the corresponding Commentaries to the UN Model. The commentaries are also considered by states when interpreting the provisions of a tax treaty that are based on the UN Model.

Modifications to the UN Model and its commentaries have an almost immediate effect on the global tax treaty network as – based on the dynamic interpretation – they

27. *Ibid.*, at m.no. 6 and Nathalie Bravo, *Interpreting Tax Treaties in the Light of Reservations and Opt-Ins under the Multilateral Instrument*, 74 BIT 231, 234 (2020) DOI: 10.59403/3swd2rw.
28. Anthony Aust, *Modern Treaty Law and Practice*, 206 (3rd ed., Cambridge University Press 2013).
29. *See* paras 3 and 32 of the Introduction to the UN Model 2001.
30. *See* Laura Turcan, *The OECD Update 2014 and Its Impact on the UN Model Convention*, in: Michael Lang et al. (eds), *The OECD-Model-Convention and its Update 2014* vol. 90, 207, 209 (Linde Verlag 2015).
31. *See* Wim Wijnen & Jan de Goede, *The UN Model in Practice 1997–2013*, 68 BIT 118, 118 et seq. (2014) DOI: 10.59403/1r99e4n.

may result in changes to the interpretation of tax treaty provisions[32] and changes in the allocation of taxing rights. This is especially true for DTCs concluded by developing countries.[33]

ii The UN Model and Its Commentaries Hereto

1 History and Legal Basis of the UN Model and the UN Tax Committee

The history of the UN Model and its commentaries originated in 1967. On the basis of Article 68 of the UN Charter, the Economic and Social Council of the United Nations (ECOSOC)[34] decided to request the secretary general to set up an ad hoc working group in 1967 with the task of exploring 'ways and means for facilitating the conclusion of tax treaties between developed and developing countries'.[35]

The Ad Hoc Group of Experts on Tax Treaties between Developed and Developing Countries that was finally established by the secretary general following the resolution by the ECOSOC consisted of independent experts and persons from tax administrations from both developed and developing countries. As requested by the ECOSOC, the Group of Experts was nominated by the respective governments but acted in their own personal capacity.[36]

Between 1968 and 1977, seven meetings were held by the Ad Hoc Group of Experts to complete the formulation of guidelines for the negotiation of bilateral tax treaties between developed and developing countries.[37] Their objective was to provide technical assistance to states with respect to the conclusion of tax treaties.[38] Although the Group of Eminent Persons recommended the establishment of guidelines for the conclusion of a worldwide multilateral tax agreement, the Ad Hoc Group of Experts explicated that the objective of these guidelines was to lay a foundation for an appropriate bilateral tax treaty network.[39]

The Secretary-General shared the position of the Ad Hoc Group of Experts in the first regular session of the ECOSOC in 1978, i.e., to complete a model bilateral convention that could be used as a template for tax treaty negotiations between developed and developing countries.[40]

---

32. *See* for a more thorough analysis: Chapter 2.B.ii.3.a.
33. *See* David Orzechowski, *The Relevance of the Commentaries on the OECD and UN Models for the Interpretation of the UN Model*, in: Michael Lang et al. (eds), *The UN Model Convention and Its Relevance for the Global Tax Treaty Network* vol. 7, 1, 1 et seq. (IBFD 2017).
34. The ECOSOC is one of the principal organs of the United Nations together with the General Assembly, the Security Council, the Trusteeship Council, the International Court of Justice, and the Secretariat.
35. Economic and Social Council, *Tax treaties between developed and developing countries*, Resolution 1273 (XLIII), E/4429 (4 August 1967).
36. *See* para. 7 of the Introduction to the UN Model 2017.
37. *See* para. 5 of the Introduction to the UN Model 2001.
38. Economic and Social Council, *Tax treaties between developed and developing countries*, Resolution 1541 (XLIX), E/4904 (30 July 1970).
39. *See* paras 6 et seq. of the Introduction to the UN Model 2001.
40. *See* para. 8 of the Introduction to the UN Model 2001.

At its eighth meeting in 1979, the Council requested the Ad Hoc Group of Experts to complete its work on the formulation of a draft model convention.[41]

Its articles were based on the guidelines produced by the Ad Hoc Group of Experts. Their views on the articles were reflected in the respective commentaries to the articles.[42] In preparing the articles, the drafters of the model convention heavily relied on the 1977 OECD Model and also included the views taken by OECD Member States on certain articles of the OECD Model.[43]

The Ad Hoc Group of Experts adopted the final text of the model convention at its eighth meeting in Geneva in 1979. The adoption of the final text led to the publication of the 1980 United Nations Model Double Taxation Convention between Developed and Developing Countries.[44]

The ECOSOC renamed the 'Ad Hoc Group of Experts on Tax Treaties between Developed and Developing Countries' to the 'Ad Hoc Group of Experts on International Cooperation in Tax Matters' in 1980. This was due to recognizing the need to also place emphasis on non-tax treaty-related matters of international cooperation.[45]

Since 2004, the Ad Hoc Group of Experts on International Cooperation in Tax Matters has been known as the UN Tax Committee. It keeps the United Nations Model Double Taxation Convention between Developed and Developing Countries under review and updates it as necessary.[46] Members of the UN Tax Committee act in their personal capacity and not as official government representatives even though they are appointed by the secretary general after nomination by their respective governments.[47] In the past, attempts were made to strengthen the status of the UN Tax Committee by upgrading it to an intergovernmental organization consisting of official government representatives. This issue was discussed at the UN's Third International Conference on Financing Development that was held in Addis Ababa in July 2015.[48] Although that plan was finally rejected, consensus was achieved for increasing the effectiveness of the work of the UN Tax Committee by increasing the number of meetings to two annually comprising four working days per meeting.[49] The UN Tax Committee, as a subsidiary body of the ECOSOC,[50] is responsible for drafting the UN Model and its

41. Based on Article 62(3) of the UN Charter, the ECOSOC 'may prepare draft conventions for submission to the General Assembly, with respect to matters falling within its competence'; *see also* para. 8 of the Introduction to the UN Model 2001.
42. *See* para. 9 of the Introduction to the UN Model 2001.
43. *See* para. 9 of the Introduction to the UN Model 2001.
44. *See* Orzechowski, *supra* n. 33, at 5.
45. *See* para. 8 of the Introduction to the UN Model 2017.
46. Economic and Social Council, *Committee of Experts on International Cooperation in Tax Matters*, Resolution 2004/69, E/2004/L.60 (11 November 2004).
47. Brian J. Arnold, *Tax Treaty News*, 65 BIT 118, 119 (2011) DOI: 10.59403/n69e31.
48. United Nations General Assembly, *Revised Draft of the Outcome Documents*, https://www.un.org/esa/ffd//wp-content/uploads/2015/05/revised-draft-outcome.pdf (accessed 17 November 2022), para. 25.
49. United Nations General Assembly, *Addis Ababa Action Agenda of the Third International Conference on Financing for Development (Addis Ababa Action Agenda)*, A/RES/69/313, https://www.un.org/en/development/desa/population/migration/generalassembly/docs/globalcompact/A_RES_69_313.pdf (accessed 5 January 2024).
50. Armando L. Yaffar & Michael Lennard, *An Introduction to the Updated UN Model (2011)*, 66 BIT 590, 591 (2012) DOI: 10.59403/3w64s5w.

commentaries. However, substantial work on the issues that are most relevant for developing countries is being done by the several different subcommittees that were founded by the UN Tax Committee itself[51] as it heavily relies on papers that are written and other work that is conducted by the subcommittees.[52]

The subcommittees have different mandates. In this respect, they play a significant role in issues related to the UN Model as it is mandated to consider, make recommendations, and provide proposed drafting for its next update.[53] The objective of the UN Model is to support developing countries in making informed sovereign decisions with respect to tax policy and administration.[54] The provisions of the UN Model are not legally binding and shall not be understood as a formal recommendation by the UN which is contrary to the OECD Model.[55] The UN Model is a recommendation of a group of experts not formally representing their governments although they express knowledge of national practices and concerns.[56] It neither inhibits governments in their tax treaty negotiations nor does it prevent them from deviating from the UN Model's provisions and negotiating provisions that are more suitable to them.

In the near future, however, the role of the UN in the field of international taxation may increase significantly, both from a political and a legal perspective. This is due to the approval of a resolution on the 'Promotion of inclusive and effective international tax cooperation at the United Nations' by the Second Committee (Economic and Financial) of the General Assembly on 22 December 2023.[57] Based on the approved resolution, an ad hoc intergovernmental committee consisting of not more than twenty geographically and among genders evenly distributed members will be established with the aim to work on a draft framework convention on international tax cooperation, i.e., a binding multilateral instrument establishing a general system

51. *See* for a list of subcommittees established in the past: Department of Economic and Social Affairs, *Subcommittees*, https://financing.desa.un.org/subcommittees (accessed 29 December 2023).
52. Yaffar & Lennard, *supra* n. 50, at 591.
53. *See* https://www.un.org/development/desa/financing/what-we-do/ECOSOC/tax-committee/subcommittees/model-tax-convention (accessed 2 July 2022).
54. Yaffar & Lennard, *supra* n. 50, at 590.
55. *See* Committee of Experts on International Cooperation in Tax Matters, *Revision of the Commentaries of the UN Model Convention – Note by the coordinator of the working group on Commentaries of the UN Model Convention*, E/C.18/2008/CRP.1, https://www.un.org/esa/ffd/wp-content/uploads/2014/10/4STM_EC18_2008_CRP1.pdf (accessed 6 January 2024), 3; Committee of Experts on International Cooperation in Tax Matters, *Note by the Secretariat on 'Country Observations, Reservations and Positions: Relevance to the United Nations Model Tax Convention'*, E/C.18/2011/4, https://digitallibrary.un.org/record/709968?ln=en (accessed 6 January 2024), para. 9; para. 12 of the Introduction to the UN Model 2017.
56. *See* Committee of Experts on International Cooperation in Tax Matters, *supra* n. 55, at para. 9.
57. *See* United Nations General Assembly, *Macroeconomic policy questions: promotion of inclusive and effective international cooperation on tax matters at the United Nations: Resolution adopted by the General Assembly on 22 December 2023*, A/RES/78/230, https://financing.desa.un.org/sites/default/files/2024-01/A.RES_.78.230_English.pdf (accessed 5 January 2024) and United Nations General Assembly, *Nigeria: revised draft resolution, Promotion of inclusive and effective international tax cooperation at the United Nations*, A/C.2/78/L.18/Rev.1 (15 November 2023).

(framework) for international tax governance between states.[58] The establishment of a framework convention was one of three options considered by the Secretary-General in the report which served as a basis for the aforementioned resolution.[59] The other two options were 1) the elaboration on a legally binding multilateral tax convention and 2) a legally non-binding commitment to a framework for international tax cooperation. While the draft resolution of 11 October 2023 proposed the elaboration on a legally binding multilateral tax convention, it was most probably due to a compromise achieved in non-public meetings between the African Group and developed countries that the legally less binding instrument of a general framework for international tax cooperation was chosen for future consideration. The adoption of the aforementioned draft resolution is nevertheless a significant achievement by developing countries to increase their political visibility in the decision-making processes of international tax policy initiatives.

2 *Relevance of the OECD Model and Its Commentaries as Basis for the UN Model and Its Commentaries*

a *Adoption and Absence of Passages from the Commentaries of the OECD Model and the Partially Autonomous Formulation of the Commentaries of the UN Model*

To a great extent, the UN Model reproduces the provisions of the OECD Model and its corresponding commentaries.[60] Main differences are ascertained in the provisions on the taxation of international shipping and air transport, passive income, fees for technical services, income from automated digital services, independent personal services, pensions and social security payments, other income, mutual agreement procedure, as well as the provisions on permanent establishments.

Neither the OECD nor the UN Model and its corresponding commentaries have a legally binding effect.[61] Nevertheless, it became common state practice among OECD and UN Member States to adopt the articles of the OECD and UN Models into their tax treaties.[62] In doing so, states often decide to include a specific provision in their

58. United Nations General Assembly, *Macroeconomic policy questions: promotion of inclusive and effective international cooperation on tax matters at the United Nations – Report of the Second Committee*, A/78/459/Add.8, https://digitallibrary.un.org/record/4030104?v=pdf, 7 (accessed 20 March 2024).
59. United Nations General Assembly, *Promotion of inclusive and effective international tax cooperation at the United Nations: Report of the Secretary-General*, A/78/235, https://digitallibrary.un.org/record/4019360?v=pdf (accessed 20 March 2024), paras 55 et seq.
60. Committee of Experts on International Cooperation in Tax Matters, *supra* n. 55, at 3.
61. *See* with respect to the legal status of the OECD Commentaries: OECD, *Recommendation of the OECD Council concerning the Model Tax Convention on Income and on Capital*, C (97)195/Final, https://one.oecd.org/document/C(97)195/FINAL/en/pdf (accessed 5 January 2024); Martti Nieminen, *OECD Commentaries under the Vienna Rules*, 18 (Tampereen Yliopisto 2014); Orzechowski, *supra* n. 33, at 2 et seq.
62. *See, e.g.*, the Preamble of the Technical Explanation to the 1985 Treaty and 2002 Protocol of the DTC Sri Lanka-United States (2003) and no. 1.4 of the Explanatory Memorandum to the DTC Australia-Israel (2019).

protocol to legally emphasize the importance of the corresponding commentaries as guidelines for the interpretation of the articles taken from the OECD and UN Models in their bilateral relationship with their treaty partner.[63]

The Commentaries to the OECD Model are often quoted by the UN Model. In doing so, the Commentaries to the UN Model use an amended text or include additions to reflect any relevant differences.[64] These are usually placed in square brackets, such as the retention of the 'fixed base' concept.[65] However, additions are not necessarily visible through the use of square brackets. These additions, not necessarily reflecting a relevant difference in comparison to the Commentaries to the OECD Models, are also commonly used in the Commentaries to the UN Models.

When quoting parts from the Commentaries to the OECD Model, the Commentaries to the UN Model also sometimes places entire paragraphs or parts of paragraphs in ellipses in order to indicate that these paragraphs or parts thereof are not applicable in interpreting the relevant article of the UN Model.[66] The omission of certain parts, however, does not necessarily mean that there is any disagreement with the displayed content. To ascertain whether the omission of certain parts of the Commentaries to the OECD Model is due to not being relevant for the interpretation of articles of the UN Model or is subject for future considerations, the context of the omitted parts must be considered.[67]

The omission of certain passages might also be explained on the basis of structural differences between the OECD and the UN Models, such as is the case for Article 21(1) UN Model due to the inclusion of a third paragraph in Article 21 of the UN Model.

b Dissenting Views to the OECD Model and Its Commentary and Their Influence on the UN Model and Its Commentary

Although the OECD Model is a legally non-binding recommendation adopted by the OECD Council on the basis of Article 5(b) of the Convention establishing the OECD as an international organization,[68] it still allows OECD Member States to make 'reservations' on the provisions of the OECD Model. These reservations, however, cannot be subsumed under Article 2(1)(d) VCLT as they are not made under an international legal instrument.[69]

Reservations under the OECD Model are recorded in the Commentaries to the OECD Model and are generally addressed to prospective treaty partners. By making a

63. *See, e.g.*, no. 7 of the Protocol to the DTC Austria-Cuba (2003) and no. 1 of the Protocol to the DTA Hong Kong-Mexico (2012).
64. *See* Orzechowski, *supra* n. 33, at 2 et seq.
65. *See* para. 3 of the Commentary on Article 15 UN Model 2011; para. 2 of the Commentary on article 17 UN Model 2011; Yaffar & Lennard, *supra* n. 50, at 592; para. 21 of the Introduction to the UN Model 2017.
66. *See* para. 21 of the Introduction to the UN Model 2017.
67. *See* Yaffar & Lennard, *supra* n. 50, at 592 and para. 21 of the Introduction to the UN Model 2017.
68. *See* Nieminen, *supra* n. 61, at 18 and Orzechowski, *supra* n. 33, at 2 et seq.
69. *See* Orzechowski, *supra* n. 33, at 12.

reservation to the OECD Model, Member States express the intention to not use or to only use an adapted version of a model provision with respect to prospective treaty negotiations.[70] Nevertheless, OECD Member States are not legally bound by their reservation and are free to deviate from them.[71] Besides reservations, OECD Member States also often make use of what is known as 'observations'. These are a tool to express a dissenting view on the interpretation of the articles of the OECD Model as expressed in the corresponding commentaries.[72]

Reservations and observations to the OECD commentaries are instruments solely available to OECD Member States. However, non-OECD Member States are also free to express dissenting views on the OECD Model and its corresponding commentaries which are referred to as 'positions'.[73] Non-OECD Member States' positions can take the form of either reservations[74] or observations.[75] However, as non-OECD Member States are not addressed by the OECD Model, it cannot necessarily be expected that these states express their dissenting view on the OECD Model and its commentaries. Therefore, caution must be used when drawing conclusions from the absence of positions of non-OECD Member States on the OECD Model and its commentaries.[76]

The UN Tax Committee has recognized that reservations, observations, and positions play a beneficial role in the interpretation and application of the OECD Model. These dissenting views, however, are not repeated in the UN Model for practical reasons.[77] The UN Tax Committee nevertheless recognizes the importance of observations to the Commentaries to the OECD Model for the interpretation of the Commentaries to the UN Model. This is especially true for those passages that are quoted and incorporated by the Commentaries to the UN Model.[78]

With respect to the UN Model and its corresponding commentaries, the concepts of reservation, observation, and position in the context of the OECD Model are not

70. *See, e.g.*, para. 117 of the Commentary on Article 1 of the OECD Model 2017: 'France, Germany, Hungary, Ireland, Luxembourg and Switzerland reserve the right not to include paragraph 3 in their conventions.'
71. David A. Ward QC, *Is There an Obligation in International Law of OECD Member Countries to Follow the Commentaries on the Model?*, in: Sjoerd Douma & Frank Engelen (eds), *The Legal Status of the OECD Commentaries*, 73, 92 et seq. (IBFD 2008).
72. *See, e.g.*, para. 25 of the Commentary on Article 4 of the OECD Model 2017: 'Chile wishes to clarify that, with respect to paragraph 8.12, entities that are not regarded as residents may also include pension funds unless expressly covered by the convention.'
73. *See, e.g.*, paras 6 and 7 of Non-Member Countries' Positions on Article 12(2) of the OECD Model 1998.
74. *See, e.g.*, para. 5 of Non-Member Countries' Positions on Article 3 of the OECD Model 2017: 'With respect to the definition of "international traffic", Bulgaria and Croatia reserve the right to extend the scope of the definition to cover road and railway transportation in bilateral conventions.'
75. *See, e.g.*, para. 9 of Non-Member Countries' Positions on Article 4 of the OECD Model 2017: 'In the opinion of Vietnam the personal relations and economic relations mentioned in paragraphs 14 and 15 of the Commentary should be separated and one given priority over the other. For Vietnam, economic relations, particularly the criterion of the country where employment is exercised, is more important to determine the country of residence for treaty purposes in the case of a dual resident individual.'
76. *See* Orzechowski, *supra* n. 33, at 15.
77. *See* para. 22 of the Introduction to the UN Model 2017.
78. *See* Committee of Experts on International Cooperation in Tax Matters, *supra* n. 55, at para. 6.

used. As pointed out in a secretariat note to the tax committee, this is due to conceptual differences between the OECD and the UN Models.[79] As the UN Tax Committee is a group of experts acting in their personal capacity and not representing formal views of the governments that have nominated them, it would not be appropriate for these experts to make reservations, observations, or positions in the OECD Model.

Therefore, the UN Model uses a different approach to make dissenting views on the UN Model and its commentaries visible. These dissenting views, i.e., known as 'minority views', are related to discussions for which no consensus has been reached by the UN Tax Committee.[80] Minority views represent the views of the experts of the UN Tax Committee and are not official government views that can be related to one specific state.

At its twenty-second session, the UN Tax Committee decided to revise paragraph 23 of the introductory part of the Commentary to the UN Model 2017 to further specify the concept of the minority view.[81] The UN Tax Committee agreed to further categorize a minority view on the proportion of present and voting members of the UN Tax Committee as 'a single member', 'a small minority of members', 'a medium-sized minority of members', and 'a large minority of members'.[82]

Minority views have little to no interpretational value. In contrast to reservations, observations and positions made in relation to the OECD Model and its commentaries, minority views cannot be ascribed to a certain Member State. As members of the UN Tax Committee act in their personal capacity and do not represent the formal views of their governments, it would – as already mentioned – also not be appropriate for them to make such official statements.

3 *Legal Relevance of the UN Model and Its Commentaries for the Tax Treaty Network*

a *General Rule of Interpretation: Article 31 VCLT*

Article 31 VCLT constitutes the general rule of interpretation of 'treaties' in the sense of Article 2(1)(a) VCLT, requiring the adoption of a textual approach.[83] According to Article 31(1) VCLT, a (tax) treaty 'shall be interpreted in good faith in accordance with the ordinary meaning given to the terms of the treaty in their context and in the light of its object and purpose'. Article 31(1) VCLT refers to the ordinary meaning of treaty terms. However, a purely literal interpretation is not intended as the ordinary meaning is to be derived from its context (systematic interpretation) and object and purpose of

79. *Ibid.*, at para. 6.
80. *See* para. 23 of the Introduction to the UN Model 2011.
81. Committee of Experts on International Cooperation in Tax Matters, *Report on the twenty-second session*, E/2021/45/Add.2-E/C.18/2021/2, https://digitallibrary.un.org/record/3930124?ln=en (accessed 6 January 2024), 9.
82. *See* for further explanations: *Ibid.*, at 9.
83. *See, e.g.*, Ulf Linderfalk & Maria Hilling, *The Use of OECD Commentaries as Interpretative Aids – The Static/Ambulatory-Approaches Debate Considered from the Perspective of International Law*, NTJ 34, 36 with further references (2015) DOI: 10.1515/ntaxj-2015-0003.

the treaty as a whole, including its preamble and annexes (teleological interpretation).[84] The ordinary meaning might also be technical, i.e., a special meaning in the context of Article 31(4) VCLT if the parties to a treaty so intend.

Article 31 VCLT also includes other relevant elements that shall be considered for treaty interpretation, i.e., preamble, annexes, agreements, or instruments made in connection with the conclusion of a treaty as part of the context,[85] and any subsequent agreements, practices, and relevant rules agreed by the parties to the treaty.[86] In this respect, it must be mentioned that the interpretation process is a uniform procedure in which all mentioned elements shall be considered. This is clarified by using the singular in the wording of the header of Article 31 VCLT.[87]

Whether and how the OECD and UN Models and their corresponding commentaries fit within the rules of Articles 31 and 32 VCLT has been highly controversial in the past.[88] The UN Model and its commentaries are – like the OECD Model and its commentaries – legally non-binding instruments under international law.

As Article 31 VCLT only applies to legally binding instruments, the UN Model and its commentaries are not within the scope of the general rule of interpretation.[89] However, when incorporating provisions of the UN Model into a tax treaty, contracting states decide to make these provisions legally binding on themselves.[90]

Several scholars opine that the OECD/UN Models and its corresponding commentaries have established an international 'tax language' and might be subsumed under either Article 31(1) or (4) VCLT as part of the ordinary or special meaning of the terms that are used.[91] If it can be established that the contracting states adopted provisions of the UN Model into their tax treaty, an interpretation in good faith[92] also

84. *See also* Article 31(2) VCLT.
85. *See* Article 31(2)(a) and (b) VCLT.
86. *See* Article 31(3)(a)-(c) VCLT.
87. *See* United Nations, *United Nations Conference on the Law of Treaties: Documents of the Conference*, A/CONF.39/11/Add.2, https://treaties.un.org/doc/source/docs/A_CONF.39_11_Add.2-E.pdf (accessed 19 January 2024), 39: 'Thus, article 27 is entitled "General rule of interpretation" in the singular, not "General rules" in the plural, because the Commission desired to emphasize that the process of interpretation is a unity and that the provisions of the article form a single, closely integrated rule.'
88. *See* John F. Avery Jones et al., *The Interpretation of Tax Treaties with Particular Reference to Article 3(2) of the OECD Model-II*, BTR 90-128 (1984); Michael Lang & Florian Brugger, *The Role of the OECD Commentary in tax treaty interpretation*, 23 Australian Tax Forum 95-108 (2008); Dietmar Gosch, *Bedeutung des OECD-Kommentars für die Auslegung des DBA Österreich-Deutschland*, SWI 505-514 (2015); Frank Engelen, *Some Observations on the Legal Status of the Commentaries on the OECD Model*, 60 BIT 105-109 (2016); Brian J. Arnold, *The Interpretation of Tax Treaties: Looking to the Future*, 75 BIT 665-672 (2021) DOI: 10.59403/3acrt4x.
89. *See* with respect to the OECD Model and its Commentary: Monica Erasmus-Koen & Sjoerd Douma, *Legal Status of the OECD Commentaries – In Search of the Holy Grail of International Tax Law*, 61 BIT 339, 346 (2007); Martti Nieminen, *Dual Role of the OECD Commentaries – Part 1*, 43 Intertax 636, 642 et seq. (2015) DOI: 10.54648/taxi2015062.
90. Evert Alkema, *The Commentaries on the OECD Model Tax Convention on Income and on Capital: Effective in Domestic Law or in Need of Alternatives?*, in: Sjoerd Douma & Frank Engelen (eds), *The Legal Status of the OECD Commentaries*, 163, 163 et seq. (IBFD 2008).
91. Steffen Lampert, *Germany*, in: Michael Lang, Pasquale Pistone, Josef Schuch & Claus Staringer (eds), The impact of the OECD and UN Model Conventions on bilateral tax treaties, 466, 468 with further references (Cambridge University Press 2012).
92. *See* Article 31(1) VCLT.

requires taking the UN Model and its commentaries into account. This is because it is only reasonable to conclude that the contracting states intended to give the treaty provisions a meaning that is in accordance with the Commentaries to the UN Model.[93] While this conclusion is easier to make, when the contracting states decide to include a provision of the UN Model that is not included in the OECD Model (e.g., Article 12A) into their tax treaty, it becomes less clear whether the contracting states intended to base the interpretation on the Commentary to the UN Model in cases in which the provision of the UN Model is identical to the OECD Model. In these cases, however, interpretational issues will only occur if the Commentaries to the UN and OECD Models substantially differ from each other which is not the case in most instances.[94]

As the UN Model and its commentaries are updated on a regular basis, the question arises of whether the commentary version available at the time of signing the treaty (static interpretation) or the most recent commentary version has to be taken into account (dynamic interpretation) in the interpretation process. In this respect, Article 31(3)(b) VCLT mentions that also subsequent practice in the application of a treaty establishing an agreement on its interpretation shall be taken into account (together with its context). As the agreement mentioned in Article 31(3)(b) VCLT does not have to be explicit,[95] subsequent changes in practice by the contracting states might also be based on changes made to the Commentary to the UN Model. The basis of such subsequent practice would then not be the Commentary itself but rather an implicit agreement between the contracting states to use the most recent commentary version of the UN Model.[96] According to *Lang*, however, commentary versions published after the conclusion of a tax treaty cannot be relevant to interpreting a previously concluded tax treaty. This is because these materials were not available to the contracting states at the time of the conclusion of the treaty and can therefore not form part of their intention.[97] In addition, it must be established that the primarily responsible tax offices conduct a certain undisputed practice, i.e., a practice that is either not disputed before courts or already confirmed by courts.[98] Such established practice is often difficult to substantiate.

93. *See* with respect to the OECD Model and its commentary: Lang & Brugger, *supra* n. 88, at 96; Álvaro de la Cueva González-Cotera & Adrián Arroyo Ataz, *Tax Treaty Interpretation: A New Beginning?*, 61 ET 60, 61 (2021) DOI: 10.59403/1719a2d.
94. *See* Orzechowski, *supra* n. 33, at 17 et seq.
95. *See* Linderfalk & Hilling, *supra* n. 83, at 46 with further references: The authors argue that the term 'agreement' in Article 31(3)(b) VCLT cannot be interpreted in a way to establish a legal obligation between the two contracting states, as – like all provisions of the VCLT – Article 31(3)(b) only applies insofar contracting states have not agreed otherwise.
96. *See*, with respect to the Commentaries to the OECD Model: Erasmus-Koch & Douma, *supra* n. 89, at 348.
97. *See* Michael Lang, *Die Auslegung von Doppelbesteuerungsabkommen als Problem der Planungssicherheit bei grenzüberschreitenden Sachverhalten*, in: Siegfried Grotherr (ed.), *Handbuch der internationalen Steuerplanung*, 1865, 1871 (3rd ed., NWB 2011); Michael Lang, *Art. 3 Abs. 2 OECD-MA und die Auslegung von Doppelbesteuerungsabkommen*, IWB 281, 286 (2011).
98. *See* Michael Lang, *Die Bedeutung des OECD-Kommentars und der Reservations, Observations und Positions für die DBA-Auslegung*, in: Jürgen Lüdicke, Rudolf Mellinghoff & Thomas Rödder (eds), *Nationale und internationale Unternehmensbesteuerung in der Rechtsordnung –*

b Supplementary Means of Interpretation: Article 32 VCLT

Irrespective of whether the UN Model and its commentaries are within the scope of the general rule of interpretation, they are at least to be considered supplementary means of interpretation in the context of Article 32 VCLT.[99] As it refers to preparatory work and circumstances of the conclusion, only materials existing before a treaty has finally been concluded can be taken into account.[100] Therefore, Commentaries to the UN Model published after the conclusion of a tax treaty cannot be subsumed under Article 32 VCLT. If it can be established that the UN Model was used as a basis for tax treaty negotiations, its accompanying commentaries may be subsumed under either 'circumstances of its conclusion'[101] or other supplementary means[102] in the sense of Article 32 VCLT.

The effect of the application of Article 32 VCLT is limited to confirming an already established meaning resulting from the application of Article 31 VCLT or determining a meaning that, after the application of Article 31 VCLT, leads to an ambiguous or obscure meaning or a manifestly absurd or unreasonable result. However, the treaty interpreter is expected to utilize all available materials to establish the true meaning of a treaty, and the VCLT does not limit the weight to be attributed to supplementary materials of a treaty. Therefore, the relevance of the Commentaries to the UN Model might be factually similar to Article 31 VCLT even if 'only' subsumed under Article 32 VCLT.[103]

Preparatory work leading to the conclusion of a treaty, such as draft versions of treaty protocols or bilaterally exchanged diplomatic notes may establish that the UN Model was used during the draft process as the basis for the wording of a tax treaty. If so, the UN Model and its commentaries would certainly be within the scope of Article 32 VCLT. In the author's opinion, however, it is also very likely that the Commentaries to the UN Model will already be used in the interpretation process to ascertain the ordinary meaning of treaty terms as referred to in Article 31(1) VCLT or the special meaning in the context of Article 31(4) VCLT, as there is no restriction in the materials used to interpret such meaning. Therefore, also less 'authentic' supplementary materials will have to be taken into account by the interpreter to 'supplement' the 'more' authentic materials as outlined in Article 31 VCLT. In the author's opinion, supplementary materials may support the assessment of whether the contracting states intended to not deviate from the UN Model and give a term a meaning that is in

Festschrift für Dietmar Gosch, 235, 239 (C.H. Beck 2016); however, *see also* Dörr & Schmalenbach, *supra* n. 26, at m.no. 78: The term 'practice' is not bound to a particular 'legal' form, so diplomatic correspondence and press releases are just as important as national acts of legislation.

99. *See* Erasmus-Koen & Douma, *supra* n. 89, at 348.
100. Nieminen, *supra* n. 89, at 643.
101. *See* with respect to the commentary to the OECD Model: Linderfalk & Hilling, *supra* n. 83, at 46.
102. Nieminen, *supra* n. 89, at 644.
103. Sir Ian McTaggart Sinclair, *The Vienna Convention on the Law of Treaties*, 117 (2nd ed., Manchester University Press 1984); Dörr & Schmalenbach, *supra* n. 26, Article 32, at m.no. 31 and Arnold, *supra* n. 88, at 665 et seq.

conformity with that outlined in the Commentary to the UN Model, i.e., a special meaning in the sense of Article 31(4) VCLT.

c Relevance of the Official Languages of the UN: Article 33 VCLT

Interpretational issues could occur when a treaty is concluded in two or more (authentic) languages. In general, it is at the discretion of the contracting states to conclude a treaty in any desired language irrespective of its national language. This accords with the principle of state sovereignty.[104]

To avoid conflicts of interpretation, contracting states often establish one of the authentic languages as taking precedence over the other authentic languages in the event of conflicts of interpretation.[105]

The UN Charter is authenticated in five languages: Chinese, English, French, Russian, and Spanish.[106] Together with Arabic, these five languages are also the UN's official languages.[107] The UN issues most of its documents in all six official languages which requires translations from the original document. This is also true for the UN Model and its updates as the UN Tax Committee intends to translate the UN Model and its commentaries into all six official languages.[108] English, together with French and Spanish, is one of the working languages and translations into the official languages are made on the basis of the original English version of the document. Therefore, it is of particular importance to put more emphasis on the original English version of the UN Model for interpretational purposes.[109]

Although Article 33(1) and (3) VCLT are based on the premise that the terms in each authentic text shall have the same meaning, exact equivalents rarely exist in different languages and variances in the meaning of two language versions of a text are inevitable. In the case that the comparison of authentic treaty texts results in dissimilar meanings and the contracting states did not establish one of the authentic languages as taking precedence over the other(s), recourse shall be had to Articles 31 and 32 VCLT to establish the intention of the contracting states.[110]

In order to ensure uniformity of interpretation of a treaty provision that is identical with a provision of the UN Model, it must be taken into account that the UN Model was originally available in the original English working language and not the other official languages as these are mere translations of the original text. Therefore, in

104. Arnold D. McNair, *The Law of Treaties* (Clarendon Press 1961) 30.
105. *See, e.g.*, DTC Italy-Spain (1977): 'Done at Rome, the 8th day of September 1977, in two original copies, in the Spanish, Italian and French languages, the three texts being equally authentic, but in case of doubt the French text shall prevail.'
106. *See* Article 111 UN Charter.
107. *See* Orzechowski, *supra* n. 33, at 10.
108. *See* Committee of Experts on International Cooperation in Tax Matters, *Report on the seventh session*, E/2011/45-E/C.18/2011/6, https://financing.desa.un.org/sites/default/files/2023-03/N1222955_0.pdf (accessed January 2024), para. 84.
109. Similarly: Michael Lang, *Auslegung von Doppelbesteuerungsabkommen und authentische Vertragssprachen*, IStR 403, 409 (2011).
110. *See* Orzechowski, *supra* n. 33, at 9.

case of divergences of interpretation between two or more authentic texts, an interpretation in accordance with Articles 31 and 32 VCLT requires giving more weight to the authentic English text of a tax treaty. This is due to the fact that the UN Model and its commentaries were originally available in the original English language version and not in the other official languages.[111] Otherwise, it is not ensured that the respective provisions of a tax treaty that are based on the UN Model will be interpreted in accordance with the original English version of the UN Model and its commentaries.[112] In addition, when states decide to adopt provisions from the UN Model into their tax treaty that are identical to those in the OECD Model, an interpretation in accordance with Articles 31 and 32 VCLT becomes relevant. It demands taking into account the English and French versions of the OECD Model and its commentaries to ensure uniformity of interpretation of the specific provisions.[113]

d Terms and Concepts Not Defined in the UN Model

What is referred to as the primacy of treaty autonomous interpretation requires that terms of a treaty are interpreted independently from concepts and definitions found in the national law of the contracting states. This view originates from the application of the dualist-approach.[114] Scholars have already intensively discussed the issue of the relevance of domestic law in interpreting unidentified terms of a tax treaty.[115] The discussion is based on Article 3(2) of the OECD and UN Models.

According to Article 3(2) of the UN Model, any term not defined in the UN Model 'shall, unless the context otherwise requires, have the meaning that it has at that time under the law of that State for the purposes of the taxes to which the Convention applies'. Article 3(2) of the UN Model is a special rule of interpretation in relation to the rules of interpretation contained in the VCLT.[116] This does not mean, however, that the VCLT is of no relevance due to the application of Article 3(2) of the UN Model. As *Avery Jones* contends, Articles 31 and 32 VCLT are an integral part of Article 3(2) UN Model itself as these scholars read the concept of 'unless the context otherwise requires' as 'unless the Vienna Convention on the Law of Treaties otherwise requires'.[117]

111. *See* Orzechowski, *supra* n. 33, at 11.
112. *See also* Lang, *supra* n. 109, at 408.
113. *See* Jacques Sasseville, *The OECD Model Convention and Commentaries*, in: Guglielmo Maisto (ed.), *Multilingual Texts and Interpretation of Tax Treaties and EC Tax Law*, 129, 130 (IBFD 2005); Lang, *supra* n. 109, at 409.
114. Anger & Wagemann, *supra* n. 25, at 611.
115. *See* Karin Heger, *The Relationship Between Tax Treaty Law and National Tax Law*, SWI 95-104 (2011); Anna Leisner-Egensperger, *DBA-Auslegung unter Rückgriff auf nationales Recht*, IStR 10-15 (2014); John F. Avery Jones, *A Fresh Look at Article 3(2) of the OECD Model*, 74 BIT 654-659 (2020) DOI: 10.59403/xgw0x3.
116. Alexander Rust, *Article 3(2) OECD and UN MC*, in: Ekkehart Reimer & Alexander Rust (eds), *Klaus Vogel on Double Taxation Conventions* vol. 1, 171, m.no. 110 (4th ed., Wolters Kluwer 2015).
117. *See, e.g.*, Frank Engelen, *Interpretation of Tax Treaties under International Law* vol. 7, 478 (IBFD 2004); also, if incorporated in a tax treaty, Article 3(2) needs to be interpreted on the basis of the rules of Arts 31-33 VCLT.

It is a matter of debate whether the term 'context' should be interpreted in a narrow or wider sense. *Leisner-Egensperger* favours a wider interpretation and therefore advocates that the context must be determined on the basis of a subjective approach considering the object and purpose of the entire treaty.[118] Therefore, before determining whether it was the intention of the contracting states to have recourse to a meaning based on national law, a systematic interpretation considering the object and purpose of the treaty must be made. As a result, the wording 'unless the context otherwise requires' in Article 3(2) of the UN Model establishes a primacy of treaty autonomous interpretation. Recourse to a meaning based on national law may only be made if an autonomous treaty interpretation is not successful. Such an outcome, however - according to *Lang* - will rarely be the case.[119] This view is also generally shared by the German Bundesfinanzhof (BFH). The BFH gives precedence to a treaty autonomous interpretation of an undefined tax treaty term. In this respect, if a treaty does not expressly stipulate that an undefined term shall have the meaning it has under the national law of the contracting states,[120] reference to national law shall only be made if a contextual interpretation is not feasible.[121]

Avery Jones, on the other hand, favours a narrower approach and does not regard the reference to the context as an alternative interpretation but rather as a simultaneous consideration of the contextual approach defined in Article 3(2) UN Model.[122] According to this view, the notion 'unless the context otherwise requires' shall not be interpreted in a manner that virtually excludes recourse to domestic law. Both references to the context and the domestic law are in a relationship of mutual reciprocity. Not every apparently convincing interpretation from the context shall take precedence over the use of national law on the basis of Article 3(2) UN Model. If an interpretation from the context is convincing enough, must be decided on a case-by-case basis.[123]

In the author's opinion, a treaty autonomous interpretation shall prevail in the situation of undefined terms of a tax treaty. It can be deduced from the application of the dualist-approach that tax treaties need to be interpreted independently from the national law of the contracting states. In this regard, treaty autonomous interpretation aims to ensure that undefined terms of a tax treaty are interpreted on the basis of common rules in order to avoid a result that is not in conformity with the object and purpose of the tax treaty, i.e., the avoidance of double taxation or double non-taxation. In contrast, hereto, an interpretation based on the domestic law of the contracting states may - due to different tax systems and definitions of a certain type of income - enhance the risk of double taxation or double non-taxation. Such an outcome,

118. Leisner-Egensperger, *supra* n. 115, at 13.
119. Lang, *supra* n. 97, at 288 and *supra* n. 109, at 410.
120. *See, e.g.*, Article 6(2) OECD and UN Models 2017: 'The term "immovable property" shall have the meaning which it has under the law of the Contracting State in which the property in question is situated.'
121. Anger & Wagemann, *supra* n. 25, at 612 and 615.
122. *See* Avery Jones, *supra* n. 115, at 656: Avery Jones refers to Article 3(2) of the OECD Model, however, as the notion 'unless the context otherwise requires' is also included in Article 3(2) of the UN Model, Avery Jones' reflections are also applicable to Article 3(2) of the UN Model.
123. Avery Jones et al., *supra* n. 88, at 106 et seq. with further references.

however, shall be avoided to the highest possible degree. Therefore, this author posits that the wording 'unless the context otherwise requires' as contained in Article 3(2) UN Model refers to the precedence of application of a treaty autonomous interpretation as referred to in the rules of interpretation in the VCLT. Due to the very nature of the rules of interpretation enshrined in Articles 31-33 VCLT, using elements from an objective and a subjective approach to interpretation, recourse to definitions and concepts of domestic law would only rarely have to be made as a treaty autonomous interpretation would regularly lead to convincing results.

CHAPTER 3

Evolution and Object and Purpose of Article 12A UN Model

A INTRODUCTION TO ARTICLE 12A UN MODEL

The UN Tax Committee introduced Article 12A on the taxation of fees for technical services to the UN Model in May 2018 in New York as part of its 2017 update. Article 12A UN Model remained unchanged since then and reads as follows:

> Article 12A
>
> FEES FOR TECHNICAL SERVICES
>
> 1. Fees for technical services arising in a Contracting State and paid to a resident of the other Contracting State may be taxed in that other State.
> 2. However, notwithstanding the provisions of Article 14 and subject to the provisions of Articles 8, 16 and 17, fees for technical services arising in a Contracting State may also be taxed in the Contracting State in which they arise and according to the laws of that State, but if the beneficial owner of the fees is a resident of the other Contracting State, the tax so charged shall not exceed ___ per cent [the percentage is to be established through bilateral negotiations] of the gross amount of the fees.
> 3. The term 'fees for technical services' as used in this Article means any payment in consideration for any service of a managerial, technical or consultancy nature, unless the payment is made:
>   (a) to an employee of the person making the payment;
>   (b) for teaching in an educational institution or for teaching by an educational institution; or
>   (c) by an individual for services for the personal use of an individual.
> 4. The provisions of paragraphs 1 and 2 shall not apply if the beneficial owner of fees for technical services, being a resident of a Contracting State, carries on business in the other Contracting State in which the fees for technical services arise through a permanent establishment situated in that other State, or performs in the other Contracting State independent personal services from a fixed base situated in that other State, and the fees for technical services are effectively connected with: (a) such permanent establishment or fixed base, or

(b) business activities referred to in (c) of paragraph 1 of Article 7. In such cases the provisions of Article 7 or Article 14, as the case may be, shall apply.

5. For the purposes of this Article, subject to paragraph 6, fees for technical services shall be deemed to arise in a Contracting State if the payer is a resident of that State or if the person paying the fees, whether that person is a resident of a Contracting State or not, has in a Contracting State a permanent establishment or a fixed base in connection with which the obligation to pay the fees was incurred, and such fees are borne by the permanent establishment or fixed base.
6. For the purposes of this Article, fees for technical services shall be deemed not to arise in a Contracting State if the payer is a resident of that State and carries on business in the other Contracting State through a permanent establishment situated in that other State or performs independent personal services through a fixed base situated in that other State and such fees are borne by that permanent establishment or fixed base.
7. Where, by reason of a special relationship between the payer and the beneficial owner of the fees for technical services or between both of them and some other person, the amount of the fees, having regard to the services for which they are paid, exceeds the amount which would have been agreed upon by the payer and the beneficial owner in the absence of such relationship, the provisions of this Article shall apply only to the last-mentioned amount. In such case, the excess part of the fees shall remain taxable according to the laws of each Contracting State, due regard being had to the other provisions of this Convention.

Article 12A(1) UN Model allocates a taxing right for fees for technical services to the residence state of the recipient of the fee (payee). The taxing right of the residence state, however, is not an exclusive one. According to Article 12A(2) UN Model, the contracting state in which fees for technical services arise (source state) has a taxing right over them. Source taxing rights on the basis of Article 12A(2) UN Model, however, are capped by a tax rate negotiated by the contracting states if the recipient of the fees is the beneficial owner of these. As explicitly provided in Article 12A(2) UN Model, the tax rate will be applied on the gross amount of the fees. This provision also establishes priority rules concerning the application of other allocation rules of the UN Model on fees for technical services. In this respect, Article 12A(2) notes that Articles 8, 16, and 17 shall take precedence over the application of Article 12A if payments for international shipping and air transport services, directors' fees and remuneration of top-level managerial officials, or payments for services of an artist or sportsperson also constitute fees for technical services.

Article 12A(3) UN Model defines fees for technical services as 'any payment in consideration for any service of a managerial, technical or consultancy'. Those technical services as broadly defined in Article 12A(3) UN Model include services requiring the application of specialized knowledge, skill, or expertise by the service provider on behalf of a client. Based on the view provided by the Commentary on Article 12A UN Model, services of a routine, standardized nature that do not involve this type of application are not within the scope of Article 12A UN Model.[124] If, however, technical services are provided on the basis of an employment relationship,

124. *See* para. 62 of the Commentary on Article 12A UN Model 2021.

for teaching services in or by an educational institution, or in a B2C relationship, such fees are – according to Article 12A(3) UN Model – outside the scope of Article 12A UN Model. This is because such payments are either already covered by another allocation rule of the UN Model or are not regarded as having a base-eroding character.[125]

The source state has a taxing right – according to Article 12A(2) UN Model – over the gross amount of fees for technical services at a tax rate negotiated by the contracting states. As Article 12A UN Model exclusively focuses on the payer-payee relationship, the place of performance of the service is not decisive for determining the source state. Therefore, it is irrelevant whether technical services are performed in the residence state of the service recipient or a third state.

Article 12A(4) UN Model establishes the precedence of the concept of a PE or fixed base. Therefore, if the payee performs technical services through a PE or a fixed base in the source state and the fees for them are effectively connected with the payee's[126] PE, fixed base, or business activities to which the force-of-attraction rule of Article 7(1)(c) UN Model applies, Articles 7 or 14 UN Model shall apply instead of Article 12A.

Article 12A(5) and (6) UN Model constitute the source rules of this article. Based on Article 12A(5) UN Model, fees for technical services arise in a contracting state when the payer of the fees is a resident of that state or if the fees are borne by a PE or fixed base therein. Regarding the latter mentioned situations, Article 12A(5) UN Model does not require that the payer is a resident of one of the contracting states. Therefore, Article 12A(5) UN Model also covers situations in which the payer is a resident of a third state, but the obligation to pay the fee is incurred by a PE or fixed base of the payer and the fees are borne by one of them. Fees for technical services, however, do not arise in a contracting state if the payer and the payee are residents of the same contracting state or if the payer has a PE or fixed base in the residence state of the payee and the fees are borne by such PE or fixed base in that state. The aforementioned rule is constituted in Article 12A(6) UN Model.

Article 12A(7) UN Model establishes that the provisions of this article shall only apply to the amount paid in consideration for the provision of technical services that are at arm's length. Any amount paid above the arm's length price shall be subject – according to Article 12A(7) UN Model – to the other allocation rules of the UN Model. This rule, however, shall only apply to associated enterprises or other persons having a special relationship with each other. The examples given for such relationships in the Commentary to Article 12A UN Model are relationships by blood, marriage or any other community of interests that are distinct from legal relationships giving rise to fees for technical services as defined in Article 12A(3) UN Model.[127]

The following subchapters intend to provide a more in-depth analysis of the aims of inclusion of Article 12A to the UN Model 2017 in the context of the historical evolution of Article 12A UN Model.

125. *See* paras 69 et seq. of the Commentary on Article 12A UN Model 2021.
126. Typically, the service provider.
127. *See* para. 130 of the Commentary on Article 12A UN Model 2021

B HISTORY OF ORIGINS OF ARTICLE 12A UN MODEL

i Third to Sixth Session of the UN Tax Committee

The issue of taxation of fees for technical services was already mentioned (but not discussed) during the third session of the tax committee in 2007 as part of possible revisions to Article 5 on permanent establishments. The aforementioned issue was presented by *Stig Sollund* on behalf of the UN Subcommittee on the Definition of Permanent Establishment.[128]

In the tax committee's fourth session in 2008, further proposals on the improvement of the text of Article 5 and its accompanying commentary were proposed by the subcommittee previously mentioned. These proposals included (i) the treatment of Article 14 and its possible deletion, (ii) the treatment of services in general and the inclusion of a provision on services in Article 5, and (iii) the taxation of fees for technical services.[129] On the issue of technical services, several participants emphasized the special characteristics of services in terms of modes of supply and the specific economic needs of source states, e.g., with respect to services provided via the internet.[130]

The way forward taken by the UN Tax Committee was to form a new subcommittee on Article 14 and the tax treatment of services. In this respect, *Liselotte Kana* agreed to be the coordinator of the subcommittee. There has been support for further work on the issue of royalties and technical fees.[131] In this respect, the UN Tax Committee conceived a draft agenda for its fifth session including the point 'royalties and technical fees: policy and technical issues'.[132]

In the tax committee's fifth session in 2009, it decided that the taxation of services (including fees for technical services) and issues on Article 14 shall not be dealt with by one subcommittee but rather by two separate ones. They would be chaired by *Kana* with the view to considering possible interactions between the issues discussed in them.[133] The subcommittee on the taxation of services aimed at submitting an initial

128. Committee of Experts on International Cooperation in Tax Matters, *Report on the third session*, E/C.18/2007/19, https://financing.desa.un.org/sites/default/files/2023-03/N0820731%20%281%29.pdf (accessed 6 January 2024), para. 51.
129. *See* Committee of Experts on International Cooperation in Tax Matters, *Report on the fourth session*, E/C.18/2008/6, https://financing.desa.un.org/sites/default/files/2023-03/N0921065%20%282%29.pdf (accessed 6 January 2024), para. 28.
130. *Ibid.*, at para. 37.
131. *Ibid.*, at para. 81.
132. *Ibid.*, at para. 88.
133. *See* Committee of Experts on International Cooperation in Tax Matters, *supra* n. 14, at para. 25; *see also* Committee of Experts on International Cooperation in Tax Matters, *Note Provided by the Coordinator of the Subcommittee on Article 14 and the Tax Treatment of Services*, E/C.18/2009/CRP.4, https://www.un.org/esa/ffd/wp-content/uploads/2014/10/5STM_E-C18-2009-CRP4.pdf (accessed 6 January 2024), para. 7: 'The subcommittee welcomes discussion on addressing the services issue in general, as well as on the particular issue of the treatment of fees for technical assistance.' It shall also be noted that, at this stage, several different terms were used within the documents of the UN: 'technical fees', 'fees for technical services', or 'fees for technical assistance'.

report for the tax committee's sixth session and having a final report completed before the end of the membership of the tax committee in 2013.[134]

The work of the UN Subcommittee on the Taxation of Services was mandated as follows:

> The Subcommittee is mandated to address the issue of the taxation treatment of services in general in a broad way including related aspects and issues. The issue of taxation of fees for technical services should also be addressed. This is the initiation of this extensive work and the Subcommittee should present at the next annual session of the Committee an initial evaluation, some possible building blocks and potential ways to go forward.[135]

In accordance with the mandate given to the UN subcommittee, a draft paper on the taxation of services under the UN Model was prepared by Prof. *Brian Arnold* 'as the first step in the Subcommittee's work'.[136] It aimed at identifying the underlying principles under the current provisions of the UN Model that are applicable to the taxation of services for elaborating any possible revisions to the UN Model and its commentaries. The paper specifically dealt with the tax treatment of fees for technical services. In addition to this paper, *Arnold* prepared a supplementary note identifying 'possible building blocks and potential ways forward' in the taxation of services.[137]

Based on the analysis conducted by *Arnold*, it was concluded that the policy reasons for the different treatment of services within and between the OECD and the UN Models were neither always clear nor consistently applied. The papers further elaborated on the issue of tax base erosion in source states in the case of fees for technical services that led a few states to include a specific provision on the taxation of the aforementioned fees in their tax treaties. Some countries also interpreted the term 'technical services' on the basis of domestic law leading to the application of paragraph 3 of the 'other income' article of the UN Model.[138] In contrast to the application of a separate provision on the taxation of fees for technical services, the application of Article 21(3) UN Model does not limit the source state in the amount of taxation of the payment. According to *Arnold*, this does not seem appropriate from a policy perspective.[139] While there was wide recognition within the forum to tax business profits in the

134. *See* Committee of Experts on International Cooperation in Tax Matters, *supra* n. 14, at para. 26.
135. *See also* Committee of Experts on International Cooperation in Tax Matters, *Note on the Taxation of Services under the United Nations Model Tax Convention*, E/C.18/2010/CRP.7, https://www.un.org/esa/ffd/wp-content/uploads/2014/10/6STM_NoteTaxationOfServices.pdf (accessed 6 January 2024), 1.
136. *See* Committee of Experts on International Cooperation in Tax Matters, *supra* n. 135, at 2.
137. Committee of Experts on International Cooperation in Tax Matters, *Note by the Secretariat: Additional Note by Mr. Brian Arnold on the Tax Treatment of Services*, E/C.18/2010/CRP.7/Add.1, https://www.un.org/esa/ffd/wp-content/uploads/2014/10/6STM_CRP7_Add1 pdf (accessed 6 January 2024).
138. *See* Article 21(3) UN-Model in its versions since the 1980 UN Model: 'Notwithstanding the provisions of paragraphs 1 and 2, items of income of a resident of a Contracting State not dealt with in the foregoing Articles of this Convention and arising in the other Contracting State may also be taxed in that other State.'
139. Committee of Experts on International Cooperation in Tax Matters, *Report on the sixth session*, E/C.18/2010/7, https://financing.desa.un.org/sites/default/files/2023-03/N1120859_0.pdf (accessed 6 January 2024), para. 69.

form of interest, royalties, and fees for technical services in the source state irrespective of the existence of a PE, there were still discussions on whether taxation in the source state shall take place on a net basis.[140] In the case of non-resident service providers that earn income from interest, royalties, and fees for technical services as part of non-business income, *Arnold* stated that a ceiling on the amount of withholding tax similar to Articles 11 and 12 UN Model should be established. The taxation of this type of income could be justified by the 'base-erosion principle'.[141]

Although no substantive discussion arose in the forum after *Arnold's* presentation, scattered comments were made by tax committee members with respect to an increased amount of services provided to developing countries from abroad. In particular, one member stated that especially services in the nature of technical assistance could – if taxed – be a significant revenue source for developing countries. According to this member, fees for such services could be collected by imposing a withholding tax on the payment. Developed countries, however, are often opposed to this approach as they are regularly exporting services to developing countries.[142]

It was decided that the Subcommittee on Taxation of Services shall draw upon the work of *Arnold* and other sources to examine the taxation of fees specifically for technical services.[143]

ii Seventh to Sixteenth Session of the UN Tax Committee

The Subcommittee on Taxation of Services issued a paper for the tax committee's seventh session summarizing the analysis made by *Arnold* in its sixth session and providing a proposal to the tax committee on the way forward with respect to the subcommittee's future work stream.[144] In the mentioned proposal, the subcommittee suggested that the tax committee discuss and make a decision in relation to the approach to the future work on 'technical fees', developing a new article and commentary on the taxation of fees for technical, management, and consulting services. In addition, it was proposed by the subcommittee to discuss the format of the outcome of the work on services. The subcommittee noted that if the outcome of the work shall be part of the Commentaries to the UN Model, the inclusion as part of the 2011 update of the UN Model would not be feasible but could be part of a future update.[145]

The tax committee's eighth session began with a note by the chair stating that the discussion on the taxation of fees for technical services was one of its most urgent

140. *Ibid.*, at para. 70.
141. *Ibid.*, at para. 70.
142. *Ibid.*, at para. 71.
143. *Ibid.*, at para. 72.
144. *See* Committee of Experts on International Cooperation in Tax Matters, *Note from the Coordinator of the Subcommittee on Tax Treatment of Services: Draft Article and Commentary on Technical Services*, E/C.18/2014/CRP.8, https://www.un.org/esa/ffd/wp-content/uploads/2014/10/10STM_CRP8_TechnicalServices1.pdf (accessed 6 January 2024).
145. *See* Committee of Experts on International Cooperation in Tax Matters, *Subcommittee on Tax Treatment of Services*, E/C.18/2011/CRP.7, https://www.un.org/esa/ffd/wp-content/uploads/2014/10/7STM_CRP7.pdf (accessed 6 January 2024), 2.

issues.[146] With respect to it, in principle, two papers and an Annex to one paper were to be discussed as part of the agenda of the meeting. These papers included a 'Follow-up note on the Taxation of Fees for Technical and other Services under the United Nations Model Convention' plus an Annex.[147] Both documents were updated by *Arnold* with additional comments on the follow-up note[148] drafted by tax committee member Mr *Diop*. As part of the introduction to the topic, *Arnold* was invited to speak on the outcome of his research on the treatment of technical and other services. In his presentation, he noted that the UN and OECD Models do not include a consistent or coherent approach to the treatment of services. He also emphasized the 'inherent difficulty' to define 'technical services' as the term is often used for managerial, consultancy, or administrative services.[149]

The UN Model – at the time it was analysed – did not include a specific provision on the taxation of fees for technical services. These were, in general, either within the scope of Article 7 or 14 UN Model. Some technical services that are more specialized have also been covered by the provision on the construction or insurance PE. In this respect, at the tax committee's eighth session, *Arnold* noted that it is very easy for a non-resident service provider to earn a substantial amount of income in the source state without being taxed therein. As fees for technical services are often deductible against the tax base at the level of the payer of the fees, an erosion of the tax base is apparent.[150] It is even more apparent in situations of intra-group transactions of multinational enterprises, leading to tax planning in order to reduce the taxable income in the source state.[151]

As the majority of tax committee members preferred the development of a new article and commentary on fees for technical services, the Follow-Up-Note[152] primarily focused on the design of the new article for this. Although not verbally expressed during the meeting of the tax committee, it was rather obvious from his Follow-Up-Note that *Arnold* was rather sceptical with the approach of the inclusion of a separate provision on the taxation of fees for technical services. In his opinion, the erosion of a tax base is not specific to them but rather to service payments in general if the services are provided by non-residents. Therefore, he concluded that 'it should be carefully considered whether a solution that focuses only on certain technical services is

146. *See* Committee of Experts on International Cooperation in Tax Matters, *Report on the eighth session*, E/2012/45-E/C.18/2012/6, https://financing.desa.un.org/sites/default/files/2023-03/N1323910_1.pdf (accessed 6 January 2024), para. 4.
147. *See* Committee of Experts on International Cooperation in Tax Matters, *Follow Up Note on Taxation of Fees for Technical Services and Comments on that Note*, E/C.18/2012/CRP.4, https://www.un.org/esa/ffd/wp-content/uploads/2014/09/8STM_CRP4-Fees-for-Technical-Services-Follow-Up-Note021012.pdf (accessed 6 January 2024).
148. *See* Committee of Experts on International Cooperation in Tax Matters, *Additional Comments on Follow-Up Note on Taxation of Fees for Technical Services*, E/C.18/2012/CRP.4/Add. 1, https://www.un.org/esa/ffd/wp-content/uploads/2014/09/8STM_CRP4_Add1.pdf (accessed 6 January 2024).
149. Committee of Experts on International Cooperation in Tax Matters, *supra* n. 146, at para. 72.
150. Committee of Experts on International Cooperation in Tax Matters, *supra* n. 147, at 11.
151. Committee of Experts on International Cooperation in Tax Matters, *supra* n. 146, at para. 54; Committee of Experts on International Cooperation in Tax Matters, *supra* n. 147, at 11.
152. *See* Committee of Experts on International Cooperation in Tax Matters, *supra* n. 147.

appropriate'.[153] In *Arnold's* view, a solution that is applicable to all types of services would be more appropriate.[154]

As a result, in his presentation at the tax committee's meeting, *Arnold* offered the members several options for consideration that are also found in the Note of the Secretariat on the 'Taxation of fees for technical and other services under the United Nations Model Convention':[155]

(1) Inclusion of a neutral discussion on the issue of treatment of technical and other services in the next update of the UN Model and its corresponding commentary with the objective of identifying the issues that arise with technical and other services.
(2) The second option complements the first one, adding and describing provisions that are already found in DTCs without offering a recommendation.[156]
(3) In addition to the first two proposals, alternative provisions that serve as a basis for treaty negotiations could be included in the Commentaries to the UN Model. The approach would be similar to that for the branch profits tax in the Commentaries to Article 10 of the UN Model.[157]
(4) Reduction of the thresholds constituted in the service PE[158] and independent services[159] provisions to less than 183 days (e.g., 120 or 90 days) thereby also expanding the taxing rights for income of business and professional services that also include technical and other services. The merits of this approach are its simplicity and straightforwardness without the need to define technical and other services if applied to all types of services. If, however, the approach is restricted to technical services, defining them would prove to be inherently difficult and, as such, possibly lead to less certainty for taxpayers and tax administrations.
(5) Inclusion of a provision on technical and other similar services related or connected to the transfer of intellectual property in Article 12 UN Model itself or its respective commentary as part of an alternative provision. In this respect, Article 12 on 'Royalties and fees for included services' of the DTC India-United States (1989) would serve as the model provision for this proposal.[160]

153. Committee of Experts on International Cooperation in Tax Matters, *supra* n. 147, at 11.
154. Committee of Experts on International Cooperation in Tax Matters, *supra* n. 147, at 11.
155. Committee of Experts on International Cooperation in Tax Matters, *supra* n. 146, at para. 55 and Committee of Experts on International Cooperation in Tax Matters, *Taxation of fees for technical and other services under the United Nations Model Convention – Note by the Secretariat*, E/C.18/2012/4, https://financing.desa.un.org/events/eighth-session-committee-experts-international-cooperation-tax-matters (accessed 6 January 2024), paras 17 et seq.
156. Committee of Experts on International Cooperation in Tax Matters, *supra* n. 147, at para. 21: 'The commentary on article 1 of the United Nations Model Convention (paras 47-56) dealing with treaty-shopping could be used as a model in this regard.'
157. Committee of Experts on International Cooperation in Tax Matters, *supra* n. 147, at para. 22.
158. *See* Article 5(3)(b) UN Model.
159. *See* Article 14(1)(b) UN Model.
160. Committee of Experts on International Cooperation in Tax Matters, *supra* n. 147, at para. 23.

(6) Revision of Article 14 UN Model to grant the source state a taxing right if the payment was made by a resident of the source state or borne by a PE of the non-resident service provider therein ('base-erosion conditions').[161] The newly included provision could be limited to technical and other similar services.
(7) Revision of Article 21(3) UN Model by limiting source taxing rights on fees for technical services by including either a fixed percentage in the UN Model or a percentage to be negotiated by the contracting states.
(8) Inclusion of a new article and corresponding commentary addressing the taxation of income arising from technical and other services. In this respect, *Arnold* noted that the draft of a new article will face several challenges. The most serious is the drafting of a definition of technical services that would provide sufficient certainty for taxpayers and tax administrations. Existing provisions found in DTCs refer to 'managerial, technical and consulting services' that mostly do not define these services. If such a definition would be chosen for the new article, additional clarification on the types of services would preferably need to be done. Another option for the new article was to apply it to all types of services which would make a definition of technical services redundant.

    In general, the new article should allow for net taxation in the source state. However, if the option of gross taxation is chosen, a limitation up to a fixed percentage should be set. The latter-mentioned option could be supplemented by a provision allowing a possibility to elect for net taxation.
(9) The last option that was presented to the tax committee is drastically different from those that were presented before: Deem a subsidiary of a non-resident parent company as a PE.[162] The reason behind this proposal is again the tax base erosion of the source state. In the case of subsidiaries, this occurs as payments in consideration for services rendered by the non-resident parent company are deductible against the tax base of the source state without being taxed therein due to the non-existence of a PE or fixed base. The proposed option would not only apply to technical but also to all types of services, however, it should – in both cases – be restricted to services that are not provided at 'arm's length'.[163]

Several participants at the tax committee meeting took the floor after *Arnold's* presentation. The opinions expressed were manifold. Participants who were not in favour of the inclusion of a new article on the taxation of fees for technical services mentioned that base erosion does not specifically occur with respect to technical services or services in general. There was an argument that large amounts of income could be earned in another economy through the provision of services without having a substantial presence therein. Hence a revision of Article 5 UN Model was suggested

161. *Ibid.*, at para. 24.
162. *Ibid.*, at para. 32.
163. Committee of Experts on International Cooperation in Tax Matters, *supra* n. 146, at para. 55.

as such a revision would not be specifically restricted to only technical but to all types of services. Participants also opined on the issue of gross taxation. They mentioned that especially technical services are highly skilled services that require a substantial amount of remuneration paid to employees or subcontractors. To keep the financial burden as low as possible, the tax rate on gross income should be kept reasonably low.[164]

The inclusion of a new article to the UN Model was recommended due to several reasons. First, as services represent a larger share of countries' GDP in the current global economy, a new article on the taxation of technical services is required to mirror the new reality. Second, fees for intra-group services result in tax base erosion of developing countries due to profit shifting activities of many multinational enterprises. Third, the Southern African Development Community introduced a new article on the taxation of fees for technical services allowing for gross taxation with a relatively low rate in their Model Convention which should suffice as a basis for bilateral negotiations.[165]

A minority of UN Tax Committee Members and observers took the view that the decision on the inclusion of a new Article on fees for technical services shall not be based on the fact that a number of tax treaties include such a provision. This is because both contracting states do not necessarily support the inclusion of an article on technical services.[166] In addition, the economic impact of the tax base erosion of developing countries as well as the exact definition of technical services and their economic relevance in developing countries still need to be elaborated. As a result, it was recommended by a minority of tax committee members to make a study on the open questions before deciding on the inclusion of a new article on the taxation of income from technical services or other options.[167]

A few tax committee members and observers were opposed to already deciding on an option as a way forward for the UN Tax Committee. However, in its eighth session, the majority of committee members agreed in principle (by majority vote) on the inclusion of a new article dealing with the taxation of fees for technical services. The new provision on the taxation of fees for technical services shall address the following issues:[168]

(1) A definition or framework on what could be understood as 'technical services'.
(2) Modalities on how the services shall be performed, including the question if physical presence needed to effectuate a taxing right for the source state and, if so, the determination of a threshold.
(3) The question on the right nexus for the allocation of source taxing rights, i.e., whether it is sufficient to base an allocation of taxing rights on the payer's

164. *Ibid.*, at para. 57.
165. *Ibid.*, at para. 58.
166. The inclusion of a provision on technical services in a tax treaty could also be the result of a compromise intending to receive another concession from the treaty partner.
167. Committee of Experts on International Cooperation in Tax Matters, *supra* n. 146, at para. 59.
168. *Ibid.*, at para. 60.

residence status or the fact that the fee is borne by a PE of the payer in the source state.

It was decided that the Subcommittee on Tax Treatment of Services shall continue its work on these issues until the end of June 2013, which was the end of the tax committee's four-year tenure. Based on this decision, the subcommittee requested *Arnold* to prepare a paper addressing the above-mentioned issues for the tax committee's ninth session.[169] The paper prepared by *Arnold* aimed at identifying the key elements of a new article on fees for technical services for future deliberations of the tax committee and does not consider other alternatives such as expanding the scope of Article 12 UN Model.

Arnold considered four key issues that must be identified as part of the drafting process of a new article on fees for technical services. These four issues basically included the most divergent issues that were identified during the tax committee's eighth session.[170] In addition, another key issue that was identified was the method of taxation in the source state, i.e., either gross or net taxation of fees for technical services.[171]

It was the general understanding that the scope of the new article shall be restricted to income from 'managerial, technical and consulting' services as opposed to a general service provision.[172] Nevertheless, there was also a range of different views among the tax committee with respect to the scope of the new article, especially on the implementation of the definition of 'technical services'. The views ranged from an inclusive definition, an exhaustive definition, a reference to a definition in domestic law, and not giving a definition in the article itself at all but providing additional guidance in the commentary to the new article. There was also a uniform view taken by several tax committee members that the new article shall not apply to services that are within the scope of Articles 7 and 14 UN Model.[173]

The coordinator of the subcommittee explained the purpose of the new article, i.e., to expand source taxing rights with respect to technical services provided therein. She proposed to the tax committee to decide on one of the options delineated in *Arnold's* paper. It shall, however, be noted that some states would prefer a different

---

169. *See* Committee of Experts on International Cooperation in Tax Matters, *Note on a new Article of the UN Model Convention dealing with the Taxation of Fees for Technical and Other Services*, E/C.18/2013/CRP.5, https://www.un.org/esa/ffd/wp-content/uploads/2014/09/9STM_CRP5_Services.pdf (accessed 6 January 2024), 2.
170. *See* Committee of Experts on International Cooperation in Tax Matters, *supra* n. 146, at para. 60.
171. *See* Committee of Experts on International Cooperation in Tax Matters, *supra* n. 169, at 5.
172. *See*, however, the comments made by *Liao*: Tizhong Liao, *Taxation of Cross border Trade in Service: A Review of the Current International Tax Landscape and the Possible Future Policy Options*, E/C.18/2013/CRP.16, https://www.un.org/esa/ffd/wp-content/uploads/2014/09/9STM_CRP16_CrossBorderTrade.pdf (accessed 4 January 2024), 28: 'The Committee should remain cautious to ensure that any changes to its approach in respect of taxing services income do not lead to inequitable distortions between the taxation treatment of trade in services and trade in goods. This is particularly true should the Committee consider the inclusion of a new article in the UN Model Tax Convention.'
173. *See* Committee of Experts on International Cooperation in Tax Matters, *supra* n. 169, at 6.

option as the basis for tax treaty negotiations. Therefore, all of the options mentioned by *Arnold* shall also be part of the commentary to the new article so that states that have reservations about the option chosen by the subcommittee are also provided with guidance.[174]

In the following discussion, several participants and observers mentioned the importance of the underlying object and purpose of the new article with respect to the expansion of source taxing rights. The formulation of the wording of the new article highly depends on the underlying object and purpose and would therefore be different if the committee intends to avoid tax base erosion of the source states or to address the issue of providing services with a minimum amount of physical presence in the source state.[175]

In addition, a few tax committee members emphasized the need to clearly define the term 'technical services' in order to avoid uncertainty for tax administrations and taxpayers that could possibly lead to double taxation.[176] Several members pointed out the fact that the inclusion of provisions on fees for technical services is on the rise, especially with respect to tax treaties concluded by Latin American and African countries. In this respect, the tax committee mentioned that it could assist those countries by providing options and a draft language.[177]

The majority of tax committee members decided that the first alternative (alternative A) provided by *Arnold* in his paper shall be the basis for the first draft of the new article. The draft article is based on the following principles and assumptions:[178]

(1) The tax treatment of payments for technical services is modelled after Article 12 UN Model. Therefore, the source country is entitled to tax payments for technical services if they are paid by a resident of the source state or borne by a PE in the source state.
(2) The source state has a taxing right on the gross payment at a rate to be determined by the contracting states.
(3) Payments for technical services are defined in a broad sense to include managerial, technical, and consultancy services. The definition shall not be determined by the domestic law of the contracting states. Specific exclusions of payments for technical services covered by Articles 7, 14, and 15 UN Model are not included in the new article.
(4) Technical services do not have to be performed in the source state for a taxing right to arise therein. Therefore, a source taxing right might arise even if technical services are utilized or consumed in another state.

174. Committee of Experts on International Cooperation in Tax Matters, *Report on the ninth session*, E/2013/45-E/C.18/2013/6, https://financing.desa.un.org/sites/default/files/2023-03/N14221 14.pdf (accessed 6 January 2024), para. 58.
175. *Ibid.*, at para. 59.
176. *Ibid.*, at para. 60.
177. *Ibid.*, at para. 61.
178. *See* Committee of Experts on International Cooperation in Tax Matters, *supra* n. 169, at 7 et seq.

Alternative A of the draft article as drafted by *Arnold* reads as follows:[179]

Article 12A – Alternative A

Income from Technical Services

1. Payments for technical services arising in a Contracting State and paid to a resident of the other Contracting State who provides those services may be taxed in that other State.
2. However, such payments may also be taxed in the Contracting State in which the payments arise, and according to the laws of that State, but the tax so charged shall not exceed ___ percent of the gross amount of the payment (the percentage to be established through bilateral negotiations).
3. The term 'payments for technical services' as used in this Article means any payment in consideration for any service of a managerial, technical or consultancy nature, unless the payment is the reimbursement of actual expenses incurred by the person providing the service or is made to an employee of the person making the payments.
4. Paragraph 2 shall not apply if a resident of a Contracting State carries on business in the other Contracting State through a permanent establishment or a fixed base situated therein and the technical services are effectively connected with such permanent establishment or fixed base. In such case, the provisions of Article 7 or Article 14, as the case may be, shall apply.
5. Payments for technical services shall be deemed to arise in a Contracting State if the payer is a resident of that State or if the person paying the technical fees, whether that person is a resident of a Contracting State or not, has in a Contracting State a permanent establishment or a fixed base in connection with which the obligation to pay the technical fees was incurred, and such technical fees are borne by the permanent establishment or fixed base.
6. [Where, by reason of a special relationship between the payer and the person providing the services or between both of them and some other person, the amount of the technical fees paid exceeds the amount that would have been agreed upon by the payer and that person in the absence of such relationship, the provisions of this Article shall apply only to the last mentioned amount. In such case, the excess part of the payments shall remain taxable according to the laws of each Contracting State, due regard being had to the other provisions of this Agreement.]

In order to address the concerns of a minority of its members and observers, the tax committee also decided to elaborate on a clear definition of the term 'technical services'. If necessary, also a list of services that are not covered by the new article shall be developed. The subcommittee's coordinator assured that the addressed concerns will be taken into account when drafting the new article and its commentary. In addition, alternatives B[180] and C,[181] which are mentioned in *Arnold's* paper, shall be taken into account as alternatives in the new commentary.[182]

---

179. *Ibid.*, at 7 et seq.
180. *See* Committee of Experts on International Cooperation in Tax Matters, *supra* n. 169, at 10: 'The *only significant difference* between Alternative A and Alternative B is that *under Alternative B the source country (the country in which the income from technical services arises) is entitled to tax the income only if the technical services are performed in the source country*. Thus, under Alternative B, a source country is not entitled to tax payments for technical services made by residents of the source country (or nonresidents with a PE or fixed base in the source country)

The discussion on service taxation and fees for technical services was concluded with the establishment of a new subcommittee that was again to be coordinated by *Kana*. It was mandated to address the issue of service taxation in a broad manner and to present a wording for the article on fees for technical services and its corresponding commentary. The mentioned texts shall be presented to the tax committee at the tenth session.[183]

The ongoing discussions on the introduction of a provision on the taxation of fees for technical services were complemented by a presentation of a paper written by Prof. *Zhu* on 'Proposed changes to the UN Model Tax Convention dealing with cyber-based services', including a proposal on the introduction of a provision on the taxation of 'fees for cyber-based technical services'.[184] They are defined as:

> any consideration for the provision of any managerial, technical or consultancy services by a resident of a contracting state *through the network to consumers in the other contracting state*, including the provision by such a resident itself or other personnel employed or engaged for such a purpose.[185]

The proposal is based on the fact that the supply of services is not necessarily connected to physical presence in a state due to the advancements of network and digitalization technologies. Therefore, according to *Zhu*, the use of network and information technology by consumers shall substitute physical presence as a connecting factor for source taxation of services.[186] It was also recognized by the tax committee that the increasing digitalization of the economy and upsurge in the use of adapted business models could raise concerns by the source state as no physical presence is needed to conduct services therein. The tax committee agreed that some of these concerns should be addressed through the inclusion of a new provision on the taxation of fees for technical services. In this respect, it was also mentioned that the relationship between Article 5 UN Model and the new article on fees for technical services must be clarified in the respective commentary to the latter.[187]

---

to residents of the other state if the services are performed outside the source country. Income from such services is taxable exclusively by the state in which the service provider is resident.' (words and word orders italicized by the author).

181. *Ibid.*, at 10 et seq.: 'There are *two major differences between Alternative C and Alternative B. First*, under *Alternative C* the source country is entitled to *tax income* from technical services only *if the technical services are performed in the source country for a minimum period of days in any 12-month period*...The *second* major difference between Alternative C and Alternative B is that Alternative C requires the source country to tax income from services on a *net basis*.' (words and word orders italicized by the author).
182. *See* Committee of Experts on International Cooperation in Tax Matters, *supra* n. 146, at para. 62.
183. Committee of Experts on International Cooperation in Tax Matters, *supra* n. 174, at para. 63.
184. *See* Yansheng Zhu, *Proposed changes to the UN Model Tax Convention dealing with the Cyber-based Services*, E/C.18/2014/CRP.9, https://www.un.org/esa/ffd/wp-content/uploads/2014/10/10STM_CRP9_CyberServices.pdf (accessed 2 January 2024), at 9.
185. *Ibid.*, at 10 (word order italicized by the author).
186. *Ibid.*, at 9.
187. Committee of Experts on International Cooperation in Tax Matters, *Report on the tenth session*, E/2014/45-E/C.18/2014/6, https://financing.desa.un.org/sites/default/files/2023-03/N1469313.pdf (accessed 6 January 2024), para. 21.

On the basis of the options discussed in the UN Tax Committee's ninth session, *Arnold* drafted an article and corresponding commentary on the taxation of technical services that was presented at the committee's tenth session. It reads as follows:[188]

Article XX – Payments for Technical Services

1. Payments for technical services arising in a Contracting State and paid to a resident of the other Contracting State who furnishes [in consideration of] those services may be taxed in that other State.
2. However, notwithstanding Article 14 and subject to the provisions of Articles 8, 17 and 20, such payments for technical services may also be taxed in the Contracting State in which the payments arise [and according to the laws of that State] but the tax so charged shall not exceed ___ percent of the gross amount of the payments (the percentage to be established through bilateral negotiations).
3. The term 'payments for technical services' as used in this Article means any payment in consideration for any service of a managerial, technical or consultancy nature, unless the payment is the reimbursement of actual expenses incurred by the person providing the service or is made to an employee, director or top-level managerial officer of the person making the payments.
4. The provisions of paragraphs 1 and 2 shall not apply if the recipient of payments for technical services [person who furnishes the technical services], being a resident of a Contracting State, carries on business in the other Contracting State in which the payments for technical services arise through a permanent establishment situated in that other State, or performs in the other Contracting State independent personal services from a fixed base situated in that other State, and the technical services [in respect of which the payments are made] are effectively connected with
   a) such permanent establishment or fixed base, or
   b) business activities referred to in I of paragraph 1 of Article 7. In such cases the provisions of Article 7 or Article 14, as the case may be, shall apply.
5. For the purposes of this Article, subject to paragraph 6, payments for technical services shall be deemed to arise in a Contracting State if the payer is a resident of that State or if the person making the payments for technical services, whether that person is a resident of a Contracting State or not, has in a Contracting State a permanent establishment or a fixed base in connection with which the obligation to make the payments for technical services was incurred, and such payments are borne by the permanent establishment or fixed base.
6. For the purposes of this Article, payments for technical services shall be deemed not to arise in a Contracting State if the payer is a resident of that State and carries on business in the other Contracting State or a third State through a permanent establishment situated in that State, or performs independent personal services through a fixed base situated in the other Contracting State or a third State and such payments are borne by that permanent establishment or fixed base.

The draft article is generally based on the wording and principles found in Articles 11 and 12 UN Model with adjustments made where necessary.[189] The new

188. Committee of Experts on International Cooperation in Tax Matters, *supra* n. 144, 2.
189. Committee of Experts on International Cooperation in Tax Matters, *supra* n. 187, at para. 75.

article allows for taxation of payments for services of a managerial, technical, or consultancy nature in the residence state of the payer of the service fees on a gross basis. The rate is to be negotiated by the contracting states of the tax treaty. As the taxing right for such payments is shared, the residence state of the payee also has a taxing right on those. In contrast to the final version of Article 12A UN Model 2017, paragraph 1 of the draft article requires that the service provider has to be the recipient of the payment.

The services do not have to be performed in the source state nor does the service provider have to be physically present therein. This is because a service provider in modern economies can be substantially involved in a country's economy without the requirement of physical presence. In this regard, the committee discussed the phrase 'furnishing of services' which is found in paragraph 1 of the draft article. The aforementioned phrase might lead to similar controversies as those already discussed with respect to the service PE provision[190] of the UN Model.[191] This is due to the fact that, for most committee members, this phrase implies the requirement of physical presence.[192]

Paragraph 3 of the draft article aims to define the term 'technical services'. They are exhaustively defined without reference to domestic law as payments made in consideration for services of a managerial, technical, and consultancy nature.[193] By including this definition in the new article, the drafter intended to replicate the same general and undefined terms as already ascertained in several tax treaties at the time of the drafting.[194] The definition found in paragraph 3 of the draft article does not provide recourse to domestic law and is intended to be exclusive.[195]

The definition does not include reimbursements of expenses, or payments to employees, directors, or top-level managerial officials. The exclusion of the latter-mentioned payments from the scope was not under debate as these payments are already in the scope of Articles 15, 16, 18, and 19 of the UN Model. However, the question of the exclusion of reimbursements of expenses from the scope of the new article was quite debatable as, according to *Arnold*, abusive situations might possibly occur due to such exclusion.[196] Additionally, it was also discussed during the meeting

190. *See* Article 5(3)(b) UN Models.
191. *See* Chapter 4.D.i.4.g.(iii) of this publication.
192. Committee of Experts on International Cooperation in Tax Matters, *supra* n. 187, at para. 86.
193. Committee of Experts on International Cooperation in Tax Matters, *supra* n. 144, at paras 42 et seq.
194. Committee of Experts on International Cooperation in Tax Matters, *supra* n. 187, at para. 77; International Chamber of Commerce, *ICC's perspectives on the taxation of technical services*, https://www.un.org/esa/ffd/wp-content/uploads/2014/10/10STM_LetterICC_perspectivesTTS.pdf (accessed 6 January 2024), 4: The ICC voiced a preference for 'a precise and specific definition' in contrast to a broad definition of the term technical services as a broad definition 'is...likely to result in a very broad taxation of services that would further weaken the principle of PE based taxation and extend beyond the aim of taxing technical services in the source country'.
195. Committee of Experts on International Cooperation in Tax Matters, *supra* n. 187, at para. 78.
196. Committee of Experts on International Cooperation in Tax Matters, *supra* n. 187, at para. 78: 'He [Arnold] indicated that, in the case of exclusion, taxpayers might be tempted to have a clause in their contract that all expenses would be reimbursed and that, therefore, the taxation

that payments made by private consumers should be excluded from the scope of the new article. In this respect, *Arnold* referred to the alternative version of paragraph 2 of the new article found in the commentary to the article. The alternative version of paragraph 2 narrows down the scope of the new article to payments made by enterprises:

> However, notwithstanding Article 14 and subject to the provisions of Articles 8, 17 and 20, such payments for technical services may also be taxed in the Contracting State in which the payments arise, [and according to the laws of that State] *if the payments are made by or in the course of an enterprise*, but the tax so charged shall not exceed ___ percent of the gross amount of the payments (the percentage to be established through bilateral negotiations).[197]

In this respect, however, no decision has yet been made on restricting the scope of the new article to payments made by enterprises.

Several committee members and observers expressed concerns about the breadth and the lack of clarity in the scope of technical services.[198] In order to determine the appropriate scope for the fees for technical services article, a discussion on the policy objectives of the aforementioned provision was held. During the discussions, some committee members pointed out that a new article might not be needed if the definition of 'royalty' was expanded.[199] In this regard, the coordinator of the subcommittee of services reminded the members that the inclusion of the new provision on payments for technical services was already discussed in the committee's ninth session and was accepted by the majority of members.[200] After some discussions, it was decided that the taxation of payments for technical services shall remain covered by the new article.[201]

Similar to the provisions of Articles 10 to 12 UN Model, paragraph 4 of the draft article states that Articles 7 or 14 UN Model shall apply if the service provider has a PE or fixed base in the other contracting state and the services are effectively connected with either of them. As a consequence, payments for technical services would be taxed on a net basis.

Payments for technical services arise – similar to Articles 11 and 12 UN Model – in the residence state of the payer or in the state in which the payer has a permanent establishment or fixed base if the payment is borne by either of the latter (paragraph 5). However, if the payment is borne by one of them in the residence state of the payer or a third state, the payment shall not be deemed to arise in a contracting state (paragraph 6).

The draft article did not include a provision dealing with excessive payments and also had no counterpart to Article 11(6) and Article 12(6) UN Model.[202] During the

---

of payments which was supposed to be on a gross basis with a reduced rate would become taxed on a net basis with the same reduced rate.'

197. Committee of Experts on International Cooperation in Tax Matters, *supra* n. 144, at para. 40 (word order italicized by the author).
198. Committee of Experts on International Cooperation in Tax Matters, *supra* n. 187, at para. 83.
199. *Ibid.*, at para. 83.
200. *Ibid.*, at para. 89.
201. *Ibid.*, at para. 90.
202. *Ibid.*, at para. 81.

meeting, opinions varied on the appropriateness of an 'excessive payment' provision in relation to service payments.[203] Additionally, the concept of 'beneficial ownership' and the 'length of stay' proposed in paragraph 4 were discussed. Regarding the inclusion of a provision referring to excessive payments, *Arnold* mentioned that Article 9 UN Model is already sufficient for covering excessive payments. However, due to the support shown for an additional provision for them, *Arnold* redrafted the article to include paragraph 7 dealing with excessive payments.[204]

Concerning the issue of 'beneficial ownership', *Arnold* stated that he did not explicitly include this concept in the draft article as other provisions of the UN Model dealing with the taxation of services do not explicitly refer to it. Additionally, the reference to the person 'who furnishes those services' with regard to the recipient of the payment can essentially be seen as the equivalent of the 'beneficial owner' test reflected in Articles 11 and 12 of the UN Model.[205] One committee member concluded that the reference to the concept of beneficial ownership is already present in the articles on the taxation of passive income and gross base taxation. In addition, the notion of 'who furnishes the services' could be misinterpreted as a physical presence requirement in the source state. As a result, the beneficial ownership concept should be a part of the new article.[206] As a response to the discussions on the beneficial ownership concept, *Arnold* presented a redrafted version of the article in order to include the beneficial ownership concept.[207] *Arnold's* redraft also included the removal of the reference to the provisions of Articles 17 and 20 UN Model in paragraph 2 of the draft article as this issue is going to be dealt with in the commentary to the new article. On the question of whether the reference to Article 8 UN Model shall be left in the article itself or only be included in the commentary, the tax committee decided to table this issue for discussion at a later date.[208]

The tax committee also comprehensively discussed the appropriateness of the adoption of a rule that is based on the residence of the payer of technical service fees even if they were not deducted from the tax base of the paying individual. To some committee members, taxation of the service payments was not seen as appropriate in this scenario as they were not deducted from the payer's tax base. Others, however, considered that there is already established state practice reflecting the discussed scenario with the view of helping to preserve the source state's tax base.[209]

Another issue that arose during the committee's session was – similar to what is already found in Articles 8, 18, 23, and 25 UN Model – the drafting of alternative provisions to the new article. *Kana*, the coordinator of the subcommittee on services proposed that committee members who are interested in the inclusion of an alternative could draft an option that might then be included by the subcommittee in the

203. *Ibid.*, at para. 82.
204. *Ibid.*, at para. 87.
205. *Ibid.*, at para. 85.
206. *Ibid.*, at para. 86.
207. *Ibid.*, at para. 87.
208. *Ibid.*, at para. 88.
209. *Ibid.*, at para. 84.

commentary to the article.[210] In this respect, the tax committee decided to not include an alternative separate provision to the UN Model itself but rather in the commentary to the new article. In addition, the latter shall also include a discussion on the pros and cons of the inclusion of the new article and its alternative provision, also making reference to the fact that several countries might not want to include the new article in their tax treaties due to policy reasons.[211]

In its eleventh session in 2015, a revised draft article and commentary were presented.[212] The following changes have been made to the draft article that was presented during the tax committee's eleventh session:

Article XX – ~~Payments~~ Fees for Technical and Other Services

1. ~~Payments~~ **Fees** for technical services arising in a Contracting State and paid to a resident of the other Contracting State ~~who furnishes [in consideration of] those services~~ may be taxed in that other State.
2. However, notwithstanding Article 14 and subject to the provisions of Articles 8, [17 and 20] ~~such payments~~ **fees for technical services arising in a Contracting State** may also be taxed in the Contracting State in which they ~~the payments~~ arise and according to the laws of that State, **but if the beneficial owner of the fees is a resident of the other Contracting State**, the tax so charged shall not exceed __ percent of the gross amount of the fees ~~payments~~ (the percentage to be established through bilateral negotiations).
3. The term '~~payments~~ **fees** for technical services' as used in this Article means any payment in consideration for any service of a managerial, technical or consultancy nature, unless the payment is ~~the reimbursement of actual expenses incurred by the person providing the service or is made to an employee, director or top level managerial officer of the person making the payments.~~ **made:**
   a. to an employee of the person making the payment;
   b. **to a director or top-level managerial official of a company;**
   c. **for teaching in or by educational institutions [as part of a degree granting program]; or**
   d. **by an individual for services for the personal use by an individual;**
   e. **[for services that are ancillary and subsidiary, as well as inextricably and essentially linked, to the sale of property].**
4. The provisions of paragraphs 1 and 2 shall not apply if the **beneficial owner** ~~recipient~~ of ~~payments~~ **fees** for technical services ~~[person who furnishes the technical services]~~, being a resident of a Contracting State in which the ~~payments~~ **fees** for technical services arise through a permanent establishment situated in that other State, or performs in the other Contracting State independent personal services from a fixed base situated in that other State, and the **fees for** technical services ~~[in respect of which the payments are made]~~ are effectively connected with
   a. such permanent establishment or fixed base, or
   b. business activities referred to in (c) of paragraph 1 of Article 7.

   In such cases the provisions of Article 7 or Article 14, as the case may be, shall apply.

210. *Ibid.*, at para. 89.
211. *Ibid.*, at para. 90.
212. Committee of Experts on International Cooperation in Tax Matters, *Report on the eleventh session*, E/2015/45-E/C.18/2015/6, https://financing.desa.un.org/sites/default/files/2023-03/N1546004.pdf (accessed 6 January 2024), paras 63 et seq.

5. For the purposes of this Article, subject to paragraph 6, ~~payments~~ **fees** for technical services shall be deemed to arise in a Contracting State if the payer is a resident of that State or if the person **paying the fees** ~~making the payments~~ for technical services, whether that person is a resident of a Contracting State or not, has in a Contracting State a permanent establishment or a fixed base in connection with which the obligation to **pay the fees** ~~make the payments for technical services~~ was incurred, and such ~~payments~~ **fees** are borne by the permanent establishment or fixed base.
6. For the purposes of this Article, ~~payments~~ **fees** for technical services shall be deemed not to arise in a Contracting State if the payer is a resident of that State and carries on business in the other Contracting State **or a third State** through a permanent establishment situated in that State **or the third State**, or performs independent personal services through a fixed base situated in ~~the~~ **that** other ~~Contracting~~ State **or the third State** and such ~~payments~~ **fees** are borne by that permanent establishment or fixed base.
7. **Where, by reason of a special relationship between the payer and the beneficial owner of the fees for technical services or between both of them and some other person, the amount of the fees, having regard to the services for which they are paid, exceeds the amount which would have been agreed upon by the payer and the beneficial owner in the absence of such relationship, the provisions of this Article shall apply only to the last-mentioned amount [the amount that would have been agreed upon in the absence of such relationship]. In such case, the excess part of the fees shall remain taxable according to the laws of each Contracting State, due regard being had to the other provisions of this Convention.**[213]

The main changes made to the draft article since the tax committee's tenth session were:

- change in the title of the article by including 'other services';
- the term 'payments' was replaced with the term 'fees' throughout the entire article;
- the concept of beneficial ownership was included in the article;
- the reference to 'reimbursement of actual expenses incurred by the person providing the service' was deleted from the definition of 'fees for technical services' in paragraph 3;
- the scope of the new article was restricted by adding new exclusions to the definition of 'fees for technical services' in paragraph 3, i.e., payments for teaching in or by educational institutions and payments by an individual for services for the personal use by an individual (B2C services);
- a new paragraph concerning the treatment of excessive fees between related persons was added to the article.

Changes were also made to the commentary of the new article, especially with respect to the inclusion of minority positions.[214,215]

213. Changes emphasized by the author.
214. *See* Chapter 2.B.ii.2.b. of this publication.
215. *See* Committee of Experts on International Cooperation in Tax Matters, *Revised Draft Article and Commentary UN Model Tax Convention – Fees for Technical and Other Services,*

At the tax committee's eleventh session, the wording of the minority positions reflected in the commentary on the new article was discussed and consensus was achieved. In this respect, the tax committee agreed to add an alternative version in the Commentary to Article 12 UN Model. Additionally, it decided to include another alternative to the new article in its corresponding commentary that allowed the source state to tax all types of services performed in and outside that state if the services are performed for a related entity.[216]

Considerable discussions were held with respect to the proposed exclusion of payments for 'teaching in or by educational institutions as part of a degree-granting program' as found in (c) of paragraph 3 of the new article. In this respect, the tax committee decided that the reference to a 'degree-granting program' shall be deleted from the draft article in order to accommodate the different country practices and broaden the scope of the exclusion. However, several members of the tax committee expressed concerns about the general exclusion of payments for teaching activities due to the possibility of abuse and the difficulty of autonomously defining the term 'teaching'. As a result, the tax committee decided to address the possibility of removing the mentioned exclusion in the commentary to the new article.[217]

The discussions on the scope of the new article led the tax committee to decide to not include a reference to Article 20 UN Model as the new article does not overlap with the provisions on the allocation of taxing rights for payments received by a student, business trainee, or apprentice for the purpose of his or her education or training. The scope of the new article, however, potentially overlaps with Article 17 UN Model. Therefore, the tax committee decided to reflect this fact in the new article.[218] It was also agreed that the new article would be made subject to Article 16 UN Model.[219]

With respect to another possible exclusion from the scope of fees for technical services, i.e., (e) of paragraph 3, the tax committee decided not to include a 'carve-out' with respect to services 'that are ancillary and subsidiary, as well as inextricably and essentially linked, to the sale of property'.[220] Instead, this option shall be addressed in the commentary to the new article.[221]

At the tax committee's twelfth session in 2016, the UN Subcommittee on Tax Treatment of Services provided a report on the taxation of services[222] that included several annexes. Annex 1 contained the text of the new article on fees for technical services that was agreed upon by the committee in the eleventh session in 2015. The

E/C.18/2015/CRP.5, https://www.un.org/esa/ffd/wp-content/uploads/2015/10/11STM_CRP.5_Services.pdf (accessed 6 January 2024), 7.

216. Committee of Experts on International Cooperation in Tax Matters, *supra* n. 212, at para. 72.
217. *Ibid.*, at para. 68.
218. *Ibid.*, at para. 67.
219. *Ibid.*, at para. 69.
220. Committee of Experts on International Cooperation in Tax Matters, *supra* n. 215, at para. 61: 'Payments for technical services that are intimately connected to the sale of property are expressly excluded from the definition of fees for technical services by paragraph 3(e) of Article XX.'
221. Committee of Experts on International Cooperation in Tax Matters, *supra* n. 212, at para. 70.
222. Committee of Experts on International Cooperation in Tax Matters, *Taxation of Services – Report of the Coordinator (Ms. Liselott Kana)*, E/C.18/2016/CRP.1, https://www.un.org/esa/ffd/wp-content/uploads/2016/10/12STM_CRP1_Services.pdf (accessed 6 January 2024).

corresponding commentary to the new article is extracted in Annex 2 for approval by the tax committee at its twelfth session. At that time, the tax committee also decided on the text of the Commentary to Article 12 UN Model relating to issues of taxation of fees for technical services in the context of taxation of royalties (Annex 3). It also concluded other necessary textual changes in the UN Model relating to the inclusion of the new article on fees for technical services (Annex 4).[223]

Discussion arose with respect to the concept of 'high-value services' found in the draft commentary to the new article:

> Paragraph 2 is not expressly subject to the provisions of Article [21] dealing with income from services provided by students, apprentices or business trainees. Given that Article [16][224] is intended to apply to specialized, *high-value services*, income from services derived by students, apprentices and business trainees should not fall within the definition of 'fees for technical services' in paragraph 3.[225]

Due to the difficult task of differentiating between low-value and high-value services with respect to services provided by students, apprentices, and business trainees, the tax committee decided to delete the entire paragraph in the commentary referring to high-value services. In addition, other minor drafting modifications were made.[226]

After renumbering the new article from Article 16 to Article 12A[227] and including a different wording in paragraph 74 of the draft commentary on reimbursement of costs, the tax committee agreed on a final text of the new article and its corresponding commentary.[228] It decided to assign the article on the taxation of fees for technical services the number '12A' as assigning the new article number '16' – as was planned during the last stage of drafting – became highly controversial. This is because it required renumbering the existing Articles 16 to 30 UN Model and their commentaries together with changes in other secondary sources relating to the UN Model.[229]

Following the tax committee's thirteenth session, however, the UN Subcommittee on Tax Treatment of Services decided to substantially revise the text of the new article and its corresponding commentary 'to render the text clearer and easier for its

223. *Ibid.*, at 2.
224. The draft article on the taxation of fees for technical services was – at that time – numbered as the 'new' Article 16 UN Model.
225. Committee of Experts on International Cooperation in Tax Matters, *supra* n. 222, at 20 (word order italicized by the author).
226. Committee of Experts on International Cooperation in Tax Matters, *Report on the twelfth and thirteenth sessions*, E/2016/45-E/C.18/2016/7, https://financing.desa.un.org/sites/default/files/2023-03/English_31.pdf (accessed 6 January 2024), para. 40.
227. *Arnold* already used the number '12A' for the new article in the Tax Committee's paper of 11 October 2013 principally prepared by him: Committee of Experts on International Cooperation in Tax Matters, *supra* n. 168, at 7 et seq.
228. Committee of Experts on International Cooperation in Tax Matters, *supra* n. 226, at para. 43.
229. Brian J. Arnold, *The UN Committee of Experts and the UN Model: Recent Developments*, 71 BIT 131, 131 et seq. (2017) DOI: 10.59403/1dz7hrf.

application'.[230] As a result, the subcommittee presented the changes to the tax committee for approval of the revision.

A substantial change referred to the elimination of the reference to 'third state' in paragraph 6 of the agreed Article 12A:

> For the purposes of this Article, fees for technical services shall be deemed not to arise in a Contracting State if the payer is a resident of that State and carries on business in the other Contracting State ~~or a third State~~ through a permanent establishment situated in that other State ~~or the third State~~, or performs independent personal services through a fixed base situated in that other State ~~or the third State~~ and such fees are borne by that permanent establishment or fixed base.[231]

Instead of extending the scope of the new article to fees arising in a third state explicitly in the article itself, the tax committee decided to provide an option for such an extension in paragraphs 125 to 127 of the commentary to the article.

Other changes were made with respect to the concept of closely related persons,[232] clarification of the relationship between Article 12A and the switch over-clause of Article 23 A (2) UN Model,[233] elucidating the relationship between Article 12A and Article 14 UN Model,[234] and the addition of an example on the reimbursement of expenses.[235] All suggested changes were ultimately approved by the tax committee, and the drafting of the new article and its commentary were regarded as being completed.[236] At the tax committee's sixteenth session in 2018, Article 12A was finally launched as part of the UN Model 2017.[237]

C OBJECT AND PURPOSE OF ARTICLE 12A UN MODEL

i Unequal Tax Treatment of Resident and Non-resident Service Providers

Before the inclusion of Article 12A to the UN Model 2017, non-resident business service providers were only subject to taxation in the source state with the existence of a PE or

230. *See* Committee of Experts on International Cooperation in Tax Matters, *Revised Commentary on Article 12A: Fees for Technical services*, E/C.18/2017/CRP.1, https://financing.desa.un.org/sites/default/files/2023-03/14STM_CRP1_Article12A_technical-services.pdf (accessed 6 January 2024), 1.
231. *Ibid.*, at 53 et seq. (changes emphasized by the author).
232. Committee of Experts on International Cooperation in Tax Matters, *supra* n. 230, at paras 28 to 31.
233. *Ibid.*, at para. 43: 'In this regard, where a country applies the exemption method under Article 23 A, it is entitled to apply the credit method under Article 23 A, paragraph (2) with respect to items of income taxable under Article 10, 11, 12 or 12A.'
234. *Ibid.*, at paras 28 to 47.
235. *Ibid.*, at paras 79 and 80.
236. Committee of Experts on International Cooperation in Tax Matters, *Report on the fourteenth session*, E/2017/45-E/C.18/2017/3, https://financing.desa.un.org/sites/default/files/2023-03/N1715746.pdf (accessed 6 January 2024), para. 37.
237. *See* Committee of Experts on International Cooperation in Tax Matters, *Report on the sixteenth session*, E/2018/45/Add.1-E/C.18/2018/7, https://financing.desa.un.org/sites/default/files/2023-03/N1818654.pdf (accessed 6 January 2024), 61.

fixed base therein. Domestic businesses, however, are subject to residence taxation based on their worldwide income. As it was not possible for source states to tax non-resident service providers unless a certain (physical) nexus was met, competitive disadvantages of domestic service providers may have occurred in the past as these were subject to domestic taxation on services provided within that state. A competitive disadvantage of domestic service providers may especially arise if the non-resident service provider is – based on its worldwide income – subject to no or only minimal taxation in its residence state, possibly leading to the provision of services at a lower price.

To increase the competitiveness of domestic service providers in the source state, the UN Tax Committee decided – among other objectives – to include Article 12A to the UN Model 2017.[238] This increases the competitiveness of domestic service providers basically by adding to the tax burden of non-resident service providers. Based on the provisions of Article 12A UN Model, non-resident service providers are subject to gross taxation of fees for technical services at a rate negotiated by the contracting states. This is, on the one hand, restricted to technical services and therefore not to all types of them and, on the other hand, only to B2B services.

Gross taxation is generally viewed as leading to excessive taxation of non-resident service providers which may even lead to unrelieved double taxation of service fees.[239] In addition, non-resident service providers might be enticed to pass on the tax burden to the service recipient by grossing-up its fees.[240] Service recipients of net importing countries, such as developing countries, would then be faced with higher prices of foreign services. Such an outcome might possibly increase the overall competitiveness of domestic service providers as customers might be tempted to choose the less expensive option in the form of services provided by domestic service providers.

The objective of the UN Tax Committee to increase the competitiveness of domestic service providers seems – initially – to be achieved through the inclusion of Article 12A to the UN Model 2017. However, while it is true that there is a possibility of more competitiveness of domestic service providers by increasing the tax burden of non-resident service providers, such a measure can have detrimental effects on the source countries' economy by discouraging cross-border trade and investments: Technical services are often cost-intensive services, especially when they are based on sophisticated R&D. They require specialized knowledge, skill, or expertise. Therefore, there is often a lack of availability of domestic service providers who are able to provide these which leads to a certain degree of dependence on service providers located abroad. The imposition of a withholding tax on the gross amount of technical service fees, however, might discourage the inbound flow of highly sophisticated and needed services. Therefore, non-resident service providers should – in the same way as domestic service providers – at least be afforded the possibility to file for net taxation

238. *See, e.g.*, para. 11 of the Commentary on Article 12A UN Model 2017.
239. Sixdorf & Leitsch, *supra* n. 6, at 241.
240. *See, e.g.*, Malan, *supra* n. 6, at 65: The risk of grossing up the fees might be mitigated by using an 'appropriate' tax rate in the corresponding DTC.

in the source state. Although this would already be possible if the non-resident service provider establishes a PE in the source state, the creation of a PE is highly unlikely with respect to technical services. The resident service provider cannot just 'easily' avoid gross taxation through the creation of a PE or a fixed base in the source state[241] as the highly specialized nature of the services often neither require a long-term engagement nor a physical presence in there. Such a nature of technical services was also a reason - among others - why base erosion of source countries' tax base was addressed and Article 12A was included to the UN Model 2017. The nature of technical services prevented the taxation of its fees in the source state as no PE or fixed base was established therein causing a base erosion of the tax base of the source state.[242] If the nature of technical services would have been of such a type that it regularly creates a PE or fixed base, the inclusion of Article 12A to the UN Model 2017 would - in the author's opinion - not have been justifiable.

ii Taxation of Technical Services in a Digitalized Economy

1 Introduction

a Global Strategic Planning of MNEs

New business models have emerged due to the increasing digitalized economy. Although modern business models may have parallels to more traditional models, advancements in information and communication technologies (ICT) have made it possible to conduct business on a significantly larger scale and longer distances than in the traditional 'brick-and-mortar'-economy. Over the years, more and more new business models emerged, as innovation in the field of ICT continued. Business models range from e-commerce in a general sense to payment services, app stores, online advertising, cloud computing, high-frequency trading and participative network platforms.[243] It is also worth mentioning that several groups of companies specifically focus on the provision of infrastructure to enable companies specialized in digitalized business to exist and prosper, as they provide the necessary hardware, software and communication technology to them (e.g., IBM, Oracle, Microsoft and Apple). Business models used in the digitalized economy share several key features relevant to taxation purposes:[244]

- Mobility of intangibles, users and business functions resulting from the higher degree of flexibility with respect to the geographical location of personnel, servers and other relevant resources.
- Use of 'big data'.

241. *See* for a different opinion: Malan, *supra* n. 6, at 66.
242. *See* Chapter 3.C.iii. of this publication.
243. *See* OECD, *Addressing the Tax Challenges of the Digital Economy – Action 1: 2015 Final Report*, paras 116 et seq. (OECD Publishing 2015).
244. *Ibid.*, at 64 et seq.

- Network effects in relation to user participation, integration and synergies.
- Use of business models in which the supply and demand markets are located in different jurisdictions (multi-sided business models).
- Tendency of mono- or oligopoly due to strong reliance on network effects.
- Low entry barriers and rapidly growing technology.

These key features of evolving business models in the digitalized economy have a huge impact on value-creation and the place of economic activity. The main challenges raise serious questions not only on income characterization gained through the use of emerging business models but also on the appropriateness of fundamental concepts upon which the allocation of taxing rights for service income or the income from the sale of goods is based. These challenges which – for the most part – still remain unsolved on a global scale,[245] led to the introduction of several unilateral measures by source states,[246] as current rules on international taxation are not able to appropriately tackle the challenges of the digitalized economy. The challenges of the digitalized economy may be divided into the following categories:[247]

- *Physical presence:* Large MNE-groups can provide services in jurisdictions where substantial value is generated without the need to establish substantial (physical) infrastructure therein. Subsidiaries located in such (market) jurisdictions may provide a broad variety of services with only basic equipment in place. These services may include high-value marketing services, customer or legal support, digital content services or cloud-computing services, all of which are rendered completely online.
- *The use of data:* As business models evolved over time, the generation, collection, and use of data have – together with their influence on the generation of business profits – increased. This raises serious questions on value creation and its characterization for tax purposes.
- *Characterization of emerging digital goods and services:* Digitalization also fostered the transformation of individual resources such as software, network infrastructure or even hardware from goods to services. Such transformation resulted in an increasing availability of these resources through the internet as services. In this respect, 'X-as-a-service' (XaaS) has been used to describe the transformation from goods to services.[248] The most prominent examples used in the business context are Software-as-a-Service (SaaS), Infrastructure-as-a-Service (IaaS) and Platform-as-a-Service (PaaS), all of which are cloud-based processes.[249] The use of cloud-computing services has been increasingly popular in recent years. In 2016, approximately 50 % of large businesses made

245. *See* Chapter 3.C.ii.1.c. of this publication.
246. *See, e.g.*, Annet W. Oguttu, *Addressing the Tax Challenges Arising from the Digitalization of the Economy – Action 1 and Subsequent Work*, in: Emily Muyaa et al. (eds), *Base Erosion and Profit Shifting: A Blueprint for Africa's Response*, 563-616 (IBFD 2021), at 14.4.1.
247. See OECD, *supra* n. 243, at 98 et seq.
248. *Ibid.*, at 41.
249. Louise F. Kjærsgaard, *Allocation of the Taxing Right to Payments for Cloud Computing-as-a-Service*, 11 WTJ 379, 386 (2019) DOI: 10.59403/3hp5yk7.

use of cloud-computing services[250] and it is expected that the use of increasingly sophisticated cloud-computing services will – partially by using artificial intelligence – increase in the future,[251] leading to challenging questions on the characterization of income from such services under current international taxation rules.

These challenges are often accompanied by a risk of Base Erosion and Profit Shifting (BEPS). The following subchapter shall give an overview of the risk of BEPS-related challenges of the digitalized economy.

b BEPS Through Digitalized Services

The rise of the digitalized economy raises substantial questions about the appropriate allocation of taxing rights. The PE-concept has arguably become redundant due to the increased mobility of the workforce and the possibility to conduct business remotely through digital means. As most of the tax treaties currently in force are based on the OECD and partially the UN Models before its 2017 update,[252] they still heavily rely on the PE-concept as a nexus to tax services in the source state. Therefore, the source states' ability to tax profits from cross-border services is increasingly challenged through the increasing digitalization of the economy.

In addition, profit allocation rules of the OECD and UN Models[253] are still highly dependent on physical features (e.g., functions performed or assets employed),[254] therefore, not taking into account the characteristics of new business models specifically arising in a digital business context.

The academic discourse has shown that certain BEPS-related risks do not specifically originate from the advancements in digitalization but are rather exacerbated by such advancements.[255] As a result, BEPS risks arising from the digitalization of the economy should not be tackled only through isolated measures. This is also reflected by the OECD BEPS Action Plan, as several BEPS Action Points are intended to counter the challenges arising from the digitalization of the economy, e.g., BEPS Action

250. *See* OECD, *Tax Challenges Arising from Digitalisation – Interim Report 2018: Inclusive Framework on BEPS*, 13 et seq. (OECD Publishing 2018).
251. Dina Scornos, *Cloud Computing: Difficulties in Applying Current and Proposed Nexus and Profit Allocation Rules in a Cross-Border Scenario*, 74 BIT 88, 88 (2020) DOI: 10.59403/2kx2mp2.
252. The introduction of Article 12A to the UN Model 2017 and Article 12B to the UN Model 2021 significantly increased the source-states' ability to tax cross-border services, especially those that are provided on a short-term basis.
253. *See* Articles 7 and 9 of the OECD and UN Models.
254. *See* Vikram Chand & Andrés Báez Moreno, *Solving the Allocation of Taxing Rights Debate for the Digitalized Economy: Shortcomings of the Digital PE Proposal and Reconsideration of the Base-Eroding Payments Proposal*, in: Pasquale Pistone & Dennis Weber (eds), *Taxing the Digital Economy: The EU Proposals and Other Insights*, 119, 121 (IBFD 2019).
255. *See, e.g.*, Georg Kofler, Gunter Mayr & Christoph Schlager, *Digitalisierung und Betriebsstättenkonzept*, RdW 369, 369 et seq. (2017); Marcel Olbert & Christoph Spengel, *Taxation in the Digital Economy – Recent Policy Developments and the Question of Value Creation*, 2 ITAXS 3, at 2.1. (2019) DOI: 10.2139/ssrn.3368092.

7 on 'preventing the artificial avoidance of permanent establishment status' or BEPS Actions 8-10 on 'aligning transfer pricing outcomes with value creation'.[256]

The digitalized economy aggravated the possibility of digital service providers artificially shifting their taxable income from high- to low-tax jurisdictions in which no to little economic activity is carried out.[257] It also made the international tax community aware of the fact that current rules of international taxation do not necessarily protect the tax base of source states due to the increased possibility of avoidance of physical presence in the source state.[258]

This concern is especially apparent in relation to the conduct of cross-border business by large MNE groups. The current policy debate amongst the international tax community hereby focuses on prominent examples of MNE groups that pay little to no amount of tax in large market jurisdictions.[259]

The OECD BEPS Action Plan did not raise the issue of tax base erosion through the deductibility of (technical) service fees. However, such tax base erosion is especially a concern for developing countries as they are major importers of 'high value' services, such as technical, managerial or consultancy services. Tax treaties of developing countries that adopt provisions based on the OECD or the UN Models before the inclusion of Article 12A to the UN Model 2017, usually don't allow for source taxation without the existence of a PE or fixed base therein. Therefore, service fees paid by a resident of a developing country for services rendered by a non-resident are not taxable by the developing country if such services are rendered completely through digital means. As such service fees may, however, be deductible as business expenses by the payer of the fee, the tax base of the developing country will be reduced, resulting in tax base erosion.

To counter such tax base erosion, developing countries favour the inclusion of rules into their domestic law that deny a deduction of the payment or the imposition of a source-based withholding-tax on payments to related entities resident in a low- or no-tax jurisdiction.[260] This rule often works in combination with a provision included in tax treaties, granting the source state a taxing right on base eroding payments, such as technical service fees as defined in Article 12A(3) UN Model, if the payment is not subject to any tax.[261]

Such countermeasures, however, are not particular to the evolution of digitalized business models. They already existed before *Doernberg* – as one of the first movers in the academic discourse on the base-erosion principle – suggested the use of a

256. Kofler, Mayr & Schlager, *supra* n. 255, at 371.
257. Annet W. Oguttu, *A Critique from a Developing Country Perspective of the Proposals to Tax the Digital Economy*, 12 WTJ 799, 800 (2020) DOI: 10.59403/3y6ybja.
258. *See, e.g.*, Alessandro Samari, *The OECD Public Consultation Document on Addressing the Tax Challenges of the Digitalization of the Economy: Strengths and Weaknesses of the Three Proposals for Revising Profit Allocation and Nexus Rules*, 26 ITPJ 265, 265 (2019) DOI: 10.59403/1gyweah.
259. Olbert & Spengel, *supra* n. 255, at 2.3.
260. *See* Chapter 3.C.iii. with reference to the base erosion principle.
261. Oguttu, *supra* n. 257, at 820.

withholding tax mechanism to counter tax base erosion in the field of e-commerce.[262] The base-erosion principle, without being named as such, was already reflected in service fee-provisions of Kenyan tax treaties as early as the 1970s.[263] Based on the mentioned provisions, the source state is allowed to levy a withholding tax on specific service fees, even in the absence of a PE or fixed base therein. Therefore, also tax base-eroding payments are subject to source taxation irrespective of the use of digital means.

The next chapter aims to provide an overview of (partially) global initiatives aiming to specifically tackle the tax challenges arising from the digitalization of the economy in the field of digitalized services, before specifically analysing the application of Articles 12A and 12B UN Model on digitalized services.

c Global Initiatives to Tax Digitalized Services

(i) OECD: From BEPS Action Plan 1 to Pillars I and II

In recognizing that the use of modern information and communication technologies might lead to tax base erosion, the OECD published a report on 'Addressing the Tax Challenges of the Digital Economy' (BEPS Action 1) in 2015.[264] BEPS Action 1 examined – amongst others – the possibilities of companies to have a significant digital presence in a state without being liable to tax therein, value creation of digital products and services, characterization of income derived from emerging business concepts and its application with respect to existing source rules.[265] One of the options developed by the OECD to address the broader tax challenges of the digitalized economy was the introduction of a withholding tax on certain types of digital transactions.[266] In this respect, scholars supported the inclusion of a WHT-mechanism to challenge the broader challenges of the digitalized economy.[267] In contrast to the UN,[268] however, the OECD did not develop plans for a mechanism that is based on gross-computation but rather a mechanism based on a profit-based computation, therefore, making the implementation of a withholding-tax system highly unlikely.[269] A withholding tax mechanism is only foreseen as an accessory mechanism to some proposals of the Pillar II-solution (see below).

262. Richard L. Doernberg, *Electronic Commerce and International Tax Sharing*, 16 TNI 1013-1022 (1998) and with explicit reference to *Doernberg's* work: Richard L. Doernberg & Luc Hinnekens, *Electronic Commerce and International Taxation*, at 315 and 319 et seq. (Wolters Kluwer 1999).
263. *See, e.g.*, Article 14 DTC Kenya-Denmark (1972) and Article 14 DTC Kenya-Norway (1972).
264. OECD, *supra* n. 243.
265. *Ibid.*, at 16.
266. *Ibid.*, at 106.
267. *See, e.g.*, Andrés Báez Moreno & Yariv Brauner, *Withholding Taxes in the Service of BEPS Action 1: Address the Tax Challenges of the Digital Economy*, at 4 et seq. (IBFD White Paper 2015); Báez Moreno, *supra* n. 6, at 323 et seq.
268. *See* Chapter 3.C.ii.2. of this publication.
269. *See, e.g.*, Graeme S. Cooper, *Building on the Rubble of Pillar One*, 75 BIT 533, 539 (2021) DOI: 10.59403/q2700q.

Based on BEPS Action 1, the OECD started to further develop concepts for measures tackling the broad tax challenges related to the digitalization of the economy. In this respect, the Task Force on the Digital Economy (TFDE) of the Inclusive Framework on BEPS (IF) issued an Interim Report on the 'Tax Challenges Arising from Digitalisation' recognizing the need for a coordinated global solution.[270] As a result, a global approach based on a two-pillar solution has been approved by the IF on 23 January 2019.[271]

The two-pillar solution aims at 1) reforming and restoring the international tax system to address the tax challenges of the digitalized economy, 2) ensuring fairness and equity of the international tax framework, 3) preventing uncoordinated unilateral tax measures, and 4) ensuring tax certainty.[272]

Pillar I of the two-pillar solution focuses on changes to profit allocation and currently established nexus rules in the international tax system by expanding taxing rights of market jurisdictions, i.e., jurisdictions where an MNE has active participation in the jurisdictions' economy through the sale of products, the provision of services or the acquirement and collection of data or contributions from users.[273] The proposed taxing right is not limited to factors of physical presence and goes beyond the current arm's length principle.[274] Pillar I establishes a new taxing right (Amount A) for market jurisdictions overlaying existing nexus and profit allocation rules.[275] Amount A's key design features include 1) a revenue threshold based on an MNE-group's annual consolidated group revenue, 2) scoping rules, 3) the use of a new nexus rule, 4) sourcing rules, 5) an approach for reallocating residual profit, 6) a loss-carry-forward regime, 7) a marketing and distribution profits safe harbour, 8) mechanisms on the elimination of double taxation, 9) a simplified administrative process, and 10) the implementation of Amount A through a Multilateral Convention (MLC) and supplementary rules for changes in domestic law.

Pillar II on the other hand, focuses on the introduction of a systemic solution with the intention to address the remaining BEPS-issues, including – amongst others – the introduction of an Income Inclusion Rule (IIR), Undertaxed Payments Rule (UTPR) and Subject to Tax Rule (STTR).[276] The IIR together with the UTPR are known as Global Anti-Base Erosion (GloBE) rules and are aimed at being implemented by IF Member States through provisions of domestic law.[277] The STTR on the other hand is a tax treaty-related rule aiming to ensure source state taxation on payments between related

270. OECD, *supra* n. 250, at 212 et seq.
271. *See* OECD, *Addressing the Tax Challenges of the Digitalisation of the Economy – Policy Note – 23 January 2019*, https://www.oecd.org/tax/beps/policy-note-beps-inclusive-framework-addressing-tax-challenges-digitalisation.pdf (accessed 1 January 2024).
272. OECD, *Tax Challenges Arising from Digitalisation – Report on Pillar One Blueprint: Inclusive Framework on BEPS*, 11 (OECD Publishing 2020).
273. *Ibid.*, at 11 et seq.
274. Doreen Liu, Jaap Reyneveld & Charlotte Straatman, *OECD's Work on the Digital Economy: Impact Far Beyond the Digital Economy*, 26 ITPJ 295, 259 (2019) DOI: 10.59403/2pm8eef.
275. OECD, *supra* n. 272, at 13.
276. *Ibid.*, at 11.
277. Belisa Ferreira Liotti, *Limits of International Cooperation: The Concept of 'Jurisdiction Not to Tax' from the BEPS Project to GloBE*, 76 BIT 63, 77 with further references (2022) DOI: 10.59403/240km9w.

entities that are subject to a low level of taxation.[278] The introduction of these measures aims to ensure that large, cross-border business-conducting enterprises pay at least a certain minimum amount of tax if their corporate income is taxed below an agreed minimum rate.[279]

The OECD's ambitious implementation plan foresaw that the necessary legal instruments to implement the concepts of Pillars I and II shall be 'in effect' already as of 1 January 2023,[280] with the exception of the UTPR.[281] Based on the ambitious timetable, it was rather expected by delegates of the Task Force on the Digital Economy (TFDE) that the implementation of Pillars I and II may be delayed by the OECD. As expected, the OECD announced the delay of implementation of Pillar I and II until 2024 through the publication of the OECD Secretary-General Tax Report to G20 Finance Ministers and Central Bank Governors on 11 July 2022 at their meeting in Indonesia.[282] On 15 November 2023, an outcome statement on the two-pillar solution was approved by 140 Member States of the IF.[283] The outcome statement aims to summarize the deliverables of the two-pillar solution as well as its remaining elements.[284] It – amongst others – informs on the intention to enable the MLC (Pillar I) to enter into force in 2025 and provides information on the possibility of signing the STTR (Pillar II) as of 2 October 2023.[285]

(ii) EU: Initiatives to Tackle the Challenges of the Digitalized Economy

With a view to ensure a 'fair and efficient corporate taxation in the Union',[286] the European Commission made a proposal for a Council Directive relating to corporate taxation of a significant digital presence (SDP) in March 2018.[287] On the same day (21

278. João F. Pinto Nogueira, *GloBE and EU Law: Assessing the Compatibility of the OECD's Pillar II Initiative on a Minimum Effective Tax Rate with EU Law and Implementing It within the Internal Market*, 12 WTJ 465, 478 et seq. (2020) DOI: 10.59403/27gh15s.
279. OECD, *supra* n. 272, at 9.
280. OECD, *Statement on a Two-Pillar Solution to Address the Tax Challenges Arising from the Digitalisation of the Economy – 8 October 2021*, https://www.oecd.org/tax/beps/statement-on-a-two-pillar-solution-to-address-the-tax-challenges-arising-from-the-digitalisation-of-the-economy-october-2021.pdf (accessed 1 January 2024).
281. *Ibid.*, at 5.
282. *OECD*, OECD Secretary-General Tax Report to G20 Finance Ministers and Central Bank Governors (2022), 4 et seq.: www.oecd.org/g20/topics/international-taxation/oecd-secretary-general-tax-report-g20-finance-ministers-indonesia-july-2022.pdf (accessed 7 August 2022).
283. See OECD, *Outcome Statement on the Two-Pillar Solution to Address the Tax Challenges Arising from the Digitalisation of the Economy*, https://www.oecd.org/tax/beps/outcome-statement-on-the-two-pillar-solution-to-address-the-tax-challenges-arising-from-the-digitalisation-of-the-economy-july-2023.pdf (accessed 30 December 2023).
284. *Ibid.*, at para. 4.
285. *Ibid.*, at paras 8 and 15.
286. European Commission, *Proposal for a Council Directive laying down rules relating to the corporate taxation of a significant digital presence*, COM(2018) 147 final, https://eur-lex.europa.eu/legal-content/DE/TXT/?uri=CELEX%3A52018PC0147 (accessed 6 January 2024), 3 with further references.
287. *Ibid.*, at 7 et seq.: Its most relevant provisions are the articles on Scope (Article 2), Definitions (Article 3), Significant digital presence (Article 4) and Profits attributable to the significant digital presence (Article 5).

March 2018), the European Commission also published its proposal for a Council Directive on the imposition of a digital services tax (DST) on revenues from certain digital services.[288] Both proposals are part of the efforts taken by the European Union to tackle the tax challenges of the digitalized economy and intend to contribute to the ongoing work conducted at the level of the OECD.[289]

The EU Commission's first proposal aimed to target corporations incorporated or established in the EU or incorporated or established in a third jurisdiction with which no tax treaty with the EU Member State in an SDP is established.[290] An SDP is established through the supply of digital services and the fulfilment of one of three user-based criteria (revenues, number of users and number of contracts) and a threshold criterion.[291] The SDP shall only cover digital services, i.e., services of essentially automated nature, involving only minimal human involvement, provided through the internet or an electronic network.[292]

The EU Commission's second proposal related to the incorporation of taxation rules with respect to revenues generated through the provision of digital services. It aimed to tax entities earning a total amount of revenues for the relevant financial year of more than EUR 750 m and as a part of it, a total amount of taxable revenues from digital services – as defined in Article 3 of the Directive's proposal – within the EU of more than EUR 50 m.[293] The tax rate of the DST shall be 3 % of the proportion of taxable revenues obtained by a taxable entity as obtained in a Member State in a tax period.[294] Taxable revenues are deemed to be obtained in a Member State if users are located therein during the tax period.[295]

In contrast to the Commission's proposal on the corporate taxation of an SDP, the DST-proposal is only referred to as a temporary intra-European solution, tackling the challenges of the digitalized economy with respect to digital services until a global solution at the level of the OECD is reached.[296]

Further work by the European Commission on both proposals is currently on hold. The future work stream will highly depend on the outcome of the two-pillar solution of the OECD. In this respect, however, it needs to be mentioned that the OECD's work on Pillar II has also been taken up by the EU. A proposal for a Council Directive to ensure a global minimum level of taxation for multinational groups in the European Union[297] was released on 22 December 2021. The final text of the Directive

288. European Commission, *Proposal for a Council Directive on the common system of a digital services tax on revenues resulting from the provision of certain digital services*, COM(2018) 148 final, https://eur-lex.europa.eu/legal-content/EN/TXT/?uri=COM%3A2018%3A148%3AFIN (accessed 6 January 2024).
289. European Commission, *supra* n. 286, at 3 and *Ibid.*, at 1 et seq.
290. European Commission, *supra* n. 286, 7.
291. *Ibid.*, at 7 et seq.
292. *Ibid.*, at 7.
293. European Commission, *supra* n. 288, at 25 et seq.
294. *Ibid.*, at 28.
295. *Ibid.*, at 28.
296. *Ibid.*, at 16.
297. European Commission, *Proposal for a Council Directive on ensuring a global minimum level of taxation for multinational groups in the Union*, COM(2021) 823 final, https://eur-lex.europa.eu/legal-content/EN/ALL/?uri=COM:2021:0823:FIN (accessed 6 January 2024).

was subsequently published in the Official Journal of the European Union on 22 December 2022, i.e., exactly one year after the release of its proposal.[298] The Directive aims at ensuring that Pillar II is implemented in a consistent and coherent manner. Its provisions reflect the global agreement by the IF and solely implement the OECD GloBE Model Rules with necessary adjustments to conform to EU law.[299]

2 *UN: Application of Articles 12A and 12B UN Model on Digitalized Services*

a Article 12A UN Model

One of the aims of the inclusion of Article 12A to the UN Model 2017 was to enable source states to tax fees for technical services provided by a non-resident service provider that has a significant economic but not physical presence within their jurisdiction.[300] This is especially true for digitalized services, as the performance of those mostly doesn't require any physical presence in the source state at all. According to *Lennard*, Article 12A UN Model 2017 constitutes 'the next frontier in addressing the realities of global services trade in a digitalized economy' as this provision does not require any physical presence in the state of the service recipient for a taxing right to arise therein.[301]

The application of Article 12A on digital services was already discussed before the introduction of Article 12A to the UN Model 2017 in a paper principally prepared by this author.[302] The author opined that the application of Article 12A UN Model 2017 in the digitalized economy might be a solution to a so-called fair allocation of taxing rights and would also reduce the source base eroding character of fees for technical, managerial and consultancy services conducted digitally, i.e., without a physical presence in the source state.[303]

As part of the discussions on the tax consequences of the digitalized economy, also *Falcão/Michel* gave input with respect to the application of Article 12A as an interim solution to 'uniformize the application of digital services taxes'.[304] As digital

298. Council of the European Union, *Council Directive (EU) 2022/2523 of 14 December 2022 on ensuring a global minimum level of taxation for multinational groups and large-scale domestic groups in the Union*, L 328/1, https://eur-lex.europa.eu/legal-content/EN/TXT/?uri=CELEX%3A32022L2523 (accessed 6 January 2024).
299. European Commission, *supra* n. 297, at 1.
300. *See* paras 2 et seq. of the Commentary on Article 12A UN Model 2017.
301. Michael Lennard, *Base Erosion and Profit Shifting and Developing Country Tax Administrations*, 44 Intertax 740, 741 (2016) DOI: 10.54648/taxi2016063.
302. Committee of Experts on International Cooperation in Tax Matters, *supra* n. 5, at paras 77 et seq.
303. *Ibid.*, at paras 106 et seq.
304. Tatiana Falcão & Bob Michel, Tax Consequences of the Digitalised Economy – Input to the United Nations Committee of Experts on International Cooperation in Tax Matters: https://www.un.org/development/desa/financing/document/comment-tatiana-falcao-and-bob-michel-20th-session-tax-committee-crp-25 (accessed 4 August 2022).

services taxes introduced by states around the globe[305] are mainly focused on targeting online advertising services, the authors focused on the possible ways of application of Article 12A on fees for online advertising services. The UN Tax Committee, however, did not follow up on the approaches suggested by *Falcão/Michel*, as it was highlighted that online advertising services should not be the main focus of the future work stream of the UN Tax Committee. Instead, a wider approach to the different revenue streams arising from the digitalized economy should be taken, also recognizing the interest of some countries in taxing companies that operate in a market without being physically present therein.[306] In this respect, support was expressed by several members of the UN Tax Committee for drafting a new model provision.[307]

Until the inclusion of Article 12A to the UN Model 2017, the attribution of source taxing rights on services was restricted to cases in which services were attributable to a PE or fixed base of the service provider in the source state. This 'more restrictive rule[s] of application'[308] on the allocation of taxing rights on cross-border services originated from a time in which international trade was mainly based on the trade of tangible goods, requiring the establishment of offices, sale facilities and storage facilities (i.e., physical presence) to provide the source state with the ability to enforce its tax law.[309] As new digital business models allow substantial economic involvement in the source state without relying on physical presence, the fixed base concept was regarded by the majority of UN Tax Committee Members as not being a sufficient nexus with respect to cross-border services due to the advancements in communication and information technologies.[310] Therefore, it was agreed by the UN Tax Committee to not include any (physical) threshold requirement in Article 12A UN Model 2017 for source taxing rights to arise but rather focus on the payer-payee relationship due to the base eroding character of fees for technical services in the source state.[311]

As Article 12A UN Model focuses on the payer-payee relationship and not on the place of performance of the service, the residence state of the payer of fees for technical services or the PE-state to which the fees are effectively attributed to, may tax these fees, even if technical services are performed in a third state, e.g., through digital means of communication.

305. *See* European Commission, *supra* n. 288, at 3; Lorenzo Bellavite, Davide Morabito & Riccardo Tognettini, *The Digital Service Tax in Italy: Main Characteristics and Practical Issues*, 60 ET 351-356 (2020) DOI: 10.59403/1er2jc5; Xeniya Yeroshenko, *Introducing a Digital Services Tax in the Czech Republic*, 27 ITPJ 199-204 (2020) DOI: 10.59403/11n5at6; Sholpan Issakova, *Taxing Automated Digital Services: Targeted Online Advertising*, 61 ET 174-178 (2021) DOI: 10.59403/3qzrv4w.
306. *See* Committee of Experts on International Cooperation in Tax Matters, *Report on the twentieth session*, E/2021/45-E/C.18/2020/3, https://financing.desa.un.org/sites/default/files/2023-03/Report%20on%2020th%20Session_EN.pdf (accessed 6 January 2024), para. 103.
307. *See Ibid.*, at para. 110.
308. *See* para. 3 of the Commentary on Article 12A of the UN Model 2017.
309. *See* Michael Kobetsky, *International Taxation of Permanent Establishments*, 125 et seq. (Cambridge University Press 2011).
310. *See* paras 2 and 16 of the Commentary on Article 12A UN Model 2021.
311. Committee of Experts on International Cooperation in Tax Matters, *supra* n. 169, at 7 et seq.

However, Article 12A does not apply to all technical services rendered digitally. As, according to the Commentary on Article 12A UN Model 2021,[312] services of a routine nature are outside the scope of Article 12A UN Model, only digitalized services of specialized nature rendered in a B2B context[313] with more than minimal human intervention[314] are within the scope of this provision. As a result, Article 12A UN Model does not apply to services that build the 'essential core of the digital economy', i.e., digital advertising or intermediation services.[315]

As Article 12 UN Model was not specifically regarded by the UN Tax Committee as a solution to tackle the challenges arising from the digitalization economy, it needed to further explore a solution that would be more capable of tackling these challenges.

b *Article 12B UN Model*

The inclusion of Article 12A to the UN Model 2017 was the result of extensive work completed by the UN Tax Committee and its Subcommittee on the Taxation of Services, starting in 2008.[316] The completion of Article 12A, however, was also 'the initiation of extensive work' for future changes to the UN Model based on potential conclusions derived from the changes made to the 2017 update of the UN Model and *in concreto* the inclusion of Article 12A on the taxation of Fees for Technical Services.[317]

The UN Tax Committee established a 'Subcommittee on Tax Challenges related to the Digitalization of the Economy' in 2017.[318] Its mandate encompassed the exploration of possibilities to tackle the challenges of the digitalized economy, including the possibility of drafting a provision related to income taxes and tax treaties.[319] To achieve its mandate, the subcommittee closely followed the discussions on Pillar I and II at the level of the OECD. After the release of the 'Statement by the OECD/G20 Inclusive Framework on BEPS on the Two-Pillar Approach to Address the Tax Challenges Arising from the Digitalisation of the Economy',[320] the co-coordinators of

312. *See* para. 62 of the Commentary on Article 12A UN Model 2021: 'Services of a routine nature that do not involve the application of such specialized knowledge, skill or expertise are not within the scope of Article 12A.'
313. *See* for the exclusion of B2C services: Article 12A(3)(c) UN Model.
314. *See* para. 3 of the Commentary on Article 12B UN Model 2021.
315. Andrés Báez Moreno, *Because not Always B Comes after A: Critical Reflections on the New Article 12B of the UN Model on Automated Digital Services*, 13 WTJ 501, 503 (2021) DOI: 10.2139/ssrn.3923508.
316. *See* Committee of Experts on International Cooperation in Tax Matters, *supra* n. 129, at para. 28.
317. *See* para. 17 of the Introduction to the UN Model 2017.
318. Committee of Experts on International Cooperation in Tax Matters, *Report on the fifteenth session*, E/2018/45-E/C.18/2018/1, https://financing.desa.un.org/sites/default/files/2023-03/N1746399.pdf (accessed 6 January 2024), para. 29.
319. Committee of Experts on International Cooperation in Tax Matters, *Tax Issues related to the Digitalization of the Economy: Report*, E/C.18/2019/CRP.12, https://financing.desa.un.org/sites/default/files/2023-03/18STM_CRP12-Work-on-taxation-issues-digitalization.pdf (accessed 6 January 2024), para. 1.
320. OECD, *Statement by the OECD/G20 Inclusive Framework on BEPS on the Two-Pillar Approach to Address the Tax Challenges Arising from the Digitalisation of the Economy – January 2020*,

the subcommittee submitted an update note on the subcommittee's recent developments. The update note was part of the agenda of the twentieth session of the UN Tax Committee in 2020.[321] It included a written proposal on the inclusion of a new article in the UN Model on automated digital services, as defined in the statement of the IF on the tax challenges arising from the digitalization of the economy.[322] The written proposal even included a proposal for the conclusion of a multilateral convention among the UN Member States. This very ambitious and questionable suggestion, however, has not been followed up subsequently. The proposal to include a new article to the UN Model, however, received support from several UN Tax Committee Members.[323] It was noted that the OECD's proposals on Pillar I and II were very complex to implement, demanding a solution that is easy to administer for developing countries, such as the introduction of a withholding tax at a reasonable rate. The offered proposal also aimed to fund any governmental initiatives as a response to the COVID-19 crisis.[324] Several members, however, noted that 'unprincipled' solutions shall be avoided and other sources of revenue shall be explored.[325]

A drafting group consisting of UN Tax Committee Members supporting the proposal to add a new provision to the UN Model was formed at the twentieth session of the UN Tax Committee.[326] Based on the general idea that the OECD Unified Approach can be modelled in a simpler way by making use of a withholding tax mechanism,[327] the UN Tax Committee has approved the addition of Article 12B to the UN Model 2021 by a majority vote in its twenty-first session, finalizing the text of the article at the twenty-second session of the UN Tax Committee in 2021.[328] Article 12B on Fees for Automated Digital Services (ADS) aims to address the challenges of the digitalized economy in the field of taxes and serves as an answer to the OECD project on Pillar I and II.

Article 12B(1) UN Model grants a taxing right for ADS to the residence state of the payee. However, such income may also be taxed in the state in which it arises according to the source rules of Article 12B(9) and (10) UN Model. In this respect, Article 12B(9) UN Model establishes that income arises in a contracting state if the payer is a resident of that state or if the payer, whether he is a resident of that contracting state or not, has a PE or fixed base in a contracting state through which the

http://www.oecd.org/tax/beps/statement-by-the-oecd-g20-inclusive-framework-on-beps-january-2020.pdf (accessed 25 July 2022).

321. Committee of Experts on International Cooperation in Tax Matters, *Co-coordinators' Paper on Tax Issues related to the Digitalization of the Economy for the 20th Session of the UN Committee of Experts on Cooperation in Tax Matters*, E/C.18/2020/CRP.25, https://financing.desa.un.org/sites/default/files/2023-03/CICTM%2020th_CRP.25%20_%20Digitalized%20Economy.pdf (accessed 6 January 2024).
322. Committee of Experts on International Cooperation in Tax Matters, *supra* n. 321, at 11 et seq.
323. Committee of Experts on International Cooperation in Tax Matters, *supra* n. 306, at para. 106.
324. *Ibid.*, at para. 107.
325. *Ibid.*, at para. 107.
326. *Ibid.*, at para. 110.
327. Committee of Experts on International Cooperation in Tax Matters, *supra* n. 321, at 8.
328. Committee of Experts on International Cooperation in Tax Matters, *Report on the twenty-first session*, E/2021/45/Add.1-E/C.18/2020/4, https://digitallibrary.un.org/record/3898885?ln=en (accessed 6 January 2024), para. 107.

income is incurred and borne. Source taxing rights are – according to Article 12B(2) UN Model – granted on the gross amount of income from ADS. If, however, the income recipient is the beneficial owner of such income, the tax rate charged on income from ADS shall not exceed a certain percentage negotiated by the contracting states.[329] However, according to Article 12B(3) UN Model, income derived from the provision of ADS will not be taxed on a gross basis if the beneficial owner requests the source state to be taxed on the basis of the qualified profits of the service provider.

The inclusion of Article 12B to the UN Model 2021 aims at a 'fair' allocation of taxing rights with respect to digital services, concretely, automated digital services. Its inclusion, however, has been accompanied by a lot of criticism from *Báez Moreno*[330] and a significant minority of UN Tax Committee Members. The issues of criticism included 1) the focus on the payer-payee relationship and not the place of performance of services as a connecting factor for source taxing rights, 2) addressing a multilateral problem with a bilateral solution,[331] 3) not awaiting the outcomes of the work of the Inclusive Framework on BEPS,[332] 4) problems of conceptual delineation between the definition of fees for technical services and ADS and the inclusion of B2C services in its scope as opposed to Article 12A UN Model 2017,[333] and the 5) non-inclusion of a payment threshold.[334]

The relationship between Article 12A and 12B UN Model will be further explored in *Chapter 4.C.* of this publication.

c *The Fast-Track Instrument*

At its twenty-fourth session in April 2022, the UN Tax Committee issued a Co-Coordinators' report on the taxation issues related to the digitalized and globalized economy, including information on workstreams elaborated by the Subcommittee on Taxation Issues Related to the Digitalized and Globalized Economy.[335] These workstreams aim to address the mandate given to the aforementioned subcommittee on identifying taxation issues of high priority for developing countries related to the digitalized and globalized economy.[336] In this respect, so-called Workstream A aims to explore options for a multilateral implementation of certain existing and prospective rules of the UN Model, such as Articles 12A and 12B, as these rules may have

329. *See* Article 12B(2) UN Model 2021.
330. *See* Báez Moreno, *supra* n. 315, at 503.
331. Committee of Experts on International Cooperation in Tax Matters, *supra* n. 328, at para. 105.
332. *Ibid.*, at para. 106.
333. *See* especially Báez Moreno, *supra* n. 315, at 501 et seq.
334. This point of criticism is reflected in para. 14 of the Commentary on Article 12B UN Model 2021: Due to the non-inclusion of a payment-threshold, Article 12B and a built-in withholding tax mechanism would also apply to small amounts of payments for ADS. This could be potentially burdensome for businesses.
335. Committee of Experts on International Cooperation in Tax Matters, *Taxation issues related to the digitalized and globalized economy: Co-Coordinators' Report*, E/C.18/2022/CRP.6, https://financing.desa.un.org/sites/default/files/2023-03/CRP.6%20Digitalized%20and%20Globalized%20Economy.pdf (accessed 13 January 2024).
336. *Ibid.*, at para. 2.

significant relevance in tackling the challenges of a digitalized and globalized economy.[337]

At its twenty-sixth session in March 2023, the UN Tax Committee addressed these two workstreams in the Co-Coordinators report for consideration. In this respect, Prof. *Baker* also gave input on a possible UN multilateral instrument as regards Workstream A, including a first draft version of such an instrument as well as draft protocols to address the multilateral implementation of Articles 12A and 12B UN Model in tax treaties.[338] The aforementioned instrument shall work as a so-called Fast-Track Instrument (FTI),[339] i.e., a state might agree to include provisions of the UN Model to tax treaties with several treaty partners at the so-called 'Conference of the Parties'[340] during one negotiation session. Participating states shall benefit from such a process from an efficiency standpoint as otherwise, they would need to negotiate several different amending protocols separately instead.[341] In this regard, the drafters also intend that participating states may add new protocols over time in order to account for possible future changes to the UN Model.[342]

At its twenty-seventh session in October 2023, the Subcommittee on Tax Challenges Related to the Digitalization of the Economy presented its Co-Coordinators' Report, reflecting the outcomes of the subcommittee meetings as well as the direction taken by the subcommittee as regards Workstream A, to the UN Tax Committee.[343] In this respect, the Secretariat advised the UN Tax Committee to 'remain focused on suggesting an approach and text for the proposed instrument [FTI]'.[344] The Secretariat also mentioned that it will seek advice from public international law experts to put the draft text of the instrument into treaty language and aims to assist developing countries in its future extension of their tax treaty network.[345] As part of the proposed next steps, the aforementioned subcommittee announced that it will work towards a final draft version of the FTI for approval by the UN Tax Committee at its twenty-eighth session.[346]

337. *Ibid.*, at 3 et seq.
338. Committee of Experts on International Cooperation in Tax Matters, *Taxation issues related to the digitalized and globalized economy: Co-Coordinators' Report*, E/C.18/2023/CRP.1, https://financing.desa.un.org/sites/default/files/2023-04/CRP.1%20Co-Coordinator%20report%20on%20Taxation%20of%20the%20Digitalized%20Economy%20CICTM%2026%20120323%20pdf%20merged.pdf (accessed 13 January 2024), 30 et seq.
339. *Ibid.*, at 7 et seq.
340. Note that this term has also already been used in the context of the Multilateral Convention to Implement Tax Treaty Related Measures to Prevent Base Erosion and Profit Shifting (BEPS MLI): https://www.oecd.org/tax/treaties/multilateral-convention-to-implement-tax-treaty-related-measures-to-prevent-beps.htm (accessed 19 January 2024).
341. *Ibid.*, at paras 25 et seq.
342. Committee of Experts on International Cooperation in Tax Matters, *Taxation issues related to the digitalized and globalized economy: Co-Coordinators' Report*, E/C.18/2023/CRP.40, https://financing.desa.un.org/sites/default/files/2023-11/CRP.40%20Combined%20Final%20with%20all%20annexes-Copy.pdf (accessed 13 January 2024), para. 11.
343. *Ibid.*, at para. 6.
344. *Ibid.*, at para. 7.
345. *Ibid.*, at para. 8.
346. *Ibid.*, at paras 32 et seq.

iii BEPS Through Deductibility of Fees for Technical Services

1 Deductibility Without Taxation as Sufficient Nexus?

The base-erosion principle, or as it is also referred to in literature as the 'single-rate withholding approach',[347] describes the ability to tax service payments at the level of the payer based on the possibility of deduction of the service payments as business expenses.[348] It is regarded as an effective means to address the main tax-related concerns stemming from the emergence of e-commerce,[349] i.e., on the one hand, the possibility for BEPS by shifting profits from a profitable MNE of a high-tax jurisdiction to another related enterprise located in a low-tax jurisdiction[350] and on the other hand the avoidance of physical presence in the source state due to higher mobility of workforce and the remote provision of services or delivery of goods, which under current international taxing rules cannot be appropriately tackled.[351]

Mentioned principle permits the source state to apply a withholding tax at a single rate on any base-eroding payment. A payment is considered base eroding, if it is either deductible at the level of the payer or forms part of the cost of goods sold, regardless of taxation of the payment at the level of the recipient. The base-erosion principle applies, in general, irrespective of the type of income. However, two notable exceptions exist: 1) Dividends are not subject to a withholding due to their non-deductibility, and 2) payments made by consumers, as consumers generally cannot deduct costs related to their private consumption.[352]

The features of the withholding mechanism based on the base-erosion principle comprise the inclusion of a considerable tax rate, the possibility to credit the tax withheld against the tax paid in the residence state, and the possibility to file for net taxation in the source state. This would reduce an excessive tax burden associated with the imposition of a gross-based withholding mechanism.[353]

A withholding tax is a simple, reliable, and efficient tax collection method that is very suitable for developing countries due to their national limitations in administrative capacity. Such a tax may be imposed in a final or non-final manner with the difference being that the latter allows filing for a refund of excessive tax withheld at source and also for a deduction of expenses paid with respect to the fees. Most

347. *See* Dale Pinto, *The Need to Reconceptualize the Permanent Establishment Threshold*, 60 BIT 266, 275 (2006).
348. *See* Miller, *supra* n. 2, at 56 et seq. and para. 33 of the Commentary on Article 12A UN Model 2021.
349. *See* Marcel Olbert & Christoph Spengel, *International Taxation in the Digital Economy: Challenge Accepted?*, 9 WTJ 3, 18 with further references (2017) DOI: 10.59403/2y70g6v.
350. Oguttu, *supra* n. 257, at 800.
351. Samari, *supra* n. 258, at 265.
352. Pinto, *supra* n. 347, at 275.
353. *See* Pinto, *supra* n. 347, at 275; *see*, however, Christian Kaeser, *Besteuerung technischer Dienstleistungen: Tendenzen*, in: *Festgabe Wassermeyer, Doppelbesteuerung*, 335-340, at m.no. 10 (C.H. Beck 2015): Although the imposition of a gross withholding tax is regarded as more burdensome with respect to taxes paid for technical services due to their cost intensive nature, filing for net taxation places greater administrative burden on the taxpayer due to the registration requirement in the source state.

developing countries, however, decide to impose a final withholding tax on fees for technical services due to a lack of the administrative resources that would be needed to assess the tax returns that are received.[354]

The base-erosion principle has been regarded in literature as a 'radical departure' from the international consensus that a withholding tax shall only apply in certain limited cases (i.e., dividends, interest and royalties) and comes into conflict with internationally accepted standards on the allocation of source taxing rights, such as the source and the threshold principles.[355] In this respect, especially the extraterritorial application of the base-erosion principle, i.e., a withholding tax will be imposed at the level of the payer, although services are rendered in a third state, has been criticized by several authors.[356] The extra-territorial application of the base-erosion principle might, however, be the only possible way to consistently apply the base-erosion principle, as both extra-territorial and territorial services are deductible against a country's tax base.[357]

2 The Application of the Base-Erosion Principle in the UN Model until the Inclusion of Article 12A to the UN Model

Taxation based on the base-erosion principle is not a newly introduced concept. On the contrary, it is already to be found in other articles of the OECD and UN Models as a nexus criterion for source taxation before Article 12A was introduced to the UN Model 2017:

Article 14 UN Model 1980

Article 14(1)(c) UN Model 1980 already included a base-erosion provision, which was then removed in the 2001 update to the UN Model:

---

354. Brian J. Arnold, *The Taxation of Income from Services, Papers on Selected Topics in Protecting the Tax Base of Developing Countries*, https://www.un.org/esa/ffd/wp-content/uploads/2014/10/20140604_Paper2_Arnold.pdf (accessed 2 January 2024), 15 and Committee of Experts on International Cooperation in Tax Matters, *supra* n. 135, at para. 86.
355. The eCom Taxpert Group, *Taxation of Electronic Commerce in India*, 8 APTB 241, 242 (2002); Arnold, *supra* n. 6, at 65 et seq.; *see also* ICC, *supra* n. 194, at 3: '…ICC believes strongly that there is no basis for a so-called "source" country to impose tax on services that are performed outside of its borders.'; *see* for a different view Báez Moreno, *supra* n. 6, at 272: *Báez Moreno*, however, takes the view that the evident link between the deductibility of expenses and the taxation of the corresponding income at the level of the payer shows enough economic allegiance to justify source taxation.
356. Kaeser, *supra* n. 353, at m.no. 9; Shee Boon Law, *Withholding Taxes on Services Income – A 21st Century Outlaw or a Necessary Evil?*, in: Carlos Gutiérrez & Andreas Perdelwitz (eds), *Taxation of Business Profits in the 21st Century: Selected Issues under Tax Treaties –Essays in Commemoration of IBFD's 75th Anniversary Written by Tax Research Staff of IBFD*, 79-102, at 4.3.4. (IBFD 2013): 'Although practical constraints that tax authorities may face in tracking down all the extra-territorial payments for services may, for the moment, restrict multiple withholding tax liabilities from becoming an unmanageable problem for multinationals, it is unwise to continue to ignore this risk. As tax authorities are looking for more revenue, payments for services that may look like extra-territorial payments and are conventionally thought of as such may come under closer scrutiny.'
357. Báez Moreno, *supra* n. 6, at 308.

(1) Income derived by a resident of a Contracting State in respect of professional services or other activities of an independent character shall be taxable only in that State except in the following circumstances, when *such income may also be taxed in the other Contracting State*:...

(c) if the remuneration for his activities in the other Contracting State *is paid by a resident of that Contracting State or is borne by a permanent establishment or a fixed base situated in that Contracting State* and exceeds in the fiscal year ... (the amount is to be established through bilateral negotiations).[358]

Article 14(1)(c) has been included in the UN Model 1980 as part of a compromise between members of developed and developing countries, taking diverging views on the appropriate nexus for source taxation into account: According to members of developing countries, the source of income should – as a deviation to the fixed base criterion – have been the only relevant criterion for source taxation. On the other hand, developed countries did not take the view that the exportation of skills alone should give rise to a taxing right in the country of destination. According to their view, the relevant nexus for independent services shall be the fixed base criterion and the length of stay, as reflected in Article 14(1)(a)-(b) UN Model 1980.[359] It was, however, agreed that the source state may have a taxing right on fees for independent personal services if the payer of the fees is a resident of that state or the fees are borne by a PE located in that state and the fees for services so performed in that state exceed a certain monetary amount.[360]

Article 15 OECD and UN Models

The object and purpose of Article 15(2)(b) and (c) OECD and UN Models is to avoid the taxation of payments based on short-term employment if the employment income is not deductible in the source state due to the fact that neither the employer is resident in that state nor has a PE therein. As a result, the source state has a taxing right on the employment income, even if the employee is only physically present for a short period of time. This result is justified on the basis of the application of the base-erosion principle,[361] as employment income is deductible against the source states' tax base at the level of the paying employer or PE. However, Article 15(2)(b) and (c) UN Model only addresses the issue of base erosion to the extent that the employment is physically exercised in the source state.[362] In this situation, according to *Arnold*, the base-erosion principle prevails over the source and threshold[363] principles.[364]

Article 16 UN Model

The taxation of Directors' Fees and Remuneration of Top-Level Managerial Officials (Article 16 UN Model) is, besides the source principle and threshold

358. *See* Article 14(1)(c) UN Model 1980 (word orders italicized by the author).
359. United Nations, *United Nations Model Double Taxation Convention between Developed and Developing Countries*, ST/ESA/102, 161 (United Nations Publication 1980).
360. *See* Article 14(1)(c) UN Model 1980.
361. Leonardo T. Pignatari, *Article 15(2) of the OECD Model and the International Hiring-Out of Labour: New Criteria Required?*, 74 BIT 487, 492 (2020) DOI: 10.59403/14h259d.
362. Malan, *supra* n. 6, at 61.
363. *See* with further general and specific explanations on the threshold principle: Andy Cools, *Article 16 of the OECD Model: A Plea to Extend the Scope of the Ratione Personae*, 70 BIT 558, 570 (2016) DOI: 10.59403/3g7vmn4.
364. Arnold, *supra* n. 6, at 66.

> principle, also based[365] on the base-erosion principle:[366] the residence state of the fee-paying company is entitled to tax the fees irrespective of the place in which the services have been rendered. Such nexus with respect to Directors' Fees and Remuneration of Top-Level Managerial Officials has been justified by the fact that the place of activity of directors and managerial officials was hard to establish due to modern information and communication technologies, enabling meetings and conferences to be held remotely without physical presence in the source state.[367] Therefore, the OEEC decided in the second half of the 1950s to deviate from the principle of place of performance as a nexus for source taxation and established that the residence state of the fee-paying company shall be entitled to tax the directors' fees.[368] The application of the base-erosion principle to justify taxation in the residence state of the company, however, has been subject to criticism by *De Jaegher*.[369] According to *De Jaegher*, there may be several situations, in which the base-erosion principle is not a valid justification for source taxing rights with regards to Article 16 UN Model: 1) non-deductibility of fees based on remuneration linked to days of performance at board meetings (*jetons de presence*), 2) non-deductibility of fees due to the attribution of a share of profits of the company (*tantièmes*), and 3) the debtor of the fees is a tax-exempt company, e.g., a non-profit organization.[370] What is more, even if the fee-paying company may likely deduct the fee paid to the director for the computation of the company's income, that deduction would be offset by the taxation of the director's income at the level of the non-resident director, avoiding erosion of tax base of the source state. Ultimately, tax base erosion in the source state will likely not be that severe to justify unlimited source state taxation over director's fees. As a result, *De Jaegher* concludes that the base-erosion principle should not serve as a suitable justification for the allocation of taxing rights of directors' fees and remuneration of top-level managers.[371] Instead, in the opinion of *De Jaegher*, the source principle should be the predominant principle upon which the allocation of taxing rights under Article 16 UN Model is based.[372]

For the sake of completeness, it has to be mentioned that the base-erosion principle is not manifested as a basis for justification of source taxation in Article 12 OECD and UN Models. The Fiscal Committee considered the deductibility of business expenses at the level of the payer as justified – with the exception of fraud – even if no source tax is levied on the payment, otherwise the beneficial effects of the measures on

365. However, see Charlotte De Jaegher, *International Taxation of Directors' Fees: Article 16 of the OECD Model or How to Reconcile Disagreement among Neighbours*, 5 WTJ 215, 266 (2013) DOI: 10.59403/212cd5t: 'The provision on directors' fees seems to be solely based on the base erosion principle, which cannot be considered as consistent with the other articles on private income in the Model.'
366. *See* Arnold, *supra* n. 6, at 66; Cools, *supra* n. 363, at 572 with further references.
367. Cools, *supra* n. 363, at 558.
368. OEEC Fiscal Committee, *The Elimination of Double Taxation: 2nd Report*, FC(59)2, Article IX (18 June 1959).
369. *See* De Jaegher, *supra* n. 365, at 255 et seq. and with explicit reference to the OECD Model: Cools, *supra* n. 363, at 572.
370. *See* De Jaegher, *supra* n. 365, at 256.
371. *See* De Jaegher, *supra* n. 365, at 266 et seq. and similarly Cools, *supra* n. 363, at 575; *see* for a different opinion: Arnold, *supra* n. 6, at 63.
372. *See also* Andy Cools, *What Is the Scope of the Concept of 'Income' in Article 16 of the OECD Model?*, 71 BIT 3/4, at 2.2. (2017) DOI: 10.59403/2f65kr5.

the avoidance of double taxation might be cancelled out.[373] However, if interest, royalties and fees for technical services do not form part of the business profits of a non-resident, taxation up to a ceiling as established in Articles 11 and 12 UN Model may also be justified based on the base-erosion principle.[374]

3 *The Application of the Base-Erosion Principle with Respect to Article 12A UN Model*

Article 12A UN Model is based on the base-erosion principle. Although the issue of tax base erosion could have been addressed through several other options proposed by *Arnold* as part of the work of the UN Subcommittee on Services,[375] the UN Tax Committee decided to draft a provision on the taxation of fees for technical services based on the base-erosion principle as a connecting factor for source taxation.

A significant minority of UN Tax Committee Members, however, did not agree with such justification. In their view, taxation of fees for technical services in the source state is only justified if the nexus requirements of Articles 5, 7 and 14 UN Model are met.[376] In addition, this significant minority took the view that focusing on the residence state of the payer does not meet the requirement of being substantially economically involved in the source state if the services are provided in a third state.[377] Also, the mere deductibility of a commercially justified payment cannot be regarded as base-eroding and therefore, be a sufficient nexus for the allocation of source taxing rights.[378] On the other hand, *Báez Moreno* argues that the application of the base-erosion principle on fees for technical services might serve to avoid unintended double non-taxation of service fees as the imposition of a withholding tax is self-enforcing, making the deductibility of a payment conditional upon an effective withholding.[379] In general, the application of the base-erosion principle through the inclusion of a withholding tax mechanism on fees for technical services is considered to be an effective and administrable solution to protect the source state from tax base erosion. However, such an approach might also be detrimental to source states. The introduction of gross taxation with respect to fees for technical services has been criticized by *Sixdorf/Leitsch* as it negatively affects the investment climate in the source state.[380] As the provision of technical services usually includes significant expenses, inbound investments might – depending on the design of the withholding tax mechanism – be

373. *See* para. 9 of the Commentary on Article 12 OECD Model 1963.
374. Committee of Experts on International Cooperation in Tax Matters, *Secretariat Note – Recent Work of the Committee on Tax Treatment of Services*, E/C.18/2013/CRP.17, https://www.un.org/esa/ffd/wp-content/uploads/2014/09/9STM_CRP17_Services.pdf (accessed 14 January 2024), 5.
375. *See* Committee of Experts on International Cooperation in Tax Matters, *supra* n. 146, at para. 55 and Committee of Experts on International Cooperation in Tax Matters, *supra* n. 155, at paras 17 et seq.
376. *See* paras 16 and 17 of the Commentary on Article 12A UN Model 2017.
377. *See* para. 16 of the Commentary on Article 12A UN Model 2017.
378. *See* para. 18 of the Commentary on Article 12A UN Model 2017.
379. Báez Moreno, *supra* n. 6, at 272.
380. *See, e.g.*, Sixdorf & Leitsch, *supra* n. 6, at 240.

discouraged by shifting the tax burden to resident companies and increasing their costs of business.[381] The tax burden from the application of a gross withholding mechanism will be increasingly higher and consequently create higher expenses. As withholding tax rates that exceed the normal net profit resulting from a transaction tend to shift the economic burden to the payer of service fees, a high withholding tax rate would increase the costs of cross-border services to the service recipient due to a gross-up of costs incurred.[382] To avoid such a situation, the ICC recommended setting a tax rate at a maximum of 3 %.[383]

As the scope of Article 12A UN Model is restricted to fees for technical, managerial and consultancy services and does not include service fees of a different nature, the base-erosion principle is not consistently applied. This fact was subject to criticism in literature, as the restriction of the scope of Article 12A UN Model to services of technical, managerial and consultancy nature is 'radically incompatible'[384] with the base-erosion principle, as B2B services generally have base-eroding character.[385] This was also already mentioned by *Arnold* during the drafting process of Article 12A UN Model.[386] However, as the UN Tax Committee did not intend to include a provision covering all types of services to the UN Model but to replicate the same scope as already found in existing treaties with respect to the taxation of fees for technical services,[387] the application of the base-erosion principle was restricted to fees for technical services as defined in the final version of Article 12A UN Model 2017. In this respect, however, it needs to be mentioned that the UN Tax Committee decided at its eleventh session to include an alternative version of Article 12A to the Commentary of the UN Model, extending the scope to 'fees for services' (technical and other services) if the services are provided to closely related enterprises.[388] Although intra-group transactions may cause the most serious base-erosion issues for developing countries, as service fees may be used to shift profits from a profitable group member to another group member located in a low-tax jurisdiction, possibly leading to non- or low-taxation of service fees, the base-erosion principle is – again – not consistently applied as base-erosion might also exist with respect to unrelated entities in a B2B context.

Article 12A(2) UN Model also includes certain carve-outs from the scope of application. These carve-outs are made with respect to Articles 8, 16 and 17 UN Model.[389] They might partially be explained by the fact that payments for services

381. Jinyan Li, *Protecting the Tax Base in the Digital Economy, Papers on Selected Topics in Protecting the Tax Base of Developing Countries*, https://www.un.org/esa/ffd/wp-content/uploads/2014/10/20140604_Paper9_Li.pdf (accessed 4 January 2024), 42.
382. *See* Sixdorf & Leitsch, *supra* n. 6, at 241.
383. ICC, *supra* n. 194, at 6.
384. Báez Moreno, *supra* n. 6, at 303.
385. *See* Committee of Experts on International Cooperation in Tax Matters, *supra* n. 147, at 11; Báez Moreno, *supra* n. 6, at 303; Sixdorf & Leitsch, *supra* n. 6, at 241; Patrícia Duarte da Conceiçao Machado, *Evolution of the Concept of Technical Services and the Policy Considerations Driving Their Development*, 4 ITAXS 2, 16 et seq. (2021) DOI: 10.59403/2y45xh1.
386. Committee of Experts on International Cooperation in Tax Matters, *supra* n. 147, at 11.
387. Committee of Experts on International Cooperation in Tax Matters, *supra* n. 187, at para. 77.
388. *See* Committee of Experts on International Cooperation in Tax Matters, *supra* n. 212, at para. 72 and paras 26 et seq. of the Commentary on Article 12A UN Model 2021.
389. Article 12A(2) UN Model 2021.

falling in the scope of Articles 16 and 17 UN Model are either already to a certain extent based on the base-erosion principle (Article 16) or are not subject to concerns of base erosion (Article 17).[390] Article 8 UN Model, however, works as an independent operative rule with respect to profits from International Shipping and Air Transport. Its aim is to exempt such profits from taxation in the source state and allocate exclusive taxing rights solely in the state in which the ship or aircraft is operated.[391] This is mostly due to the fact that enterprises engaged in shipping and air transport services earn income in the open sea and air space, leading to exposure to several different tax jurisdictions, likely resulting in a difficult allocation of taxing rights.[392] Therefore, the application of the base-erosion principle for (B2B) payments with respect to international shipping or aircraft services would not be appropriate for the allocation of taxing rights.

It is inherent to the base-erosion principle that B2B transactions are intended to be covered by its scope, as private expenses for services are usually not deductible at the level of an individual consumer. Therefore, the allocation of source taxing rights for service payments made regarding a B2C transaction is not justifiable on the basis of the base-erosion principle. As a result, Article 12A(3)(c) UN Model excludes B2C payments from the scope of source taxation due to the non-base-eroding character of such payments.

As the base-erosion principle aims to cover B2B transactions, it has its flaws in tackling the challenges to the digitalized economy, as a significant number of services rendered digitally are B2C transactions. This is also the reason, why some authors argue that the scope of Article 12A UN Model is rather limited in the digitalized economy.[393] This might also be the reason, why the UN Tax Committee did not seriously consider Article 12A as being a considerable option to tackle the challenges of the digitalized economy, as proposed by this author in the fifteenth session of the UN Tax Committee in Geneva.[394] In this respect, however, *Kapur* argues that the base-erosion principle shall also apply to B2C transactions, resulting in a source states' taxing right for service payments based on base erosion resulting from deductions claimed by consumers.[395] In this respect, however, scholars like *Kaeser* disagree that the taxation of service payments of consumers may be justified on the basis of the base-erosion principle, as consumers incur such expenditures to generate a higher income, leading to a higher tax base in the source state and therefore not eroding its tax base.[396] Also, the exclusion of non-business payments based on the base-erosion principle necessarily leads to non-neutral outcomes. Such outcomes, however, might

390. Arnold, *supra* n. 6, at 65.
391. *See* para. 8 of the Commentary on Article 8 of the UN Model 2021.
392. *See* para. 9 of the Commentary on Article 8 of the UN Model 2021.
393. *See* Tatiana Falcão & Bob Michel, *Scope and Interpretation of Article 12A: Assessing the Impact of the New Fees for Technical Services Article*, BTR 422, 438 et seq. (2018).
394. *See* Committee of Experts on International Cooperation in Tax Matters, *supra* n. 5, at para. 87 and *supra* n. 318, at para. 23.
395. Dhruv Sanghavi, *Report IFA 68th Congress in Mumbai – Seminar F: UN Matters – UN and OECD Differences in Model, TP, etc.* (accessed online on the IBFD-Tax Research Platform on 16 July 2022).
396. *Ibid.*

be justified not only based on easier administrability and efficiency[397] but also on the fact that the base-erosion principle does not intend to generate a higher tax revenue[398] but to allocate taxing rights between contracting states.[399]

4 *The Application of the Base-Erosion Principle with Respect to Article 12B UN Model*

One of the main purposes of the inclusion of Article 12A to the UN Model was the concern of base-erosion of the tax base of the source state through the deductibility of technical service fees at the level of the payer.[400] As payments for the provision of technical services are usually not deductible at the level of an individual for services for personal use, such payments were excluded from the scope of Article 12A. The exclusion was explained by the fact that such payments were not incentivizing base erosion.[401]

Although B2C services are within the scope of Article 12B UN Model,[402] base-erosion and profit-shifting aspects were – during the draft process – still considered by the majority of UN Tax Committee Members as justification to justify source taxation of income from automated digital services.[403] It was noted by the UN Subcommittee on Tax Issues related to the Digitalization of the Economy – with reference to the BEPS Action 1 Report – that 'digital economies' aggravate BEPS.[404] In addition, the subcommittee also mentioned that an inadequate level of taxation in the residence state might also be seen as enough justification for the inclusion of Article 12B to the UN Model.[405] Such reference, which was originally included in the Draft Commentary on Article 12B was finally deleted with respect to the final version of the Commentary on Article 12B UN Model. The deletion was based on criticism by observers during the consultation process, as according to their view, an inadequate level of taxation in the residence state would not be an adequate justification for the allocation of taxing rights.[406]

Another point of criticism concerned the inclusion of B2C services in the scope of Article 12B UN Model as such inclusion leads to significantly higher administrative complexity due to the imposition of a WHT at the level of the individual consumers and

397. Stjepan Gadžo, *Nexus Requirements for Taxation of Non-Residents' Business Income – A Normative Evaluation in the Context of the Global Economy* vol. 41, at 7.3.3.3.2. (IBFD 2018).
398. Báez Moreno, *supra* n. 6, at 310 with further references.
399. Doernberg, *supra* n. 262, at 1017.
400. *See* Chapter 3.C.iii.3 of this publication.
401. *See* para. 72 of the Commentary on Article 12A UN Model 2017.
402. *See* for explanations on Article 12B: Chapter 4.C.ii. of this publication.
403. *See*, Committee of Experts on International Cooperation in Tax Matters, *Co-coordinators' Paper on Tax Issues related to the Digitalization of the Economy for the 20th Session of the UN Committee of Experts on Cooperation in Tax Matters*, E/C.18/2020/CRP.41, https://financing.desa.un.org/events/21st-session-committee-experts-international-cooperation-tax-matters (accessed 6 January 2024), 45 et seq.
404. *Ibid.*, at 46.
405. *Ibid.*, at 42.
406. *Ibid.*, at 58 et seq.

inconsistencies with the approach taken for Article 12A UN Model.[407] A large minority of UN Tax Committee Members was also concerned that the application of Article 12B on payments of small amounts and payments made by consumers would lead to a higher administrative burden in the application of the Article by developing countries and the inclusion of so-called gross-up clauses.[408]

After several comments were made by the public on the inclusion of B2C payments and its inconsistencies with the base-erosion principle, the Drafting Group responded by changing the wording of the relevant commentaries, removing those parts referring to BEPS as an underlying principle on the justification of source taxation and also made clear that the 'allocation of taxing rights is the justification'.[409] It was observed by one of the coordinators of the Drafting group that the inclusion of Article 12B is 'a tax treaty solution to what was considered a tax treaty problem, that is, the lack of taxing rights where a permanent establishment did not exist but where significant economic activity was taking place'.[410] It was further noted by the UN Tax Committee that 'it cannot be disregarded that many multinational enterprises that rely on digital business models derive a very significant portion of income from the provision of automated digital services generally to individual consumers'.[411] Article 12B UN Model was therefore rather introduced as a measure towards the allocation of taxing rights than as a safeguard against BEPS.[412]

The relevant nexus to justify source taxation based on Article 12B UN Model is the residence of the payer receiving the digital service and not the user location.[413] The mentioned nexus' ability to deal with the challenges of the digitalized economy has been questioned by several UN Tax Committee Members and observers during the sessions of the UN Tax Committee. Several UN Tax Committee Members would have preferred the users' location, i.e., the place to which the services are rendered, as a relevant connecting factor. What is more, *Collier/Devereux/Vella* question the intention that the introduction of Article 12B intends a general reform of allocation of taxing rights due to the very specific scope of this provision, only targeting highly specialized digital businesses and excluding Consumer-Facing-Businesses (CFBs).[414]

The different justifications for source taxation with respect to Articles 12A and 12B UN Model are ambiguous and, in most parts, inconsistent. As has been mentioned in *Chapter 4.C.ii.*, source taxation of fees for technical services has been justified by the application of the base-erosion principle. The base-erosion principle or single-rate withholding approach,[415] allows the imposition of a withholding tax on base-eroding payments. Although one could rightfully argue that Article 12A UN Model does not

407. Committee of Experts on International Cooperation in Tax Matters, supra n. 328, at paras 104 and 111
408. *See, e.g.*, para. 15 of the Commentary on Article 12B UN Model 2021.
409. Committee of Experts on International Cooperation in Tax Matters, *supra* n. 403, at 43 and 58.
410. Committee of Experts on International Cooperation in Tax Matters, *supra* n. 81, at para. 80.
411. Committee of Experts on International Cooperation in Tax Matters, *supra* n. 403, at 24.
412. *Ibid.*, at 42.
413. *Ibid.*, at 37.
414. Richard Collier, Michael P. Devereux & John Vella, *Comparing Proposals to Tax Some Profit in the Market Country*, 13 WTJ 405, at 3.1.1. (2021) DOI: 10.59403/vj9y4k.
415. *See* Pinto, *supra* n. 347, at 275.

fully implement the base-erosion principle as it only applies to fees for technical services and not all types of services,[416] the exclusion of B2C services has been rightfully implemented into Article 12A UN Model 2017 due to the non-base-eroding character of B2C payments. In addition, a single-rate withholding tax on B2C payments is also not justified on the background of the arising administrative difficulties in requiring consumers or financial intermediaries to withhold a tax on payments of a low amount.[417] This fact has also been acknowledged by the UN Tax Committee, as the Commentary on Article 12A to the UN Model 2017 states that the:

> ...imposition of withholding tax obligations on such payments by individuals under domestic law would be difficult to enforce and might cause serious compliance problems for individuals utilizing technical services supplied remotely [!] by non-residents.[418]

Based on the fact that the UN Tax Committee completely abandoned the application of the base-erosion principle during the draft process of Article 12B UN Model, the question arises whether the imposition of a withholding tax obligation to consumers or financial intermediaries on the basis of payments for automated digital services is less burdensome and more justified than for fees for technical services? The UN Tax Committee justifies the inclusion of B2C services in the scope of Article 12B UN Model by referring to the fact that MNEs derive a significant portion of their income from digital activities from consumers.[419]

While it is true that the imposition of a withholding tax on payments for services provided by non-resident taxpayers might be a simple, efficient and reliable method for developing countries to collect the tax imposed by a state, in the author's opinion, such a withholding tax requirement at the level of individuals or financial intermediaries might, however, possibly outweigh its benefits (i.e., profit generation). This is because withholding tax requirements at the level of an individual might be difficult to enforce under the domestic law of developing countries, causing serious compliance problems. This applies to Article 12A as well as 12B UN Model. The imposition of a withholding tax requirement based on Article 12B is also not less burdensome than in relation to Article 12A, as the UN Tax Committee already mentioned with respect to technical services that MNEs may provide 'substantial services' to customers in a Contracting State without being physically present therein,[420] using a similar explanation but a different approach on the imposition of withholding tax to B2C services.

416. *See* Committee of Experts on International Cooperation in Tax Matters, *supra* n. 212, at para. 72.
417. *See* Báez Moreno, *supra* n. 6, at 310.
418. *See* para. 72 of the Commentary on Article 12A UN Model 2021; exclamation mark in brackets inserted by the author.
419. *See* para. 63 of the Commentary on Article 12B UN Model 2021.
420. *See, e.g.*, para. 2 of the Commentary on Article 12A UN Model 2017.

iv Legal Certainty

1 Minimization of Tax Disputes

Several non-OECD members allocate taxing rights for fees for technical services on the basis of the royalties' article of the respective DTC in order to expand source taxing rights. This interpretation is – as will be shown in *Chapter 4.B.ii.2.* of this publication – mostly based on the fact that several countries take the view that certain technical (assistance) services are within the scope of the notion 'information concerning industrial, commercial or scientific experience' (know-how).[421] Therefore, several non-OECD members tax income of such services at source even if no explicit wording with respect to technical or other similar services is included in the treaty definition of royalties. In addition to the inclusion of technical services in the scope of Article 12 UN Model, some states also take the view that technical services might fall within the scope of Articles 14[422] or 21[423] UN Model. Moreover, numerous non-OECD members from Asia, Africa, and South America include separate provisions on the taxation of 'Technical Fees',[424] 'Management Fees',[425] 'Management and Technical Fees',[426] and others alike.[427]

The emergence of a wide variety of different provisions on the taxation of fees for technical and other similar services in tax treaties might be explained by the non-existence of explicit treaty provisions on the taxation of fees for technical services in the OECD and UN Models before the introduction of Article 12A to the UN Model 2017. The non-existence of such a model provision that might serve as a basis for tax treaty negotiations in conjunction with a corresponding means of interpretation as found in the Commentaries to the OECD and UN Models led – in the author's opinion – to an increasing level of uncertainty for tax authorities and taxpayers.

The uncertainty of the treatment of fees for technical services through the application of different allocation rules was one of the key drivers for the UN Tax Committee to include a separate provision to the UN Model 2017 on the taxation of fees for technical services.[428] Therefore, the introduction of Article 12A aimed – amongst

421. *See, e.g.*, para. 4 of the Commentary on Article 12A UN Model 2021.
422. *See, e.g.*, Edwin van der Bruggen, *Source Taxation of Consideration for Technical Services and Know-How*, 7 APTB 42, 48 (2001) and Rocha, *supra* n. 12, at 338 with further references, DOI: 10.1023/a:1010689322152.
423. *See*, with reference to the approach taken by the Brazil tax authorities before 2014: Freitas de Moraes e Castro & Moraes do Rego Monteiro, *supra* n. 13, at 54 et seq.; *see also* the inclusion of technical services in the 'Other Income' article of the DTC Egypt-Italy (1979), i.e., Article 22(3): 'For the purposes of this Article the term "management fees" means payments of any kind to any person, other than to an employee of the person making the payments, for, or in respect of, the provision of industrial or commercial advice, or management or technical services, or similar services or facilities, or hire of plant or equipment, but it does not include payments for independent personal services mentioned in Article 14.'
424. *See, e.g.*, Article 11 DTC Bulgaria-Zimbabwe (1988).
425. *See, e.g.*, Article 13 DTC Ivory Coast-UK (1985).
426. *See, e.g.*, Article 17 DTC Ghana-UK (1993).
427. *See*, for a comprehensive study: Chapter 4.A.ii.1. of this publication.
428. *See* para. 6 of the Commentary on Article 12A UN Model 2017.

others – at increasing tax certainty with respect to the legal treatment of fees for technical services. *Wijnen/de Goede/Alessi*[429] examined – at the request of the UN Tax Committee – provisions on the taxation of services in more than 1,500 tax treaties concluded between 1 April 1997 and 1 January 2011. Based on their research, the authors concluded that tax treaty provisions covering the taxation of fees for technical services can basically be distinguished into 'included services' provisions[430] (that form part of the royalty's article) and autonomous provisions on the taxation of fees for technical services.[431] An attempt to display a more thorough categorization concerning provisions on the taxation of fees for technical services as part of the royalty's article, however, was abandoned due to a comprehensive variety of different tax treaty provisions on included services.[432]

The following chapters attempt to display uni- and bilateral-state practices with respect to the taxation of fees for technical services. Special focus will be placed on state practice before the inclusion of Article 12A to the UN Model 2017.

2 *Interpretation of Technical Services by Non-OECD Members*

a *Brazil*

Fees for technical services and management fees paid by a resident of Brazil to a non-resident service provider are – without the requirement of the services being performed in Brazil[433] – subject to a 15% withholding tax rate that could possibly increase to 25% if the recipient of the payment is a resident of a low-tax jurisdiction. The definition of fees for technical services is found in Article 17(1) subparagraph 2(a) of Normative Instruction 1,455/2014. According to this provision, technical services generally require the application of specialized technical knowledge, the involvement of administrative assistance or consulting, or be automated services with clear technological content.[434] Normative Instruction 1,455/2014 also defines technical assistance which – although described differently in comparison to technical services – also effectuates a liability to being subject to withholding tax for domestic law purposes in Brazil. Technical assistance is specified as permanent assistance through technicians, drawings, studies, or other similar services provided by one party that

429. Wijnen, de Goede & Alessi, *supra* n. 3, at 27.
430. Wijnen, de Goede & Alessi, *supra* n. 3, at 32: The authors emphasized the similarities of the examined provisions with Article 12 (Royalties and fees for included services) of the DTC India-United States (1989).
431. Orzechowski, *supra* n. 5, at 640.
432. Wijnen, de Goede & Alessi, *supra* n. 3, at 33.
433. *See, e.g.*, Fernando Souza de Man, *Taxation of Services in Treaties between Developed and Developing Countries: A Proposal for New Guidelines* vol. 39, 238 et seq. (IBFD 2017).
434. *See* Maria F. Furtado, Henny Verboom & Cedrik Lütter, *No Brazilian Withholding Tax on Payments for Technical Services?*, 69 BIT 558, 558 (2015) DOI: 10.59403/2n1ptgx: Private ruling 99001/2021 establishes that payments in consideration for Software-as-a-Service (SaaS) are payments in consideration for technical services due to the application of specialized knowledge in computer sciences.

affords a recipient the effective use of a process or secret formula.[435] In the opinion of the Brazilian tax authorities, fees for technical assistance are regularly within the scope of the provision of know-how, i.e., the tax treaty article on royalties.[436] This view is also often clarified by including a protocol provision extending the scope of the royalties article to fees for technical assistance and technical services.[437]

Exceptions from the scope of technical services and technical assistance apply to fees paid for educational, scientific, or cultural purposes. These payments are not subject to a withholding tax.[438] However, payments in consideration for training services provided to professionals who are residing in Brazil are subject to a 15% withholding tax rate.[439]

Before 2014, Brazil's tax authorities argued that taxing rights for fees for technical services and technical assistance without the transfer of technology shall not be allocated on the basis of Article 7 on business profits but rather on the basis of the application of Article 21 on other income.[440] As Brazil usually does not adopt Article 21 OECD Model but rather Article 21 UN Model it had – based on this view – a taxing right on the gross amount of fees for technical services arising therein. Brazil's tax authorities made a change of opinion regarding the qualification of fees for technical services and technical assistance in 2014. According to the tax authorities, these fees should be subject to the business income article of Brazil's tax treaties. This is based on the formal opinion issued by Brazil's National Treasury Attorney's Office (PGFN)[441] on the interpretation of the article on business profits in Brazil's tax treaties with respect to the qualification of fees for technical services and technical assistance.[442]

With a ruling issued in 2014,[443] the Brazil tax authorities expressed the view that:

435. *See Ibid.*, at 558.
436. *See Ibid.*, at 560.
437. *See, e.g.*, para. 8 of the Protocol to the DTC Brazil-Canada (1984): 'It is understood that the expression "for information concerning industrial, commercial or scientific experience" mentioned in paragraph 3 of Article 12 includes income derived from the rendering of technical assistance and technical services.' and for further references and explanations on Brazil's tax treaty policy: Freitas de Moraes e Castro & Moraes do Rego Monteiro, *supra* n. 13, at 56.
438. Receita Federal, *Instrução Normativa (Normative Instruction) 1,645/2016*, http://normas.receita.fazenda.gov.br/sijut2consulta/link.action?visao = anotado&idAto = 74319 (accessed 5 January 2024).
439. *See* Vanessa Arruda Ferreira, *Outbound Payment for Training Services – Clarified*, IBFD Report of 9 March 2018, https://research.ibfd.org/#/doc?url = /data/tns/docs/html/tns_2018-03-09_br_2.html (accessed 28 August 2022).
440. Freitas de Moraes e Castro & Moraes do Rego Monteiro, *supra* n. 13, at 58.
441. PGFN & CAT, *Nota No. 2363/2013*, https://www.ibet.com.br/wp-content/uploads/2019/06/Parecer_2363-2013.pdf (accessed 5 January 2024).
442. The change of opinion is also based on several judicial judgments: *see* Luis E. Schoueri & Mateus C. Barbosa, *Brazil: Technical Services and the Application of Article 7 under Brazilian Treaty Practice – A Case Study*, in Michael Lang et al. (eds), *Tax Treaty Case Law Around the Globe 2013* vol. 81, 103-116 (Linde Verlag 2013); Freitas de Moraes e Castro & Moraes do Rego Monteiro, *supra* n. 13, at 54 et seq.
443. Receita Federal, *Instrução Normativa (Normative Instruction) 1,455/14*, http://normas.receita.fazenda.gov.br/sijut2consulta/link.action?idAto = 50414&visao = anotado (accessed 5 January 2024).

(1) The royalties' article of the tax treaty shall apply if technical services and technical assistance are explicitly covered by it, e.g., by extending the definition on royalties through the inclusion of a specific provision in the protocol to the DTC.[444]
(2) The article on independent personal services shall apply if technical services and assistance are related to the technical capacity of a person or a group of persons.
(3) The article on business profits shall apply in all remaining cases.[445]

Since then, Brazil's tax authorities have been consistently applying these principles with respect to the taxation of fees for technical services and technical assistance paid to non-residents irrespective of whether know-how is transferred.[446]

b *India*

India's domestic law defines technical services in a broad context. According to Explanation 2 of section 9(1)(vii) of the Indian Income Tax Act, they are defined as any 'service of a technical, managerial or consultancy nature'. Consideration paid for any construction, assembly, mining, or similar project conducted by the service provider or any compensation that would be qualified as a recipient's salary is explicitly excluded from the scope of fees for technical services.[447] In addition, services for online advertising do not fall within their scope. This was one of the reasons why India introduced the equalization levy on online advertising services.[448]

India uses a similar definition of technical services as that used in its domestic law in several of their negotiated tax treaties. Such a broad definition is usually found in tax treaties that do not include a make-available clause in the article on royalties,[449] i.e., making technical knowledge, skill, or expertise available to the payer of the

444. Several Brazilian DTCs include a provision extending the scope of royalties to technical services and technical assistance, e.g., no. 3 of the Protocol to the DTC Brazil-South Africa (2003, 2015): 'It is understood that the provisions of paragraph 3 of Article 12 shall apply to payments of any kind received as a consideration for the rendering of technical services and technical assistance.'
445. Rocha, *supra* n. 12, at 336.
446. *See* in this respect Furtado, Verboom & Lütter, *supra* n. 434, at 559 and the following private rulings: Receita Federal, *Instrução Normativa (Normative Instruction) 155/2016*, http://normas.receita.fazenda.gov.br/sijut2consulta/link.action?visao=anotado&idAto=78944 (accessed 5 January 2024), *Instrução Normativa (Normative Instruction) 5/2017*, http://normas.receita.fazenda.gov.br/sijut2consulta/link.action?idAto=79701&visao=anotado (accessed 6 January 2024), *Instrução Normativa (Normative Instruction) 99006/2020*, http://normas.receita.fazenda.gov.br/sijut2consulta/link.action?visao=anotado&idAto=111584 (accessed 6 January 2024), *Instrução Normativa (Normative Instruction) 99001/2021*, http://normas.receita.fazenda.gov.br/sijut2consulta/link.action?visao=anotado&idAto=116528 (accessed 6 January 2024).
447. Sanghvi & Shaktawat, *supra* n. 22, at 453.
448. Mansi Agrawal, *India at the Forefront in Implementing BEPS-Related Measures: Equalization Levy in Line with Action 1*, 23 ITPJ 323, 324 (2016) DOI: 10.59403/23w4pz7.
449. *See also* Jyoti Pal, *Taxation of Fees for Technical Services: An Analysis of Indian Tax Treaties and Their Journey Through the Courts*, 23 APTB 1, at 3.3. (2017) DOI: 10.59403/1qf8hby.

royalties.[450] The Indian tax authorities regularly refer to its provisions of domestic law when interpreting the term 'fees for technical services'. This view is also reflected in its position made in the OECD Model 2008 which is also found in the OECD Model 2017:

> India reserves the right to: tax royalties and fees for technical services at source; define these, particularly by reference to its domestic law; define the source of such payments, which may extend beyond the source defined in paragraph 5 of Article 11, and modify paragraphs 3 and 4 accordingly.[451]

The Indian Income Tax Act and most of India's tax treaties[452] do not include a definition of technical, managerial, and consultancy services. As a result, as will be shown in *Chapter 4.A.iii.3*, the interpretation of these terms in the context of the application of a tax treaty has been subject to numerous litigation cases before India's administrative and judicial courts. This has led to very extensive case law on the interpretation of 'fees for technical services', providing tax authorities and taxpayers with guidance on the correct interpretation and application of the mentioned term.

Payments in consideration for technical services provided by Indian residents are generally taxable in India. According to section 9(1)(vii)(b) of the Indian Income Tax Act, however, fees for technical services are deemed to not arise in India if the services are utilized in a business or profession carried on outside of the country by a resident. This is also applicable if fees for technical services are utilized for purposes of making or earning any type of income from any source outside of India. Therefore, a tax liability for an Indian resident arises if the services are utilized abroad for a resident's personal purposes. However, no tax liability would arise if the same service would be utilized in a business or profession abroad. To avoid such an incongruent outcome, Indian tax treaties often exclude services of personal use of individuals from the scope of the fees for technical services article.[453]

According to section 9(1)(vii)(c) of the Indian Income Tax Act, fees for technical services are payable by a non-resident service provider if they are utilized in a business or profession carried on by the non-resident in India or for the purposes of making or earning any income from any source in India.

The Supreme Court of India held that fees for technical services are only taxable in India if the service is rendered and utilized therein.[454] However, India enacted Finance Bill 2010 to counteract this decision in *Ishikawajima-Harima Heavy Industries*

---

450. *See, e.g.*, Joint Committee on Taxation, *Explanation of proposed Income Tax Treaty (and proposed Protocol) between The United States of America and The Republic of India*, JCS-20-90, paras 18 et seq. (14 June 1990).
451. *See* para. 4.1 of Non-Member Countries' Positions on Article 12(1) OECD Models 2008 and 2017.
452. *See*, however, for a definition of 'Royalties and Fees for Included Services': Joint Committee on Taxation, *supra* n. 450, at 42 et seq.
453. *See also* Pal, *supra* n. 449, at 3.1.2.
454. With reference to the interpretation of the supreme court in *Ishikawajima-Harima Heavy Industries Ltd. v. Director of Income Tax*: Mohammed M. Chishty & Sumangala A. Chakalabbi, *Royalties and Fees for Technical Services in International Trade*, 18 APTB 40, 42 (2009) DOI: 10.59403/2xrq97.

Ltd. v. Director of Income Tax[455] in favour of the tax authorities enabling taxation of fees for technical services in India without the need of performing the services within that territory.[456] As a result, similar to the source rule of Article 12A UN Model, the place of performance of the service is not relevant for taxing fees for technical services based on India's domestic law. The only relevant factor for such fees to arise in India is the residence status of the payer.

c *Other Non-OECD Members*

Provisions on the taxation of fees for technical services are regularly found in domestic law of most African[457] and several Asian and South American countries.[458] This might – as already mentioned in previous chapters – partly be explained by the fact that developing countries attempt to address the issue of tax base erosion through the deductibility of (technical) service fees by imposing a withholding tax at source.[459]

In addition, as royalty and service payments are often difficult to differentiate from each other, large taxpayers might be encouraged to reclassify certain intra-group payments to benefit from a more beneficial tax regime based on the various tax treatment of royalties and service payments. In this respect, the Chinese SAT broadened the treaty definition of royalties in the context of protecting national tax revenue to also include 'technical fees' within its scope.[460]

On the background of the aforementioned issues, it seems reasonable – according to *Dubut* –to impose a withholding tax on fees for technical services.[461] The following list provides an overview of domestic provisions found in the national law of selected non-OECD Member States:

- Payments for services of any nature (including technical services) to non-residents are subject to a final withholding tax at a rate of 6.5 % in Angola. The

455. See Supreme Court of India, *Ishikawajima-Harima Heavy Industries Ltd. v. Director of Income Tax*, 288 ITR 408 (4 January 2007).
456. *See* Souza de Man, *supra* n. 433, at 238 et seq.
457. *See*, for an overview: Nazreen Begg, *A Technical Analysis of the Difference in Treatment of Technical Fees in Relation to the Receipt of Management Fees by a Resident of South Africa Sourced from Botswana and Zambia Including the Impact of Domestic and Treaty Relief*, 40 (University of Cape Town 2019); in more detail with respect to the domestic treatment of service fees in Angola, Mozambique, Cape Verde, and São Tomé and Príncipe: Tiago Machado Graça, *Portuguese-Speaking African Countries: Same Background, Different Solutions*, 70 BIT 717-723 (2016) DOI: 10.59403/sp0dd5.
458. *See also* Committee of Experts on International Cooperation in Tax Matters, *supra* n. 5, at paras 28 et seq.
459. Although transfer pricing adjustments that are in conformity with the arm's length principle might – to a great extent – deal with the mentioned issue of tax base erosion in the source state, such adjustments are difficult for most developing countries to monitor and administer.
460. *See* Shimeng Lan, *A Comparative Study of the 'Royalties' Provisions in the Tax Treaties Concluded by China*, 72 BIT 142, 149 (2018) DOI: 10.59403/1jbwz65.
461. Thomas Dubut, *The International Tax Policy of the Least Developed Countries: The Case of the Partner States of the East African Community – Burundi, Kenya, Rwanda, Tanzania and Uganda*, in: Yariv Brauner & Pasquale Pistone (eds), *BRICS and the Emergence of International Tax Coordination*, 327, 340 et seq. (IBFD 2015).

withholding tax will be imposed when the services are provided in Angola or are paid by an Angolan resident entity.[462] Therefore, the place of performance is not decisive as long as the payment is made by an Angolan entity.

- Fees for technical and management services paid to a non-resident service provider are taxed in Indonesia by imposing a 20% withholding tax at source[463] irrespective of the place of performance of the services.[464]
- According to section 109B(1)(b) of the Malaysian Income Tax Act, payments derived from Malaysia and paid to a non-resident service provider for 'technical advice assistance or services rendered in connection with technical management or administration or any scientific, industrial or commercial undertaking, venture, project or scheme' are taxable in Malaysia by way of a withholding tax for the payer. These payments are subject to a withholding tax of 10% on the gross amount of the payment.[465] By issuing Finance Act 2016,[466] Malaysia expanded its source taxing rights by amending its domestic law to deem service fees to arise in Malaysia irrespective of the place of performance or the existence of a PE therein. Therefore, fees for technical services are taxed in Malaysia even if the services are rendered abroad.[467]
- According to the national law of Uruguay, fees for technical services are subject to a withholding tax of 12% if they are provided by a non-resident service provider to Uruguayan taxpayers that are liable to the IRAE (Impuesto a las Rentas de las Actividades Económicas)[468] or the IRPF (Impuesto a las Rentas de las Personas Físicas)[469]. If technical services are provided to the aforementioned taxpayers, fees for such services are deemed to arise in Uruguay irrespective of the place of performance therein or a third state.[470]

462. Machado Graça, *supra* n. 457, at 718.
463. Based on Direktorat Jenderal Pajak Circular Letter SE03/PJ.101/1996, Indonesia did not impose a withholding tax on fees for technical services if the non-resident service provider did not have a PE in Indonesia. However, as the mentioned regulation was revoked in 2009, the existence of a PE is no longer decisive for imposing a withholding tax on technical services; *see also* Pieter de Ridder, *Indonesia – Taxation of Cross-Border Dividends, Interest, Royalties and Service Fees*, 19 APTB 323, 326 (2013).
464. Henrietta Kristanto, *Indonesia – Corporate Taxation – Country Tax Guides* (accessed online on the IBFD-Tax Research Platform on 6 January 2024), at 7.3.4.4.
465. *See* Section 109B (2) and Part V of Schedule 1 of Malaysia's Income Tax Act 1967.
466. *See* Clause 6 of the Finance Act 2016 and the deletion of the notion 'Provided that in respect of paragraphs (a) and (b), this section shall apply to the amount attributable to services which are performed in Malaysia.' contained in section 15A of the Income Tax Act.
467. Committee of Experts on International Cooperation in Tax Matters, *supra* n. 5, at para. 41.
468. Income Tax on Economic Activities.
469. Personal Income Tax.
470. Rodrigo Barrios Correa, *Uruguay's Treaty Policy*, 71 BIT 137, 152 (2017) DOI: 10.59403/1b6tv5g.

CHAPTER 4

Article 12A UN Model: Overlap with Other Allocation Rules of the UN Model

A ARTICLE 12A UN MODEL: SCOPE

i Article 12A UN Model: Application Requirements

1 *'Any Payment'*

According to Article 12A(3) UN Model, the term 'fees for technical services' includes 'any payment'. In this respect, the term 'payment' has a broad meaning. It refers to 'the fulfilment of the obligation to put funds at the disposal of the service provider in the manner required by contract or custom'.[471]

The term 'payment' not only refers to money but also to other considerations of monetary value.[472] Although Article 12A(3) UN Model refers to the plural form, a one-time payment also fulfils the established requirements.[473]

2 *'Resident of the Other Contracting State'*

a Eligible 'Persons'

Article 12A(1) UN Model covers fees for technical services 'paid to a resident of the other Contracting State'. In this regard, Article 12A(1) UN Model refers to the concept of residence as established under Article 4 UN Model. The mentioned concept has,

471. *See* para. 40 of the Commentary on Article 12A UN Model 2021.
472. *See* with regards to Article 12 on royalties: Reinhard Pöllath, *Art. 12 Lizenzgebühren*, in: Moris Lehner (ed.), *Doppelbesteuerungsabkommen*, 1143, m.no. 44 (4th ed., Beck 2003).
473. *See* with regards to Article 12 on royalties: *Ibid.*, at m.no. 44.

among others, the function of entitling a person[474] to the benefits of a DTC.[475] In addition, it also intends to resolve cases of double taxation in situations in which a conflict arises due to taxation in the residence and the source states.[476]

According to Article 4(1) UN Model, a 'resident of a Contracting State' is any person who is subject under the laws of that contracting state to full[477] tax liability based on the connecting factors of 'domicile, residence, place of incorporation, place of management or any other criterion of a similar nature'. It excludes persons from its scope who are not subject to full tax liability in a state and are only liable to tax due to income sources therein.[478]

In this respect, Article 12A(1) UN Model allows for taxation in the residence state of the payee who does not necessarily have to be the service provider. This provision, however, only refers to a shared and not an exclusive taxing right: 'may be taxed' in contrast to 'shall be taxable only'.[479] As Article 12A(1) UN Model refers to a shared taxing right, the residence state is obligated to eliminate possible double taxation for fees for technical services that may also be taxed within the limits of Article 12A(2) UN Model in the state where the fees arise.

As has already been mentioned in *Chapter 3.B.ii.*, the wording and structure of Article 12A UN Model is, in essence, based on Articles 11 and 12 UN Model.[480] In this respect, Articles 11(1), 12(1) and 12A(1) UN Model refer to payments made 'to a resident of the other Contracting State'. These provisions therefore do not specifically refer to the requirement that the payments need be made to their beneficial owner. In contrast hereto, e.g., Article 12(1) OECD Model specifically establishes the requirement that royalties need to be 'beneficially owned by a resident of the other Contracting State'. The different wording used in Articles 11(1), 12(1) and 12A(1) UN Model, however, does not intend to have a different meaning from the wording used in the OECD Model. This is, among other reasons, reflected by the fact that the Commentary on Articles 11 and 12 UN Model expressly cites the relevant passages of the Commentaries of the OECD Model on the beneficial ownership requirement.[481] The addition of the beneficial ownership requirement to the OECD Model merely intends to clarify[482] and emphasize that the source state is not obligated to forfeit taxing rights for passive income solely because of the fact that the person who receives royalties is a resident of the other contracting state. In addition to being a resident of the other contracting state, such a resident also has to be the economic owner of the passive income.[483] This is –

474. *See* Article 3(1)(a) UN Model 2021.
475. *See* Article 1(1) UN Model 2021.
476. *See* para. 1 of the Commentary on Article 4 OECD Model 2017.
477. *See* para. 3 of the Commentary on Article 4 UN Model 2021.
478. *See* Article 4(1) second sentence UN Model 2021.
479. *See, e.g.*, Article 19(1)(a) UN Model 2021.
480. *See also* Committee of Experts on International Cooperation in Tax Matters, *supra* n. 187, at para. 75.
481. *See* para. 5 of the Commentary on Article 12 UN Model 2021.
482. *See* para. 12.1 of the Commentary on Article 10 OECD Model 2017.
483. *See* US Tax Court, *Aiken Industries Inc. v. Commissioner of Internal Revenue*, Docket No. 292-69 (5 August 1971).

although not being passive income – also true for fees for technical services received by a resident of the other contracting state.[484]

Such limitation of treaty benefits, however, is already inherent to the object and purpose of a tax treaty which is the avoidance of double taxation and prevention of fiscal evasion and avoidance. In this regard, in the author's opinion, the wording 'paid to a resident of the other Contracting State' needs to be read in light of the object and purpose of the tax treaty. As a result, it can be argued that the beneficial ownership requirement is already included in the notion of 'paid to a resident of the other Contracting State'.[485] Therefore, no explicit inclusion of the beneficial ownership requirement is specifically needed in the wording of, e.g., the royalty's article as has been done by the OECD. In addition, according to *Lang* it also remains questionable whether the OECD's aim to increase legal certainty through the addition of the beneficial ownership requirement has been met due to the globally (nearly) weekly arising court decisions on the interpretation of the wording 'beneficial ownership'.[486]

Concerning fees for technical services, usually the service provider will be the recipient of the fee. However, according to the Commentary on Article 12A UN Model, domestic law must determine 'the proper taxpayer' if the service provider is not designated as such.[487] Nevertheless, if the recipient of the service fee is not the beneficial owner of the fee, Article 12A(1) would still apply. In such a case, however, the source state would no longer be restricted by the tax rate negotiated by the contracting states as Article 12A(2) UN Model expressly states that the beneficial tax rate in the source state shall only apply 'if the beneficial owner of the fees is a resident of the other Contracting State'.

b *Beneficial Ownership Requirement*

As aforementioned, the source state is restricted in the application of its tax rate on fees for technical services if these fees are paid to its beneficial owner. According to the Commentaries to the OECD and UN Models, the beneficial ownership requirement functions as an anti-abuse rule against treaty shopping.[488] It concretely addresses the situation of imposing a payment on a receiving person who has the obligation to pass on payments to another person with the aim of tax avoidance.[489]

The term 'beneficial ownership' is not defined in the OECD and UN Models. Nevertheless, the OECD included a definition of it in 2001 in the 'Report of the Steering Group on Corporate Governance on the use of Corporate Entities for Illicit Purposes.'[490] According to the report, uncovering the beneficial owner of an entity such as a

484. *See* para. 52 of the Commentary on Article 12A UN Model 2021.
485. *See* para. 52 of the Commentary on Article 12A UN Model 2021.
486. *See* Michael Lang, *Schweizer Grundsatzurteil zum Beneficial Owner nach DBA-Recht*, SWI 226, 230 (2012).
487. *See* para. 39 of the Commentary on Article 12A UN Model 2021.
488. *See* para. 97 of the Commentary on Article 1 UN Model 2021.
489. *See, e.g.*, para. 35 of the Commentary on Article 12B UN Model 2021.
490. *See* OECD, *Behind the Corporate Veil: Using Corporate Entities for Illicit Purposes*, 14 (OECD Publications 2001).

corporation or partnership means 'piercing through various intermediary entities and/or individuals until the true owner who is a natural person is found' in order to find the person ultimately exercising effective control of the entity.[491] The report concluded that persons exercising effective control are – depending on the legal form of the entity – shareholders or members of a corporation, general and limited partners of a partnership, or beneficiaries of trusts and foundations. Focusing on effective control instead of legal ownership is important as, in any constellation of misuse, the beneficial owner is exercising effective control over an entity. Although the outward appearance might suggest control by a third party, e.g., directors of a corporation acting as mere 'nominees', the entity is passing on their duties to and accepting instructions from the beneficial owner.[492]

Another definition of 'beneficial ownership' focusing on effective control over a legal person or arrangement was established by the Financial Action Task Force on International Standards on Combating Money Laundering and the Financing of Terrorism & Proliferation (FATF) in its recommendations with respect to anti-money laundering:

> the natural person(s) who ultimately owns or controls a customer and/or the person on whose behalf a transaction is being conducted. It also incorporates those persons who exercise ultimate effective control over a legal person or arrangement.[493]

The term 'beneficial owner' as referred to by the OECD and UN Models is not used in a narrow technical sense but rather has to be interpreted in the context of the wording 'paid to a resident' and the object and purpose of the treaty which is to avoid double taxation and prevent fiscal evasion and avoidance.[494] *Baker* assumes that the beneficial ownership requirement as used in the Commentaries to the OECD and UN Models is derived from international tax practice and relates to an 'international fiscal meaning' that is not dependent on provisions of domestic law.[495]

Judicial decisions by international courts also point out that the beneficial ownership requirement shall be based on the substance of the matter. In this regard, in the case *Prévost Car Inc. v. Herr Majesty the Queen*,[496] the Court of Canada defined a beneficial owner of income as a person who receives the income for his or her own use

491. *Ibid.*, at 14.
492. *Ibid.*, at 14.
493. Financial Action Task Force on International Standards on Combating Money Laundering and the Financing of Terrorism & Proliferation, *International Standards on Combating Money Laundering and the Financing of Terrorism & Proliferation*, 119 (2012-2022).
494. *See also* para. 53 of the Commentary on Article 12A UN Model 2021: When trustees of a discretionary trust decide to not distribute fees earned from the provision of technical services, these trustees could be regarded as beneficial owners for the purposes of Article 12A, notwithstanding the qualification under the applicable trust law.
495. *See* Philip Baker, *The Meaning of 'Beneficial Ownership' as Applied to Dividends under the OECD Model Tax Convention*, in: Guglielmo Maisto (ed.), *Taxation of Intercompany Dividends under Tax Treaties and EU Law* vol. 8, 87, 93 (IBFD 2012).
496. The Court of Canada, *Prévost Car Inc. v. Her Majesty the Queen*, 2004-2006(IT)G and 2004-4226(IT)G (22 April 2008).

and assumes risk and control of the income received.[497] These requirements were also repeated in following court decisions such as *Velcro Canada v. Her Majesty the Queen*.[498] In the mentioned case, the Tax Court of Canada had to decide whether a Dutch resident (Velcro Holdings) was the beneficial owner of royalties paid by a Canadian taxpayer under Article 12 of the DTC Canada-Netherlands (1986). As already established in *Prévost Car Inc. v. Her Majesty the Queen*, the tax court decided to base its decision on the aforementioned requirements and concluded that Velcro Holdings 1) had the legal rights to receive the royalties, 2) had exclusive possession and control over the funds through their own account, 3) had ownership on the interest from funds, and 4) did not need to seek instructions on the use of the funds and the amount of royalties paid to Velcro Holdings that was different from the amount that was forwarded to another related entity.[499] According to *Prévost Car Inc. v. Her Majesty the Queen*, only with 'absolutely no discretion' over the use of funds can 'the draconian step of piercing the corporate veil' be taken.[500] As Velcro Holdings had discretion over the use of the funds, the Tax Court of Canada was prevented from piercing the corporate veil.

3 *'Arising in a Contracting State'*

According to Article 12A(2) UN Model, fees for technical services may also be taxed in the state where they arise. In this respect, Article 12A(5) UN Model provides that fees for technical services deem to arise in the payer's residence state or in the state in which the payer has a PE or a fixed base and the liability to pay the royalties or fees was incurred and borne by such PE or fixed base. The latter-mentioned requirement shall – due to the unmistakable wording of Article 12A(5) UN Model – also be fulfilled if the payer is a resident of a third state. Furthermore, technical services do not need to be provided in the residence state of the payer or the state where the payer has a PE or fixed base for fees to arise therein.[501] Therefore, the place of performance is not a decisive criterion for establishing source taxing rights as regards fees for technical services.

The source rule of Article 12A(5) UN Model is equivalent to Articles 11(5) and 12(5) UN Model as the UN Tax Committee decided during the drafting process of Article 12A to base the wording and structure of the article on Articles 11 and 12 UN Model.[502] With reference to the source rule of Article 12A(5) UN Model, the commentary refers to the need for a 'clear economic link' between fees for technical services and the PE or fixed base in the source state.[503] Only if such a close economic

497. *Ibid.*, at para. 100.
498. The Court of Canada, *Velcro Canada v. Her Majesty the Queen*, 2007-1806(IT)G (24 February 2012).
499. *Ibid.*, at paras 27 et seq.
500. *Ibid.*, at para. 52.
501. *See* para. 108 of the Commentary on Article 12A UN Model 2021.
502. *See* Committee of Experts on International Cooperation in Tax Matters, *supra* n. 187, at para. 75.
503. *See* para. 110 of the Commentary on Article 12A UN Model 2021.

link is absent, do fees for technical services deem to arise in the residence state of the payer if that state is a contracting state. Article 12A(5) UN Model, however, does not apply to fees that are paid by a resident of a contracting state if such state is also the residence state of the payee. In such a case, fees for technical services do not arise in a contracting state and as will be argued by the author in *Chapter 4.E.iv.3.*, Article 21(1) UN Model shall apply.

The aforementioned 'economic link' points to the deductibility of fees for technical services in the state of the PE or fixed base:

> The deductibility of the fees for technical services provides an objective standard for determining that the payments have a close economic connection to the State in which the permanent establishment or fixed base is situated.[504]

The source rule of Article 12A(5) UN Model is therefore based on the base-erosion principle that has been examined by the author in *Chapter 3.C.iii*. In this respect, mere entitlement to deduct fees for technical services at the level of the PE or fixed base is sufficient enough to fulfil the economic link requirement. Therefore, the economic link is not determined by an actual deduction for the payer.[505] The Commentary on Article 12A does not specifically relate to an economic link at the level of the deductibility of the fees of the payer if that payer, such as a company, has no PE or fixed base in a contracting state. However, it may be deduced from the object and purpose of the inclusion of Article 12A to the UN Model 2017 that the UN Tax Committee intended to introduce a source rule on the basis of the possibility of deducting technical service payments in a B2B context. This is because these payments are, at least according to the majority view of the committee, of a base-eroding character.[506] Therefore, also in relation to the 'payer', it seems decisive that the fees are deductible at the level of the payer thus establishing the necessary link leading to source taxing rights.

The application of the source rule of Article 12A(5) UN Model is subject to paragraph 6. 12A(6) UN Model deems fees for technical services to not arise in a contracting state if they are borne by a payer's PE or fixed base in the other contracting state. In cases in which Article 12A(6) UN Model deems fees for technical services as not arising in a contracting state due to an insufficient economic link therein, Article 12A(1) and (2) UN Model do not lead to source taxing rights as fees for technical services do not arise in a contracting state. However, Article 12A(6) UN Model does not apply if the payer and payee are residents of the contracting states and the former has a PE or fixed base in a third state that bears the fees. In such a case, fees for technical services are deemed to arise in the payer's residence state due to the application of Article 12A(5) first sentence UN Model.[507] The mentioned fees will – in such a triangular case – most probably be subject to double taxation as the third state will be allocated a taxing right under current international taxation rules for the fees (either

504. *See* para. 113 of the Commentary on Article 12A UN Model 2021.
505. *See* para. 114 of the Commentary on Article 12A UN Model 2021.
506. *See* Chapter 3.C.iii.3.
507. *See also* para. 125 of the Commentary on Article 12A UN Model 2021.

under Articles 7, 14, 12A or less likely 12B of the respective treaty). However, double taxation might be avoided by including the following provision in a tax treaty:

> For the purposes of this Article, fees for technical services shall be deemed not to arise in a Contracting State if the payer is a resident of that State and carries on business in the other Contracting State *or a third State* through a permanent establishment situated in that other State *or the third State*, or performs independent personal services through a fixed base situated in that other State *or the third State* and such fees are borne by that permanent establishment or fixed base.[508]

Taking into account the aforementioned case, the inclusion of such a provision in a tax treaty has the effect that fees for technical services do not arise in the payer's residence state as the amended version of Article 12A(6) UN Model extends its scope to a PE or fixed base situated in a third state. As a result, this amended provision excludes the application of Article 12A(5), first sentence UN Model, leading to exclusive residence taxation of fees for technical services.

The functioning of the source rules shall be illustrated with a few examples:[509]

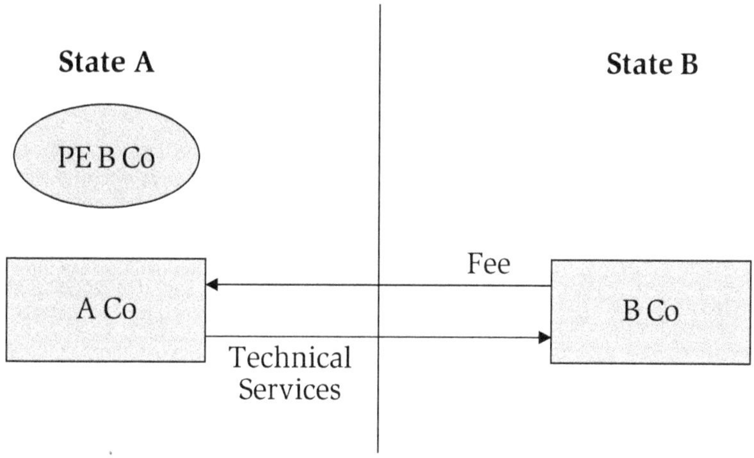

Example 1: States A and B concluded a tax treaty including a provision corresponding to Article 12A UN Model. B Co, a resident of State B, receives technical services in consideration of a fee. As the payment is made by B Co, a resident of State B, and fees for technical services are not borne by a PE of B Co in State A, Article 12A(5), the first sentence of the UN Model applies. As a result, the mentioned fees arise in State B.

Alternative to Example 1. Fees for technical services are paid by B Co but borne by the PE of B Co in State A. Due to the fact that the fees are borne by a PE of the payer, B Co in State A, Article 12A(6) UN Model applies, and fees for technical

508. *See* para. 127 of the Commentary on Article 12A UN Model 2021; changes to the original version of Article 12A(6) UN Model 2021 were italicized by the author.
509. The illustrated examples are based on the examples displayed in paras 116 et seq. of the Commentary on Article 12A UN Model 2021.

services are deemed to not arise in State B due to an insufficient economic link therein. As a result, Article 21(1) UN Model applies, leading to an exclusive taxing right of State A.[510]

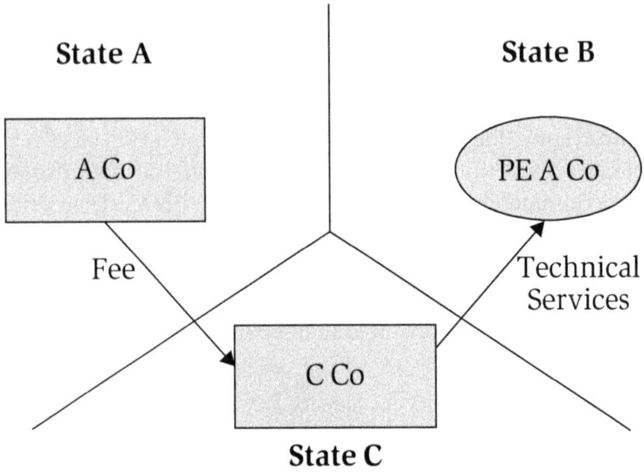

Example 2: States A and B concluded a tax treaty including a provision based on Article 12A UN Model. A Co, a resident of State A, pays a fee for technical services provided by C Co, a resident of State C, to a PE of A Co in State B. The payment made by A Co is deductible at the level of its PE in State B. Although the payment is made by A Co, fees for technical services are not deemed to arise in State A as the fees are borne by a PE of A Co in State B. Due to the close economic link with income earning activities of A Co in State B, fees for technical services are deemed to arise in State B and State B is allowed to tax the fees in accordance with Article 12A(2) UN Model.[511]

ii Definition of Fees for Technical Services under Article 12A UN Model

1 Fees for Technical Services in Bilateral Tax Treaties

A survey conducted by *Miller* on the basis of 2,534 tax treaties in force in August 2012 shows that, from a historical perspective, source taxation of service fees on income of non-residents is, to the greatest extent, an issue of developing countries.[512] OECD

510. *See*, however, paras 118 et seq. of the Commentary on Article 12A UN Model 2021: In the authors opinion, the Commentary on Article 12A UN Model 2021 erroneously considers Article 12A(1) UN Model as being applicable in such a case. Although, according to the commentary, the application of Article 12A(1) would in such a case – just as in the case of Article 21(1) – lead to exclusive residence taxation, Article 12A(1) is not applicable. This is because the fees are not 'arising in a Contracting State' due to the application of Article 12A(6) UN Model. For a more thorough analysis of the interaction between Articles 12A and 21 UN Model, *see* Chapter 4.E.iv.
511. *See* paras 121 et seq. of the Commentary on Article 12A UN Model 2021.
512. Miller, *supra* n. 2, at 174.

Member States, on the other hand, are more reluctant to include a provision granting source taxing rights for fees for technical and other similar services as part of their tax treaty policy. This conclusion mostly stems from the fact that the OECD Model – which is regularly the basis for tax treaty negotiations for the OECD Member States – only grants source taxing rights for service fees if certain 'physical' thresholds are met, such as the PE threshold in Article 5 OECD Model 2017. These, however, seem – as displayed through tax treaty practice – to be inappropriately high for developing countries with respect to the taxation of fees for technical and other similar services.

Before the inclusion of Article 12A to the UN Model 2017, the wording of provisions on the taxation of fees for technical and other similar services was mostly based on provisions of national law. This is because the OECD and UN Models did not provide any wording that contracting states were keen to include in their tax treaties. Such diverging wording is basically found 1) in the respective article on royalties as part of an extension of its definition to fees for technical services or 2) as part of the inclusion of a stand-alone provision on the taxation of fees for technical and other similar services. To a lesser extent, specific provisions are also found in the articles on business profits,[513] shipping and air transport[514] and other income.[515,516]

The following chapters will describe tax treaty practice before the inclusion of Article 12A to the UN Model 2017[517] with respect to provisions on the taxation of fees for technical and other similar services, including a display of the various differences found in such provisions. For this purpose, the author will have recourse to already available surveys conducted on tax treaty practice of service taxation. In addition, a complementary study will be referenced that was conducted by the author on the basis

513. *See, e.g.*, Article 11(7) Income, Inheritance, Registration and Stamp Tax Treaty Tunisia-France (1973): '…technical fees…arising in the other State shall be taxable in that last-mentioned State even in the absence of a permanent establishment in the said State where any other provision of the Convention grants the said State the right to levy taxes under the conditions laid down in that other provision.' and Article 7(6) DTC Tunisia-Togo (1987): '…technical fees…arising in the other state shall be taxable in that last-mentioned state even in the absence of a permanent establishment' in case any other provision of the convention grants the said state the right to levy taxes under the conditions laid down in that other provision.

514. *See, e.g.*, Article 9(3) nos 3 and 4 DTC Gambia-UAE (2015) and Article 9(4) nos 3 and 4 DTC Senegal-UAE (2015): '…profits derived from:…3) income from training schemes; 4) income from selling of technical engineering to a third party.'

515. *See, e.g.*, Article 22(3) DTC Egypt-Italy (1979): 'For the purposes of this Article the term "management fees" means payments of any kind to any person, other than to an employee of the person making the payments, for, or in respect of the provision of industrial or commercial advice, or management or technical services, or similar services or facilities, or hire of plant or equipment, but it does not include payments for independent personal services mentioned in Article 14.'

516. Although payments for services mentioned in other articles of the UN Model 2017 might also be covered by the term 'fees for technical services' as defined in Article 12A(3) UN Model (e.g., Articles 16 and 17), for the purposes of this chapter, the author only refers to provisions specifically including fees for technical and other similar services.

517. The UN Model 2017 was 'launched' during the sixteenth session of the UN Tax Committee: Committee of Experts on International Cooperation in Tax Matters, *supra* n. 237, at 18 et seq.

of 369 tax treaties concluded by nineteen African countries[518] that are geographically evenly distributed across the continent.[519]

a Provisions in the Article on Royalties

The taxation of fees for technical and other similar services was never expressly included in the scope of Article 12 of the OECD and UN Models. Especially developing countries, however, have established tax treaty practices over the past fifty years for taxing fees for technical and other similar services. This was accomplished either on the basis of a broad understanding of the term 'know-how' or through extending the scope of Article 12 to technical and other similar services such as technical assistance.[520] As already shown by *Wijnen/de Goede/Alessi*[521] and *Miller*,[522] provisions permitting source taxation of fees for technical and other similar services on the basis of the article on royalties show a significant variety of wording. One of the most prominent examples to which literature[523] regularly refers with respect to the taxation of fees for technical services in the royalties' article is India's tax treaty practice. As already mentioned in *Chapter 3.C.iv.2.b.*, India regularly refers to provisions of domestic law when interpreting the term 'fees for technical services'. Most of its tax treaties define technical services as 'managerial, technical or consultancy services'.[524] This very broad definition is narrowed down in several Indian tax treaties due to the inclusion of the make-available clause.[525] Those Indian treaties including such a clause either use the term 'fees for included services' or 'fees for technical services'.[526]

The concept of fees for included services is most prominently displayed in Article 12(4) of the DTC India-USA (1989):[527]

> For purposes of this Article, 'fees for included services' means payments of any kind to any person in consideration for the rendering of any technical or consultancy services (including through the provision of services of technical or other personnel) if such services:

518. Angola, Benin, Botswana, Cape Verde, Congo, Egypt, Gabon, Gambia, Ghana, Kenya, Lesotho, Mauritius, Nigeria, Rwanda, Senegal, South Africa, Tunisia, Uganda and Zimbabwe.
519. The analysis made is also displayed in Appendices 1 to 6. The relevant data was extracted from the IBFD Tax Research Platform by examining each tax treaty individually. Tax treaties covered by the author's study only include those that were concluded (signed) before the publishing of the UN Model 2017 (May 2018).
520. *See* for a more thorough explanation: Chapter 4.B.ii.2. of this publication.
521. Wijnen, de Goede & Alessi, *supra* n. 3, at 27.
522. Miller, *supra* n. 2, at 147 et seq.
523. van der Bruggen, *supra* n. 422, at 42 et seq.; Wijnen, de Goede & Alessi, *supra* n. 3, at 32 et seq.; Wolfgang W. Fischer, Christian Klein & Matthias Eilers, *Quellensteuerproblematik bei produktbegleitenden technischen Dienstleistungen in DBA-Outbound-Fällen*, IStR 483, 485 et seq. (2012); Báez Moreno, *supra* n. 6, at 310 et seq.
524. *See, e.g.*, Article 13(4) DTC India-Poland (1989), Article 12(4) DTC India-South Africa (1996) and Article 12(3)(b) DTC India-Sweden (1997).
525. *See, e.g.*, Joint Committee on Taxation, *supra* n. 450, at 47; ITAT Mumbai, *supra* n. 23, at paras 18 et seq.
526. Sanghvi & Shaktawat, *supra* n. 22, at 454.
527. *See also* Article 12(5) DTC India-United States (1989).

(a) are ancillary and subsidiary to the application or enjoyment of the right, property or information for which a payment described in paragraph 3 is received; or
(b) make available technical knowledge, experience, skill, know-how, or processes, or consist of the development and transfer of a technical plan or technical design.[528]

As mentioned, the DTC India-USA offers detailed explanations of the concept of 'fees for included services' in its technical explanation. These are often cited by Indian courts[529] to interpret provisions of other tax treaties including a similar provision as that found in the DTC India-USA (1989). *Wijnen/de Goede/Alessi*[530] also concluded that tax treaty provisions including source taxation for (technical) services are inspired – in one way or another – by Article 12 DTC India-USA (1989). However, due to the immense variety of different included services provisions in the royalties' article of tax treaties examined by *Wijnen/de Goede/Alessi*, an attempt to categorize these different provisions was abandoned.[531]

The examination of tax treaties concluded by African countries shows a similar situation. Among those examined, source taxation of technical and other similar services is found in the articles on 'Royalties',[532] 'Royalties and fees for technical services',[533] 'Royalties and technical services fees',[534] 'Royalties and services fees',[535] and 'Royalties and management fees'.[536,537] In this respect, various services are covered by these provisions, even in the articles on 'Royalties'. Most commonly, technical assistance performed in a contracting state by a resident of the other contracting state in relation to the transfer of IP rights (without the requirement of being ancillary to these rights) has been included as part of the definition of the royalties' article, such as in Article 12(3) DTC Egypt-Spain (2005):

> It also includes payments for technical assistance performed in a Contracting State by a resident of the other Contracting State where it is connected only to the application of the above mentioned rights, properties or information.

Such a definition is also included in an adapted form in other examined treaties such as the DTC Egypt-Indonesia (1998). In this respect, Article 12(3) DTC Egypt-Indonesia only allows source taxation of technical assistance of ancillary or subsidiary nature to the enjoyment of IP rights.[538] This might either be the case when such

528. *See* for a similar provision: Article 12(4) DTC Canada-India (1996).
529. *See, e.g.*, ITAT Delhi, *NQA Quality Systems Registrar Ltd. v. Deputy Commissioner of Income Tax*, ITA No. 394 to 397 (Delhi) of 2002 (22. December 2004) and ITAT New Delhi, *ONGC as Representative Assessee of Shell International Exploration & Production BV Netherlands v. Assistant Commissioner of Income Tax*, ITA No. 4942 Delhi of 2004 (31 March 2006).
530. Wijnen, de Goede & Alessi, *supra* n. 3, at 27.
531. Wijnen, de Goede & Alessi, *supra* n. 3, at 33.
532. *See, e.g.*, Article 12 DTC Botswana-China (2012) and Article 13 DTC Benin-UAE (2013).
533. *See* Article 12 DTC India-Uganda (2004) and Article 12 DTC Morocco-Rwanda (2016).
534. *See* Article 12 DTC Ghana-Netherlands (2008).
535. *See, e.g.*, Article 12 DTC Germany-Ghana (2004) and Article 12 DTC Ghana-Switzerland (2008).
536. *See* Article 12 DTC Germany-Kenya (1977).
537. *See also* Appendices 1 to 6 for a complete analysis.
538. *See* similarly Article 12(3) DTC Egypt-Greece (2004).

assistance is performed in a contracting state[539] or irrespective of the place of performance.[540]

Especially Tunisia also included payments for technical or economic studies and technical assistance in the scope of the article on royalties.[541] Such assistance is sometimes connected to the transfer of IP rights[542] or the performance in a contracting state.[543] In addition, the inclusion of technical services instead of technical assistance is used in the definition of royalties in a few Tunisian tax treaties.[544]

The definition of royalties in other examined tax treaties is considerably diverse. It includes payments for 'technical services',[545] 'technical and consultancy services',[546] 'any services of a technical, managerial, administrative or consultancy nature rendered in the State of which the payer is a resident',[547] 'technical assistance and the services delivery and staff services',[548] 'consultancy and technical assistance',[549] 'technical services and technical assistance',[550] 'technical services and the furnishing of services', 'studies of a scientific, geological or technical nature and for engineering projects with plans pertaining thereto',[551] 'technical and economic studies',[552] 'studies or in exchange of technical assistance',[553] 'the supply of any assistance that is ancillary and subsidiary to, and is furnished as a means of enabling the application or enjoyment of, any such property or right',[554] 'information concerning industrial, commercial or scientific experience including consultancy and technical assistance',[555] and 'technical assistance in connection with the use of, or the right to use, any copyright, goods or information'.[556]

Source taxing rights for technical and other services are also included in articles on 'Royalties and fees for technical services',[557] 'Royalties and technical services fees',[558] 'Royalties and services fees'[559] and 'Royalties and management fees'.[560] In

539. *See* Article 12(3) DTC Egypt-Mauritius (2012).
540. *See* Article 12(4) DTC Egypt-Saudi Arabia (2016).
541. *See, e.g.*, Article 12(3) DTC Korea-Tunisia (1988) and Article 12(3) DTC Malta-Tunisia (2000).
542. *See* Article 12(3)(d) DTC Tunisia-USA (1985).
543. *See, e.g.*, Article 12(3) DTC Luxembourg-Tunisia (1996).
544. *See* Article 12(3)(a) DTC Czech Republic-Tunisia (1990) and Article 12(3) DTC Netherlands-Tunisia (1995).
545. *See* Article 12(2)(a) DTC Tunisia-Singapore (2018).
546. *See* Article 12(3) DTC Botswana-China (2012).
547. *See* Article 12(3) dash 2 DTC France-Zimbabwe (1993).
548. *See* Article 13(2) DTC Benin-UAE (2013).
549. *See* Article 12(3) DTC Kuwait-Mauritius (1997).
550. *See* no. 3 of the Protocol to the DTC Brazil-South Africa (2003, 2015).
551. *See* Article 20(4) DTC France-Senegal Income, Inheritance, Registration, Stamp and Gift Tax Treaty (1974).
552. *See* Article XII (4) DTC Canada-Tunisia (1982).
553. *See* Article 12(3) DTC Cameroon-Tunisia (1999).
554. *See* Article 12(3)(d) DTC Indonesia-South Africa (1997) and Article 12(3)(d) DTC Australia-South Africa (1999).
555. *See* Article 12(3) DTC Kuwait-Mauritius (1997).
556. *See* Protocol on Article 12 of the DTC Cape Verde-Mauritius (2017).
557. *See* Article 12(4) DTC Morocco-Rwanda (2016).
558. *See* Article 12(5) DTC Ghana-Netherlands (2008).
559. *See* Article 12 DTC Germany-Ghana (2004), Article 12 DTC Ghana-Switzerland (2008), Article 12 DTC Denmark-Ghana (2014) and Article 12 DTC Czech Republic-Ghana (2017).
560. *See* Article 12 DTC Germany-Kenya (1977).

contrast to the articles on 'Royalties', the mentioned services are also defined in the respective article independently from the definition of royalties.

In this respect, 'fees for technical services' and 'technical services fees' are nearly identically defined. They include 'services of a managerial, technical or consultancy nature',[561] or 'managerial, technical or consultancy services'.[562] In addition, the term 'services fees' as found in a few examined tax treaties shares the same definitions.[563] Interestingly, the description of the term 'management fees' in Article 12(4) DTC Germany-Kenya (1977) not only includes services of a managerial nature – as it would seem obvious – but also those of a technical or consultancy character and independent activities of physicians, lawyers, engineers, architects, dentists, and accountants in its scope.

The mentioned definitions often explicitly exclude certain activities from their scope. In this respect, the definition of 'services fees' regularly excludes supervisory activities in connection with a building site, construction, assembly, or installation project and supervisory activities connected to installation services that are incidental to the sale of machinery or parts thereof from its scope. Additionally, Article 12(4) DTC Ghana-Switzerland (2008) and Article 12(4) DTC Ghana-Germany (2004) also exclude remuneration as referred to in the respective article on independent personal services from its scope.

Similar exclusions are also found in the articles on 'Royalties and fees for technical services' and 'Royalties and technical services fees'. According to Article 12(4) DTC Pakistan-South Africa (1998), services mentioned in the provisions on the construction and service PE[564] as well as those falling within the scope of the respective articles on (in)dependent personal services are outside the scope of technical services. Exclusions with respect to services of a(n) (in)dependent nature as defined in the treaty are also included in Article 12(4) DTC Morocco-Rwanda (2016) and Article 12(3)(b) DTC India-Uganda (2004).

It is noteworthy that the aforementioned provisions are found in 12.5 % of examined tax treaties concluded by African countries[565] which is a significantly higher percentage in comparison to the overall global percentage[566] of tax treaties including service provisions in the royalties' article as examined in the past.[567]

561. *See* Article 12(5) DTC Ghana-Netherlands (2008) and Article 12(4) DTC Morocco-Rwanda (2016).
562. *See* Article 12(4) DTC Pakistan-South Africa (1998) and Article 12(3)(b) DTC India-Uganda (2004).
563. *See* Article 12(3)(b) DTC Czech Republic-Ghana (2017): 'provision of technical, consultancy and managerial services' and Article 12(4) DTC Germany-Ghana (2004), Article 12(4) DTC Ghana-Switzerland (2008) and Article 12(4) DTC Denmark-Ghana (2014): 'consideration for any services of a managerial, technical or consultancy nature'.
564. *See* in this respect Article 12(5) DTC Ghana-Netherlands (2008): 'Provided that the term "technical service fees" shall not include any payments in consideration for supervisory activities in connection with a building site or construction, assembly or installation project or for supervisory activities in connection with installation incidental to the sale of machinery or parts thereof....'
565. *See* Appendices 4 and 6.
566. Wijnen, de Goede & Alessi, *supra* n. 3, at 33: Approximately 5.2 %.
567. *See* especially: Wijnen, de Goede & Alessi, *supra* n. 3, at 27.

b Autonomous Provisions

Autonomous provisions on the taxation of fees for technical and other similar services as broadly defined in Article 12A(3) UN Model are already found in African tax treaties as early as the 1970s. Kenia's DTCs concluded in the 1970s with Denmark, the United Kingdom, and Norway include a provision on the taxation of 'management or professional fees',[568] 'management fees',[569] and 'management or professional services'.[570] Irrespective of the wording of the article, all of these mentioned provisions include services of a managerial, technical, or consultancy nature within their scope.

Provisions on source taxation of technical and other similar services without the existence of a PE have also been included in model treaties in the past. In this respect, the Andean Model has already provided for source taxation of fees for services rendered by 'employees, professionals, technicians or for personal services' without the existence of a PE since 1971.[571] Aside from this model, the CARICOM tax treaty of 1994 specifically addresses the taxation of 'industrial or commercial advice or for management or technical services or similar services or facilities' in a separate article on 'Management fees'.[572]

In the study conducted by *Wijnen/de Goede/Alessi*, it was concluded that non-OECD Member States are seemingly more interested in the inclusion of autonomous provisions on the taxation of technical and other similar services in contrast to including these services under the article on royalties.[573] Based on the study of African country practice, the author's opinion is in accordance with that of *Wijnen/de Goede/Alessi*. The share of autonomous treaty provisions among examined tax treaties is nearly twice as high as in relation to service provisions found in the respective article on royalties.[574]

The inclusion of an article on the taxation of fees for technical and other similar services comes under different labels: 'Fees for technical services',[575] 'Technical fees',[576] 'Remuneration for technical services',[577] 'Fees for technical and other services',[578] 'Management, consultancy and technical fees',[579] 'Management fees',[580]

568. *See* Article 14 DTC Denmark-Kenya (1972).
569. *See* Article 14 DTC Kenya-UK (1973).
570. *See* Article 14 DTC Kenya-Norway (1972).
571. *See* The Commission of the Cartagena Agreement, *Standard Agreement to avoid double taxation between Member Countries and other States outside the Subregion*, http://www.sice.oas.org/trade/junac/decisiones/dec040e.asp (accessed 19 January 2024), Article 13.
572. *See* Article 14 of the Agreement Among the Governments of the Member States of the Caribbean Community for the Avoidance of Double Taxation and the Prevention of Fiscal Evasion with Respect to Taxes on Income, Profits or Gains and Capital Gains and for the Encouragement of Regional Trade and Investment (1994).
573. Wijnen, de Goede & Alessi, *supra* n. 3, at 33.
574. 20.5% (share of autonomous provisions found in examined tax treaties) compared to 12.5% (share of services provisions found in examined tax treaties in the article on royalties).
575. Article 14 DTC Gambia-UK (1980), Article 12 DTC Egypt-Pakistan (1995), Article 13 DTC Malaysia-South Africa (2005, 2011), Article 13 DTC Iran-Senegal (2010), Article 13 DTC Malaysia-Senegal (2010), Article 14 DTC Cameroon-South Africa (2015), Article 13 DTC Ghana-Morocco (2017).
576. Article 13 DTC UK-Zimbabwe (1982), Article 11 DTC Bulgaria-Zimbabwe (1988), Article 13 DTC Sweden-Zimbabwe (1989), Article 13 DTC Norway-Zimbabwe (1989), Article 13 DTC

'Management and technical fees',[581] 'Services fees',[582] 'Technical services fees',[583] 'Management or professional fees',[584] 'Management, professional or technical fees',[585] 'Fees for management, professional and technical services',[586] 'Administration and management fees',[587] and 'Technical and management fees'.[588]

While the articles on the taxation of fees for technical and other similar services are titled differently, in one way or another, they commonly include services of a technical, managerial, and consultancy nature as part of their definition.[589] The analysed tax treaties also generally define the term 'fees' as payments of any type[590]

Zimbabwe-Canada (1992), Article 13 DTC Uganda-UK (1992), Article 13 DTC Malaysia-Zimbabwe (1994), Article 13 DTC Serbia and Montenegro-Zimbabwe (1996), Article 13 DTC South Africa-Uganda (1997), Article 12A DTC South Africa- Tunisia (1999), Article 13 DTC Italy-Uganda (2000), Article 13 DTC Indonesia-Zimbabwe (2001), Article 14 DTC Rwanda-South Africa (2002), Article 13 DTC Congo-Zimbabwe (2002), Article 20 DTC Botswana-South Africa (2003, 2013), Article 13 DTC Mauritius-Uganda (2003), Article 21 DTC Botswana-Namibia (2004), Article 21 DTC Botswana-Seychelles (2004), Article 13 DTC South Africa-Swaziland (2004), Article 13 DTC Botswana-Zimbabwe (2004), Article 13 DTC Botswana-UK (2005), Article 21 DTC Barbados-Botswana (2005), Article 13 DTC Botswana-India (2006), Article 13 DTC Belgium-Rwanda (2007), Article 21 DTC Botswana-Mozambique (2009), Article 13 DTC Botswana-Swaziland (2010), Article 13 DTC Botswana-Lesotho (2010), Article 13 DTC Lesotho-Seychelles (2011), Article 13 DTC Serbia-Tunisia (2012), Article 13 DTC Botswana-Zambia (2013), Article 13 DTC Ghana-Seychelles (2014), Article 13 DTC Lesotho-South Africa (2014), Article 20 DTC Botswana-Ireland (2014), Article 13 DTC South Africa-Zimbabwe (2015), Article 20 DTC Botswana-Malawi (2016), Article 20 DTC Botswana-Malta (2017), Article 13 DTC China-Kenya (2017).

577. Article 13 DTC Portugal-Senegal (2014).
578. *See* Article 14 DTC Angola-UAE (2018).
579. Article 21 DTC Botswana-Sweden (1992), Article 22 DTC Botswana-Mauritius (1995), Article 21 DTC Botswana-France (1999), Article 21 DTC Botswana-Russian Federation (2003).
580. Article 14 DTC Kenya-UK (1976), Article 13 DTC France-Ghana (1993), Article 14 DTC Gambia-Norway (1994), Article 13 DTC Ghana-Serbia and Montenegro (2000), Article 20 DTC Ghana-South Africa (2004), Article 18 DTC Belgium-Ghana (2005), Article 13 DTC Barbados-Ghana (2008).
581. Article 17 DTC Ghana-UK (1993).
582. Article 13 DTC Ghana-Singapore (2017).
583. Article 14 DTC Nigeria-UAE (2016) and Article 13 DTC Ghana-Mauritius (2017).
584. Article 14 DTC Denmark-Kenya (1972), Article 14 DTC Kenya-Norway (1972), Article 14 DTC Canada-Kenya (1983), Article 13 DTC Mauritius-Rwanda (2013), Article 13 DTC Barbados-Rwanda (2014), Article 13 DTC Rwanda-Singapore (2014), Article 13 DTC Jersey-Rwanda (2015), Article 14 DTC Rwanda-UAE (2017).
585. Article 13 DTC Kenya-Seychelles (2014).
586. Article 13 DTC India-Kenya (2016).
587. Article 13 DTC Norway-Uganda (1999) and Article 13 DTC Denmark-Uganda (2000).
588. Article 12B DTC Seychelles-Zimbabwe (2002).
589. *See, e.g.*, Article 14(3) DTC Kenya-UK (1976), Article 14(3) DTC Gambia-UK (1980), Article 17(3) DTC Ghana-UK (1993), Article 13(3) DTC France-Ghana (1993), Article 12(3) DTC Egypt-Pakistan (1995), Article 20(3) DTC Ghana-South Africa (2004), Article 18(3) DTC Belgium-Ghana (2005), Article 13(3) DTC Barbados-Ghana (2008), Article 13(3) DTC Iran-Senegal (2010), Article 13(3) DTC Malaysia-Senegal (2010), Article 13(3) DTC Senegal-Portugal (2014), Article 14(3) DTC Cameroon-South Africa (2015), Article 13(3) DTC Ghana-Morocco (2017), Article 13(3) DTC Ghana-Morocco (2017).
590. *See, e.g.*, Article 14(3) DTC Denmark-Kenya (1972), Article 14(3) DTC Kenya-Norway (1972), Article 14(3) DTC Kenya-UK (1976), Article 14(3) DTC Gambia-UK (1980), Article 17(3) DTC Ghana-UK (1993), Article 13(3) DTC France-Ghana (1993), Article 14(3) DTC Gambia-Norway (1994), Article 13(3) DTC Ghana-Serbia and Montenegro (2000), Article 20(3) DTC Botswana-South Africa (2003, 2013), Article 21(3) DTC Botswana-Namibia (2004), Article 20(3) DTC

(including lump sum payments)[591] to any person.[592] However, the design of the aforementioned provisions shows – similar to that in the context of examined provisions on royalties – numerous varieties concerning their wording and respective scope. In this respect, the term 'Technical service fees' as defined in Article 14(3) DTC Nigeria-UAE (2016) also specifically includes professional services within their scope.[593] Similarly, Article 14 DTC Rwanda-UAE (2017), Article 12B DTC Zimbabwe-Seychelles (2002), and Article 14 DTC Rwanda-South Africa (2002) include professional services within the scope of 'Technical fees', 'Technical services fees', and 'Technical and management fees'. However, there is a requirement that the payment is not for the reimbursement of actual expenses.

The definition of the term 'technical fees' in numerous examined tax treaties also includes administrative services in addition to technical, managerial, and consultancy services. These either have to be performed in the residence state of the payer,[594] outside that state[595] or have no geographical requirement at all.[596] Tax treaties including a provision on the taxation of 'Technical fees' also partially explicitly include technical and economic studies and technical assistance in their definition.[597] Article 13(3) DTC Ghana-Seychelles (2014) defines technical fees very broadly thereby also including elements in subparagraphs (ii) and (iii) that are usually found in provisions on the taxation of royalties and not in an autonomous article on the taxation of fees for technical and other services:

Ghana-South Africa (2004), Article 21(3) DTC Botswana-Seychelles (2004), Article 13(3) DTC Botswana-Zimbabwe (2004), Article 13(3) DTC Botswana-UK (2005), Article 21(3) DTC Botswana-Barbados (2005), Article 18(3) DTC Belgium-Ghana (2005), Article 13(3) DTC Barbados-Ghana (2008), Article 21(3) DTC Botswana-Mozambique (2009), Article 13(3) DTC Iran-Senegal (2010), Article 13(3) DTC Botswana-Swaziland (2010), Article 13(3) DTC Botswana-Lesotho (2010), Article 13(3) DTC Malaysia-Senegal (2010), Article 13(2) DTC Malaysia-South Africa (2005, 2011), Article 13(3) DTC Botswana-Zambia (2013), Article 20(3) DTC Botswana-Ireland (2014), Article 13(3) DTC Portugal-Senegal (2014), Article 14(3) DTC Cameroon-South Africa (2015), Article 20(3) DTC Botswana-Malawi (2016).

591. Article 12(3) DTC Egypt-Pakistan (1995).
592. *See, e.g.*, Article 14(3) DTC Denmark-Kenya (1972), Article 14(3) DTC Kenya-Norway (1972), Article 14(3) DTC Kenya-UK (1976), Article 14(3) DTC Gambia-UK (1980), Article 13(3) DTC France-Ghana (1993), Article 13(3) DTC Ghana-Serbia and Montenegro (2000), Article 20(3) DTC Botswana-South Africa (2003, 2013), Article 21(3) DTC Botswana-Namibia (2004), Article 20(3) DTC Ghana-South Africa (2004), Article 21(3) DTC Botswana-Seychelles (2004), Article 13(3) DTC Botswana-Zimbabwe (2004), Article 13(3) DTC Botswana-UK (2005), Article 18(3) DTC Belgium-Ghana (2005), Article 21(3) DTC Barbados-Botswana (2005), Article 13(2) DTC Malaysia-South Africa (2005, 2011), Article 13(3) DTC Botswana-India (2006), Article 13(3) DTC Barbados-Ghana (2008), Article 21(3) DTC Botswana-Mozambique (2009), Article 13(3) DTC Malaysia-Senegal (2010), Article 13(3) DTC Botswana-Swaziland (2010), Article 13(3) DTC Botswana-Lesotho (2010), Article 13(3) DTC Botswana-Zambia (2013), Article 20(3) DTC Botswana-Ireland (2014), Article 14(3) DTC Cameroon-South Africa (2015), Article 20(3) DTC Botswana-Malawi (2016).
593. According to this provision, these services also have to be performed by a resident of a contracting state for a resident of the other contracting state.
594. *See* Article 13(3) DTC Indonesia-Zimbabwe (2001).
595. *See* Article 21(3) DTC Botswana-Namibia (2004).
596. *See, e.g.*, Article 13(3) DTC Norway-Zimbabwe (1989).
597. *See* Article 12A South Africa-Tunisia (1999) and Article 13(3) DTC Serbia-Tunisia (2012).

> The term 'technical fees' as used in this Article means an amount whether periodical or lump sum as consideration for:
>
> (i) rendering any managerial, technical or consultancy services including the services of technical or other personnel;
> (ii) the supply of any technical, industrial, commercial or scientific knowledge, experience or skill;
> (iii) the supply of services which are ancillary and subsidiary for which technical fees are received.

The definition of 'services fees' or 'technical services fees' as found in a few tax treaties also requires the rendering of services of a technical, managerial, or consultancy nature in a contracting state. Such a narrow definition, however, is only found in a few tax treaties concluded by Ghana.[598]

The term 'Management fees' as defined in Article 14(3) DTC Gambia-Norway (1994) also explicitly includes remuneration 'in respect of the provision of industrial or commercial advice...or similar services or facilities' within its scope.

Although the inclusion of a make-available provision is generally specific to 'included services' provisions in the article on royalties,[599] it was also found in an autonomous treaty provision in one examined tax treaty. In this respect, the tax treaty concluded by Uganda with Denmark includes an article on the taxation of 'Administration and management fees'.[600] These are defined as:

> ...consideration for any services of an administrative or managerial nature, if such services make available administrative or managerial knowledge, experience, skills or know-how, but only to the extent that the services are performed on a regular basis or for a period of more than six months.[601]

Certain payments are commonly excluded from the scope of technical and other similar services. In this respect, payments to employees are those most commonly excluded.[602] In addition, also exclusions for payments for teaching in or by an educational institution,[603] B2C services,[604] supervisory activities in connection with a

598. *See* Article 13(3) DTC Ghana-Singapore (2017), Article 13(3) DTC Ghana-Mauritius (2017) and Article 13(3) DTC Ghana-Ireland (2018).
599. Especially India aims to include such a provision in its tax treaties.
600. *See* Article 13 DTC Norway-Uganda (1999) and also Article 13 Denmark-Uganda (2000), however, with a different definition.
601. Article 13(3) DTC Norway-Uganda (1999).
602. *See, e.g.*, Article 14(3) DTC Denmark-Kenya (1972), Article 14(3) DTC Kenya-UK (1976), Article 14(3) DTC Gambia-UK (1980), Article 13(3) DTC France-Ghana (1993), Article 17(3) DTC Ghana-UK (1993) Article 13(3) DTC Ghana-Serbia and Montenegro (2000), Article 20(3) DTC Botswana-South Africa (2003, 2013), Article 21(3) DTC Botswana-Namibia (2004), Article 21(3) DTC Botswana-Seychelles (2004), Article 13(3) DTC Botswana-Zimbabwe (2004), Article 20(3) DTC Ghana-South Africa (2004), Article 13(3) DTC Botswana-UK (2005), Article 18(3) DTC Belgium-Ghana (2005), Article 13(2) DTC Malaysia-South Africa (2005, 2011), Article 21(3) DTC Barbados-Botswana (2005), Article 13(3) DTC Barbados-Ghana (2008), Article 21(3) DTC Botswana-Mozambique (2009), Article 13(3) DTC Malaysia-Senegal (2010), Article 13(3) DTC Botswana-Swaziland (2010), Article 13(3) DTC Botswana-Lesotho (2010), Article 13(3) DTC Botswana-Zambia (2013), Article 20(3) DTC Botswana-Ireland (2014), Article 14(3) DTC Cameroon-South Africa (2015), Article 20(3) DTC Botswana-Malawi (2016).
603. *See* Article 14(3)(b) DTC Angola-UAE and Article 13(3)(b) DTC Ghana-Morocco (2017).

building site or construction, assembly or installation project or supervisory activities in connection with installation incidental to the sale of machinery or parts thereof,[605] royalties,[606] directors' fees and remunerations of company managers,[607] reimbursement of expenses incurred by the service provider,[608] and for professional services are found in the examined tax treaties.[609]

c Analysis of Study Outcomes

As already expressed by *Wijnen/de Goede/Alessi*[610] and *Miller*,[611] provisions on source taxation of fees for technical and other similar services take a vast variety of forms. Moreover, the analysis made by the author with a set of chosen tax treaties concluded by African countries also shows that provisions on technical and other similar services are highly diverse and challenging to cluster. In general, those for the mentioned services are either found in the article on royalties or in an autonomous article.

If technical or other similar services are included in the article on 'royalties', no definition is included in the article itself. These services are – although being active income – part of the definition of royalties themselves which, in fact, is contradictory to the original nature of royalties as passive income. However, if specifically mentioned in the header of the article, i.e., 'Royalties and fees for technical services', 'Royalties and technical services fees', 'Royalties and services fees' and 'Royalties and management fees', the treaty provides a definition of the respective services independently from the definition of royalties.

Whether administrative, professional, or other types of services are explicitly included in the definition of technical or other types of services is highly dependent on the tax treaty policy of the contracting states. In this respect, no concrete conclusions can be drawn by simply examining the labelling of the article such as, e.g., 'Royalties and management fees', 'Fees for technical services', 'Management fees' or 'Services fees'. It also cannot be determined whether a certain definition is directly attributable to a specific labelling of respective fees as the attribution of a certain name to an article in a tax treaty including its definition is subject to negotiations between the contracting states. However, when analysing the definitions of examined tax treaties, certain types

604. *See* Article 14(3)(c) DTC Angola-UAE and Article 13(3)(c) DTC Ghana-Morocco (2017).
605. *See, e.g.*, with respect to the definition of 'management fees': Article 13(3) DTC France-Ghana (1993), Article 13(3) DTC Ghana-Serbia and Montenegro (2000), Article 20(3) DTC Ghana-South Africa (2004), Article 18(3) DTC Belgium-Ghana (2005), Article 13(3) DTC Barbados-Ghana (2008); with respect to 'Services fees': Article 13(3) DTC Ghana-Singapore (2017) and 'Technical services fees': Article 13(3) DTC Ghana-Mauritius (2017).
606. *See* Article 13(3) DTC Iran-Senegal (2010).
607. *See* Art 18 para. 3 DTC Belgium-Ghana (2005).
608. *See, e.g.*, Article 13(3) DTC Canada-Zimbabwe (1992) and Article 14(3) DTC Rwanda-South Africa (2002).
609. *See, e.g.*, Article 13(3) DTC India-Serbia and Montenegro (2006) and Article 13(3) DTC India-Malaysia (2012).
610. Wijnen, de Goede & Alessi, *supra* n. 3, at 27.
611. Miller, *supra* n. 2, at 147 et seq.

of services are commonly found in the definition of aforementioned services: Technical, managerial, and consultancy services. These services are also those that the UN Tax Committee decided to include in the definition of fees for technical services of Article 12A(3) UN Model 2017. Additionally, the exclusions from the scope of technical services as included in Article 12A UN Model are commonly found in numerous tax treaties. The UN Tax Committee was surely inspired by Article 12 DTC India-USA (1989) in its drafting process due to the thorough explanations to the DTC.[612] However, it still decided to draft an autonomous provision on the taxation of fees for technical services for the purposes of its inclusion to the UN Model 2017. It also considered a provision based on Article 12 DTC India-USA (1989) as an option in the Commentaries to the UN Model. The UN Tax Committee attempts – with the inclusion of Article 12A to the UN Model 2017 – to provide greater tax certainty with respect to the taxation of technical and other similar services. This is based on the assumption that the wide variety of different provisions on the taxation of fees for technical and other services is contingent upon a missing model provision that provides certain factual authority as a basis for tax treaty negotiations.

Although there must be an expectation that the number of tax treaties including a provision on fees for technical services will increase,[613] the acceptance of such an inclusion by the vast majority of OECD Member States has yet to be observed. In the past few years, several tax treaties signed by them include a provision on the taxation of fees for technical services that are (seemingly) based on Article 12A UN Model 2017.[614] Other OECD Member States like France, Germany, or the Netherlands, however, still attempt to ensure taxation of fees for technical services on the basis of the article on business profits[615] or independent personal services.[616] Therefore, these states are very much in favour of explicitly ensuring that these fees are partly subject to the article on business profits.[617]

France and Mauritius specifically included a provision in the protocol to their tax treaty of 1980 that is also similarly included in several other tax treaties concluded by OECD Member States with African countries. It considers fees for technical and other similar services as payments to which Article 7 shall apply:

> Similarly, payments received as a consideration for technical services, including studies or surveys of a scientific, geological or technical nature, or for engineering

612. *See* Chapter 3.B.ii. of this publication.
613. This is especially true for tax treaties signed between non-OECD members.
614. *See, e.g.*, Article 13 DTC Brazil-Switzerland (2018), Article 13 DTC Ghana-Norway (2020) and Article 13 DTC Ireland-Kenya (2021).
615. *See, e.g.*, Article 7(9) DTC Iraq-Netherlands (2019): 'Payments received as a consideration for technical services, including studies or surveys of a scientific, geological or technical nature, or for consultancy or supervisory services shall be deemed to be payments to which the provisions of this Article apply.'
616. *See, e.g.*, Article V of the Protocol to the DTC Algeria-Netherlands (2018): 'Payments received as a consideration for technical services, including studies or surveys of a scientific, geological or technical nature, or for consultancy or supervisory services shall be deemed to be payments to which the provisions of Article 7 or Article 14, as the case may be, apply.'
617. *See, e.g.*, Miller, *supra* n. 2, at 174.

> contracts including blue prints related thereto, or for consultant or supervisory services shall be deemed to be profits to which the provisions of Article 7 apply.[618]

Another provision found in the Protocol to the DTC France-Nigeria (1990) also specifically excluded fees for technical services and other similar services such as consultancy or supervisory services from the scope of know-how. This makes Article 12 DTC France-Nigeria (Royalties) inapplicable to such service fees.[619]

Although especially OECD members might be reluctant to source taxation for fees for technical services as provided by Article 12A UN Model, it must still be borne in mind that this provision mainly addresses non-OECD members. As already mentioned,[620] the UN Model and its corresponding commentaries are in no way legally binding, however, states still heavily rely on them as a basis for tax treaty negotiations and means of interpretation. In this respect, it needs to be mentioned that the Commentaries to the OECD and UN Models did not include any guidance – except for the explanations on mixed contracts – on the taxation of fees for technical services upon which OECD and non-OECD members could have relied upon in the past. Therefore, the inclusion of Article 12A to the UN Model 2017 might serve as a means to foster a more consistent approach in tax treaty practice among non-OECD Member States in the future. In addition, its corresponding commentary will also be of high value as a means of interpretation.

2 *Technical, Managerial and Consultancy Services*

Article 12A(3) UN Model defines the term 'fees for technical services' as 'any services of a managerial, technical or consultancy nature'. The latter definition is found in

618. *See* Article 1(2)(b) of the Protocol to the DTC France-Mauritius (1980); *see also* Article II of the Protocol to the DTC Netherlands-Nigeria (1991) and paragraph 4(c) of the Protocol to the DTC Germany-Mauritius (2011), including the same wording as found in the DTC France-Mauritius; no. 3 of the Protocol to the DTC Egypt-Korea (1992): '...Similarly, payments received by corporations as a consideration for studies or surveys of a scientific, geological or technical nature, or for consultant or supervisory services shall be deemed to be payments to which the provisions of Article 7 apply.'; *see also* no. III of the Protocol to the DTC Egypt-Netherlands (1999): 'Payments received as a consideration for technical services, including studies or surveys of a scientific, geological or technical nature, or for consultancy or supervisory services, shall be deemed to be payments *to which the provisions of Article 7 or Article 14 apply.*' (word order italicized by the author); similarly Article V of the Protocol to the DTC Netherlands-South Africa (2005): 'Payments received as a consideration for technical services, including studies or surveys of a scientific, geological or technical nature, or for consultancy or supervisory services shall be deemed to be payments to which the provisions of Article 7 apply.'; similarly no. 1 (c) of the Protocol to the DTC Germany-Tunisia (2018), however, with the exception that the contracting states specifically exclude technical assistance from the scope of Article 7 due to its inclusion in the scope of Article 12(3) on royalties.
619. *See* no. 5 of the Protocol to the DTC France-Nigeria (1990); similarly, no. 4 of the Protocol to the DTC Belgium-Uganda (2007), explicitly excluding payments for technical assistance and technical services from the scope of know-how: 'In applying Article 12, paragraph 3 of the Convention payments constituting consideration for technical assistance or technical services shall not be considered to be payments for information concerning industrial, commercial or scientific experience, but shall be taxable in accordance with the provisions of Article 7 or Article 15 [independent personal services], as the case may be.'
620. *See* Chapter 2.B.ii.1. of this publication.

several tax treaties concluded by African countries before the inclusion of Article 12A to the UN Model 2017.[621] However, as shown by literature[622] and the author,[623] state practice on the taxation of fees for technical services has been highly heterogeneous since the 1970s. Therefore, the UN Tax Committee intended to increase tax certainty through the inclusion of an article on the taxation of fees for technical services as a basis for tax treaty negotiations. One means to achieve this goal is to provide a definition of the term 'fees for technical services' that is clear, exhaustive, and excludes – as far as possible – reference to domestic law. In this respect, the Commentary on Article 12A UN Model states that 'fees for technical services' are limited to those services mentioned in Article 12A(3) UN Model. As a result, Article 12A UN Model does not aim to apply to all service payments but only technical, managerial, and consultancy services.[624]

The UN Model does not include a definition of the term 'services'. However, the Commentary on Article 12A UN Model suggests giving the term a broad meaning on the basis of its ordinary use. Therefore, the term 'services' shall be understood as any activity that is carried on by one person for the benefit of another in exchange for a fee.[625]

Although the UN Model provides a definition of the term 'technical', it includes an inherent difficulty as the term is used twice in the form of A = A + B + C.[626] The Commentary on Article 12A of the UN Model attempts to solve this equation by expressing that technical, managerial, and consultancy services have one underlying concept in common, i.e., the involvement of application of specialized knowledge, skill, or expertise on behalf of a client.[627]

According to the Cambridge Dictionary, the term 'technical' is ascribed a meaning as 'having, or relating to, a particular science or skill, especially of a mechanical or industrial kind'.[628] Similarly, the Merriam-Webster Dictionary refers to the term 'technical' as 'having special and usually practical knowledge especially of a mechanical or scientific subject' and is also 'marked by or characteristic of specialization'.[629] Based on the ordinary meaning of the term 'technical', the Commentary on Article 12A UN Model concludes that fees for services provided by regulated professions[630] such as law, accounting, and engineering would be covered by the definition of the term 'technical' as found in Article 12A(3) UN Model.[631] In addition, Article 12A(3) UN Model shall also cover services rendered by professions outside of

621. *See* in this respect: Chapter 4.A.1. of this publication.
622. Miller, *supra* n. 2, at 174 et seq. and Wijnen, de Goede & Alessi, *supra* n. 3, at 32 et seq.
623. *See* Chapter 4.A.1. and Appendices 1 to 6 of this publication.
624. *See* para. 62 of the Commentary on Article 12A UN Model 2021: 'Article 12A applies only to fees for technical services, and not to all payments for services.'
625. *See* para. 84 of the Commentary on Article 12A UN Model 2021.
626. *See, e.g.*, Pal, *supra* n. 449, at 3.1.1.
627. *See, e.g.*, para. 62 of the Commentary on Article 12A UN Model 2021.
628. Cambridge University Press & Assessment, *Cambridge Dictionary*, https://dictionary.cambridge.org/de/worterbuch/englisch-deutsch/technical (accessed 5 September 2022).
629. Merriam-Webster, *Dictionary*, https://www.merriam-webster.com/dictionary/technical (accessed 5 September 2022).
630. *See* Article 14(2) UN Model 2021.
631. *See* para. 64 of the Commentary on Article 12A UN Model 2021.

Article 14(2) UN Model as long as such services involve the provision of specialized knowledge, skill, or expertise.[632] Therefore, based on the ordinary meaning of the term 'technical', standardized routine services shall not be within the scope of Article 12A UN Model. In this respect, the Commentary on Article 12A UN Model aims to clarify the scope of this article through the illustration of several examples of the delineation between standardized and routine services:[633]

> *Example 3*: Company A, a resident of State A, is engaged in the business of collecting, organizing, and maintaining various databases. In the course of its business, Company A sells access to various databases to Company B, a resident of State B. State A and State B concluded a tax treaty based on the UN Model 2021.
>
> The payments made by Company B for access to various databases are not subject to the application of Article 12A, as Company A does not apply its specialized knowledge, skill, or expertise at the moment of providing its service, i.e., granting access to the database. Although the development of the databases might have required the application of specialized knowledge, skill or expertise, the mere granting of access to the databases is a service of a routine nature.
>
> *Alternative to Example 3*: Company A creates a customized database on behalf of Company B. As the creation of a customized database on behalf of its client, Company B, requires the application of specialized knowledge, skill and expertise by Company A, fees paid in consideration for the customization of the database can be considered fees for technical services.
>
> *Example 4:* Company A, a resident of State A, provides insurance through standard form insurance contracts to customers in State B. The tax treaty concluded between State A and State B includes a provision that is based on Article 12A UN Model. The insurance premiums received from residents of State B are not considered fees for technical services, as Company A does not provide services directly for the benefit of each of its clients.
>
> *Example 5:* Company A, a resident of State A, is a financial institution that provides various financial services to customers of State B, such as acceptance of deposits, payments and transmission services, guarantees and advisory services. States A and B included Article 12A UN Model in its tax treaty. Whether fees received for financial services are fees for technical services in the sense of Article 12A(3) DTC A-B depends on the nature of the particular service, i.e., whether the service requires the application of specialized knowledge, skill or expertise on behalf of a specific client. According to the Commentary on Article 12A UN Model, services such as payment and transmission services, banker's drafts, foreign exchange, debt and credit card services and negotiable instruments are regularly routinely provided to clients. As a result, such services are not considered fees for technical services. If, however, advisory services are provided to a particular client with respect to a merger & acquisition involving the client, fees paid for such service could be regarded as fees for technical services.

The examples illustrated in the Commentary on Article 12A UN Model emphasize the need to apply specialized knowledge, skill, or expertise at the moment of the provision of the service. While the development of certain products such as databases or software might require the application of these, granting access to these products is

632. *See* para. 65 of the Commentary on Article 12A UN Model 2021.
633. *See* in this regard: paras 90 et seq. of the Commentary on Article 12A UN Model 2021.

only of a routine nature and does not require any customization of the product.[634] The latter-mentioned service, therefore, does not meet the requirement 'technical' according to the Commentary on Article 12A UN Model.[635]

The explanations found with regards to the application of specialized knowledge, skill, or expertise in the Commentaries on Article 12A UN Model are already similarly found in a report of the OECD Technical Advisory Group (TAG) to Working Party 1 (WP 1).[636] While the OECD did not include an article on the taxation of fees for technical services and no definition of technical services in the Commentaries to the OECD Model can be found, the TAG acknowledged the existence of treaty provisions specifically addressing the allocation of taxing rights for fees for technical services. To clarify the scope of these provisions on e-commerce, the TAG examined three types of services that are regularly found in bilateral treaty definitions of fees for technical services provisions, i.e., technical services, managerial services, and consultancy services.[637]

According to the TAG, technical services are characterized by the use of 'special skills or knowledge related to a technical field'.[638] A service can be regarded as 'technical' when special skills or knowledge are used at the moment that the service is provided to the customer. Although special skills or knowledge are used during the process of developing software or a troubleshooting database, the specialized service for the process is not to be regarded as technical as they are not directly provided to the customer. In the context of data and software, the provision is related to granting access and making data and software available to the customer. These types of services, however, do not require any special skills or knowledge. Therefore, the TAG concludes that neither the development of software or databases nor the granting of access to software or databases relates to technical services as the services provided to the customer do not relate to the creation of such software or database but rather to making the software or database available to a customer.[639]

Similarly, the TAG applies these principles to managerial services as it concludes that the application of 'substantial management expertise' is required when providing the service to the customer.[640] Finally, the definition of the term 'consultancy services'

634. Similarly, according to the AAR, managerial, technical or consultancy services in the form of routine data entry, application sorting, document handling, and data capturing services are not regarded as 'technical' as they do not involve the use of any sophisticated technology: AAR New Delhi, *R R Donnelley India Outsource Pvt. Ltd. v. Commissioner of Income Tax*, AAR No. 003 of 2010, at para. 6.1. (16 May 2011)
635. *See, e.g.*, para. 90 of the Commentary on Article 12A UN Model 2021.
636. *See* OECD Technical Advisory Group on Treaty Characterization of Electronic Commerce Payments, *Tax Treaty Characterisation Issues Arising from E-Commerce: Report to Working Party No. 1 of the OECD Committee on Fiscal Affairs*, https://web-archive.oecd.org/2012-06-15/167336-1923396.pdf (accessed 5 January 2024).
637. *Ibid.*, at paras 36 et seq.
638. *Ibid.*, at para. 39.
639. *Ibid.*, at paras 41 et seq.
640. *Ibid.*, at para. 44.

has to be understood as advice given by, e.g., a professional, who has 'special qualifications' to do so.[641]

Although the TAG explicitly only refers to the requirement of special skills or knowledge with respect to technical services in a narrow sense, i.e., services related to applied science or craftsmanship.[642] It can also be concluded from the explanations of the definition of managerial and consultancy services as found in their report to WP 1 that the TAG also requires these services to be of a specialized nature regarding the fulfilment of the definition of 'technical fees' as found in tax treaties.[643] Therefore, in the author's opinion, the Commentary on Article 12A UN Model in essence adheres to a similar approach as only services that require the use of specialized knowledge, skill, or expertise are within its scope.[644]

The requirement of 'specialised knowledge, skill or expertise' has been subject to criticism in literature. Due to the broad definition of 'technical', the question arises of 'which service does not actually involve the application of (at least a certain) degree of specialized knowledge, expertise or skill'.[645] In this respect, *Malan* mentions that 'it is difficult to conceive of a service that is not 'technical'.[646] Finally, also *Sixdorf/Leitsch* cannot 'imagine a service that does not involve the application of at least a certain degree of specialized knowledge, expertise or skill'.[647]

In the author's opinion, the meaning of the term 'technical' as defined in Article 12A(3) UN Model is twofold. As mentioned previously, the term 'technical' is used twice; once in the header of the article to describe all services covered by Article 12A UN Model and a second time in the definition of 'fees for technical services' as services of a 'technical nature' (Article 12A(3) UN Model). This leads to a circular definition that is not solved by the Commentary on Article 12A UN Model as it only defines the term 'technical' once based on its ordinary meaning:

> The ordinary meaning of the term 'technical' involves the application of specialized knowledge, skill or expertise with respect to a particular art, science, profession or occupation. Therefore, fees received for services provided by regulated professions such as law, accounting, architecture, medicine, engineering and dentistry would be fees for technical services within the meaning of paragraph 3.[648]

This broad definition, however, would make the addition of 'managerial' or 'consultancy' services to the definition of Article 12A(3) UN Model obsolete. They

641. *Ibid.*, at para. 45; *see also* AAR New Delhi, *Intertek Testing Services (P.) Ltd.*, AAR No. 751 of 2007, at para. 10.7 (7 November 2008): A certain level of expertise is inherent to consultancy services.
642. *See* OECD Technical Advisory Group on Treaty Characterization of Electronic Commerce Payments, *supra* n. 636, at para. 39.
643. *See* the wording in *Ibid.*, at paras 36 et seq. and paras 44 and 45: 'require substantial management expertise' and 'provision of advice by someone, such as a professional, who has special qualifications allowing him to do so'.
644. *See* para. 61 of the Commentary on Article 12A UN Model 2021.
645. *See* Báez Moreno, *supra* n. 6, at 300 and Malan, *supra* n. 6, at 64.
646. *See* Malan, *supra* n. 6, at 64.
647. *See* Sixdorf & Leitsch, *supra* n. 6, at 240.
648. *See* para. 64 of the Commentary on Article 12A UN Model 2021.

would already be covered by the definition of 'technical' as found in the Commentary to the UN Model, due to the mere requirement of the application of specialized knowledge, skill, or expertise in relation to some sort of occupation, e.g., a consultant or manager.

The definition of the term 'technical' as referred to by the Commentary on Article 12A UN Model seems to disregard the historical context and traditional meaning of the term 'technical'. As mentioned by the TAG, technical services are typically those that relate to the technical field of engineering or applied sciences in general[649] and exclude services by occupations from human sciences such as psychologists.[650] The reference to the field of applied sciences stems from the fact that, historically speaking, services of a 'technical' nature were closely related to the transfer of some sort of IP rights or, more concretely, know-how. Their transfer often required additional auxiliary services from the grantor to the grantee and its employees so that the grantee would be able to make use of them. Through the provision of such services, however, no specialized knowledge skill or expertise was transferred. The challenging delineation between the transfer of IP rights and the mentioned services, however, led to the evolution of the term 'technical assistance' and explanations on what is referred to as 'mixed contracts'. These explanations are included in the Commentaries on Article 12 of the OECD Model since its update of 1977 and are still relevant for the interpretation of tax treaties concluded after the release of the update.[651]

The narrow understanding of the term 'technical' as being only related to the technical field of engineering excluded several other types of services, such as professional services, from the scope of 'technical assistance'.[652] As the term 'technical' traditionally has a rather narrow scope,[653] it was in the interest of several non-OECD members to broaden the scope of 'fees for technical services' to also include other types of services, such as management, professional, or consultancy services in

649. *See also* Madras High Court, *Skycell Communications Ltd. v. Deputy Commissioner of Income Tax*, 2001 251 ITR 53 Mad, at para. 10 (23 February 2001): 'Having regard to the fact that the term is required to be understood in the context in which it is used, "fee for technical services" could only be meant to cover such things technical as are capable of being provided by way of service for a fee. The popular meaning associated with "technical" is "involving or concerning applied and industrial science".'
650. OECD Technical Advisory Group on Treaty Characterization of Electronic Commerce Payments, *supra* n. 636, at para. 39.
651. *See* para. 12 of the Commentary on Article 12 OECD Model 1977; for further explanations, *see* the following chapters of this publication; *see also* Chapter 2.B.; Only the commentary versions available at the time of signing a tax treaty shall be relevant for the interpretation of a tax treaty.
652. *See* in this respect para. 12 of the Commentary on Article 12 OECD Model 1977 that mentions advice given by an advocate or accountant separately from the provision of technical assistance.
653. With respect to impact testing using a vehicle front unit: ITAT Delhi, *Maruti Udyog Ltd. v. Assistant Director of Income Tax*, IT Appeal Nos 4217, 4219 and 4221 (Delhi) of 2005, paras 11.2 et seq. (31 August 2009); referring to the field of science and technology: ITAT Jaipur, *Modern Insulator Ltd. v. Assistant Commissioner of Income Tax*, ITA No. 281/Jp/2010, para. 3.13. (13 April 2011).

the scope of an autonomous provision on the taxation of 'Fees for technical services',[654] 'Fees for technical and other services',[655] 'Management, consultancy and technical fees',[656] 'Management fees',[657] 'Management and technical fees',[658] 'Services fees'[659] and so forth.[660] In this respect, Article 12A(3) UN Model accords with common state practice as it also includes consultancy and managerial services within its scope.

The addition of additional categories of services, however, raises the question of whether these categories have to be linked to the traditional concept of 'technical', i.e., whether consultancy and managerial services have to be linked to the technical engineering field. In this respect, the Austrian Ministry of Finance (BMF) argued that the term 'technical' in the definition of 'fees for technical services' in Article 12(4) of the DTC Austria-India (1999) has to be interpreted in a narrow sense and refer to engineering services such as mechanical or constructional engineering.[661] Additionally, the terms 'managerial' and 'consultancy' as included in the definition of 'fees for technical services' in the aforementioned DTC, are only subject to its definition if they are connected to the technical field of engineering even if they are exclusively mentioned in the definition of the term itself. A different understanding of these terms would be inconsistent with the header of the article 'Royalties and fees for technical services'.[662] Therefore, advice given by a consultant regarding prospective repair work of a steel mill would be within the scope of the definition of 'fees for technical services' as the consultancy service is related to the technical field.[663]

In the mentioned example analysed by the BMF, the term 'technical services' was embedded in the context of Article 12 on royalties and not in an autonomous provision on 'fees for technical services'. Therefore, it was more reasonable for the BMF to conclude that also the categories of managerial and consultancy services have to be interpreted in light of the narrow meaning of 'fees for technical services', i.e., relating to the field of engineering. Similar to *Valta/Langner*, the author also argues that, in such a case, the contracting states could have chosen a different wording that is much clearer and broader to underline the independence of managerial and consultancy

654. Article 14 DTC Gambia-UK (1980), Article 12 DTC Egypt-Pakistan (1995), Article 13 DTC Malaysia-South Africa (2005, 2011), Article 13 DTC Iran-Senegal (2010), Article 13 DTC Malaysia-Senegal (2010), Article 14 DTC Cameroon-South Africa (2015), Article 13 DTC Ghana-Morocco (2017).
655. *See* Article 14 DTC Angola-UAE (2018).
656. Article 21 DTC Botswana-Sweden (1992), Article 22 DTC Botswana-Mauritius (1995), Article 21 DTC Botswana-France (1999), Article 21 DTC Botswana-Russian Federation (2003).
657. Article 14 DTC Kenya-UK (1976), Article 13 DTC France-Ghana (1993), Article 14 DTC Gambia-Norway (1994), Article 13 DTC Ghana-Serbia and Montenegro (2000), Article 20 DTC Ghana-South Africa (2004), Article 18 DTC Belgium-Ghana (2005), Article 13 DTC Barbados-Ghana (2008).
658. Article 17 DTC Ghana-UK (1993).
659. Article 13 DTC Ghana-Singapore (2017).
660. *See* Chapter 4.A.ii.1. and Appendices 1 to 6 of this publication.
661. *See* Austrian Ministry of Finance, *Express Antwort Service 3224*, BMF-010221/1104-IV/4/2011 (17 June 2011); *see also* Matthias Valta & Stella Langner, *Article 12: Income from Royalties*, in: Ekkehart Reimer & Alexander Rust (eds), *Klaus Vogel on Double Taxation Conventions* vol. 1, 1097, m.no. 277 (5th ed., Wolters Kluwer 2021).
662. *See* Article 12 DTC Austria-India (1999).
663. *See* Austrian Ministry of Finance, *supra* n. 661 and Valta & Langner, *supra* n. 663, at m.no. 277.

services as a separate category from the field of engineering.[664] Therefore, if it was the intention of the contracting states to include 'consultancy' and 'managerial' services as separate categories from the term 'technical', the contracting states could have chosen to include a broader wording such as 'Fees for technical and other services'[665] or 'Services fees'[666] as, e.g., part of an autonomous article in the tax treaty.

In contrast to the aforementioned explanations on the rather narrow scope of the term 'technical', Article 12A(3) UN Model ascribes it a very broad meaning that goes beyond the technical field of engineering, as it 'involves the application of specialized knowledge, skill or expertise with respect to a particular art, science, profession or occupation'. In the author's opinion, Article 12A(3) UN Model includes three categories of services: 'technical services of managerial nature', 'technical services of technical nature' and 'technical services of consultancy nature'. Based on the definition of 'technical' as found in the Commentary on Article 12A UN Model, all managerial and consultancy services, irrespective of whether they are connected to the field of engineering, would be covered by Article 12A as the application of specialized knowledge, skill, or expertise is inherent to the provision of such services.[667] Therefore, in the author's view, the term 'technical' should not be ascribed a universal meaning in the context of Article 12A UN Model, i.e., without differentiating between the use of 'technical' in the super category on the one hand and the subcategory of Article 12A(3) UN Model on the other. Based on the ordinary meaning of the term 'technical', fees for technical services relate to a 'particular science or skill'.[668] This super category is – in the context of Article 12A UN Model – related to services of a technical, managerial or consultancy nature.[669] The term 'technical' as defined in the subcategory of Article 12A(3) UN Model, therefore, necessarily needs to have a different meaning than the one found in the super category. Otherwise, the additionally included subcategories of managerial and consultancy services as defined in the Commentary on Article 12A(3) UN Model would be redundant as they would already be covered by the subcategory-definition of the term 'technical', i.e., services of a specialized nature.[670] As a result, the author argues that the term 'technical' as found in the subcategory of Article 12A(3) UN Model should be ascribed a narrow meaning relating to the technical field.[671] In this respect, fees for 'technical services of technical nature' would be defined as services in the technical field requiring the application of specialized knowledge, skill, or expertise. Similarly, in the author's opinion, 'technical services of managerial nature' and

664. *See* Valta & Langner, *supra* n. 663, at m.no. 279.
665. *See* Committee of Experts on International Cooperation in Tax Matters, *supra* n. 212, at paras 63 et seq. and Article 14 of the DTC Angola-UAE (2018).
666. *See* Article 13 DTC Ghana-Singapore (2017).
667. *See, e.g.*, OECD Technical Advisory Group on Treaty Characterization of Electronic Commerce Payments, *supra* n. 636, at paras 43 et seq. and para. 62 of the Commentary on Article 12A UN Model 2021.
668. *See* Cambridge University Press & Assessment, *supra* n. 628.
669. *See* Article 12A(3) UN Model 2021.
670. *See* para. 64 of the Commentary on Article 12A UN Model 2021.
671. Similarly, Pal, *supra* n. 449, at footnote 25: 'The word "technical", used inside the definition, probably refers to technical services in the narrow sense, which requires expertise in applied or industrial science.'

'technical services of consultancy nature' would include managerial and consultancy services that require the application of specialized knowledge, skill, or expertise, i.e., services carried out by the profession as a manager or consultant.[672] In contrast to the explanations found in the Commentary on Article 12A UN Model, however, the author opines that the definition 'fees for technical services' should not cover activities carried out by a heart surgeon[673] or academics in general[674] simply under the assumption that these persons apply specialized knowledge, skill or expertise in all their activities. Their activities shall, however, be within the scope of the definition of Article 12A(3) UN Model if their specific activity relates to either of the aforementioned subcategories of Article 12A(3) UN Model.

3 *Indian Jurisprudence as Guidance for the Interpretation of Technical Services?*

As has already been mentioned in *Chapter 3.C.iv.2.b.*, section 9(1)(vii) of the Indian Income Tax Act defines fees for technical services as 'any consideration...for the rendering of any managerial, technical or consultancy services'. This definition is essentially also used in Article 12A(3) UN Model. As the Indian Tax Authorities regularly refer to this definition when interpreting the articles on fees for technical services in its tax treaties, it is of utmost importance to analyse Indian jurisprudence and obtain a broader perspective on a possible delineation with respect to technical and non-technical services.

The High Court of Delhi had to decide in 2008 whether payments for the provision of interconnection access/ports to a network are regarded as 'fees for technical services' according to section 9(1)(vii) of the Indian Income Tax Act.[675] Based on the ordinary meaning of the terms 'manager' and 'consultant', it held that one element that is inherent to both terms and subsequently to 'managerial services' and 'consultancy services' is the provision by humans. Applying the rule of *noscitur a sociis* to interpret the term 'technical', technical services are those that involve a human element as this term 'takes colour from the expressions "managerial services" and "consultancy services" which necessarily involve a human element'.[676]

Based on the explanations on the interpretation of 'fees for technical services' in the aforementioned case, automated services without human involvement are outside this scope. This has also been confirmed by the ITAT Agra in *Metro & Metro v. Additional Commissioner of Income Tax*.[677] The ITAT Agra expressed that services cannot be regarded as 'technical services' when they do not include an element of

672. *See also* Chapters 4.E.ii. and 4.E.iii.
673. *See* para. 89 of the Commentary on Article 12A UN Model 2021.
674. *See* para. 65 of the Commentary on Article 12A UN Model 2021.
675. High Court of Delhi, *Bharti Cellular Ltd. v. Commissioner of Income Tax*, I.T.A. Nos 1120/2007, Nos 1120, 1121, 1129, 1135, 1154, 1155, 1159, 1171, 1177/2007 and 697, 698, 1020/2008, paras 4 et seq. (31 October 2008).
676. *Ibid.*, at para. 15.
677. ITAT Agra, *Metro & Metro v. Additional Commissioner of Income Tax*, I.T.A. No. 393/Agra/2012 (1 November 2013).

human intervention.[678] On the question of the degree of human involvement, the ITAT Agra noted that it is 'not a question of more of, or less of, human involvement. It is in our humble understanding, the question of presence of or absence of human involvement'.[679] However, the adoption of such a high benchmark on the qualification of services as 'technical' might be inappropriately high due to the increasing use of modern technologies in the provision of services. Therefore, the AAR New Delhi referred to other court decisions on the interpretation of 'technical services', such as *Kotak Securities Ltd. Mumbai v. Department of Income Tax*,[680] and concluded that the more appropriate test to apply was whether the service was provided through a standard facility.[681] This concept has evolved in Indian jurisprudence based on the decision of the Madras High Court in *Skycell Communications Ltd. v. Deputy Commissioner of Income Tax*.[682] In it, the high court concluded that:

> Installation and operation of sophisticated equipment [facilities] with a view to earn income by allowing customers to avail of the benefit of the user of such equipment [facility] does not result in the provision of technical service to the customer for a fee.[683]

Therefore, the mere receipt of transmission of television signals through cable, the subscription to a mobile phone service to have access to a facility that allows communicating with each other, and the subscription to internet services do not lead to 'technical services'.[684] In this respect, the AAR of New Delhi also decided that transaction processing services are not in the nature of technical services as the service provider made use of a standard facility, i.e., a bank, as a medium for processing a payment.[685] Similarly, in *Flag Telecom Group Ltd. v. Deputy Director of Income Tax*, the ITAT Mumbai decided that payments for the use of a high-capacity telecommunication cable system do not constitute fees for technical services as the mere usage of such equipment did not require the provision of technical skills involving a human element by the service provider.[686] In addition, according to Indian jurisprudence, payments in consideration for the use of bulk text messaging services, internet bandwidth, and an automated leather testing process were payments for the use of a standard facility without human intervention.[687] Therefore, it may be concluded that the use of a

678. *Ibid.*, at para. 20.
679. *Ibid.*, at para. 21.
680. ITAT Mumbai, *Kotak Securities Ltd. Mumbai v. Department of Income Tax*, ITA No. 4644/Mum/2010, para. 25 (17 March 2010).
681. AAR New Delhi, *MasterCard Asia Pacific Pte Ltd. v. Assistant Director of Income Tax*, A.A.R. No 1573 of 2014, para. 25.3 (6 June 2016).
682. Madras High Court, *supra* n. 649.
683. Madras High Court, *supra* n. 649, at para. 14; brackets inserted by the author.
684. *Ibid.*, at paras 13, 15 and 16.
685. *See* AAR New Delhi, *supra* n. 681, at para. 25.3.2.
686. *See* ITAT Mumbai, *Flag Telecom Group Ltd. v. Deputy Director of Income Tax*, ITA No. 2255/Mum/2006 (15 June 2015).
687. *See* with regards to an analysis of Indian jurisprudence on human intervention: Amar Mehta, *Importance of Human Involvement for Income Characterization as Fees for Technical Services*, 22 APTB 2 (2016) DOI: 10.59403/2rdwd6x.

standard facility is characterized by its routine nature that does not require any customization towards the service recipient by a human.[688]

In this respect, it is important to note that not just any human intervention suffices to meet the requirements established by the Indian jurisprudence. They must be interventions from technical personnel possessing technical know-how. In the case, *GlaxoSmithKline Pharmaceuticals Ltd. v. Income Tax Officer*, a company engaged in manufacturing medicine made payments for the provision of security services.[689] According to the tax authorities, the security services were skilled services that can be categorized as technical services.[690] The medical company, however, argued that the provision of security services to guard the company's factory premises was in the nature of a supply of work.[691] The ITAT Pune decided that the payments made for the provision of security services were not in the nature of managerial, technical, or consultancy services[692] as technical services are characterized by the use of technical know-how which was apparently not present in the case in question.[693]

In this regard, another key decision also has to be mentioned: *Lufthansa Cargo India Pvt. Ltd. v. Director of Income Tax.*[694] The High Court of Delhi had to decide whether service fees for repairs and overhauls of aircraft were in the nature of technical services.[695] While the ITAT New Delhi[696] held that these fees are not fees for technical services as the repair and overhaul of aircraft amounts to 'contracts of work', the high court took a different position in this case. According to it, aircraft maintenance and repairs need to be differentiated from other contracts for maintenance and machine repair as the former mentioned services are characterized by a high-level of expertise and specialization that can only be rendered by a few entities. Therefore, the exclusive nature of these services leads to the conclusion that the 'technical' nature of these services cannot be denied.[697]

In a more recent decision, the High Court of Delhi manifested its view on the requirement of specialization to qualify a service as 'technical'. In *The Commissioner of Income Tax v. Springer Nature Customer Services Centre GmbH*, the high court contemplated that 'for a service to be categorised as a technical service, it had to be

688. ITAT Mumbai, *Merchant Shipping Services Pvt. Ltd. v. Assistant Commissioner of Income Tax*, ITA No.192/Mum/2010 (24 November 2010); para. 14; *see also* ITAT New Delhi, *Amazon Web Services Inc. v. ACIT*, ITA Nos 522 & 523/Del/2023 (1 August 2023) para. 27.
689. ITAT Pune, *GlaxoSmithKline Pharmaceuticals Ltd. v. Income Tax Officer*, ITA Nos 552 to 555/PN/2010 (7 October 2011).
690. *Ibid.*, at para. 2.
691. *Ibid.*, at para. 6.
692. *Ibid.*, at para. 7.
693. *Ibid.*, at paras 10 et seq.
694. High Court of Delhi, *Lufthansa Cargo India Pvt. Ltd. v. Director of Income Tax*, ITA 95/2005 (27 May 2015).
695. *Ibid.*, at paras 2 et seq.
696. ITAT New Delhi, *Lufthansa Cargo India Pvt. Ltd. v. Department of Income Tax*, ITA Nos 661 to 663/D/2001 (30 June 2004).
697. High Court of Delhi, *supra* n. 694, at para. 20.

concerned with applied science, i.e., using scientific knowledge for practical applications, or industrial science concerning, relating to or derived from industry'.[698] As the provision of underlying support services, e.g., customer services, order handling, invoicing and subscriptions management on behalf of the publishing house, did not – in the view of the High Court of Delhi require the application of specialized skills or knowledge, it took the view that these services were not of 'technical' nature.[699]

Based on an analysis of Indian jurisprudence, it has to be concluded that the characterization of services as 'technical' requires that they are provided by technical personnel possessing technical expertise, i.e., personnel in the field of engineering or applied and industrial sciences. These services must also have a certain degree of specialization as provided in *Lufthansa Cargo India Pvt. Ltd. v. Director of Income Tax* or *The Commissioner of Income Tax v. Springer Nature Customer Services Centre GmbH*, otherwise, the activities are qualified as routine work falling outside the scope of being 'technical'. In addition, the provision of services using equipment or facilities of a standardized nature that are available to the wide public is excluded from the scope of technical services. Examples would be the use of public transport services[700] or online advertising services provided through the internet.[701] Therefore, one of the main characteristics of a technical service is its customization to the needs of the customer.[702]

The approach used for the characterization of technical services by Indian courts is similar to the one found in the Commentaries on Article 12A UN Model. The definition of fees for technical services based on Article 12A UN Model requires the provision of services of a specialized nature. Article 12A UN Model, therefore, excludes services of a routine nature from its scope. Although the Commentary on Article 12A UN Model does not explicitly exclude fees for automated services, the newly introduced Article 12B UN Model distinctly covers automated services requiring minimal human involvement within its scope thereby establishing an explicit allocation rule for such services.[703] Specialized services provided by technical personnel are also clearly covered by the scope of Article 12A UN Model. As has been mentioned in *Chapter 4.A.ii.2.*, however, the scope of Article 12A UN Model is not restricted to services provided by technical personnel possessing technical expertise. The extent to which the provision of services by other professions outside the technical field shall be covered by Article 12A UN Model will be subject to the analysis found in *Chapters 4.B. to e.* of this publication.

698. High Court of Delhi, *The Commissioner of Income Tax v. Springer Nature Customer Services Centre GmbH*, ITA 306/2023, para. 22 (12 July 2023).
699. *Ibid.*, at para. 22.
700. ITAT Mumbai, *supra* n. 688, at para. 14.
701. Agrawal, *supra* n. 448, at 324.
702. Chishty & Chakalabbi, *supra* n. 454, at 45.
703. *See* Article 12B(5) UN Model and Chapter 4.C. of this publication.

4 *Exceptions from the Scope*

a *Introduction*

Article 12A(3)(a)-(c) UN Model excludes certain types of payments from the definition of 'fees for technical services' as they are either already covered by another allocation rule of the UN Model or are not regarded as incentivizing base erosion and profit shifting. The excluded payments are payments made to employees (a), payments for teaching in or by an educational institution (b), or payments made by an individual for services of personal use, i.e., B2C services (c).

b *Payments to Employees*

The first exclusion mentioned in Article 12A(3)(a) UN Model concerns payments made by employers to their employees. This provision was inserted into Article 12A UN Model as these payments are already covered by Articles 15 and 19 UN Model.[704] Additionally, pensions that are subject to Articles 18 and 19 UN Model shall be covered by Article 12A(3)(a) UN Model.[705] The aforementioned provision also applies to employment concerning activities covered by the scope of 'fees for technical services'.[706] As a result, also payments made for (past) employment involving the provision of technical, managerial, or consultancy services are covered by the exclusion of Article 12A(3)(a) UN Model:[707]

> *Example 6*: Mr A is a resident of State A and a heart surgeon who regularly provides surgeries in a clinic of corporation B in State B (not as an employee). The tax treaty concluded between States A and B includes a provision based on Article 12A UN Model. Therefore, payments made by the corporation to Mr A for surgeries provided in State B, would – according to the Commentary on Article 12A UN Model – be regarded as fees for technical services. If, however, Mr A would act as an employee of corporation B, the mentioned payments would be excluded from the definition of fees for technical services according to Article 12A(3)(a) UN Model with the result being that Article 15 UN Model would apply.

To distinguish fees for technical services rendered under a contract of services from those rendered on the basis of an employment relationship, recourse may be made to the criteria established by the Commentaries of the OECD and UN Models with respect to Article 15(2) on the economic employer. In this respect, the following criteria might – amongst others – be used:[708]

704. *See, e.g.*, Committee of Experts on International Cooperation in Tax Matters, *supra* n. 169, at 7 et seq.
705. *See* para. 69 of the Commentary on Article 12A UN Model 2021.
706. *Ibid.*
707. *See* para. 89 of the Commentary on Article 12A UN Model 2021.
708. *See* para. 8.14 of the Commentary on Article 15 OECD Model 2017 and para. 5 of the Commentary on Article 15 UN Model 2021 with reference to para. 8.14 of the OECD Model 2017.

- Who has the authority to instruct when and where the services have to be performed?
- Who supplies the individual with relevant working materials and tools?
- Who bears the remuneration paid and the costs incurred by the services?
- Who can impose sanctions related to the work of the individual?
- Who can determine the holiday and work schedule of the individual?

As India regularly excludes employment income from the scope of fees for technical services in its tax treaties, numerous decisions from Indian courts have also emerged in the last decades.[709] These decisions often concern the secondment of employees to an Indian company from an Indian non-resident company. In this regard, it is common practice - especially for brief periods - that the Indian company reimburses the non-resident company seconding its employees for salary costs incurred. The main question that commonly arises in these cases is whether such payments made for the secondment of employees are subject to the application of the technical services article or is a mere reimbursement of expenses.[710]

In this regard, the ITAT Kolkata held that the mere fact that the Indian taxpayer company withheld tax in its function as an employer based on the issued certificate of deduction of tax at source was sufficient enough to establish an employer-employee relationship.[711] In *Centrica India Offshore Private Ltd. v. Commissioner of Income Tax*, the High Court of Delhi noted that, although the Indian company had operational control over the seconded employees in terms of their daily work and was held responsible for the outcome by the seconded employees, these factors might be disregarded in the context that these persons were only seconded to India for a limited period of time in order to utilize their technical expertise for the Indian company. In addition, the high court also held that they were employees of their legal non-resident employers as the Indian taxpayer could not terminate the employment of the secondees.[712] In the light of the aforementioned considerations, the High Court of Delhi held that - based on the respective 'Royalties and fees for technical services'[713] and 'Royalties and fees for included services'[714] provisions of the reviewed tax treaties - the fees in question amounted to fees for technical services.[715]

In *A. T. & S. India P. Ltd. v. Commissioner of Income Tax*, the Authority for Advance Rulings (AAR) New Delhi had to decide on the question of whether payments made for the reimbursement of salary costs from an Indian resident to an Austrian company were subject to the exclusion from the definition of fees for technical services

709. *See* Sanghvi & Shaktawat, *supra* n. 22, at 458.
710. *See, e.g.*, High Court of Delhi, *Centrica India Offshore Private Ltd. v. Commissioner of Income Tax*, W.P. (C) No. 6807/2012 (25 April 2014) and ITAT Kolkata, *Reckitt Benckiser (India) Ltd. v. Joint Commissioner of Income Tax*, ITA No. 1671/Kol/2008 (25 May 2016).
711. Based on Articles 10(1), 13(4), 16(1) and (2) DTC India-UK 1993: ITAT Kolkata, *supra* n. 710, at para. 9.
712. *See* Brian J. Arnold, *Tax Treaty Case Law News*, 69 BIT 53, 55 (2015).
713. *See* Article 13 DTC India-UK (1993).
714. *See* Article 12 DTC Canada-India (1996).
715. *See* High Court of Delhi, *supra* n. 710, m.nos 29 et seq.

according to Article 12(4) DTC Austria-India (1999).[716] In this respect, personnel was seconded by an Austrian company to an Indian resident on the basis of a secondment agreement. The seconded personnel worked under the direct control and supervision of the Indian company. In addition, the Austrian company did not charge any additional fee for the secondment of the employees than the mere actual expenditure incurred for the Austrian company.

The AAR held that the payments made for the secondment of the employees were covered by the term 'fees for technical services' as defined in Article 12(4) DTC Austria-India (1999). In this regard, it did not place any weight on the fact that the Austrian company did not charge any additional fee for the secondment or that the seconded personnel was under the direct control and supervision of the Indian company.[717] The AAR considered it decisive that the Austrian company had the power to recall and replace any seconded personnel and that the Indian company had no margin of freedom to remunerate any amount above or below the salary that was established by the Austrian company. The AAR therefore concluded 'that the role of AT&S Austria [the Austrian company] is not of a mere employment agent and that in effect the seconded personnel remain the employees of AT&S Austria'.[718]

c Payments for Teaching Services

Article 12A(3)(b) UN Model includes an exclusion for payments for teaching in or by an educational institution from the scope of fees for technical services. It was already included in the draft article of Article 12A UN Model[719] in preparation for the eleventh session of the UN Tax Committee.[720] The reason behind the inclusion of this exclusion was, on the one hand, the low risk of base erosion and, on the other hand, also the fact that the activities behind such payments are regarded as desirable by states.[721] The term 'educational institution' is not defined in the UN Model. However, according to the Commentary on Article 12A(3) UN Model, universities, colleges, and other post-secondary educational institutions should generally be covered by this term.[722] In addition, this commentary also suggests that contracting states shall clarify the meaning of the term 'educational institution' if they have a very broad or unusual meaning of this term within their respective national law.[723] As some states may view the exclusion of Article 12A(3)(b) as overly excessive and therefore susceptible to

716. *See* AAR New Delhi, *A. T. & S. India P. Ltd. v. Commissioner of Income Tax*, A.A.R. No. 670 of 2005 (6 November 2006).
717. *Ibid.*, at para. 17.
718. *Ibid.*, at para. 12.
719. At that time, the draft article was presented as 'Article XX'.
720. Committee of Experts on International Cooperation in Tax Matters, *supra* n. 212, at paras 63 et seq.
721. Committee of Experts on International Cooperation in Tax Matters, *Summary of the United Nations Practical Portfolio on Protecting the Tax Base of Developing Countries against Base Erosion: Income from Services*, E/C.18/2018/9, https://financing.desa.un.org/sites/default/files/2023-03/N1824764.pdf (accessed 6 January 2024).
722. *See* para. 70 of the Commentary on Article 12A UN Model 2021.
723. *See* para. 70 of the Commentary on Article 12A UN Model 2021.

abuse, they might omit the exclusion entirely or narrow the scope to teaching services such as 'teaching in or by educational institutions as part of a degree-granting program'.[724]

d B2C Services

Article 12A(3)(c) UN Model expressly provides that payments by individuals for services for their personal use[725] shall be excluded from the definition of fees for technical services as these do not entail a risk of tax base erosion. As mentioned in *Chapter 3.C.iii.*, the base-erosion principle only intends to cover B2B transactions as private expenses are usually not deductible at the level of the individual consumer. As a result, the application of the base-erosion principle on B2C transactions with respect to fees for technical services would not be justifiable. Furthermore, the imposition of a withholding tax on payments made by individuals would be too difficult to enforce and might also cause serious compliance problems.[726] It is for all of these reasons that the UN Tax Committee therefore decided to include the exclusion of B2C payments to Article 12A(3) UN Model.

B ARTICLE 12A UN MODEL: DEFINITION OF FEES FOR TECHNICAL SERVICES AND OVERLAP WITH ARTICLE 12 UN MODEL

i Preliminary Remarks on Article 12 UN Model and Potential Overlaps with Article 12A UN Model

Article 12 UN Model reproduces Article 12 OECD Model to a great extent. However, the former still substantially deviates from the latter in certain parts. In this respect, substantial differences are found in paragraphs 1 and 3. In addition, paragraphs 2 and 5 of the UN Model are not included in Article 12 OECD Model.[727]

Both Article 12 UN and OECD Models include the phrase 'information concerning industrial, commercial or scientific experience' (know-how) in the scope of the definition of royalties. The interpretation and the scope of the 'use of' know-how, however, is very controversial among non-OECD Member States as some of them opine that certain fees for technical services are generally within the scope of the transfer of

724. *See* Committee of Experts on International Cooperation in Tax Matters, *supra* n. 212, at para. 68 and para. 71 of the Commentary on Article 12A UN Model 2021.
725. *See* para. 87 of the Commentary on Article 12A UN Model 2021 for an example of 'personal use of an individual': 'X is a resident of State R and a heart surgeon. X's practice is carried on primarily in State R, although X occasionally travels to other countries to provide heart surgery. X performs surgery in State R on an individual resident in State S. The tax treaty between State R and State S contains a provision identical to Article 12A of the United Nations Model Convention. Although the payments made by the patient, a resident of State S, to X would be considered to be fees for technical services that arise in State S, they are explicitly excluded from the definition by subparagraph (c) of paragraph 3. As a result, the payments would not be taxable by State S in accordance with Article 12A, paragraph 2.'
726. *See* Committee of Experts on International Cooperation in Tax Matters, *supra* n. 215, at 17.
727. *See* para. 1 of the Commentary on Article 12 UN Model 2021.

know-how and therefore taxable as royalties.[728] In addition, as has already been shown in *Chapter 4.A.ii.1.*, several tax treaties of developing countries also either specifically include technical services in the definition of royalties or extend the scope of the article on royalties to also include service fees separately defined from royalties, such as 'royalties and technical services fees'.[729]

In addition, Article 12(3) UN Model specifically includes the concept 'for the use of, or the right to use, industrial, commercial or scientific equipment' in the definition of royalties. The mentioned wording was deleted from the OECD Model in its update of 1992. The reason for this was to ensure that such payments would solely fall under the allocation rule on business profits (Article 7 OECD and UN Models).[730] In this respect, however, it is worth noting that also fees for certain types of services may be regarded as being covered by 'for the use of, or the right to use, industrial, commercial or scientific equipment'.[731] This is especially true for cloud-computing services such as IaaS, SaaS, or PaaS. Their commonality is that they include the letting of certain IP rights like the use of software and certain (automated) services. Since the 2017 update of the UN Model, however, the Commentary on Article 12 UN Model clarifies that the term 'equipment' only refers to tangible goods such as ships or aircraft.[732] In addition, the recipient also needs to have possession or control of such equipment.[733] Therefore, several services in the field of cloud-computing are most probably excluded from the scope of the use of or the right to use industrial, commercial, or scientific equipment as they primarily concern intangible equipment, such as software.[734] Nevertheless, these services could fall under either Article 12A UN Model or Article 12B UN Model if they are provided on a customized basis by applying specialized knowledge, skill, or expertise (Article 12A UN Model) or in an automated, generic manner with minimal human involvement (Article 12B UN Model).

The following chapters aim to display the historical connection between royalties and fees for technical services. In this respect, the author will analyse the historical evolution of the article on royalties and make reference to the academic and judicial discourse on the inclusion of technical services as part of the notion of 'know-how'. In addition, an analysis of the term 'technical' in the context of Articles 12 and 12A UN Model shall be made in order to further elucidate the rather ambiguous concept of 'technical services'.

728. *See* paras 4 and 5 of the Commentary on Article 12A UN Model 2021.
729. *See* Article 12(5) DTC Ghana-Netherlands (2008).
730. *See* para. 9 of the Commentary on Article 12 OECD Model 1992.
731. Kjærsgaard, *supra* n. 249, at 403 et seq.
732. *See* para. 19 of the Commentary on Article 12 UN Model 2021.
733. *See* para. 21 of the Commentary on Article 12 UN Model 2021 and para. 9.1 of the Commentary on Article 12 OECD Model 2017.
734. *See* for a more thorough analysis: Kjærsgaard, *supra* n. 249, at 379 and Aleksandra Bal, *The Sky's the Limit – Cloud-Based Services in an International Perspective*, 68 BIT 515, 516 (2014) DOI: 10.59403/2mkwnac.

ii Technical Services Covered by Article 12 UN Model

1 Origins and Causes of Conflicts of Qualification Between Royalties and Technical Services

a The Work of the League of Nations (The 1923 Four Economists' Report, the 1925 Technical Experts Report, the 1928 and 1931 Draft Model Conventions, the 1943 Mexico and 1946 London Models)

The League of Nations did not expressly consider specific references on the taxation of intellectual property until the preparatory works on the draft of a multilateral convention in 1930. Based on the 1923 Four Economists' Report, the 1925 Technical Experts Report, and the 1927 Draft Convention, it seemed that royalties were subject to exclusive residence taxation. This result, however, has neither been expressly discussed nor mentioned in the reports.[735] Based on responses to a country questionnaire on the tax treatment of intellectual property, the fiscal committee reached the conclusion that 'income from authors' rights or patents' shall not be classified as industrial or commercial income and taxed by the domicile state of the 'intitule'.[736] As a result, a subcommittee was appointed to submit a draft multilateral convention including a provision on the taxation of 'Authors' royalties or rights' taxable only in the recipient's domicile state or that of the creditor earning such income.[737] The mentioned draft convention was finally presented as part of the fourth session of the fiscal committee in 1931. However, the presented alternative drafts on the signing of two plurilateral conventions of different types and the adoption of the draft multilateral convention did not find enough support and appeared to be impracticable at that point in time. One of them exclusively dealt with the allocation of taxing rights on business profits. The draft plurilateral convention on the allocation of business profits expressly excluded 'Rentals or royalties arising from leasing personal property or from any interest in such property' from the scope of business income.[738]

The 1943 Mexico and 1946 London Models departed from the general principle of exclusive residence taxation of intellectual property that was advocated by the fiscal committee in its proposals for the adoption of a multilateral convention. Nevertheless, both models adhered to a different approach to establishing a taxing right on payments received with respect to the right to use intellectual property.

According to Article X of the 1943 Mexico Model, royalties other than those paid 'in consideration for the right to use a musical, artistical, literary or other cultural work

735. Jacques Sasseville, *Source vs Residence Taxation of Royalties: A Historical Perspective*, in: Guglielmo Maisto (ed.), *Taxation of Intellectual Property under Domestic Law, EU Law and Tax Treaties* vol. 16, 97, 97 (IBFD 2018).
736. *See* League of Nations Fiscal Committee, *Report to the Council on the Work of the Second Session of the Committee*, C.340.M.140.1930.II., at 6 (31 May 1930).
737. *Ibid.*, at 8.
738. *See* Sasseville, *supra* n. 735, at 99 with reference to League of Nations Fiscal Committee, *Report to the Council on the Fourth Session of the Committee*, C.399.M.204 1933.II.A., at 2 (June 1933).

or publication' shall be taxable exclusively in the state of exploitation of such rights.[739] In contrast hereto, Article X of the 1946 London Model narrowed the scope of source taxing rights on royalties as understood in its general meaning to considerations paid between associated enterprises. In the mentioned case, the source state has an exclusive taxing right without being limited by a certain rate.[740]

The difference in the approach to the allocation of taxing rights of royalties is explained in the Commentaries to the Mexico and London Models. The Mexico Model applies the principle of immediate economic origin to justify source taxation of royalty payments. According to the mentioned principle, the state in which patents or other similar rights are exploited is entitled to tax the considerations paid in return for their use.[741] The London Model, however, restricted source taxing rights on royalties and justified this on the same principle as that being applied in the Mexico Model, i.e., the principle of immediate economic origin, to payments made between associated enterprises subject to deductibility of expenses related to royalties in the state of exploitation.[742]

It was therefore concluded by *Sasseville* that the League of Nations, in general, took a neutral position on the allocation of taxing rights between the residence and source state by recognizing two possible approaches, i.e., exclusive source taxation or residence taxation, with the exception of 'copyright royalties from artistic and scientific productions', royalty payments between associated enterprises, and royalties derived from the right to exploit naturals deposits and resources, for all of which a clear non-neutral position on the allocation of taxing rights was taken.[743]

b The Work of the OEEC and the 1963 OECD Model

(i) Preparatory Works of WP 8 of the OEEC

The predecessor of the OECD, i.e., the OEEC, established Working Party 8 (WP 8) at the fourth meeting of the fiscal committee in 1957 to further investigate the 'direct taxation of royalties'.[744] WP 8 consisted of members from Germany and Luxembourg and had the purpose of drafting a model provision on the taxation of royalties that could be included in conventions on the avoidance of double taxation. The draft article on royalties provided for exclusive residence taxation of royalty payments except for amounts exceeding an adequate consideration and in the presence of a PE or fixed base

739. *See* League of Nations Fiscal Committee, *Second Regional Conference in Mexico – Report on the work of the Conference*, F/Fiscal/131, 6 (29 July 1943): Article X (3) and League of Nations Fiscal Committee, *London and Mexico Model Tax Conventions – Commentary and Text*, C.88.M.88.1946.II.A., 66 (November 1946).
740. *See* League of Nations Fiscal Committee, *supra* n. 739, C.88.M.88.1946.II.A., at 65 and 67.
741. *See Ibid.*, at 27.
742. *See Ibid.*
743. *See* Sasseville, *supra* n. 735, at 100.
744. *See* Fiscal Committee, *Minutes of the 4th Session*, FC/M(57)2, 8 (3 July 1957).

in the source state.[745] WP 8 justified its approach to exclusive residence taxation of royalty payments with reference to taxation principles on royalties adopted in most recently concluded tax treaties of OEEC Member States.[746] Based on the tax treaty policy of OEEC Member States, the taxing right on 'patent royalties and similar payments' stays with the grantor's state of domicile unless mentioned payments are derived from industrial or commercial activities derived through a PE or in connection with professional services performed by the grantor. In the latter-mentioned cases, the royalty payments shall be taxed in accordance with the principles on the taxation of industrial or commercial income or income derived from the performance of professional activities.[747]

The surprising and unusual part of the report was a reservation made by the Luxembourg delegation that was part of the subcommittee responsible for drafting the article on the underlying principle of exclusive residence taxation of royalties. In Luxembourg's view, exclusive residence taxation is inconsistent with economic realities and would result in a unilateral relinquishment of taxing rights. Therefore, as long as their allocation is governed in a bilateral context, a draft article on royalties should include the possibility of agreeing on source taxing rights, i.e., the state in which the patent, copyright, or other right is used. For the sake of laying the foundations for a multilateral convention, however, the Luxembourg Delegation has consented to withdraw its reservation.[748] The reservation made by Luxembourg also found support from Belgium during the eighth meeting of the fiscal committee in 1958.[749]

The WP 8 prepared a follow-up report that was discussed during the ninth session of the OEEC Fiscal Committee in September 1958.[750] Just like in its first report, it advocated exclusive residence taxation of royalty payments. However, during the ninth session, it became clear that several Member States such as Austria, Belgium, Luxembourg, Portugal, and Italy were in favour of deviating from the principle of exclusive residence taxation in certain circumstances.

Given the fact that several delegates expressed concerns about the proposed solution of the allocation of taxing rights between the residence and the source state, delegates supporting source taxation of royalty payments were invited to send comments to the WP 8 who then attempted to determine a compromise. Based on the written submissions of delegates, the WP 8 submitted a supplementary memorandum to the second report on direct taxation of patent royalties and similar payments in November 1958.[751] The WP 8 proposed granting the source state a taxing right on the gross amount of royalties of up to 5% as such a threshold would only be considered a minor deviation from the general principle of exclusive residence taxation. The

745. *See* Working Party No. 8 of the Fiscal Committee, *Report on the Direct Taxation of Patent Royalties and Similar Payments*, FC/WP8(58)1, 2 (12 February 1958), https://www.taxtreatieshistory.org/data/html/FC-WP8(58)1E.html (accessed 6 November 2022).
746. *Ibid.*, at 1 and 4 et seq.
747. *Ibid.*, at 4 et seq.
748. *See* Fiscal Committee, *Minutes of the 8th Session*, FC/M(58)3, 8 (16 June 1958).
749. *Ibid.*, at 8.
750. *See* Fiscal Committee, *Minutes of the 9th Session*, FC/M(58)4, at 7 and 8 (31 October 1958).
751. *See* Fiscal Committee, *Minutes of the 10th Session*, FC/M(58)5, 10 (16 December 1958).

proposed solution, however, did not help to foster agreement on the basic principles underlying the design of an article on the taxation of royalties. Although the delegates of Austria and Luxembourg were in support of the proposal, other states like Switzerland and the United Kingdom were strongly opposed to source taxing rights.[752] The strongly contrasting views among the delegates led to a situation in which consensus could not easily be reached, therefore, the fiscal committee decided to table this issue for approximately fifteen months and continue discussions at the fiscal committee's seventeenth session in March 1960.[753] Between the seventeenth and the twenty-first sessions, attempts were made to reach a consensus based on draft proposals submitted by the WP 8. It was not until the delegates met at the fiscal committee's twenty-second session in January 1961, however, that a compromise solution was found.[754] By a majority of only one state (including those states that abstained), the principle of residence taxation was adopted.[755] The decision, however, was conditional upon the adoption of a declaration according to which Member States favouring residence taxation commit themselves to grant a source taxing right in the amount of 5% in bilateral negotiations with those Member States that were recognized as supporters of source taxation, i.e., Greece, Luxembourg, Portugal, and Turkey.[756] The declaration that was later also published as a recommendation of the OEEC also found inclusion in the Commentary to Article 12 of the 1963 Draft Convention by using the wording 'special derogation' instead of 'declaration'.[757] It is also notable that Austria made a reservation on Article 12(1) OECD Model 1963 stating that it is unable to accept a provision in a tax treaty that would preclude it in bilateral negotiations to negotiate a source taxing right on royalties of up to 10%.[758]

(ii) 'Know-How' and 'Show-How'

As has already been mentioned in *Chapter 3.C.iv.* of this publication, several states interpret 'the use of...information concerning industrial, commercial or scientific experience' (know-how)[759] in such a way that it also includes services in the definition of royalties. Such an interpretation, however, raises the possibility of conflicts of qualification as it is advocated by only a minority of non-OECD members.[760]

The definition of royalties as found in the preparatory works of the former OEEC's WP 8 – that led to the drafting of the OECD Model 1963 – included payments '...for the renting of cinematograph films (including cinematograph films intended to be exhibited by television), for the use of industrial, commercial or scientific equipment and for

752. *Ibid.*, at 9.
753. *Ibid.*, at 10.
754. *See* Sasseville, *supra* n. 735, at 111.
755. *See* Fiscal Committee, *Minutes of the 22nd Session*, FC/M(61)1, 11 (17 February 1961).
756. *Ibid.*, at 8 et seq.
757. *See* paras 25 et seq. of the Commentary on Article 12 OECD Model 1963.
758. *See* para. 28 of the Commentary on Article 12 OECD Model 1963.
759. *See* Articles 12(2) OECD Model 2017 and 12(3) UN Model 2021.
760. *See, e.g.*, para. 22 of the Commentary on Article 12 UN Model 2021.

the supply of information concerning industrial or commercial experience.'[761] The term 'scientific experience' was later added in the drafting process[762] and was eventually found in the definition of royalties in Article 12(2) OECD Model 1963. In contrast hereto, the term '[for] the supply of [information]' that was part of the draft version of the royalties' definition was not included in the final version of Article 12(2) OECD Model 1963.

After thorough research of the draft documents that led to the conclusion of the final text of the royalties' Article of the OECD Model 1963, *Jiménez* concluded that, in the first stages of the drafting process, the definition of royalties was - with reference to the notion 'supply of information' - also meant to cover technical assistance, show-how, and most probably also some technical services.[763]

c The 1977 OECD Model and Thereafter

(i) Know-How Payments and Service Fees

In its report 'Transfer Pricing: Rights and Services' of 12 September 1974, the WP 6 acknowledged that payments for the provision of 'know-how' are often regarded as service fees which means a different tax treatment of the payments.[764]

Payments in consideration for the supply of 'know-how' are payments connected to 'information concerning industrial, commercial or scientific experience' as enshrined in Article 12(3) UN Model.[765] The concept of 'know-how' was not explained in the Commentaries to the OECD Model nor did a unanimous agreement on the scope of 'know-how' exist. In 1977, however, a definition for the term 'know-how', i.e., 'information concerning industrial, commercial or scientific experience', was included in the Commentary on Article 12 OECD Model. To define such information, the Commentary on Article 12 OECD Model referred to the definition provided by the 'Association des Bureaux pour la Protection de la Propriété Industrielle' (ANBPPI):

> know-how is all the undivulged technical information, whether capable of being patented or not, that is necessary for the industrial reproduction of a product or process, directly and under the same conditions; inasmuch as it is derived from experience, know-how represents what a manufacturer cannot know from mere examination of the product and mere knowledge of the progress of technique.[766]

In contrast to its predecessor version, the Commentary on the OECD Model 1977 makes a clear distinction between payments in the consideration for 'know-how' and those for technical assistance. The latter shall generally be taxable under Articles 7 or

761. *See* Working Party No. 8 of the Fiscal Committee, *supra* n. 745, at 2.
762. *See* Working Party No. 8 of the Fiscal Committee, *Second Report on the Direct Taxation of Patent Royalties and Similar Payments*, FC/WP8(58)2, 5 (3 September 1958), https://www.taxtreatieshistory.org/data/html/FC-WP8(58)2E.html (accessed 6 November 2022).
763. *See* Jiménez, *supra* n. 10, at 132 et seq.
764. Working Party No. 6 of the Fiscal Committee, *Transfer Pricing: Rights and Services*, DAF/CFA/74.13, 3 (12 September 1974).
765. *See* Article 12(2) OECD Model 1977.
766. *See* para. 12 of the Commentary on Article 12 OECD Model 1977.

14 OECD Model.[767] However, if technical assistance is only of an ancillary and largely unimportant character and the supply of know-how is ultimately the principal purpose of a contract, the provision of technical assistance may be taxed on the basis of the royalty's provision of a tax treaty in accordance with the principal part of the contract (supply of know-how).[768]

Taking into account the developments at the level of the OECD, the UN included the OECD's wording on the definition of royalties in Article 12(3) UN Model 1980. The relevant passages of the Commentary on Article 12(2) OECD Model regarding 'know-how' and mixed contracts were also included in the Commentary on Article 12(3) UN Model 1980. In this respect, *Jiménez* noted that the unchanged adoption of Article 12(2) OECD Model 1977 and its corresponding commentaries has been controversial with respect to the differentiation of know-how and technical assistance.[769] This is, according to *Jiménez*, based on the fact that the Eighth Report of the UN Group of Experts on tax treaties between developed and developing countries noted that the adoption of Article 12 of the OECD Model - amongst others - needed further discussion before finalization.[770] In the author's opinion, however, based on the following statement in the Eighth Report, this assumption is a mild exaggeration beyond what is likely the case:

> (c) Articles reproducing guidelines formulated by the Group of Experts which, judging from the comments submitted to the Secretariat by the members of the Group, would seem to call for further discussion before finalization (arts. 5, 7, 8, 10, 12, 13, 14, 16, 18, 19, 20, 21, 25 and 26).[771]

The Eighth Report does not specifically provide information on lengthy discussions with respect to the inclusion of passages relating to 'know-how' and mixed contracts. It merely states that further discussions on the final draft version of Article 12 UN Model 1980 and other articles needed to occur before the finalization of the draft version of the UN Model 1980. In contrast hereto, other articles such as Articles 1, 3 and 4 UN Model 1980 were simply adopted without changes from the OECD Model 1977.[772]

In the final version of the Commentary on Article 12 UN Model 1980, the Group of Experts recognized the difficulty of distinguishing royalty income from business profits.[773] As a result, it agreed to include subparagraph b) in Article 5(3) UN Model 1980 providing that:

> The furnishing of services, including consultancy services, by an enterprise through employees or other personnel engaged by the enterprise for such purpose, but only where activities of that nature continue (for the same or a connected

767. Note, however, that Article 14 has been removed from the OECD Model as part of its 2001 update.
768. *See* para. 12 of the Commentary on Article 12 OECD Model 1977.
769. *See* Jiménez, *supra* n. 10, at 132 et seq.
770. *See* Committee on Fiscal Affairs, *Eighth Report of the U.N. Group of Experts on Tax Treaties between Developed and Developing Countries*, DAF/CFA/80.5, 5 (19 March 1980).
771. *Ibid.*, at 5.
772. *Ibid.*
773. *See* United Nations, *supra* n. 359, at 140 et seq.

project) within the country for a period or periods aggregating more than six months within any 12-month period.[774]

The reasons for the inclusion of this service PE to the UN Model 1980 were manifold. On the one hand, the inclusion aimed to address the need of developing countries to tax management and consultancy services originating from industrialized countries as these included substantial amounts of remuneration.[775] On the other hand, it intended to clarify that the provision of services shall be subject to the allocation of taxing rights on the basis of Article 7 icw Article 5 UN Model 1980. With respect to the latter-mentioned issue, the Commentaries on Article 12 UN Model 1980 also acknowledged different views taken by Member States. In this regard, it was mentioned that certain states view 'brain-work' and technical services as being covered by the provision of know-how and therefore being subject to source taxation according to Article 12 UN Model 1980.[776] In this regard, a member representing a developed country in the former Group of Experts, however, suggested clarifying in a protocol to a tax treaty that payments made in consideration for 'studies or surveys of a scientific or technical nature, such as geological surveys, or for consultant or supervisory services' are not regarded as payments for know-how but those to which Article 7 UN Model 1980 shall apply.[777]

The Commentaries on Article 12 UN Models 2001, 2011, 2017, and 2021 repeated the aforementioned explanations on the problem of distinguishing technical services from the 'use of' know-how.[778]

(ii) Reservations and Positions on Article 12 OECD Model Regarding Technical Services

Over the years, states have increasingly made use of reservations and positions[779] on Article 12 OECD Model to express dissenting views with respect to its scope and the intention of its inclusion in prospective tax treaties. Beginning with the OECD Model 1992, especially non-OECD members expressed reservations in the form of positions regarding the inclusion of fees for technical assistance and services within the definition of Article 12(2) OECD Model. They also expressed the intention to reserve the right to include a separate provision on the taxation of fees for technical services in their prospective tax treaties. As the OECD Model does not expressly address non-OECD members, conclusions must be cautiously drawn from the absence of positions.

774. *Ibid.*, at 141.
775. *Ibid.*, at 64.
776. *Ibid.*, at 144.
777. *Ibid.*, at 144 et seq.; *see* for such mentioned provision Article 1(2)(b) of the Protocol to the DTC France-Mauritius (1980): 'Similarly, payments received as a consideration for technical services, including studies or surveys of a scientific, geological or technical nature, or for engineering contracts including blue prints related thereto, or for consultant or supervisory services shall be deemed to be profits to which the provisions of Article 7 apply.'
778. *See* paras 15 et seq. of the Commentary on Article 12 UN Models 2001 and 2011, paras 14 et seq. of the Commentary on Article 12 UN Model 2017 and paras 22 et seq. of the Commentary on Article 12 UN Model 2021.
779. *See* Chapter 2.B.ii.2.b.

However, the presence of positions expressed by non-OECD members provides a beneficial indication of a country's tax policy with respect to a certain type of income and its treatment under domestic law. This is because the allocation of taxing rights for a specific type of income to a state is purposeless and might even lead to unintended double non-taxation if no corresponding taxing laws are established domestically. With respect to the taxation of royalty income, the following reservations and positions were expressed in each OECD Model, starting from the publication of the OECD Model 1992:

- Portugal and Spain made a reservation to Article 12(1) OECD Model 1992[780] to also tax technical assistance that is closely associated with the transfer of royalties at source.[781]
- According to their position on Article 12 of the OECD Model 1998 and its corresponding commentaries, Argentina, Brazil, Philippines, and Thailand reserved the right to include fees for technical services in the definition of royalties.[782] In addition, Brazil also posited including fees for technical assistance in the scope of the royalties' definition.[783] Another position has also been made by Malaysia, Russia, and Vietnam to include the taxation of fees for technical services in a separate article.[784]
- Brazil, Gabon, Ivory Coast, and Tunisia reserved the right to include fees for technical assistance and technical services in the definition of 'royalties' in Article 12(2) OECD Model 2005.[785] With respect to the same provision, Morocco reserved the right to include payments in consideration for all types of services, technical assistance, and technical and economic studies in the mentioned definition.[786] Albania expressed its intention to include a separate article on the taxation of fees for technical services in their tax treaties.[787]
- With respect to the OECD Model 2008, Portugal expressed that it reserves the right to tax income arising from technical assistance in connection with the use of or the right to use industrial, commercial, or scientific equipment or containers at source.[788] In addition, India reserved the right to tax fees for technical services at source and to define these by reference to its domestic law.[789] Similarly, Argentina, Brazil, Gabon, Ivory Coast, the Philippines, Thailand, Tunisia, and Vietnam expressed the view to include fees for technical services in the definition of 'royalties' of Article 12(2) OECD Model 2008.[790] In addition, Brazil, Gabon, Ivory Coast, and Tunisia also prefer that

780. *See* para. 38 of the Commentary on Article 12 OECD Model 1992.
781. Such reservation is absent in the OECD Model 2017.
782. *See* paras 6 and 7 of Non-Member Countries' Positions on Article 12(2) OECD Model 1998.
783. *See* para. 7 of Non-Member Countries' Positions on Article 12 OECD Model 1998.
784. *See* para. 11 of Non-Member Countries' Positions on Article 12 OECD Model 1998.
785. *See* para. 7 of Non-Member Countries' Positions on Article 12 OECD Model 2005.
786. *See* para. 7.1 of Non-Member Countries' Positions on Article 12 OECD Model 2005.
787. *See* para. 7.1 of Non-Member Countries' Positions on Article 12 OECD Model 2005: Malaysia, Russia and Vietnam also expressed the same position.
788. *See* para. 43.1 of the Commentary on Article 12 OECD Model 2008.
789. *See* para. 4.1 of Non-Member Countries' Positions on Article 12 OECD Model 2008.
790. *See* para. 6 of Non-Member Countries' Positions on Article 12 OECD Model 2008.

technical assistance be covered by the royalties' definition. Morocco repeated its view with respect to the OECD Model 2005.[791]

- In addition to its reservation expressed in relation to the definition of Article 12(2) OECD Model 2008, Portugal reserved the right to tax technical assistance in connection with the use of or the right to use it related to Article 12(2) OECD Model 2010.[792] Similar to their position on Article 12(2) OECD Model 2005, Albania, Malaysia, and Vietnam reserved the right to include a separate article on the taxation of fees for technical services in their tax treaties.[793] In this respect, Serbia shared the same position.[794]
- Colombia made a reservation regarding the definition of 'royalties' of Article 12 OECD Model 2014 as it expressed that it reserves the right to include considerations received for technical assistance, technical services, and consulting services in its definition.[795] Besides the mentioned reservation, the OECD Model 2014 did not include any other additional reservations than those that were already expressed with respect to its previous versions.
- No positions or reservations – other than those already made in relation to its predecessor versions – were made concerning the OECD Model 2017.

2 *'Know-How' and Fees for Technical Services*

a *Differentiation 'Know-How', Technical Assistance, and Technical Services*

The definition of 'royalties' in Articles 12(2) OECD Model and 12(3) UN Model includes payments for 'the use of, or the right to use … information concerning industrial, commercial or scientific experience'. These types of payments are also known as payments in consideration for the provision of 'know-how', i.e., to know how to do something. Know-how usually needs to be made tangible, such as via blueprints or drawings, to be transferred. However, a transfer might also occur through verbal explanations by the grantor of the know-how or his employees.[796]

According to the Commentary on Article 12 OECD Model, only the transfer of non-patented information that does not fall within other categories of IP rights is covered by the scope of know-how.[797] Its definition shall also only cover information arising from previous experience which means that Article 12 of the OECD and UN Models is not applicable to payments for (new) information obtained from the

791. *See* para. 7.1 of Non-Member Countries' Positions on Article 12 OECD Model 2008.
792. *See* para. 44 of the Commentary on Article 12 OECD Model 2010.
793. *See* para. 11 of Non-Member Countries' Positions on Article 12 OECD Model 2010.
794. *See* para. 11 of Non-Member Countries' Positions on Article 12 OECD Model 2010.
795. *See* para. 7.2 of Non-Member Countries' Positions on Article 12 OECD Model 2014.
796. *See* Alejandro Garcia Heredia, *Who Knows the Riddle of Know-How? Spain Becomes Entangled in the Web of Intangibles*, 45 European Taxation 103, 105 (2005).
797. *See* para. 11 of the Commentary on Article 12 OECD Model 2017 and para. 13 of the Commentary on Article 12 UN Model 2021.

rendering of services requested by the payer.[798] However, some members of the UN Tax Committee and also some authors[799] opine that no (legal) grounds exist to limit the scope of know-how to previous experience.[800]

As already mentioned in *Chapter 4.B.ii.1.b(ii)*, WP 6 already acknowledged in 1974 that payments made for the transfer of know-how are often qualified as service payments by states.[801] While the difference between know-how and service payments is clear in theory, making an unambiguous distinction is difficult in practice. Therefore, states often unilaterally expand the scope of know-how to also include certain types of services, such as technical services, within its scope. Such an approach is justified on the basis that know-how still needs to be made available to the transferee in order to be imparted by him. In this respect, the transferor of know-how often uses – but does not transmit – his specialized knowledge, skill, or expertise in the form of training or consultancy services to the transferee to empower the latter to use the transferred know-how. Therefore, several states view the provision of services as an indispensable part of the transfer of know-how that cannot be considered separately for taxation purposes.[802] In this regard, the United States also acknowledges that, in certain cases, know-how may also include 'technical information that is conveyed through technical or consultancy services'.[803] In the view of the United States, however, general training to the employees of the transferee and payments for professional services shall not be included in the definition of know-how.[804]

The most common term that is used by the Commentaries to the OECD and UN Models[805] to describe services that are connected to the transfer of know-how is 'technical assistance'. This term is not defined in the Commentaries to the OECD and UN Models, however, the OECD established criteria on the distinction between service payments such as 'pure' technical assistance and payments for the supply of know-how:[806]

- Although the provision of services might require the use of specialized knowledge, skill, or expertise, these are not transferred by the provision of services.[807] In contrast, hereto, the transfer of know-how is based on making knowledge, skill, or expertise available to the transferee.

798. *See* para. 11 of the Commentary on Article 12 OECD Model 2017 and para. 13 of the Commentary on Article 12 UN Model 2021.
799. *See, e.g.*, Báez Moreno, *supra* n. 6, at footnote 264.
800. *See* para. 13 of the Commentary on Article 12 UN Model 2021 with reference to a modified version of para. 11 of the Commentary on Article 12 OECD Model 2017.
801. Working Party No. 6 of the Fiscal Committee, *supra* n. 764, at para. 2.
802. *See, e.g.*, Lan, *supra* n. 460, at 149 with further references.
803. *See* U.S. Department of the Treasury, *United States Model Technical Explanation accompanying the United States Model Income Tax Convention of November 15, 2006)*, https://home.treasury.gov/system/files/131/Treaty-US-Model-TE-2006.pdf (accessed 18 November 2022), 43.
804. *Ibid.*
805. *See* para. 11.6 of the Commentary on Article 12 OECD Model 2017 and para. 13 of the Commentary on Article 12 UN Model 2021.
806. *See* paras 11.1 et seq. of the Commentary on Article 12 OECD Model 2017 and para. 13 of the Commentary on Article 12 UN Model 2021 with reference to paras 11.1 et seq. of the Commentary on Article 12 OECD Model 2017.
807. *See* para. 85 of the Commentary on Article 12A UN Model 2021.

- The transferor of know-how has no obligation to take part in the application of know-how granted to the transferee and also does not guarantee any result thereof. Under a service contract, however, the service provider guarantees a specific result to the service recipient.
- Contracts for the provision of know-how regularly either include already existing information or information that is being developed or created (including a confidentiality clause).
- Based on a contract for the provision of know-how, in general, only the relevant know-how would have to be transferred without more involvement by the transferor. The client carries out the work himself with the use of specialized knowledge, skill, or expertise that has been made available to him by the transferor of know-how. In contrast, hereto, a service provider carries out the work by himself and has a substantially higher level of costs than a transferor of know-how (e.g., salaries and wages for employees, research expenses, and payments to subcontractors).

Based on the aforementioned criteria, the OECD provides a non-exhaustive list of examples of payments that should be considered service payments and not payments for the transfer of know-how. The examples include payments for:[808]

- after-sale-service;
- service payments to a seller for services rendered under a warranty;
- pure technical assistance;
- the development of a specific list of customers to the payee created on the basis of information that is generally available to the public;[809]
- opinions given by engineers, advocates, or accountants;
- electronically provided advice;
- electronic communication with technicians; and
- accessing a troubleshooting database through computer networks, such as a database that provides its users with publicly available information on frequently asked questions (FAQs).

The Commentaries on Article 12 of the OECD and UN Models do not include 'pure' technical assistance in the scope of Article 12 as payments for such assistance are either covered by Article 7 OECD Model or Articles 7, 12A, or 14 UN Model. Neither 'technical assistance' nor 'pure technical assistance' are defined in the Commentaries of Article 12 OECD and UN Models. However, the intentional addition of the term 'pure' in the paragraphs on the delineation of services and transfer of know-how clearly indicates that certain activities in the form of technical assistance are covered by Article 12 OECD and UN Models. In this respect, the explanations in the Commentaries to the OECD and UN Models concerning the tax treatment of 'mixed-contracts' make it clear

808. *See* para. 11.4. of the Commentary on Article 12 OECD Model 2017.
809. In contrast hereto, payments for a list developed on the basis of past experience with customers to which the payer has provided specific products or services shall be considered payments in consideration for the supply of know-how.

that payments for services that are of ancillary and largely unimportant nature to the supply of know-how are covered by Article 12 OECD and UN Models.[810] Although these services are – in relation to the transfer of know-how – only of a largely insignificant nature regarding the contractual obligations, they are still necessary to impart the transferred know-how to the transferee:[811]

> *Example 7*: States A and B signed a tax treaty including provisions based on Articles 12 and 12A UN Model. A Company, a resident of State A transfers know-how in the form of a secret formula and process to B Company, a resident of State B. In addition, A Company provides training to B Company's employees that is necessary to make use of such secret formulas and processes at the level of B Company. Payments made by B Company for the transfer of know-how and training provided by Company A would be covered by Article 12. Payments provided for the training services would only fall outside the scope of Article 12 if the training was not necessary to transfer the secret formula and process to B Company. In such a case, Article 12A would apply.

Example 7 showed that 'technical assistance' is generally covered by Article 12 UN Model if it is necessary to impart know-how to the transferee. Therefore, these types of technical assistance need to be distinguished from 'pure technical assistance' as Article 12 OECD and UN Models remain unapplicable for the latter mentioned services.[812] In the author's opinion, the term 'pure technical assistance' as used in the Commentaries to the OECD and UN Models refers to services that are not necessary for imparting know-how at the level of the transferee. These services would regularly not be of an ancillary nature and consequently form a category of income that is separate from the transfer of know-how.[813] An example of pure technical assistance would be consultancy services provided by the transferor of know-how to improve the effectiveness of the process that is transferred.[814] Such services would, in the author's opinion, be covered by Article 12A UN Model.

The provision of know-how also needs to be distinguished from that of studies. As elaborated in *Chapter 4.A.ii.1.a.*, several states mention income from technical studies as a separate category within the treaty definition of royalties.[815] In this regard,

810. *See* para. 11.6 of the Commentary on Article 12 OECD Model 2017 and para. 13 of the Commentary on Article 12 UN Model 2021 with reference to para. 11.6 of the Commentary on Article 12 OECD Model 2017.
811. *See* paras 102 and 103 of the Commentary on Article 12A UN Model 2021.
812. *See* para. 11.4 of the Commentary on Article 12 OECD Model 2017 and para. 13 of the Commentary on Article 12 UN Model 2021 with reference to Article 11.4 of the Commentary on Article 12 OECD Model 2017.
813. *See* para. 11.4 of the Commentary on Article 12 OECD Model 2017 and para. 13 of the Commentary on Article 12 UN Model 2021 with reference to para. 11.4 of the Commentary on Article 12 OECD Model 2017.
814. *See* ITAT Mumbai, *Preroy AG v. Deputy Director of Income Tax*, ITA Nos 4252, 4256, 5820, 5821, 6575/Mum/2004, paras 23 et seq. (16 April 2010).
815. *See, e.g.*, Article 12(3) DTC Korea-Tunisia (1988), Article 12(3) DTC Malta-Tunisia (2000) and Morocco's position in para. 7.1 of Non-Member Countries' Positions on Article 12 OECD Model 2005.

the term 'studies' is often referred to as a 'technical service'[816] or included besides the term 'technical assistance' as part of an additional inclusion to the treaty definition of royalties.[817]

As shown in *Chapter 4.B.ii.2.a.*, the term 'technical assistance' is mainly used in the context of the article on royalties and refers to assistance provided as part of the transfer of IP rights. The term 'technical services', however, is a broader term most commonly used as part of an autonomous treaty provision and also explicitly including other types of services such as administrative, consultancy, or managerial services.[818] Although state practice shows that both terms are not used interchangeably,[819] *Valta* contends that no practical difference between technical assistance and technical services exists.[820]

In the author's opinion, however, this view would require that technical assistance that is connected to the transfer of IP rights is equivalent to the term technical services. In this regard, nevertheless, technical assistance is substantially different from technical services. As mentioned in *Chapter 4.A.ii.2.*, the ordinary meaning of the term 'technical' relates to a particular science or skill, especially in the technical field.[821] With reference to technical assistance, the term clearly relates to the application of particular skills in the context of the transfer of know-how, i.e., a technical field. To 'assist' means to 'help someone to do something' or 'to give usually supplementary support or aid' to someone.[822] In *Bovis Lend Lease Pvt. Ltd. v. Income Tax Officer*, the ITAT Bangalore argued that the term 'assistance' has to be interpreted as helping or supporting another person to do the same in the future.[823] Such a view requires the transfer of know-how to the (service) recipient. In contrast to 'pure' technical assistance that also includes technical services, the former requires facilitating the

816. *See* Article V of the Protocol to the DTC Netherlands-South Africa (2005); similarly, Article V of the Protocol to the DTC Algeria-Netherlands (2018); *See also* para. 22 of the Commentary on Article 12 UN Model 2021.
817. *See, e.g.*, Article 12(3) DTC Korea-Tunisia (1988), Article 12(3) DTC Cameroon-Tunisia (1999) and Article 12(3) DTC Malta-Tunisia (2000).
818. *See, e.g.*, Article 12(4) DTC Pakistan-South Africa (1998), Article 12(3)(b) DTC India-Uganda (2004), Article 12(5) DTC Ghana-Netherlands (2008) and Article 12(4) DTC Morocco-Rwanda (2016).
819. *See, e.g.*, no. 3 of the Protocol to the DTC Brazil-South Africa (2003, 2015): 'It is understood that the provisions of paragraph 3 of Article 12 shall apply to payments of any kind received as a consideration for the rendering of technical services and technical assistance.' and no. 4 of the Protocol to the DTC Belgium-Uganda (2007), explicitly excluding payments for technical assistance and technical services from the scope of know-how: 'In applying Article 12, paragraph 3 of the Convention payments constituting consideration for technical assistance or technical services shall not be considered to be payments for information concerning industrial, commercial or scientific experience, but shall be taxable in accordance with the provisions of Article 7 or Article 15 [independent personal services], as the case may be.'
820. *See* Matthias Valta, *Article 12: Income from Royalties*, in: Ekkehart Reimer & Alexander Rust (eds), *Klaus Vogel on Double Taxation Conventions* vol. 1, 955, m.no. 180 (4th ed., Wolters Kluwer 2015).
821. *See* Cambridge University Press & Assessment, *supra* n. 628.
822. *See* Oxford University Press, *Oxford Learner's Dictionaries*, https://www.oxfordlearnersdictionaries.com/definition/american_english/assist_1 (accessed 10 September 2022).
823. ITAT Bangalore, *Bovis Lend Lease (India) Pvt. Ltd. v. Income Tax Officer*, ITA Nos 636, 637, 665, 1452/Bang/2008 and 676, 677, 678, 679/Bang/2009, para. 102 (28 August 2009).

transferee to use know-how in a strict context. As explained in the Commentary on Article 12A UN Model, the transfer of know-how often requires the provision of technical assistance as the transferee could not make use of it if it was not available.[824] Know-how as defined by the ANBPPI includes 'undivulged technical information...that is necessary for the industrial reproduction of a product or process, directly and under the same conditions'.[825] Assisting with such specialized undivulged information, therefore, primarily requires the use of specialized knowledge, skill, or expertise by the transferor or his technical personnel. This use is required in the technical field as it refers to technical information on a product or process that is not publicly available. Therefore, the transferee also relies on a certain degree of specialized assistance from the transferor of know-how in order to impart such undivulged knowledge and use it.

The qualification of technical assistance as a technical service depends on the fact of whether specialized knowledge, skill, or expertise is transferred due to the process of assistance. In this respect, only 'pure' technical assistance is regarded as a service as it does not make any specialized knowledge, skill, or expertise available.[826] Therefore, only technical assistance that is not necessary to impart know-how in the sense of Article 12 OECD and UN Models might, in the author's opinion, fall under the allocation rule of Article 12A UN Model. Technical assistance that makes specialized knowledge, skill, or expertise available to the transferee is subject to the application of Article 12 UN Model.[827]

As will be demonstrated in *Chapter 4.B.ii.3.c.*, especially India includes a make-available clause in several of its tax treaties to explicitly include all types of technical and consultancy services in the scope of Article 12 on 'Royalties and fees for technical services'.[828] Other states, such as Argentina and Austria, also included 'pure' technical assistance, i.e., assistance that does not require the transfer of specialized knowledge, skill, or expertise within the scope of their article on royalties through the inclusion of a specific provision to their tax treaty, as such assistance would otherwise – in the author's opinion – not be covered by the article on royalties:

> The term 'technical assistance' referred to in paragraph 3 is understood as the rendering of customized services involving the application by the provider of any non-patentable specialized knowledge, ability or experience, and not necessarily requiring the transmission of such knowledge to the client. It is understood that the rendering of standardized services is not covered by the term 'technical assistance'.[829]

824. *See* para. 103 of the Commentary on Article 12A UN Model 2021.
825. *See* para. 12 of the Commentary on Article 12 OECD Model 1977.
826. *See* para. 11.4 of the Commentary on Article 12 OECD Model 2017 and para. 13 of the Commentary on Article 12 UN Model 2021 with reference to para. 11.4 of the Commentary on Article 12 OECD Model 2017.
827. *See* para. 103 of the Commentary on Article 12A UN Model 2021.
828. *See, e.g.*, Article 12(4) DTC India-United States (1989).
829. *See* no. 5 of the Protocol to the DTC Argentina-Austria (2019).

b Mixed Contracts

As mentioned previously, the differentiation between the provision of technical services and the transfer of 'know-how' often gives rise to interpretational difficulties. In this regard, 'mixed contracts' often include elements of both a service contract and a contract for the transfer of know-how.[830] The need to distinguish these different types of payments is especially necessary for states that do not include explicit provisions on the taxation of technical services in their tax treaties. This is because technical services are usually subject to source taxation only in case of the existence of a PE or fixed base in the source state (Articles 7 and 14 UN Model).

The application of Articles 7 and 14 UN Model also leads to different tax consequences in contrast to technical services provisions as taxation on the basis of the former mentioned articles is based on net income. If the respective tax treaty includes a provision on the taxation of technical services, however, the differentiation between the supply of know-how and the provision of technical services becomes less relevant as a withholding tax on the gross amount of the payment would apply for the provision of both. In addition, if the contracting states agree to the application of the same tax rate for payments in consideration of know-how and technical services in their tax treaty, the need to distinguish both types of payments becomes practically irrelevant. Nevertheless, without the application of the same tax rate for payments for know-how and technical services, a distinguishment of these two types of payments still needs to be made.[831]

The Commentaries on Article 12 of the OECD and UN Models recognize that the conclusion of 'mixed contracts' is common business practice. They are characterized by the fact that specialized knowledge and experience are supplied by the transferor together with technical assistance, however, often without an indication of how the remuneration is split between the transfer of know-how and the provision of technical assistance.[832] In this respect, the Commentaries on Article 12 OECD and UN Models suggest breaking down the entire stipulated contractual amount by way of information given in the contract or through reasonable apportionment. This is often done in practice on the basis of the apportionment between services and intellectual property suggested by the OECD Transfer Pricing Guidelines.[833] Each part of the negotiated amount that has been broken down shall then be subject to 'proper' taxation. The stipulated contractual amount shall not be reasonably broken down, however, if one part is being considered 'by far' the principal purpose of the contract and the other parts are only of ancillary and unimportant nature. In such a case, the tax treatment that is aimed at the principal part of the contract shall also be applied to the other parts

830. *See* para. 11.6 of the Commentary on Article 12 OECD Model 2017 and para. 13 of the Commentary on Article 12 UN Model 2021 with reference to para. 11.6 of the Commentary on Article 12 OECD Model 2017.
831. *See* paras 4 and 100 of the Commentary on Article 12A UN Model 2021.
832. *See, e.g.*, Priestley, *Australia*, in: *Cahiers de droit fiscal international* vol. 97a, 87, 95 (Sdu 2012).
833. *See* Miller, *supra* n. 2, at 255.

of the contract.[834] The principal purpose of a contract will have to be determined on a case-by-case basis. However, neither the Commentaries to the OECD Models nor the Commentaries to the UN Models give guidance on how to determine the principal purpose of the contract.[835]

The ambiguous rules on how and when to break down parts of a contract lead to an exacerbation of problems in breaking down complex contracts that include a broad range of service components rendered via electronic means such as SaaS, IaaS and PaaS.[836] Even if payments made under these contracts are not qualified as royalties, they might still include different types of service components falling under Articles 7 and 12A or possibly the recently introduced Article 12B UN Model.[837] In the author's opinion, the complexity of the classification of different service components may lead to the application of simplified approaches by tax administrations on the taxation of these types of services, i.e., the application of withholding tax on the entire contractual amount based on the article on royalties irrespective of whether the contract also involves the provision of various types of services.[838] Such simplified approaches unilaterally broaden the scope of the article on royalties to also cover service fees that would not have been taxed in the source state due to the non-existence of a PE or fixed base therein. Such shift in the allocation of taxing rights in favour of the source state on the basis of the provision on royalties, however, is generally not intended by the Commentaries of the OECD and UN Models regarding 'pure' technical assistance, i.e., services that do not make any specialized knowledge, skill, or expertise available.[839] The taxation of these services based on the article on royalties might also possibly lead to negative economic consequences for the taxpayer, as – in contrast to Articles 7 and 14 UN Model – the taxation of royalties is based on the gross amount of the payment. Therefore, in the author's opinion, tax administrations should strengthen their efforts on receiving the necessary facts of the case from the taxpayer in order to be able to break down the different parts of the contract and make an analysis of these. They could then conclude whether services provided in connection to the transfer of know-how are actually only of ancillary and unimportant nature and therefore be taxed according to the principal part of the contract, i.e., royalties.

The difficulty in classifying the different parts of a contract might – from a practical point of view – be mitigated through the inclusion of tax treaty provisions similar to Articles 12A and 12B UN Model with a tax rate that is the same as the one in the article on royalties. While this solution would still not completely solve the

834. *See* para. 11.6 of the Commentary on Article 12 OECD Model 2017 and para. 13 of the Commentary on Article 12 UN Model 2021 with reference to para. 11.6 of the Commentary on Article 12 OECD Model 2017.
835. *See* Bal, *supra* n. 734, at 516: One approach to break down the separate service components of a contract would be to determine whether the service component in question could be purchased individually on the basis of a separate contractual agreement.
836. These three forms are so-called cloud-computing services. *See* for a more thorough analysis: Kjærsgaard, *supra* n. 249, at 386.
837. Article 12B UN Model 2021 will be applied instead of Article 12A if services are provided without human intervention.
838. *See, e.g.,* for the practice of certain Chinese tax authorities: Lan, *supra* n. 460, at 151.
839. *See* Chapter 4.B.ii.2.a.

complexity of the characterization of service payments in connection with mixed contracts, it ensures that a wide range of specialized or automated digital services that are provided in connection to the transfer of know-how are subject to the same gross taxation as royalties.

Ultimately, if tax administrations, after assessment of all the facts of a case, take different legal opinions leading to double taxation, the initiation of a mutual agreement procedure by the taxpayer would be advisable to ensure taxation in accordance with the respective tax treaty.

3 *Royalty-Related Approaches*

a Fees for Included Services

In the UN Tax Committee's eleventh session, it agreed to include an 'included services' provision as an alternative to the inclusion of Article 12A UN Model to the Commentary on Article 12 UN Model.[840] Its inclusion was already proposed by *Arnold* at the eighth session of the UN Tax Committee, however, the majority of committee members ultimately decided to introduce an autonomous article on fees for technical services.[841] Nevertheless, an 'included services' provision based on Article 12 on 'Royalties and fees for included services' of the DTC India-United States (1989) – as proposed by *Arnold* – is now included in the commentaries to also reflect a minority position among the members of the UN Tax Committee favouring its inclusion instead of an autonomous article on fees for technical services. In addition, with regards to the explanations found in the Commentary on Article 12 UN Model on the 'included services' provision, the UN Tax Committee also basically decided to duplicate the explanations from the Technical Explanations on Article 12 of the DTC India-USA (1989).[842]

The provision on included services only covers 'technical' and 'consultancy' services without mentioning 'managerial' services.[843] In this respect, the definition of the term 'technical' is different and much narrower from the one found in the Commentary on Article 12A(3) UN Model. According to the Commentary on Article 12 of the UN Model, technical services are those requiring 'expertise in a technology'.[844] Consultancy services, when understood as advisory services, are also covered by the 'included services' provision of the Commentary on Article 12 UN Model even if no expertise in a technology is required to render advice.[845] However, as opined in *Chapter 4.B.ii.2.a.*, such consultancy services need to refer to specialized assistance in the technical field due to the transfer of technical information on a product or process that is not publicly available.

840. Committee of Experts on International Cooperation in Tax Matters, *supra* n. 212, at para. 72.
841. *See* for the reasoning of the inclusion of an autonomous article: Committee of Experts on International Cooperation in Tax Matters, *supra* n. 146, at para. 58.
842. *See* Joint Committee on Taxation, *supra* n. 450, at 42 et seq.
843. *See* para. 34 of the Commentary on Article 12 UN Model 2021.
844. *See* para. 35 of the Commentary on Article 12 UN Model 2021.
845. *See* para. 35 of the Commentary on Article 12 UN Model 2021.

The provision on fees for included services covers payments for the rendering of any technical or consultancy services if they are either 'ancillary and subsidiary to the application or enjoyment of the right, property or information for which a payment described in paragraph 3 [definition of royalties] is received' or 'make available technical knowledge, experience, skill, know-how, or processes, or consist of the development and transfer of a technical plan or technical design'.[846]

The following chapters aim to describe the aforementioned concepts together with explanations on the interpretation of the term 'technical' on the background of judicial decisions of international but especially Indian courts.

b *Ancillary Activities*

According to paragraph 4(a) of the alternative version of Article 12 UN Model, technical and consultancy services are included in the scope of royalties as 'included services' under the condition of being 'ancillary and subsidiary to the application or enjoyment of the right, property or information for which' a royalty is received. Although not specifically expressed by the Commentaries on Article 12 of the OECD and UN Models, the author shares the opinions of *Báez Moreno*[847] and *Pal*[848] that this category of services is already covered by Article 12 OECD and UN Models. This is clarified through the explanations on mixed contracts as services such as technical assistance are covered by Article 12 OECD and UN Models if they are of an ancillary and largely insignificant character to the transfer of IP rights.[849] Services that clearly form the principal part of an arrangement, such as regularly conducted cleaning services in relation to the lease of equipment, are not considered 'ancillary and subsidiary' and are therefore not in the scope of the 'included services' provision.[850] As a result, the notion 'ancillary and subsidiary to the application or enjoyment of the right, property or information for which' is a mere clarification of an already existing concept in the OECD and UN Models.[851]

c *Make-Available Clauses*

Non-OECD members, especially India, often include a 'make available' provision in the respective article on royalties and fees for technical services[852] or even as part of an autonomous provision[853] in their tax treaties. According to *Jiménez*, the inclusion of

846. *See* para. 34 of the Commentary on Article 12 UN Model 2021.
847. *See* Báez Moreno, *supra* n. 6, at 311.
848. Pal, *supra* n. 449, at footnote 28.
849. *See* para. 11.6 of the Commentary on Article 12 OECD Model 2017 and para. 13 of the Commentary on Article 12 UN Model 2021 with reference to para. 11.6 of the Commentary on Article 12 OECD Model 2017.
850. Chishty & Chakalabbi, *supra* n. 454, at 49.
851. *See also* Wijnen, de Goede & Alessi, *supra* n. 3, at 32.
852. *See, e.g.*, Article 12(4) DTC India-United States (1989) and Article 12(4) DTC Canada-India (1996).
853. *See* Article 13(3) DTC Norway-Uganda (1999).

such a clause in tax treaties concluded by India is based on its non-acceptance of the more restrictive changes to the OECD Model 1977 in comparison to its predecessor version of 1963. In the opinion of *Jiménez*, the preparatory works of the OECD Model 1963 also intended to include certain technical services within the scope of the provision on royalties.[854]

The alternative provision on fees for included services as found in the Commentary on Article 12 UN Model also includes a 'make available' provision. Payments for technical and consultancy services are covered by this provision if they 'make available technical knowledge, experience, skill, know-how, or processes'[855] without the requirement of being auxiliary to the transfer of such knowledge, experience, skill, know-how or process.

Making technical services available means that the service recipient is able to benefit from the use of the knowledge, skills, or expertise that was provided to him without the aid of the service provider. The term 'make available' is independent of the acceptance of the service recipient and only refers to the service provider's willingness.[856] As knowledge, skills, or expertise have been made available to the service recipient, they remain at his disposal even after the expiration of a contract.[857] As a result, the service recipient is able to use the knowledge, skills, or expertise provided on, e.g., certain technologies, without being dependent upon the service provider.[858] Therefore, the requirements of the 'make available' clause are not fulfilled if the substantive scope of work of an engineer is based on a service contract that limits him to reviewing and opining on a project rather than designing and directing it and the suggestions that are incidentally made by the engineer are not adopted by the service recipient as a result.[859] In this regard, the mere provision of feasibility reports with respect to the development of coal mines also does not lead to a transfer of technical know-how and the fulfilment of the 'make available' provision.[860]

Therefore, a twin test of the provision of services and making technical knowledge available needs to be satisfied to fulfil the requirement of 'fees for technical services' in regards to the 'make available' provision.[861] Technical input given by the service provider such as reviewing or opining[862] does not necessarily mean that technical knowledge, skills, or expertise have been made available to the recipient of

854. *See* with reference to the preparatory works of the 1980 UN Model and its Commentary: Jiménez, *supra* n. 10, at 132 et seq.
855. *See* para. 34 of the Commentary on Article 12 UN Model 2021.
856. ITAT Bangalore, *supra* n. 823, at para. 101.
857. ITAT Mumbai, *supra* n. 23, at paras 19.18 et seq.
858. *See* Joint Committee on Taxation, *supra* n. 150, at 17: 'The memorandum of understanding states that generally technology will be considered "made available" when the person acquiring the service is enabled to apply the technology.'
859. *See* ITAT Kolkata, *Cesc Ltd. v. Deputy Commissioner of Income Tax*, ITA No 527 (Cal.) of 1998, para. 22 (6 August 2003).
860. ITAT Mumbai, *Charbonnages De France International SA v. Deputy Commissioner of Income Tax*, IT Appeal No 98 (Mum) of 2002, para. 24 (27 July 2007).
861. ITAT Delhi, *Guy Carpenter & Co. Ltd. v. Additional Director of Income Tax*, IT Appeal No. 2443 (Delhi) of 2011, para. 29.1 (30 September 2011).
862. ITAT Kolkota, *supra* n. 859, at paras 19 et seq.

the services.[863] In the case *Mahindra and Mahindra Ltd. v. Deputy Commissioner of Income Tax*,[864] the Special Bench of Mumbai observed with respect to the meaning of the term 'make available' according to Article 13(4)(c) DTC India-UK (1993) that technical information or advice needs to be submitted to the service recipient in a way that he is able to take benefit therefrom once or on a continuous basis. In contrast hereto, if the service recipient only benefits (in)directly from the services and the service provider solely uses technical services at its own end, such services are not deemed to be made available to the service recipient. As a result, the Special Bench of Mumbai decided that payments in the form of management and sales commission do not fulfil the 'make available' requirement. This is because the service recipient merely derived a benefit from the technical services without receiving any technical knowledge, skill, or expertise.[865] In this respect, also training services relating to the operation of an accounting system, management information system, and other internal reporting or safety regulations do not make technical knowledge, experience, skill, or know-how available as such training services merely facilitate employees to work in accordance with expected company standards.[866] The fulfilment of the 'make available' provision is therefore subject to a certain degree of durability and stability so that the transfer of technology, knowledge, skill, or expertise is not only of a transient character.[867]

As has been mentioned in *Chapter 4.B.ii.2.*, the transfer of technology, knowledge, skill or expertise often requires the provision of services to enable the transferee to make use of such technology, knowledge, skill or expertise. If assistance – in the form of services – is needed to impart such technology, knowledge, skill or experience, the term 'technical assistance' is used. This assistance is usually auxiliary to the transfer of technology, knowledge, skill, or expertise. It may also be the case, however, that by making available technology, knowledge, skill, or expertise, services are provided that are connected to such transfer but are not only of an auxiliary and unimportant character to the transfer of IP rights, i.e., not merely 'technical assistance' as already covered by Article 12 UN Model. In the author's opinion, such services that are referred to as 'pure technical assistance' in the Commentaries on Article 12 UN and OECD Model, may form a principal part of a contract and would not be covered by Article 12 UN and OECD Models without the existence of a specific make-available clause. Therefore, in the absence of such a clause, the application of Article 12A UN Model on the aforementioned services would need to be considered.

863. *See* Joint Committee on Taxation, *supra* n. 450, at 47 et seq.
864. ITAT Mumbai, *Mahindra and Mahindra Ltd. v. Deputy Commissioner of Income Tax*, ITA Nos 2606, 2607, 2613 and 2614/Mum/2000 (9 April 2009).
865. *See* ITAT Delhi, *supra* n. 861, at para. 28.1 and ITAT Mumbai, *Armayesh Global v. ACIT*, ITA No. 8822/Mum/2010, paras 14 et seq. (4 May 2012).
866. ITAT Bangalore, *supra* n. 823.
867. *Ibid.*, at para. 57.

C ARTICLE 12A UN MODEL: OVERLAP WITH ARTICLE 12B UN MODEL

i Preliminary Remarks on Potential Overlaps

As already mentioned in *Chapter 3.C.ii.2.b.*, the UN Tax Committee decided to include Article 12B as part of its 2021 revision to the UN Model, with the aim of specifically addressing tax issues stemming from the provision of ADS in the digitalized economy. The UN Tax Committee justified the inclusion of Article 12B on the possibility of service providers being substantially economically involved in a jurisdiction's economy through the provision of services that do not require the establishment of a physical presence therein.[868]

Article 12B(1) UN Model grants a taxing right for ADS to the residence state of the service provider. However, according to Article 12B(2) UN Model, ADS arising in a contracting state may also be taxed therein. In this respect, Article 12B(9) UN Model establishes that ADS arise in a contracting state if the payer is a resident of that state or if the payer, whether he is a resident of that contracting state, has a PE or fixed base therein through which the income is incurred and borne. According to Article 12B(2) UN Model, the source state has a taxing right for income from ADS up to a percentage established through bilateral negotiations, if the recipient of the income is the beneficial owner. However, as provided by Article 12B(3) UN Model, such fees will not be taxed on a gross basis if the beneficial owner requests the source state to being taxed on the basis of the qualified profits of the service provider.

Article 12B(7) UN Model provides that Article 12A shall take precedence over the application of Article 12B if income from ADS also qualifies as fees for technical services. Therefore, the UN Model assumes that a certain degree of overlap between these types of services might occur. Whether or not this is the case, will be explained in the following chapters.

ii Technical Services Covered by Article 12B UN Model

1 Scope of Article 12B UN Model

Article 12B UN Model covers – similar to most Digital Services Taxes (DST) – only ADS and not CFBs.[869] It, therefore, specifically targets highly digitalized businesses. The reason behind the establishment of such a scope is that the taxation of ADS provided by large MNEs to market jurisdictions reflects a common state consensus.[870] What is more, *Michel* takes the view that ADS payments have – due to their prevalence in a B2B context – a greater base-erosion potential than CFB payments. Therefore, Article 12B

868. Similarly, para. 2 of the Commentary on Article 12A UN Model 2021.
869. Collier, Devereux & Vella, *supra* n. 414, at 417.
870. Bob Michel, *Developing Countries Put Their Cards on the Table in the Digital Economy Tax Debate – But Is the UN Committee of Experts Playing a Winning Hand?* (published online on the IBFD – Tax Research Platform on 15 June 2021) DOI: 10.59403/12rzbtg.

UN Model rightfully restricts its scope to ADS.[871] However, as the author showed in *Chapter 3.C.ii.2.b.*, the base-erosion principle as a justification for source taxing rights of ADS payments has been incrementally scrapped by the UN Tax Committee during the drafting process of Article 12B UN Model. The UN Tax Committee ultimately decided that Article 12B UN Model is based on an 'allocation of taxing rights issue'.[872]

The definition of ADS heavily relies on the work done by the OECD Inclusive Framework, in order to avoid spill overs relating to divergent scoping.[873] ADS are defined as services provided via the Internet or any other electronic network, requiring only minimal human involvement from the service provider in the provision of the service.[874] Mentioned services are characterized by the fact that they are obtained automatically by a large and global group of users without the need for individual customization by the service provider.[875] Therefore, once the ADS is developed, it can be provided to either one or several thousand users on a standardized basis, without or only minimal additional human involvement.[876] In addition, ADS are also characterized by the possibility to scale up and provide such services to new users without the need for significant human involvement.[877]

In this respect, it needs to be mentioned that the Commentary on Article 12B UN Model emphasizes that human involvement needs to be present in the moment of application of the service to another person. Therefore, the presence of substantial human involvement in creating an ADS, such as the development of algorithms, maintaining and updating the system environment or other generic adjustments that are not related to an individual user request, are not relevant for the qualification of a service as ADS.[878] As Article 12B(5) UN Model 2021 only requires minimal human involvement from the ADS provider, it is also detrimental to note that automated services requiring substantial human involvement from another entity, such as a third party, do not hinder the qualification of a service as ADS.[879]

Article 12B(6) UN Model provides a non-exhaustive list of services that 'often constitute' ADS.[880] The services mentioned in the list include, *inter alia*, online advertising services, online search engines, online intermediation platform services, social media platforms, cloud computing services and standardized online teaching services.[881]

871. *Ibid.*
872. Committee of Experts on International Cooperation in Tax Matters, *supra* n. 403, at 43.
873. *Ibid.*, at 34.
874. *See* para. 53 of the Commentary on Article 12B UN Model 2021.
875. The Commentary on Article 12B UN Model also refers to a 'bespoke interaction' with the service provider: para. 53 of the Commentary on Article 12B UN Model 2021; also OECD, *supra* n. 272, at 19 et seq.
876. *See* para. 54 of the Commentary on Article 12B UN Model 2021 and OECD, *supra* n. 272, at 24.
877. *See* para. 54 of the Commentary on Article 12B UN Model 2021.
878. *See* para. 53 of the Commentary on Article 12B UN Model 2021; OECD, *supra* n. 272, at 20.
879. Committee of Experts on International Cooperation in Tax Matters, *supra* n. 403, at 50.
880. *See* para. 57 of the Commentary on Article 12B UN Model 2021.
881. *See* Article 12B(6) UN Model 2021.

The Commentary on Article 12B UN Model explicitly emphasizes that the list of activities that might qualify as ADS is only of an indicative nature.[882] Therefore, these mentioned services still need to fulfil the requirements of Article 12B(5) UN Model, i.e., provided digitally via the internet or another electronic network with only minimal human involvement. As the Commentary on Article 12B UN Model shows, listed services – and in this context especially cloud-computing and teaching services – might fall outside the scope of Article 12B UN Model as soon as these services are humanly customized to the needs of a specific client.[883]

The definition of ADS as described in Article 12B(5) UN Model requires 'minimal' human involvement in the application of ADS. The term 'minimal', however, is neither explicitly defined in Article 12B UN Model nor its corresponding commentary. In this respect, the Commentary on Article 12B UN Model only mentions the following situations to distinguish digital services requiring only a 'minimal' or a 'high degree' of human involvement:

- Customization of cloud-computing services to the specific needs of a particular client requires a high-degree of human involvement. If, however, a standardized cloud-computing-package is only configurated or integrated into a customer's existing IT-Infrastructure or if human involvement relates only to ancillary customer support, the degree of human involvement is regarded as being only ancillary to the cloud-computing service, therefore including only a 'minimal' degree of human involvement in the sense of Article 12B(5) UN Model.[884]
- Article 12B(6) UN Model refers to standardized online teaching services as an example of ADS. The characteristics of such services include non-customized, pre-packaged products, such as pre-recorded lectures. Such packages often allow students to communicate with each other within a discussion forum that is tutored by a student instructor. In this respect, the requirement of minimal human involvement is fulfilled, when the student instructor interacts with students within that forum only in a limited way.[885] Such involvement by the instructor is then referred to as being only of ancillary nature.[886]
- Independent professional services as referred to in Article 14(2) UN Model as well as specialized expert consultancy services are regarded as services that

882. This so-called 'positive list' was developed by the OECD as part of the Pillar I and II project and taken over by the UN for the purposes of developing Article 12B UN Model 2021. In contrast to the views taken by the Commentary to the UN Model 2021, however, such positive list is intended to constitute services that are automatically qualified as ADS without the need to test its fulfilment with the general definition of ADS. Only if services do not fall within those mentioned on the positive and the negative list, the fulfilment of the general definition needs to be tested; *see* for this purpose: OECD, *supra* n. 272, at 19 et seq.
883. *See* para. 58 subparas (f) and (h) of the Commentary on Article 12B UN Model 2021 that make reference to SaaS ('Software-as-a-Service').
884. *See* para. 58 subpara. (h) of the Commentary on Article 12B UN Model 2021.
885. *See* para. 58 subpara. (i) of the Commentary on Article 12B UN Model 2021.
886. *See* para. 60 subpara. (ii) of the Commentary on Article 12B UN Model 2021.

exceed the threshold of requiring only minimal human involvement. This is due to the need of customization of their service to a specific client.[887]

The Commentary on Article 12B(5) and (6) UN Model explicitly excludes customized professional services and customized online teaching services from its scope, as these services require a high degree of human involvement.[888] Therefore, the Commentary on Article 12B UN Model tries to distinguish the degree of human involvement via the concept of customization. This concept is also present in the Commentary on Article 12A UN Model, as fees for technical services are distinct from other routine services through the use of specialized knowledge, skill or expertise on behalf of a specific customer. However, the degree of customization and, therefore, the threshold of use of human involvement to deprive a service of its qualification as ADS is not precisely defined. On the contrary, the Commentary on Article 12B UN Model often uses different undetermined terms to describe the degree of human involvement: 'minimal',[889] 'ancillary',[890] 'limited',[891] 'high',[892] 'significant',[893] or 'additional'.[894]

Under the assumption that Article 12B UN Model will be included in a tax treaty, the unclear and vague guidance found in the Commentary on Article 12B UN Model with respect to the concepts of the degree of 'customization' and 'human involvement' will raise difficulties in the interpretation of services as ADS. In this regard, services provided through the internet – independently of the degree of human intervention – might simply be qualified as ADS without any further investigation, possibly leading to double taxation. The degree of human involvement will then ultimately need to be answered either in a mutual agreement procedure or by a court based on a free assessment of evidence.

2 *Differentiation Between Automated Digital Services and Fees for Technical Services*

An analysis of the definition and the examples described in Article 12B(5), (6) UN Model and its corresponding commentaries, shows that the definition of ADS focuses on standardized, routine services that only involve ancillary human involvement with respect to the application of a digital service. In contrast hereto, standardized routine services without customization to a particular client, shall not be within the scope of Article 12A UN Model. This is due to the fact that – according to the Commentaries on Article 12A UN Model – fees for technical services are characterized by the application of specialized knowledge, skill or expertise on behalf of a specific customer.

887. *See* para. 60 subpara. (i) of the Commentary on Article 12B UN Model 2021.
888. *See* para. 59 subparas (i) and (ii) of the Commentary on Article 12B UN Model 2021.
889. *See* para. 58 subpara. (f) of the Commentary on Article 12B UN Model 2021.
890. *See* para. 58 subparas (h) and (i) of the Commentary on Article 12B UN Model 2021.
891. *See* para. 58 subpara. (i) of the Commentary on Article 12B UN Model 2021.
892. *See* para. 58 subpara. (h) of the Commentary on Article 12B UN Model 2021.
893. *See* para. 60 subpara. (v) of the Commentary on Article 12B UN Model 2021.
894. *See* para. 60 subpara. (iv) of the Commentary on Article 12B UN Model 2021.

In this regard, Article 12B UN Model actually has some sort of a complementary function to Article 12A UN Model. As has been described in *Chapter 4.A.ii.*, the provision of services through a standard facility, such as access to a database through the internet, is out of the scope of Article 12A UN Model.[895] This view, as found in the Commentaries on Article 12A UN Model, is based on the decision of the ITAT Mumbai in *Kotak Securities Ltd. Mumbai v. Department of Income Tax*.[896] Therefore, also income of a service provider from the use of a search engine would not be qualified as fees for technical services.[897] Such services provided through a standard facility are, however, within the scope of Article 12B UN Model, as this provision specifically covers routine services provided through a standard facility. Such standard facility is – in the case of the services mentioned in the list of Article 12B(6) UN Model – commonly a digital interface.

Although the concept of 'human intervention' has not explicitly been mentioned in the Commentary on Article 12A UN Model, it has already been subject to several Indian court proceedings in relation to the question of whether certain types of services fulfil the criteria of 'fees for technical services'. In this regard, Indian jurisprudence heavily relies on the existence of a human element to qualify payments as fees for technical services as defined in section 9(1)(vii) of the Indian Income Tax Act ('any consideration ... for the rendering of any managerial, technical or consultancy services').

The threshold of human involvement to deem services technical services or ADS, however, seems to differ when comparing Indian jurisprudence and the approach taken by the Commentaries on Article 12A and Article 12B UN Model.

As mentioned in *Chapter 4.A.ii.3.*, the ITAT Agra argued that it is 'not a question of more of, or less of, human involvement' but rather a 'question of presence of or absence of human involvement'.[898] Therefore, *Sengupta* opines that the condition of human involvement would already be sufficed in the case of 'indirect human interface', i.e., even if human intervention is present in relation to non-core activities of a company, such as the preparation of a report that is made available through a standard facility.[899] In contrast hereto, Article 12B(5) UN Model does not seem to take such a strict approach as already its wording refers to 'minimal human involvement', i.e., some degree of human involvement does not necessarily deprive a service of its status as ADS. It is, however, important that such human involvement is not used to customize a service to a user, as the definition of ADS requires the absence of a human element within the customization process. Therefore, if a service recipient is able to get

895. *See, e.g.*, paras 92 and 95 of the Commentary on Article 12A UN Model 2021; Sagar Wagh, *The Taxation of Digital Transactions in India: The New Equalization Levy*, 70 BIT 538, 545 (2016) DOI: 10.59403/1tg2kb5.
896. ITAT Mumbai, *supra* n. 680, at para. 25.
897. *See* Amar Mehta, *'Equalization Levy' Proposal in Indian Finance Bill 2016: Is It Legitimate Tax Policy or an Attempt of Treaty Dodging?*, 22 APTB 2, at Chapter 3 (2016) DOI: 10.59403/2dz6sry.
898. *See* ITAT Agra, *supra* n. 677, at para. 21.
899. D. P. Sengupta, *India: Siemens Ltd – To Be Taxed as Fees for Technical Services Some Human Intervention Is a Must*, in: Eric C.C.M. Kemmeren et al. (eds), *Tax Treaty Case Law Around the Globe 2014* vol. 89, 211, 218 (Linde Verlag 2015).

a customized automated result after giving input on certain parameters, such an automated result would be within the scope of the definition of Article 12B(5) UN Model.[900]

In contrast, hereto, the definition of fees for technical services requires the application of specialized knowledge, skill or expertise on behalf of a customer.[901] Therefore, the Commentaries on Article 12A UN Model explicitly include services of a professional nature as referred to in Article 14(2) UN Model within its scope.[902] Such professional services are, however, explicitly excluded from the definition of ADS, due to the fact that professional services require bespoke interactions with and customization by the service provider.[903] Customization on behalf of a client, or what the Commentary of the UN Model often refers to as providing services 'for the benefit'[904] of a client, is a key part of the definition of fees for technical services found in Article 12A(3) UN Model. Although not specifically mentioned in the Commentary on Article 12A UN Model, it seems that the UN Tax Committee implicitly assumed that 'relevant' customization for the purposes of fees for technical services requires specialized knowledge, skill or expertise as may only be applied by a human and not an automated solution. The Commentary on Article 12A UN Model, however, acknowledges that several professional services may not require the application of specialized knowledge, skill or expertise on behalf of a particular client.[905] Such services, however, are commonly found in the field of professional services. They might include general products that are developed on the basis of specialized knowledge, skill or expertise, but are – when provided to the client – of a routine nature, such as the provision of legal document templates or certain payment and transmission services.[906] In practice, such services might also be automatically provided in consideration of a fee based on the input of a client. Such services would – due to their routine character and use of a standard facility – not be within the scope of Article 12A UN Model. In addition, taking into account the explanations found on the exclusion of professional services (including financial services) from the scope of Article 12B in its commentary, Article 12B would also not apply.[907]

In the author's opinion, however, the exclusion of certain routinely provided professional services from the application of Article 12B UN Model is neither consistent with the approach taken by Article 12B itself nor with respect to the explanations on the definition of fees for technical services in the Commentary on Article 12A UN Model. In this regard, already the wording of Article 12B UN Model does not explicitly exclude routine professional services provided through standard facilities from its scope. To the contrary, Article 12B(2) UN Model explicitly foresees that Article 12B applies to ADS notwithstanding the application of Article 14 UN Model if services are within the scope

900. *See* para. 53 of the Commentary on Article 12B UN Model 2021.
901. *See* paras 62 et seq. Commentary of Article 12A UN Model 2017.
902. *See* para. 64 of the Commentary on Article 12A UN Model 2021.
903. *See* para. 60 subpara. (i) of the Commentary on Article 12B UN Model 2021.
904. *See, e.g.*, the examples in paras 90 et seq. of the Commentary on Article 12A UN Model 2021.
905. *See* para. 95 of the Commentary on Article 12A UN Model 2017.
906. Similarly, with regards to certain transmission services: AAR New Delhi, *supra* n. 681.
907. *See* para. 60 subpara. (i) of the Commentary on Article 12B UN Model 2021.

of both allocation rules. In addition, the definition of ADS in Article 12B(5) UN Model does not per se exclude professional services from its scope, as these services might also meet the requirements stated therein, i.e., provision through the internet or another network and application of minimal human involvement.[908] Therefore, in the author's opinion, several professional services as mentioned in Article 14(2) UN Model but also other independent activities which are out of the scope of Article 12A UN Model (as they do not require the application of specialized knowledge, skill or expertise on behalf of a particular client) would still be within the scope of Article 12B UN Model.

The inconsistent treatment of professional services in relation to the application of Articles 12A and 12B UN Model might, according to *Báez Moreno*, be explained by the fact that the UN Tax Committee basically almost completely incorporated the concept of ADS from the OECD Pillar I project, without considering the delineation with technical services to the fullest possible extend.[909] It is, therefore, not of surprise that the explanations found in the Commentary on Article 12B UN Model do not fully deliberate on all possible interactions with regard to the application of Article 12A UN Model. In this regard, the relatively short time period to design an article on the taxation of ADS also certainly did not help to consider all possible delineations from the concept of fees for technical services.[910]

iii Room for Applicability of Article 12A UN Model

The scope of Article 12A UN Model with respect to online services is restricted in several ways. First, it has to be mentioned that Article 12A UN Model only possibly applies to online services conducted in a B2B context, as B2C services are explicitly excluded from the scope of Article 12A UN Model.[911] In this regard, just like Article 12B UN Model, Article 12A UN Model does also not apply to CFBs, as CFBs commonly generate revenue from the provision of services to consumers. In addition, customized online teaching services provided by educational institutions are also out of the scope of Article 12A UN Model.[912] The same applies to such services provided 'in' educational institutions, even if such teaching is not provided physically, as teaching services – whether or not being provided digitally – are not considered to have a base-eroding character.

Except for the aforementioned (explicit) exclusions, however, the scope of Article 12A UN Model in the field of online services generally includes a huge variety of services humanly customized to the needs of a specific client. Several of such services are already mentioned by the Commentary on Article 12B UN Model. They include

908. *See* para. 57 of the Commentary on Article 12B UN Model 2021.
909. *See* Báez Moreno, *supra* n. 315, at 519; OECD, *supra* n. 272, at 19 et seq.
910. *See* in this respect and regarding other inconsistencies found with respect to Article 12A UN Model: Báez Moreno, *supra* n. 315, at 519.
911. *See* Article 12A(3)(c) UN Model 2021.
912. *See* Article 12A(3)(b) UN Model 2021.

humanly customized professional services, technical support of machinery and industrial products that contain a digital component,[913] cloud-computing services that involve a higher degree of human intervention for customization, and other online services that require human involvement that is not only incidental to the automated service.

Whether or not such services are within the scope of Article 12A UN Model and whether they overlap with ADS, however, highly depends on the interpretation of the concepts of 'human involvement' and subsequently of the relevant degree of 'customization', as the latter mentioned concept is highly linked with the former, according to the Commentary on Article 12B UN Model.[914]

The Commentary on Article 12A UN Model clearly links the concept of customization to the use of specialized knowledge, skill or expertise, excluding standardized services from its scope. In contrast hereto, however, the Commentary on Article 12B UN Model does not consistently apply such concept of customization throughout the entirety of the commentary. Such inconsistent application of the aforementioned concept can be displayed by an analysis of the relevant passages of the commentary on cloud-computing services. As mentioned in *Chapter 4.C.ii.*, the Commentary on Article 12B UN Model explains that cloud-computing services require substantial human involvement to customize these services for a particular customer. However, on the other hand, 'standardized' cloud computing services might be provided to configure such services to the needs of a particular customer.[915] Therefore, the explanations on cloud-computing services do not base the concept of customization solely on the provision of specialized services, as also standardized services might be used to customize a specific service.

In contrast hereto, the explanations of the Commentary on Article 12A UN Model clearly provide – through the concept of customization – that standardized, routine services need to be distinguished from those services, requiring specialized knowledge, skill or expertise.[916] Therefore, the Commentary on Article 12B UN Model contradicts the explanations on Article 12A UN Model, as the former also expresses the possibility of customization through standardized, routine services. In addition, as customization might not only be provided by a human but also by automated solutions, the differentiation between technical services and ADS solely based on the concept of customization would not be appropriate.[917] As a result, the concept of customization does not function as a sufficient stand-alone concept to differentiate between technical services and ADS.

In the author's opinion, although not expressly included in the Commentaries on Article 12A UN Model, based on Indian jurisprudence, it seems that the criterion of human involvement would be the most decisive criterion to distinguish, whether a specific activity is regarded as technical service or ADS. In this respect, however, the

913. *See, e.g.*, para. 60 subpara. (v) of the Commentary on Article 12B UN Model 2021.
914. *See, e.g.*, para. 53 of the Commentary on Article 12B UN Model 2021.
915. *See* para. 58 subpara. (h) of the Commentary on Article 12B UN Model.
916. *See, e.g.*, para. 90 of the Commentary on Article 12A UN Model 2021.
917. *See, e.g.*, para. 53 of the Commentary on Article 12B UN Model 2021: '...for example where the user may input certain parameters into an automated system to obtain a customized result.'

degree of such involvement will be crucial to differentiate between the two aforementioned types of services. In this regard, it repeatedly needs to be mentioned that the Commentary on Article 12B UN Model does not give clear guidance on how to ascertain a 'minimal' degree of human involvement as provided in Article 12B(5) UN Model. While fully automated services will regularly be within the scope of Article 12B and not Article 12A UN Model, services that require at least some human element in the process of customization may potentially be within the scope of both allocation rules. This is because – based on Indian jurisprudence – it might be argued that already the mere existence of an (indirect) human element within the customization process, independently of its degree, suffices the requirements of the definition of technical services. In such a case, the application of Article 12A UN Model shall take precedence over Article 12B according to Article 12B(7) UN Model.

The Commentary on Article 12B UN Model also mentions situations in which some services 'amongst a bundle of automated digital services' might fall within the definition of fees for technical services and ADS.[918] In general, the approach taken by the Commentary on Article 12B UN Model is, to apply the allocation rule governing the separate service amongst such bundle of services, i.e., Article 12A and Article 12B UN Model separately.[919] However, as certain activities might not be separable from each other, the overall activity needs to be broken down into a 'substantial' part and its 'remaining elements'.[920] Where such remaining elements derive 'significant benefits' from parts that fulfil the requirements of Article 12B(5) UN Model, then the overall activities shall be covered by Article 12B UN Model. If, however, the characteristics of Article 12B(5) UN Model are only ancillary to the activity, Article 12B UN Model shall not apply.[921] In such a case, Article 12A UN Model might be applicable to the whole amount paid for the services if the service fulfils the definition of Article 12A(3) UN Model.

Unfortunately, the wording used in the Commentary on Article 12B UN Model differs from the historically evolved approach taken on 'mixed contracts' in Articles 12 and 12A UN Model,[922] possibly leading to uncertainty in the interpretation and application of complex contracts including several different service components: Although one could argue that the approach taken with respect to the breaking down of contracts including elements of Article 12B(5) UN Model only differs in nuances and is nothing more than the ancillary principle as found in the Commentaries on Articles 12 and 12A UN Model, the former mentioned concept clearly refers to 'benefits' derived from parts of the contract. The concept of 'mixed contracts' as originally found in the explanations on Article 12 OECD and UN Models, however, refers to parts that are of 'ancillary and largely unimportant character' without any reference to a specific benefit with respect to the principal part of the contract. Whether or not, however, the UN Tax Committee intended to use an approach in the Commentaries on Article 12B UN Model

918. *See* para. 61 of the Commentary on Article 12B UN Model 2021.
919. *Ibid.*
920. *See* para. 62 of the Commentary on Article 12B UN Model 2021.
921. *See* para. 62 of the Commentary on Article 12B UN Model 2021.
922. *See* Chapter 4.B.ii.2.b.

that is substantially different from the one taken on 'mixed contracts', is ultimately not determinable. However, it is certain, that the unclear distinction of services as ADS or fees for technical services and the different approaches used in the Commentaries to Articles 12A and 12B UN Model on contracts that include several different service elements, will ultimately lead to significant qualification conflicts in the future.

Lastly, it needs to be mentioned that states also have the choice to include the alternative version of Article 12A UN Model in their tax treaties. The alternative provision extends its scope to all types of services, therefore also including ADS.[923] Nevertheless, as the alternative version of Article 12A still excludes B2C payments from the definition of 'fees for services',[924] it does not fully cover the entire scope of Article 12B UN Model. The UN Tax Committee itself recognized in its proposed changes to the 2021 revision of the UN Model that the alternative provision of Article 12A significantly overlaps with Article 12B UN Model. However, the changes made to the commentary as part of its 2021 revision did not include further explanations for overlaps with respect to the scope. The text of the commentary version of Article 12A UN Model merely recommends that contracting states who are interested in the inclusion of both, the alternative version of Article 12A and Article 12B UN Model, shall fully consider whether any changes to both provisions need to be made.[925]

The alternative provision of Article 12A UN Model would provide more certainty due to the elimination of the need to define the terms 'fees for technical services' and 'automated digital services' as the alternative provision applies to all types of services. However, it only relates to payments to closely related persons as services provided to these persons may – in the view of the Commentary on Article 12A UN Model – pose the highest risk of tax base erosion in the source state.[926] In addition, source taxing rights on the basis of the alternative version of Article 12A UN Model are limited to those services that are provided in the residence state of the payer or the state where he has a PE or fixed base respectively. Therefore, the alternative version significantly deviates from Articles 12A and 12B UN Model as such a criterion is absent in these articles. It is because of these reasons that the Commentary on Article 12A UN Model suggests to 'carefully consider' the inclusion of the alternative version and Article 12B UN Model.

923. *See* for the alternative 'fees for services' provision: para. 26 of the Commentary on Article 12A UN Model 2021.
924. The alternative version of Article 12A UN Model also – just like its original version – excludes payments made to employees and for teaching in or by an educational institution in its version of paragraph 3 from the scope of Article 12A.
925. *See* Committee of Experts on International Cooperation in Tax Matters, *Proposed Changes to the UN Model including the Commentaries thereon as a consequence of the proposed inclusion of Article 12B on automated digital services*, E/C.18/2021/CRP.15 Rev.1, https://financing.desa.un.org/sites/default/files/2023-03/CRP15_Rev.1%20_Article%2012B%20Consequential%20Changes%20final.pdf (accessed 15 January 2024), para. 10.
926. *See* para. 27 of the Commentary on Article 12A UN Model 2021.

D ARTICLE 12A UN MODEL: OVERLAP WITH ARTICLES 7 AND 14 UN MODEL

i Overlap with Article 7 UN Model

1 Preliminary Remarks on Potential Overlaps

Article 7(6) UN Model gives precedence to the application of other articles of the UN Model in cases when (business) profits include items of income such as royalties[927] or fees for technical services[928] that are dealt with separately in other articles of the UN Model. The mentioned provision therefore specifically acknowledges that business profits – as a broad category of income – might also include specific income categories that are subject to the more specific allocation rules of the UN Model, leading to a primacy of application of the latter mentioned rules. Therefore, Article 7(6) UN Model gives primacy to the application of Article 12A over Article 7 UN Model with respect to fees for technical services arising in a state. The application of Article 12A UN Model results in the withholding of a tax on the gross amount of a payment up to a percentage established by the contracting states.[929] Article 12A(4) UN Model, however, provides that the application of Article 7 takes precedence over Article 12A UN Model if fees for technical services arise in the state in which the service provider has a PE, and the fees are effectively connected with such PE.[930]

2 General Remarks on Article 7 UN Model

Article 7(1) UN Model 2021 is based on the primacy of residence taxation. If an enterprise conducts business in another state through a PE situated therein, however, such state (source state) has a taxing right on the business profits of the enterprise. Therefore, source taxing rights in the context of Article 7 are inextricably linked with the existence of a PE as defined in Article 5 UN Model.

The PE principle reflects the general international consensus upheld until the inclusion of Article 12A to the 2017 update of the UN Model that business activities may only be taxed in the source state in the presence of proper participation in the source state's economic life. As will be shown in *Chapter 4.D.i.4.a.*, the PE concept was established on the basis of the brick-and-mortar economy with its characteristic being the focus on physical representation in a state either through a branch or personnel therein. Such physical representation is also reflected in the provisions of Article 5 UN Model such as through the service PE provision in Article 5(3)(b) UN Model.[931]

927. *See* Article 12 UN Model 2021.
928. *See* Article 12A UN Model 2021.
929. *See* Article 12A(2) UN Model 2021.
930. In this respect, Article 12A(4) UN Model 2021 is very similar to Articles 10(4), 11(4), 12(4), and 12B(4) UN Model 2021.
931. *See* Article 5(3)(b) UN Model 2021: 'The furnishing of services, including consultancy services, by an enterprise through employees or other personnel engaged by the enterprise for such

As Article 5 UN Model does not serve as a basis to allocate taxing rights, it must be read in conjunction with other allocation rules such as Article 7 UN Model. In this respect, it is also important to determine the object and amount of taxation that the source state is allowed to tax. Article 7(1) UN Model constitutes that the source state may only tax profits of an enterprise in the amount that is attributable to the PE (a), the sales of goods or merchandise in the source state of the same or similar kind as those sold via the PE (b), or other business activities carried on in the source state of the same or similar kind as those effected via the PE (c). Article 7(1)(b) and (c) UN Model are specific to the UN Model and are not included in the OECD Model.[932] Besides its function as a nexus requirement for the allocation of the taxing rights of business profits, the PE concept is also the basis for the attribution of profits allocated to the source state.

3 *Technical Services Covered by Article 7 UN Model*

Article 7 UN Model covers the allocation of taxing rights for business profits of an enterprise of a contracting state. The term 'business' is not defined in the UN Model. The OECD Model 2017, however, includes the following definition of the term 'business' in Article 3(1)(h):

> (h) The term 'business' includes the performance of professional services and of other activities of an independent character.

The definition was included in the OECD Model 2000 because Article 14 was deleted from it. It intends to ensure that the term 'business' is not interpreted in a restrictive way and therefore also explicitly including income from the performance of professional services or other activities of an independent character in its scope.[933]

As the UN Model still specifically addresses the allocation of taxing rights for income from professional or other independent activities through Article 14, the inclusion of a definition of the term 'business' in Article 3 UN Model does not seem to be necessary. However, in the case that contracting states decide to deviate from the provisions of the UN Model and not include Article 14 UN Model in their tax treaty, the Commentary on Article 5 UN Model recommends including Article 3(1)(h) OECD Model 2017 in their tax treaty.[934] This inclusion should then ensure that income from professional services and other independent activities is covered by the provisions of Articles 5 and 7 UN Model.

Whether technical services as defined in Article 12A(3) UN Model are covered by Article 7 UN Model is also dependent upon the interpretation of the term 'business'. From a historical perspective, services such as technical services were regularly

---

purpose, but only if activities of that nature continue within a Contracting State for a period or periods aggregating more than 183 days in any 12-month period commencing or ending in the fiscal year concerned.'

932. *See* para. 6 of the Commentary on Article 7 UN Model 2021.
933. *See* para. 10.2 of the Commentary on Article 3 OECD Model 2017.
934. *See* paras 45 et seq. of the Commentary on Article 5 UN Model 2021.

covered by either the article on business profits or independent personal services. Since the 1928 Draft Model Treaty of the League of Nations, no distinction has been made between the sale of goods or the provision of services as any income from industrial, commercial, and agricultural undertakings or trade or professions has been regarded as business income.[935] *Sasseville,* however, pointed out that an issue arose in the past with respect to the question of whether 'technical fees' are within the scope of Article 7 OECD and UN Models due to their specific treatment under domestic law of developing countries. Some developing countries concluded that 'technical fees' are subject to source taxation based on Article 21 UN Model and disregard Article 7's applicability.[936] This is mainly due to the fact that tax administrations and courts often referred to concepts of domestic law in the past based on the logic that, when a tax treaty does not address a specific type of income (such as fees for technical services), it cannot be automatically concluded that it corresponds to business income.[937] This view is also based on the fact that the term 'includes' in the definition of 'business' in Article 3(1)(h) OECD Model implies a non-exhaustive definition. Therefore, except for professional services or other activities of an independent character, it would still be possible to have recourse to an interpretation based on domestic law.[938]

However, before there can be recourse to domestic law, the context in which business profits are embedded within the OECD and UN Models must be considered.[939] Based on the interaction between Article 7 and the other allocation rules, Article 7 OECD and UN Models apply to all independent activities of a short- or long-term character with the exception of holding or asset management activities.[940] Therefore, also fees for technical and other similar services, such as construction or maintenance work on submarine cables,[941] would be covered by Article 7 UN Model as a 'species of business profits'.[942]

Article 7 UN Model does not restrict its scope to business profits provided in a B2B context.[943] It therefore also applies to technical services provided to individual customers. In addition, Article 7 UN Model is relevant for routine and specialized services provided on behalf of a customer as part of its regular course of business. As

935. *See* with a thorough analysis of the treatment of taxation of services in the Model Treaties drafted by the League of Nations: Souza de Man, *supra* n. 433, at 56 et seq.
936. Jacques Sasseville, *'Enterprise', 'Business' and 'Business Profits': From the League of Nations to the Current OECD Model Tax Convention*, in: *Maisto* (ed.), *The Meaning of 'Enterprise', 'Business' and 'Business Profits' under Tax Treaties and EU Tax Law* vol. 7, 85, at footnotes 13 and 14 (IBFD 2011).
937. *See, e.g.*, Eduardo Orellana Polo, *The 'Other Income' Article in Tax Treaties as Interpreted by the Courts: A Case Law Analysis*, 71 BIT 3/4, at footnote 13 (2017) DOI: 10.59403/3e6qpy0.
938. Alexander Rust, *'Business' and 'Business Profits'*, in: *Maisto* (ed.), *The Meaning of 'Enterprise', 'Business' and 'Business Profits' under Tax Treaties and EU Tax Law* vol. 7, 85, 94 (IBFD 2011); *see also* Supreme Court of the United Kingdom, *Fowler v. The Commissioners for Her Majesty's Revenue and Customs*, [2020] UKSC 22, para. 106 (20 May 2020).
939. *See* Article 3(2) OECD Model 2017 and UN Model 2021.
940. *See, e.g.*, Rust, *supra* n. 938, at 95.
941. *See, e.g.*, Superior Tribunal de Justiça, *Alcatel-Lucent Submarine Networks S.A. v. Fazenda Nacional*, Case 1.618.897 - RJ 2016/0208110-5 (26 May 2020).
942. *See* ITAT Ahmedabad, *Welspun Corporation Ltd. v. Deputy Commissioner of Income Tax*, ITA No. 48/Rjt/2015, para. 28 (3 January 2017).
943. *See* Article 12A(3)(c) UN Model 2021.

a result, it can be mentioned that Article 7 UN Model applies to all technical services covered by Article 12A UN Model. Whether source taxing rights are established, however, depends on the existence of a PE in the source state.[944] The following chapters will provide an overview of the requirements to establish a PE and will particularly also display the application of the service PE concept of the UN Model.

4 *Precedence of the Fixed Place of Business Concept*

a The Application of the Fixed Place of Business Concept to Services in the UN Model

Article 5(1) UN Model defines the term permanent establishment as a 'fixed place of business through which the business of an enterprise is wholly or partly carried on'. This definition therefore emphasizes the essential nature of a PE as a 'fixed place of business'.[945] The PE concept was first established by German states in the nineteenth century. The term that was used to describe the concept of a PE was 'stehendes Gewerbe' which might be translated as 'a trade with a fixed place of business'.[946] What is known as the 'Betriebsstätte' is that the German term for permanent establishment was also used in the area of non-tax law and was codified into Prussian tax law in 1891.[947] This concept was first used in the context of a tax treaty in the tax treaty between the Austro-Hungarian Empire and Prussia that was signed on 21 June 1899. Based on its provision, business profits were to be taxed in the state in which the 'Betriebsstätte' was located.[948] The Austro-Hungarian Empire and Prussia also included examples of the types of establishments that may constitute a PE in their tax treaty.[949]

In its preparations for a draft model treaty, the League of Nations included a provision on the taxation of business profits attributable to a PE in 1927.[950] The term 'permanent establishment' was broadly defined as 'real centres of management,...branches, factories, agencies, warehouses, offices, depots' and also included 'affiliated companies' within its scope.[951] The reference to 'affiliated companies', however, was ultimately deleted for the purposes of the 1928 Draft Model Treaty.

944. *See* Article 7(1) UN Model 2021.
945. *See* para. 3 of the Commentary on Article 5 UN Model 2021.
946. *See* Arvid A. Skaar, *Permanent Establishment: Erosion of a Tax Treaty Principle* vol. 13, 72 with further references (Kluwer Law and Taxation 1991).
947. *See* John F. Avery Jones et al., *The Origins of Concepts and Expressions Used in the OECD Model and Their Adoption by States*, 60 BIT 220, 233 (2006) DOI: 10.59403/ryv1h1.
948. Kobetsky, *supra* n. 309, at 110.
949. Avery Jones et al., *supra* n. 947, at 234: '... Branch offices, factories, storage facilities, offices, purchase and sale facilities and other business establishments used for the performance of standing enterprises by the entrepreneur himself, business partners, authorised agents or other permanent agents.'
950. League of Nations, *Double Taxation and Tax Evasion: Report presented by the Committee of Technical Experts on Double Taxation and Tax Evasion*, C.216.M.85 (12 April 1927).
951. Kobetsky, *supra* n. 309, at 122 et seq.

In the following decades, the needs of developing countries were especially considered in the 1943 Mexico Model. It was mainly drafted by a subcommittee of the League of Nations Fiscal Committee based on the result of two meetings in Mexico City in 1940 and 1943. As the subcommittee meetings were mostly attended by representatives from the least developed Latin-American states, the result of a more source-based draft model was therefore expected.[952]

Based on the 1943 Mexico Model, the source state had a taxing right on the profits of an enterprise if it did more than just carry out 'isolated or occasional transactions' in the source state.[953] The 1946 London Model reintroduced the PE principle as it required the existence of a fixed place of business to allocate a taxing right for business profits to the source state.[954] The PE concept is defined in Article 5(1) of the Protocol to the 1946 London Model and requires the existence of a fixed place of business that contributes to the business earnings of an enterprise.[955]

Based on Article 5 of the Protocol to the 1946 London Model, further work has been performed by Working Party 1 (WP 1) with the ultimate goal to finalise a provision on the allocation of taxing rights on business profits for the 1963 OECD Model. In parallel, Working Party 10 (WP 10) worked on a provision on 'professional services' that was greatly influenced by the PE principle of the 1946 London Model and of the state practice of former OEEC[956] Member States.[957]

In contrast to the 1943 Mexico and the 1946 London Models, the 1963 OECD Model included a PE definition directly in the text of the model itself. According to Article 5(1) OECD Model 1963, a PE is 'a fixed place of business in which the business of the enterprise is wholly or partly carried on'. The PE definition has basically remained unchanged until today and is – with a small textual change[958] – also found in the OECD Model 2017. The essential characteristic of a PE is its distinct *situs*, i.e., a fixed place of business.[959] With the OECD Model 1963, the OECD also introduced the concept of 'fixed base' in relation to independent personal services to the OECD Model.[960] The concepts of 'permanent establishment' and 'fixed base' are not substantially different from each other as Articles 7 and 14 are based on the same principles. The OECD, however, expressed the view that the term 'permanent establishment' shall be reserved for commercial and industrial activities.[961] The concept of a 'fixed base' has

952. Skaar, *supra* n. 946, at 88.
953. League of Nations Fiscal Committee, *supra* n. 739, C.88.M.88.1946.II.A., at 13.
954. Skaar, *supra* n. 946, at 90.
955. League of Nations Fiscal Committee, *supra* n. 739, C.88.M.88.1946.II.A., at 14.
956. The Organization for European Economic Co-Operation (OEEC) was the predecessor organization of the Organization for Economic Co-operation and Development (OECD) until 1961.
957. Souza de Man, *supra* n. 433, at 77 et seq.
958. According to the OECD Model 2017, a PE is a fixed place of business 'through' which business activities are carried out. In contrast hereto, Article 5(1) OECD Model uses the term 'in'. The word 'through' has been added to the PE definition as part of the 1977 revision of the OECD Model.
959. *See* para. 2 of the Commentary on Article 5 OECD Model 1963.
960. *See* Article 14 OECD Model 1963.
961. *See* para. 3 of the Commentary on Article 14 of the OECD Model 1963.

neither been defined in the OECD Model itself nor in its commentaries which led to increasing uncertainty in interpreting it.[962]

While the Commentaries to the OECD Model 1963 did not provide additional thorough explanations on the definition of a 'fixed place of business', the Commentaries to the OECD Model 1977 specified its criteria:[963]

- 'fixed': the establishment of a certain degree of permanence at a distinct geographical point, and
- 'place of business': a physical facility such as a premise or even machinery.

The wording of Article 5(1) OECD Model 1977 has been adopted by the UN for the purposes of its first UN Model without deviations. It also accepted the OECD's interpretation of the PE definition by incorporating the text of the Commentary on Article 5 OECD Model 1977 to the corresponding commentary of the UN Model 1980. The same is true with respect to the concept of a 'fixed base'.

In relation to the tax treatment of services, however, it must be mentioned that the concept of a 'fixed place of business' is less relevant within the UN Model than under the OECD Model. This is owed to the inclusion of a 'deemed' service PE provision in Article 5(3)(b) to the UN Model 1980. As it does not require the existence of a fixed place of business in the source state, the cited explanations from the commentary to the OECD Model on commercial and geographical coherence carry less significance than under the traditional concept of a PE.[964]

Nevertheless, the concepts of and explanations for 'permanent establishment' and 'fixed base' remained basically unchanged until the UN Model 2021. Their relevance to the taxation of services, however, has been significantly reduced since the addition of Article 12A to the UN Model 2017, on the one hand, and the inclusion of Article 12B to the UN Model 2021 on the other hand. This is because the UN Tax Committee regarded the concepts of a PE and a fixed base as being overly restrictive in a digitalized business environment as enterprises are able to have a significant economic presence in a state without the need of establishing a fixed (physical) place of business therein.[965] Therefore, taxing rights for fees for technical services and income from automated digital services are allocated to the payer's residence state without any requirement of physical activity of the service provider therein. At the same time, the UN Tax Committee also included alternative wordings and changes to the text of other articles if states wished to delete or not include Article 14 UN Model on independent personal services in their tax treaties.[966]

The introduction of Articles 12A and 12B to the UN Model, however, does not mean that the concepts of a PE and fixed base have been abolished or have become completely redundant. Articles 12A and 12B UN Model still include a rule referring to the precedence of the PE and the fixed base concept in the event that activities are

962. Souza de Man, *supra* n. 433, at 80.
963. *See* paras 2 and 4 of the Commentary on Article 5 of the OECD Model 1977.
964. *See* para. 9 of the Commentary on Article 5 of the UN Model 2021.
965. *See* para. 2 of the Commentary on Article 12A UN Model 2021.
966. *See* paras 15.1 et seq. of the Commentary on Article 5 UN Model 2021.

within the scope of application of Article 12A or 12B UN Model. The payee must constitute a PE or fixed base in the source state to which fees for technical services or income from automated digital services are effectively connected.[967] Nevertheless, increasing digitalization and a change in business models of enterprises force policy-makers to rethink the traditional PE and fixed-base concepts. In this respect, it remains to be seen how the PE concept will evolve as the Pillar I and II project of the OECD develops and how the UN Tax Committee will further respond to it. It has already prematurely incorporated a provision on the allocation of taxing rights for income from automated digital services to the UN Model 2021, i.e., Article 12B. In addition, more recently, the UN Tax Committee also published a Co-Coordinators' Report informing on the discussions of so-called Workstream B which addresses 'the function and relevance or otherwise of physical presence tests in the context of an increasingly digitalized and globalized economy'.[968] In this respect, after being consulted by *Arnold*, the Subcommittee on Taxation Issues Related to the Digitalized and Globalized Economy suggests further considering Arnold's proposal on merging Articles 5(3)(b), 12A and 14 UN Model into a new Article XX.[969] The new article XX on 'Fees for Services' will basically mirror the structure of Article 12A without the need for defining 'fees for technical services', as all types of services shall be covered by it. Just as the source rules of Article 12A UN Model, the corresponding rules of Article XX will focus on the payer-payee relationship and not the place of (physical) performance for source taxing rights to arise therein.[970] Therefore, with the adoption of proposed Article XX, the UN Tax Committee might move further away from the concept of physical presence for the reasons being 'simplification and increased coherence'.[971]

In this author's opinion, however, the proposal doesn't have a novelty character. Before the drafting process on Article 12A UN Model started, *Arnold* already preferred the inclusion of a solution addressed by the UN Tax Committee that is applicable to all types of services – and not only to those of a technical nature – in his follow-up note which was presented during the eighth session of the UN Tax Committee.[972] Two highly relevant reasons behind *Arnold's* preference were on the one hand that a definition of the term 'technical' is inherently difficult and on the other hand that the underlying principle upon which Article 12A UN Model is based, i.e., the base-erosion principle, is generally applicable to all types of services. The new proposal will address both of these issues, as the proposed Article XX will apply to fees paid in consideration for the provision of all types of services in a B2B-context[973] and will therefore also go beyond the scope of the alternative provision on 'fees for services' as already found in the Commentary on Article 12A UN Model.[974]

967. *See* Articles 12A(4) and 12B(8) UN Model 2021.
968. *See* Committee of Experts on International Cooperation in Tax Matters, *supra* n. 342, at 1.
969. *Ibid.*, at 5.
970. *Ibid.*, at 67 et seq.
971. *Ibid.*, at para. 13.
972. Committee of Experts on International Cooperation in Tax Matters, *supra* n. 147, at 4 et seq., 11 and 16.
973. *See Ibid.*, at 67 et seq.
974. *See* paras 26 et seq. of the Commentary on Article 12A UN Model 2021.

b *'Fixed' Place of Business*

One of the characteristics of the 'fixed place of business concept' is the establishment of a business at a 'distinct place'.[975] Therefore, the place of business needs to be connected to a certain geographical point.[976] Such a connection, however, does not mean that the place of business needs to be fixed to the soil. It is sufficient that it remains at a specific geographical location. Therefore, even a ship that is – by its nature – not connected to the soil might fulfil the requirement of being 'fixed' if its operation is restricted to a certain geographical area.[977] The same might apply to drilling rigs on the sea if they are operated in a specific geographical area within one state. These – as well as ships – however, still need to fulfil the temporal threshold test which is inherent to the 'fixed place of business' concept.[978]

c *The Temporal Threshold Test*

Article 5(1) OECD and UN Models do not set a temporal threshold for a fixed place of business to exist. The term 'fixed', however, implies that business activities connected to a place of business are required to exist for a specific period of time, i.e., they need to have a certain degree of permanency.[979] In this respect, the Commentaries to the OECD and UN Models mention that state practice has shown that the criterion of permanency is fulfilled if business is carried on in a state through a place of business for more than six months.[980]

Nevertheless, the Commentaries on Article 5 OECD and UN Models also acknowledge the fact that, due to the nature of certain businesses or seasonal environmental conditions, activities might only be conducted for periods of less than six months. One example might be the provision of drilling operations in an arctic location that are expected to be conducted yearly for approximately three months over a period of several years. In such a case, the seasonal conditions do not allow drilling operations for more than three months. Therefore, the six-month threshold cannot be strictly applied in such a case as it would disregard the specific nature of the business and the inherent surrounding seasonal environmental conditions. In those cases in which activities of more than six months are not achievable due to environmental conditions but are recurring on a yearly basis ('recurring activities'), each period of business activities needs to be considered in combination with the number of times during

975. *See* para. 3 of the Commentary on Article 5 UN Model 2021.
976. *See* para. 21 of the Commentary on Article 5 OECD Model 2017.
977. *See* para. 26 of the Commentary on Article 5 OECD Model 2017.
978. *See* Maximilian Görl & Christoph Gradl, *Artikel 5 Betriebstätte*, in: Roland Ismer (ed.), *Doppelbesteuerungsabkommen*, at m.no. 31 (7th ed., C.H. Beck 2021).
979. *See* para. 28 of the Commentary on Article 5 OECD Model 2017 and para. 11 of the Commentary on Article 5 UN Model 2021 with reference to the relevant provisions of the Commentary on Article 5 OECD Model 2017.
980. *See* para. 28 of the Commentary on Article 5 OECD Model 2017 and para. 11 of the Commentary on Article 5 UN Model 2021 with reference to the relevant provisions of the Commentary on Article 5 OECD Model 2017.

which the place of business is used.[981] In this regard, the temporal requirement would be met due to the recurring nature of activities over several years irrespective of the fact that the six-month threshold is not met within one specific year.

The application of the proposed six-month threshold is also offset in cases in which a business is carried out solely in one state. For example, Mr A who is a resident of State A solely carries on catering services in State B for approximately four months and uses his house as place of business for this purpose. As Mr A's catering business is solely carried out in State B, the economic link is sufficient to justify the fulfilment of the 'permanency' criterion.[982] A small minority of members of the UN Tax Committee, however, do not agree with the fact that the test of permanency is not met in State B if Mr A also carries out catering services in other states. These members still consider that the fulfilment of the proposed six-month threshold would also be offset in such a case.[983]

While the Commentaries on Article 5 OECD and UN Models indicate that the conduct of business activities above the six-month threshold fulfils the criterion of permanency, they do not set a minimum threshold that has – in any case – to be met in order to fulfil the temporal threshold test. Such a minimum threshold is controversial in the international context due to differing state practices and jurisprudence and also cannot be derived from the explanations in the Commentaries to the OECD and UN Models.[984]

d *'At the Disposal Of'*

The concept of 'at the disposal of' is not defined in the OECD and UN Models. The commentaries to both models, however, mention it as a requirement that must be fulfilled to ascertain whether a 'place of business' exists.[985]

Technical services in the sense of Article 12A(3) UN Model are often partly or wholly conducted on the premises of the service recipient in the source state. Whether such activities constitute a service provider's place of business in the source state is subject to the availability of a certain amount of space therein. In addition, such space needs to be at the disposal of the service provider and used for the conduct of his or her

981. *See* para. 29 of the Commentary on Article 5 OECD Model 2017 and para. 11 of the Commentary on Article 5 UN Model 2021 with reference to the relevant provisions of the Commentary on Article 5 OECD Model 2017; *see also* with respect to illustrative examples: Jonathan Schwarz, *Permanent Establishment: Geographic and Temporal Issues*, in: Guglielmo Maisto (ed.), *New Trends in the Definition of Permanent Establishment* vol. 17, 15, at footnote 20 (IBFD 2019).
982. *See* para. 29 of the Commentary on Article 5 OECD Model 2017 and para. 11 of the Commentary on Article 5 UN Model 2021 with reference to the relevant provisions of the Commentary on Article 5 OECD Model 2017.
983. *See* para. 12 of the Commentary on Article 5 UN Model 2021.
984. Stefan Bendlinger, *Art 5 Betriebstätte*, in: Dietmar Aigner, Georg Kofler & Michael Tumpel (eds), *DBA-Kommentar*, at m.no. 116 (Linde Verlag 2017).
985. *See* paras 10 et seq. of the Commentary on Article 5 OECD Model 2017 and para. 4 of the Commentary on Article 5 UN Model 2021 with reference to the relevant provisions of the Commentary on Article 5 OECD Model 2017.

business activities.[986] The existence of a formal right to use such a place, however, is not required.[987]

Whether the place of business is at the disposal of a service provider depends on 1) the effective power to make use of the location, 2) the time of presence at the location, and 3) the activities performed therein.[988] These requirements are fulfilled if the service provider is allowed to use premises belonging to the service recipient at a specific location on a continuous basis for a longer period of time. Therefore, if a painter performs his or her most important business functions (i.e., painting) three days a week for approximately two years in the main client's office building, the painter constitutes a PE therein.[989] A different result might be achieved if the painter provided his services in the same office building for different unrelated clients. In such a case, no coherent economic entity exists, and the office building could – irrespective of the geographic coherence – not be considered a place of business constituting a PE.[990] In the author's opinion, such logic may also be applied in regard to the constitution of a PE by a consultant who regularly provides technical services in the sense of Article 12A(3) UN Model to a client at their premises for a longer period of time.

Not all OECD Member States, however, share such a view as they included an observation on the interpretation of Article 5(1) OECD Model as expressed by the aforementioned 'painter example'.[991] The 'painter example', as reflected in the commentary, does not specifically make reference to the possibility of the location at which services are provided being at the disposal of the painter. It merely stipulates that the core business activities need to be rendered during a specific period of time at the location of the service recipient. It therefore emphasizes the importance of 'geographic' and 'economic' coherence as requirements that need to be fulfilled for a place of business to exist. It also indicates that the requirement 'at the disposal of' is – more or less – just the mere possibility of using a place, such as an office building, for the business purposes of an enterprise during a specific period of time. Contrary to this view, the German Bundesfinanzhof (BFH) decided that the mere use of a place for business purposes is not sufficient enough to have 'disposal of' such a place.[992] In accordance with the view of the BFH, an enterprise needs to have the possibility to use the relevant business place irrespective of the presence of another enterprise or customer therein.[993]

The question of fulfilment of the criteria to establish a PE is of significant importance. This is because Article 12A(4)(a) UN Model gives precedence to the application of Article 7 UN Model if fees for technical services are effectively connected with a PE and borne by it. In this respect, the inclusion of the aforementioned 'painter

986. *See* para. 10 of the Commentary on Article 5 OECD Model 2017 and para. 4 of the Commentary on Article 5 UN Model 2021 with reference to the relevant provisions of the Commentary on Article 5 OECD Model 2017.
987. *See* para. 11 of the Commentary on Article 5 OECD Model 2017.
988. *See* para. 12 of the Commentary on Article 5 OECD Model 2017.
989. *See* para. 17 of the Commentary on Article 5 OECD Model 2017.
990. *See, e.g.*, Bendlinger, *supra* n. 984, at m.no. 41 with further references.
991. *See, e.g.*, para. 178 of the Commentary on Article 5 OECD Model 2017.
992. *See* Bundesfinanzhof, X R 174/96, BStBl. II 2001, 734 (13 September 2000).
993. *See* Görl & Gradl, *supra* n. 978, at m.no. 27.

example' to the OECD Model in 2003 shows that – even among OECD members – the mere continuous presence of a service provider in the payer's residence state to provide services therein may already establish a PE without the requirement of having an own fixed place of business therein. This view is already reflected in the UN Model through the inclusion of a service PE provision in Article 5(3)(b) UN Model since the UN Model 1980 and by the OECD through the inclusion of one in the commentary update of 2008. As will be shown in *Chapter 4.D.i.g.*, the service PE provision of Article 5(3)(b) UN Model played a crucial part in the taxation of fees for technical services up until the inclusion of Article 12A to the UN Model 2017.

e *Fees Effectively Connected with a Fixed Place of Business in the Source State*

Whether fees for technical services are 'effectively connected' with a PE as provided in Article 12A(4) UN Model must be determined on a case-by-case basis and depends on the degree that these services are closely related or connected with a PE and their similarity to the activities carried out through it.[994] The terminology used in Articles 10(4), 11(4), 12(4), 12A(4), and 12B(8) UN Model is different from that in Article 7(1) UN Model as the latter-mentioned provision refers to profits 'attributable to' a PE. According to *Báez Moreno*, however, both concepts should not be interpreted differently.[995] This view is supported by the fact that the Commentaries on Articles 10(4), 11(4), 12(4), and 21(2) OECD Model include clarification that 'effectively connected' should be understood as being in accordance with the explanations on Article 7 OECD Model, i.e., on the attribution of profits according to the Authorized OECD Approach (AOA).[996] However, as the UN Model does not incorporate the AOA in its commentaries, such explicit clarifications or statements are omitted.[997] Nevertheless, *Pijl* considers that the paragraphs introduced to the commentary of the OECD Model 2010 are also perfectly applicable to the pre-2010 interpretation of Article 7 OECD Model which would, in the author's opinion, then also apply to Article 7 UN Model 2021 as the latter-mentioned provision is largely based on Article 7 OECD Model 2008.[998] This is due to the fact that the aforementioned explanations are only a clarification from what has already been understood during the time the concept of 'effectively connected' was developed in the 1950s and 1960s, i.e., as 'forming part of the business property'.[999] As a result, the rules on the attribution of profits to a PE as understood in relation to Article 7 OECD Model 2008 would also apply to the interpretation of the term 'effectively connected' in Article 12A(4) UN Model.

994. *See* para. 106 of the Commentary on Article 12A UN Model 2021.
995. *See* Báez Moreno, *supra* n. 6, at 295.
996. *See* Hans Pijl, *Capital Gains: The History of the Principle of Symmetry, the Internal Order of Article 13 and the Dynamic Interpretation of the Changes in the 2010 Commentary on 'Forming Part' and 'Effectively Connected'*, 5 WTJ 3, 7 (2013) DOI: 10.59403/6ajcts.
997. *See* para. 1 of the Commentary on Article 7 UN Model 2021.
998. *See* para. 1 of the Commentary on Article 7 UN Model 2021.
999. *See* Pijl, *supra* n. 996, at 7.

f Force-of-Attraction Rule

The limited force-of attraction-rule of Article 7(1)(b) and (c) is distinctive for the UN Model as a similar rule is not present in the OECD Model.[1000] It allows source states to not only tax business profits directly attributable to a PE but also those profits that arise from the sale of goods or merchandise of the same or similar type as those sold via the PE[1001] or other business activities as those effected via the PE.[1002] The application of the limited force-of-attraction rule, however, is restricted to business activities falling under Article 7 UN Model and does not extend to income from capital such as dividends, interest, and royalties.[1003] The limited force-of-attraction rule, however, applies to services of all kinds. Consequently, it also applies to technical services. If fees for technical services are therefore similar to those activities effected through a PE, such services are – if not already directly connected to a PE – taxable in the source state through the application of the limited force-of-attraction rule.[1004]

The limited-force-of-attraction rule is controversial among members of the UN Tax Committee as some members pointed out that this rule was abandoned in a certain number of tax treaties due to the undesirable outcome of taxing income from activities that were totally unrelated to the PE.[1005] On the other hand, however, such an outcome was welcomed by other members due to the ease of administrability and the abandonment of the need to consider whether specific activities are related to the PE.[1006]

Neither under Article 7(1)(b) nor (c) UN Model do the mentioned activities need to be conducted through or connected with a PE – including a service PE as defined in Article 5(3)(b) UN Model – in the source state. Therefore, several practical problems might occur for projects such as engineering or construction that are rendered cross-border. For these projects, technical services in the form of architectural or other engineering services are often rendered from an office in the residence state of the service provider and therefore outside the source state. Therefore, the question arises of how much of the profits arising from these activities are taxable in the source state based on the limited force-of-attraction rule.

Clearly, under the current rules of Articles 5 and 7 UN Model, activities falling under Article 7(1)(b) and (c) must be performed in the source state. Therefore, any activities performed in the residence state of the service provider would not be within the scope of Article 7(1)(b) and (c) UN Model.[1007] Nevertheless, it must be mentioned that architectural and engineering services will most likely fall under the definition of Article 12A(3) UN Model and grant the source state a taxing right on the gross amount of the fees paid for such services. If the service provider, however, finally establishes

1000. The OECD described the general force-of-attraction-rule as being rejected in international tax treaty practice: para. 10 of the Commentary on Article 7 OECD Model 2010.
1001. *See* Article 7(1)(b) UN Model 2021.
1002. *See* Article 7(1)(c) UN Model 2021.
1003. *See* para. 6 of the Commentary on Article 7 UN Model 2021.
1004. *See* para. 106 of the Commentary on Article 12A UN Model 2021.
1005. Michael Lennard, *The UN Model Tax Convention as Compared with the OECD Model Tax Convention – Current Points of Difference and Recent Developments*, 15 APTB 4, 7 (2009).
1006. *See* para. 6 of the Commentary on Article 7 UN Model 2021.
1007. *See* paras 13 et seq. of the Commentary on Article 7 UN Model 2021.

a PE in the source state (e.g., through construction activities), the rules of Article 7(1)(c) shall apply to any technical services carried on in the source state related to such PE. In that case, gross taxation will switch to net taxation.

g *Relationship with the Deemed Services PE of the UN Model*

(i) General Remarks

The UN Model had included a service PE provision in Article 5(3)(b) already since the UN Model 1980. The deemed service PE provision of Article 5(3)(b) UN Model encompasses all types of services, 'including consultancy services' that are also explicitly covered by the definition of Article 12A(3) UN Model. Although consultancy services would already be covered by the general term 'furnishing of services', the explicit inclusion of consultancy services in the wording of Article 5(3)(b) UN Model is – from a historic point of view – based on the fact that non-resident service providers generate significant revenue from the performance of management and consultancy services in developing countries.[1008] This argument was, *inter alia*, also used to initiate discussions on the inclusion of a separate article on the taxation of fees for technical services (including management and consultancy services) as part of the 2017 revision of the UN Model.[1009]

The inclusion of a deemed service PE provision was of the utmost importance for developing countries before Article 12A was introduced to the UN Model 2017 as especially consulting and management services are commonly provided without a fixed place of business in the source state. Therefore, the general PE provision of Article 5(1) UN Model would not have been applicable to such services due to the missing degree of permanence at a distinct geographical point in the source state.

As a result, the application of the service PE shall especially ensure source taxing rights for payments in consideration for technical, management, and consultancy services provided (with)in the source state without a fixed base therein. Bearing in mind that the state practice of several non-OECD Member States to tax fees for technical and other similar services dates back to the 1970s, it is not unexpected that these states were inclined to introduce a service PE provision that reflects their state practice on source taxation of technical and other similar services to some degree.

In contrast hereto, the OECD Model does not include a service PE provision. In this respect, the Commentary on Article 5 OECD Model notes that payments in consideration for services should generally be subject to source taxation in the same way as other business activities.[1010] Therefore, the fixed place of business concept as embedded in Article 5(1) OECD and UN Models shall also apply to (technical) services. The concept behind the equal treatment of the provision of services and other business

1008. *See* para. 23 of the Commentary on Article 5 UN Model 2021.
1009. *See* Committee of Experts on International Cooperation in Tax Matters, *supra* n. 139, at para. 71.
1010. *See* para. 132 of the Commentary on Article 5 OECD Model 2017.

activities, such as the export of goods, is to not increase the compliance or administrative burden of taxpayers and tax administrations.[1011] In addition, the OECD also considers difficulties in the determination of profits and tax collection as reasons why the taxation of profits derived from services in the source state without the existence of a fixed place therein as not necessarily representing an optimal tax treaty policy.[1012] It is, *inter alia*, for these reasons that the OECD did not include a specific service PE provision in the OECD Model.

Nevertheless, the OECD recognized that several OECD- and non-OECD Member States do not necessarily agree with the application of the principle of exclusive residence taxation if service providers are substantially involved within their countries' economies by providing services therein. Therefore, the OECD concluded that source taxation might be justified under certain circumstances. According to the Commentary on Article 5 OECD Model 2008, taxation of services: 1) shall not extend to services performed outside the source states' territory, 2) shall apply to profits and not to payments arising from the provision of services, and 3) a certain degree of (physical) presence shall be required to allow source taxation.[1013] Based on the aforementioned characteristics, the OECD drafted a service PE provision that has been included in the Commentary on Article 5 OECD Model since its 2008 update.

(ii) Differences and Similarities Between the Deemed Service PE Provision in the UN Model and the Alternative Version of the Commentary to the OECD Model 2008

The service PE provision of Article 5(3)(b) UN Model encompasses:

> the furnishing of services, including consultancy services, by an enterprise through employees or other personnel engaged by the enterprise for such purpose, but only if activities of that nature continue within a Contracting State for a period or periods aggregating more than 183 days in any 12-month period commencing or ending in the fiscal year concerned.

Article 5(3)(b) UN Model addresses situations in which the mere furnishing of services 'within' a contracting state might lead to the establishment of a PE even in the absence of a fixed place of business therein. The service PE provision therefore extends the scope of the general PE rule of Article 5(1) UN Model to also deem a PE to exist if an enterprise furnishes services in a contracting state for a period of 183 days or more within a twelve-month period. As already mentioned, such an extension is specifically relevant for the provision of technical and other similar services as the provision of such often does not require the establishment of a fixed place of business in the source state.

1011. *See* para. 133 of the Commentary on Article 5 OECD Model 2017.
1012. *See* para. 134 of the Commentary on Article 5 OECD Model 2017.
1013. *See* para. 42.22 of the Commentary on Article 5 OECD Model; the requirements found in the Commentary to the OECD Model 2008 remained unchanged since then and are also found in the most recent Commentary to the OECD Model 2017.

Article 5(3)(b) UN Model has been subject to textual changes as part of the 2017 revision of the UN Model. As part of latter mentioned revision, the notion 'for the same or a connected project' has been deleted as this wording was, on the one hand, easy to manipulate and, on the other hand, subject to interpretational problems and increasing administrative difficulties for developing countries.[1014]

As mentioned previously, an alternative service PE provision was included to the OECD Model as part of its 2008 update. It reads as follows:

> Notwithstanding the provisions of paragraphs 1, 2 and 3, where an enterprise of a Contracting State performs services in the other Contracting State:
>
> (a) through an individual who is present in that other State for a period or periods exceeding in the aggregate 183 days in any twelve-month period, and more than 50 per cent of the gross revenues attributable to active business activities of the enterprise during this period or periods are derived from the services performed in that other State through that individual, or
>
> (b) for a period or periods exceeding in the aggregate 183 days in any twelve-month period, and these services are performed for the same project or for connected projects through one or more individuals who are present and performing such services in that other State
>
> the activities carried on in that other State in performing these services shall be deemed to be carried on through a permanent establishment of the enterprise situated in that other State, unless these services are limited to those mentioned in paragraph 4 which, if performed through a fixed place of business (other than a fixed place of business to which paragraph 4.1 would apply), would not make this fixed place of business a permanent establishment under the provisions of that paragraph. For the purposes of this paragraph, services performed by an individual on behalf of one enterprise shall not be considered to be performed by another enterprise through that individual unless that other enterprise supervises, directs or controls the manner in which these services are performed by the individual.[1015]

Just as with Article 5(3)(b) UN Model, this alternative service PE provision is an extension of the general PE provision as it does not require a fixed place of business to exist in the source state. The alternative service PE provision is divided into two subparagraphs:

- Subparagraph a) aims to address situations in which a sole proprietor, partner of a partnership, or employee of an enterprise provides one or several unconnected projects in another contracting state, however, each of these projects by themselves does not exceed the 183-day threshold. In such a case, a service PE is deemed to exist if the enterprise derives more than 50% of the gross revenues from such projects, and the individual providing the services is physically present in that state for more than 183 days. Subparagraph a) therefore places emphasis on an individual's days of presence in the other contracting state instead of days of service provision. Therefore, also days in

1014. *See* para. 31 of the Commentary on Article 5 UN Model 2021.
1015. *See* para. 144 of the Commentary on Article 5 OECD Model 2017.

which no business activities are conducted will be counted for the computation of the 183-day threshold. This 'counting' rule is consistent with the principles applicable to Article 15(2)(a) OECD Model.[1016]
- Subparagraph b) differs from subparagraph a) as, on the one hand, it obviously excludes the reference to the 50% revenue threshold and, on the other hand, also refers to one or more individuals instead of just one individual as mentioned in the previous subparagraph.[1017] In addition, subparagraph b) still includes the reference to 'the same project or for connected projects' as similarly found in the service PE provision of the UN Model before its 2017 update. Moreover, in contrast to subparagraph a), subparagraph b) puts emphasis on exceeding the 183-day threshold through the provision of services and not the presence of an individual in the other contracting state.

The alternative service PE provision of the Commentary on Article 5 OECD Model does not apply if the activities are limited to those mentioned in Article 5(4) OECD Model. Therefore, services of exclusively preparatory or auxiliary character shall not be within the scope of the alternative service PE provision.[1018] Furthermore, if an enterprise enters into a contract with another enterprise to subcontract the provision of services to a third party or an associated enterprise, the provision of services by employees of the subcontractor to such third party or associated enterprise will not be taken into account for the application of subparagraph b) to the enterprise that entered into a service contract with the third party or associated enterprise.[1019]

The alternative OECD service PE provision therefore differs from Article 5(3)(b) UN Model in several aspects. One contrast is that the former does not specifically refer to 'consultancy services'. However, as already mentioned in the previous chapter, the inclusion of the wording 'including consultancy services' to Article 5(3)(b) UN Model is a mere clarification with the purpose of reflecting state practice on the taxation of fees for technical and other services of non-OECD members before Article 12A was introduced to the UN Model. What is more, besides the non-exclusion of the aforementioned aspects with respect to auxiliary activities and services carried on by subcontractors to neither Article 5(3)(b) UN Model nor its commentary thereof, the alternative OECD service PE provision also explicitly constitutes that the provision of services in the other contracting state needs to be made through individuals actually present therein.[1020] It can therefore be deduced that the general approach taken by Article 5(1) OECD Model that only activities that are actually performed within the

1016. *See* para. 157 of the Commentary on Article 5 OECD Model 2017.
1017. *See* Florian Rosenberger, Marco Vitali & Ulrich Ziehr, *Die Dienstleistungsbetriebsstätte: Internationale Entwicklungen und ihre Rezeption im Internationalen Steuerrecht Deutschlands, Österreichs und der Schweiz*, IStR-Beiheft 1, 4 et seq. (2010): Contrary to the wording of this provision, the authors still regard subparagraph a) as *a fortiori* applicable if the services are performed by more than one individual. According to para. 155 of the Commentary on Article 5 OECD Model 2017, however, this would only be the case if the enterprise derives most of its revenues from services rendered by one individual.
1018. *See* para. 169 of the Commentary on Article 5 OECD Model 2017.
1019. *See* para. 164 of the Commentary on Article 5 OECD Model 2017.
1020. *See, e.g.*, para. 152 of the Commentary on Article 5 OECD Model 2017.

territory of a state with a minimum level of (physical) presence therein shall be relevant to possibly establish a PE therein.[1021]

The requirement of the provision of services within the territory of a state with a minimum level of presence therein, however, is controversial with respect to the application of Article 5(3)(b) UN Model. The reasons thereof will be explained in the following subchapter.

(iii) 'Furnishing of Services' and 'Continue Within a Contracting State'

Article 5(3)(b) UN Model deems a PE to exist if services are furnished 'for a period or periods aggregating more than 183 days in any twelve-month period commencing or ending in the fiscal year concerned'.[1022] This provision uses the term 'furnishing' instead of 'performs' as used in the alternative service PE provision of the OECD Model. According to a minority of UN Tax Committee Members, the term 'furnishes' implies that services are 'used' or 'consumed' in the source state, therefore, also including services that are not physically rendered within the territory of the source state.[1023] In this regard, the question also arises of whether the concept of 'activities of that nature continue within a Contracting State' has to be interpreted to require the physical rendering of services in the source state. Alternatively, does the mere continuation of such activities, even if not physically performed therein, suffice for the mentioned requirement?

In this regard, the former Indian member of the UN Tax Committee - who was formally appointed in her own 'personal capacity' - expressed the following opinion during the eighth session of the UN Tax Committee:[1024]

> Ms. Kapur indicated that she agreed that the service has to be furnished to an entity in the source State, but she disagreed with the fact that the performance of the service had to take place in the source State. Ms. Kapur considered that the physical presence of personnel or employees is not required by the wording of the article, which talks about where the service is furnished and not where it is performed. The requirement that 'activities of that nature continue within a Contracting State' did not, in her view, imply 'performance' in that State — it would meet this test if the service was furnished to the Contracting State.

The UN Model does not provide clear guidance on whether the term 'furnishes' and the notion of 'activities of that nature continue within a Contracting State' require services to be physically performed in the source state. However, in the author's opinion, the term 'furnishes' does not require being read differently from other similar

1021. *See, e.g.*, para. 143 of the Commentary on Article 5 OECD Model 2017.
1022. *See* Article 5(3)(b) UN Model 2021.
1023. *See* Guillermo O. Teijeiro & Juan Manuel Vázquez, *Taxation of the Ride-Sharing Economy: Source Taxation Through Service Permanent Establishment Provisions Revisited – The Case under the Argentine Treaty Network*, 73 BIT 667, 675 (2019) DOI: 10.59403/1g1hrba.
1024. *See* Committee of Experts on International Cooperation in Tax Matters, *supra* n. 146, at para. 66; this view, however, is not supported by Indian jurisprudence: *see* ITAT New Delhi, *JC Bamford Excavators Ltd. v. Deputy Director of Income Tax*, ITA No. 540/Del/2011, at para. 6.10.1 (14 March 2014).

terms such as 'performs'. To furnish something (such as a service) to someone means to supply or provide something to someone.[1025] Similarly, the ordinary meaning of the term 'perform' means 'to do an action', such as a service.[1026] In addition, Article 5(3)(b) UN Model also includes an activity-threshold that must be met to establish a service PE. This activity threshold, in the author's opinion, implies that services need to be physically rendered in the source state. This is supported by the fact that the Commentary on Article 5 UN Model uses the concept of 'provide...in' instead of 'furnish' or 'within' to describe the involvement of non-resident service providers in the source state: 'if a non-resident provides services in a country for more than 183 days'.[1027] Lastly, the OECD also emphasizes that service PE provisions 'should not extend to services performed outside the territory of a State'.[1028] This view is also in accordance with the majority view taken by members of the UN Tax Committee as the majority view that is expressed still regards physical presence in the source state as a requirement to establish a service PE.[1029]

Nevertheless, as also stated by the minority view in the UN Model, certain non-OECD Member States do not agree with such an approach. This is reflected by the positions taken on Article 5 OECD Model 2017 of *Argentina*, *Brazil*, and *India*.[1030] Especially the last-mentioned state expressed that 'for furnishing services in a State, physical presence of an individual is not essential'.[1031] In addition, it also does not agree with the conclusion that taxation of services should not extend to services performed outside its own territory.[1032] This view is also supported by Saudi Arabia. The Saudi Arabian tax administration (DZIT) favours a broad interpretation of the service PE provision. In their opinion, a physical presence in Saudi Arabia is not required to constitute a service PE.[1033] Whether a service PE is deemed to exist depends upon the duration of the service contract between the non-resident service provider and the Saudi-Arabian service recipient. If the contract between these two foresees the performance of services in or outside Saudi Arabia that exceeds the time threshold provided in its national law, it is considered that a service PE exists.[1034]

Based on the aforementioned considerations, it appears that several non-OECD members already interpreted the UN Model's service PE provision as broadly as to tax service fees on the basis of two distinctive features of Article 12A UN Model, i.e., physical presence is not decisive to establish source taxing rights, and services

1025. *See* Oxford University Press, *Oxford Learner's Dictionaries*, https://www.oxfordlearnersdictionaries.com/definition/english/furnish?q=furnish (accessed 7 October 2022).
1026. *See, e.g.*, Cambridge University Press & Assessment, *Cambridge Dictionary*, https://dictionary.cambridge.org/dictionary/english/perform (accessed 7 October 2022).
1027. *See* para. 31 of the Commentary on Article 5 UN Model 2021.
1028. *See* para. 143 of the Commentary on Article 5 OECD Model 2017.
1029. *See* Committee of Experts on International Cooperation in Tax Matters, *supra* n. 146, at paras 68 et seq.; in line with the majority view, *see also* Chiles state practice: Sandra Benedetto & Liselott Kana, *Chile*, in: *Cahiers de droit fiscal international* vol. 97a, 191, -192 (Sdu 2012).
1030. *See* paras 34.1 et seq. of Non-Member Countries' Positions on Article 5 OECD Model 2017.
1031. *See* para. 39 of Non-Member Countries' Positions on Article 5 OECD Model 2017.
1032. *See* para. 38 of Non-Member Countries' Positions on Article 5 OECD Model 2017.
1033. *See* Teijeiro & Vázquez, *supra* n. 1023, at 675 with further references.
1034. Vladimir A. Gidirim, *Taxation of Foreign Multinational Enterprises Conducting Business in and with Saudi Arabia*, 70 BIT 230, 234 (2016) DOI: 10.59403/1kebcyg.

performed outside the source state may be taxed therein even if performed in a third state.

5 Room for Applicability of Article 12A UN Model

Article 7 UN Model covers the allocation of taxing rights for business profits. The term 'business' generally includes independent activities of a short- and long-term character.[1035] Therefore, technical services are also covered by Article 7 UN Model.[1036] While Article 12A UN Model does not apply to B2C services,[1037] Article 7 UN Model does not include a differentiation between B2C and B2B services. Article 7 UN Model therefore also applies to technical services provided in a B2C context. The applicability of Article 12A UN Model is, as a result, already on a general scale restricted to only those technical services provided in a B2B context.

Article 7(6) UN Model describes the interaction with the general rule of Article 7 UN Model and other rules that are more specific on certain types of income. In this respect, the aforementioned provision notes that income that is within the scope of business profits but also subject to allocation rules of the UN Model that are more specific shall be dealt with under these rules. Therefore, if technical services fulfil the requirements established by Article 12A UN Model, such services shall be subject to the rules described therein.

Article 12A(4) UN Model gives precedence to the application of Article 7 UN Model if technical services are provided through a PE, and fees for such services are effectively connected with it. As Article 12A(4) and Article 7(6) are interconnected with each other, Article 12A(4) needs to be construed in the context of Article 7(6) UN Model. The purpose of Article 12A(4) UN Model was to give the state in which fees for technical services are effectively connected with the permanent establishment of a non-resident service provider an uncapped taxing right. Otherwise, in the mentioned situation, the source taxing right would be constrained by Article 12A(2) UN Model.[1038] In this respect, it also needs to be mentioned that the force-of-attraction rule of Article 7(1)(c) UN Model applies to technical services. This broadens the scope of Article 7 in relation to Article 12A UN Model to technical services of the same or similar kind as those effected through a PE in the source state.[1039]

Article 5 UN Model on PEs has a broader scope than its parallel version of the OECD Model. This is, *inter alia*, due to the inclusion of a service PE provision in Article 5(3)(b) UN Model which can be considered an extension of the general principle that a fixed place of business needs to be established in the source state for a taxing right to arise therein. This provision explicitly includes consultancy services within its wording. This is due to the fact that the treaty policy of non-OECD Member States has

1035. *See, e.g.*, Rust, *supra* n. 938, at 95.
1036. *See* ITAT Ahmedabad, *supra* n. 942, at para. 28.
1037. *See* Article 12A(3)(c) UN Model 2021.
1038. *See* for a similar reasoning with respect to the allocation of taxing rights of royalty income: Federal Court of Australia-Full Court, *Tech Mahindra Ltd. v. Commissioner of Taxation*, [2016] FCAFC 130 (22 September 2016).
1039. *See* Article 12A(4)(b) UN Model 2021.

already included provisions on source taxation of these services – as well as technical and managerial services – without the fixed base requirement in its tax treaties since the 1970s. The inclusion of Article 5(3)(b) to the UN Model 1980 was therefore partially an acknowledgement of the tax treaty practice of those states including such a provision and other similar provisions in their tax treaties.

The deletion of the wording 'for the same or connected project' in Article 5(3)(b) as part of the 2017 revision of the UN Model broadens the scope of the service PE provision leading to narrowing down the scope of Article 12A UN Model in certain circumstances.[1040] Those circumstances might include situations in which technical services are provided by an enterprise for several unrelated projects during a time span of more than 183 days in the source state. As a service PE might – since the 2017 provision of the UN Model – be constituted in such a case due to the deletion of the concept 'for the same or connected project', Articles 7(1) and 5(3)(b) UN Model would take precedence over Article 12A UN Model due to the application of Article 12A(4) UN Model.

Several states, such as India, exclude considerations for any construction, assembly, mining, or like project from the definition of fees for technical services in its domestic law.[1041] From a treaty perspective, however, supervisory activities in connection with a building site, construction, assembly, or installation project as covered by Article 5(3)(a) UN Model could also be within the scope of Article 12A UN Model. Therefore, several states that wish to align the treaty definition of fees for technical services with its definition in domestic law, explicitly exclude supervisory activities in connection with these types of projects from the scope of the definition of the respective fees for technical services provision.[1042]

As already mentioned, fees for technical services are a narrower subcategory of business profits. Therefore, from a systematic point of view, Article 12A UN Model shall apply to considerations paid with respect to the aforementioned services. Article 12A UN Model allocates source taxing rights for fees for technical services already from the first payment made. In contrast hereto, Article 7 icw Article 5 UN Model will allocate taxing rights only after the fulfilment of certain thresholds such as the general criteria on the establishment of the fixed place of business (Article 5(1) UN Model) or the exceeding of the 183-day threshold of the service PE provision of Article 5(3)(b) UN Model. Article 12A UN Model is therefore also a concession to those developing countries that are opposed to the application of the 183-day threshold due to the possibility of a service provision of a brief duration without the requirement of being

1040. *See* para. 32 of the Commentary on Article 5 UN Model 2021.
1041. *See* section 9(1)(vii) of the Indian Income Tax Act.
1042. *See* in this respect: Article 12(5) DTC Ghana-Netherlands (2008): 'Provided that the term 'technical service fees' shall not include any payments in consideration for supervisory activities in connection with a building site or construction, assembly or installation project or for supervisory activities in connection with installation incidental to the sale of machinery or parts thereof…'; *see also* with respect to the definition of 'management fees': Article 13(3) DTC France-Ghana (1993), Article 13(3) DTC Ghana-Serbia and Montenegro (2000), Article 20(3) DTC Ghana-South Africa (2004), Article 18(3) DTC Belgium-Ghana (2005), Article 13(3) DTC Barbados-Ghana (2008); with respect to 'Services fees': Article 13(3) DTC Ghana-Singapore (2017) and 'Technical services fees': Article 13(3) DTC Ghana-Mauritius (2017).

physically present in a state. The reason for the time limit, however, is, *inter alia*, to encourage foreign enterprises to increasingly engage in a foreign state's economy through establishing activities of preparatory or auxiliary character such as those mentioned in Article 5(4) UN Model. These activities would then be the basis for further engagement in a developing country and the regular establishment of a PE therein.[1043]

While the application of Article 12A UN Model to services covered by the exclusion of Article 5(4) UN Model needs to be examined on a case-by-case basis, in the author's opinion, the former would generally not cover activities of mere preparatory or auxiliary character as these are mostly of a routine nature and not provided on a customized basis. The latter is especially true as the activities covered by Article 5(4) UN Model specifically aim to support the core business activities of the enterprise itself. Such activities may therefore not cover services that are rendered on behalf of another enterprise such as advertising services on its behalf.[1044] Moreover, the furnishing of plans and activities of a similar character specifically developed for an individual customer or managing an enterprise through a 'management office', including supervisory and coordinating activities, are also not regarded as being of a 'preparatory or auxiliary character'.[1045] These services form an essential component of an enterprise's business activities and therefore exceed the threshold of being merely 'preparatory or auxiliary'. They would, in most cases, fulfil the definition of fees for technical services according to Article 12A(3) UN Model and therefore be subject to taxation on a gross basis, i.e., a tax is imposed on the full amount of the service fee without a deduction of any expenses. Such a tax will – in most cases – be collected by withholding the taxable amount at the level of the payer.[1046] In contrast, hereto, net taxation would allow the source state to tax fees for technical services at a tax rate not limited by the tax treaty. Such net taxation is usually applicable if fees for these services are effectively connected with a PE of the payee therein.[1047] This is due to the fact that net taxation in the source state on the basis of the application of Article 7 UN Model may be required due to the application of the non-discrimination provision of Article 24(3) UN Model.[1048]

1043. *See* para. 25 of the Commentary on Article 5 UN Model 2021.
1044. *See* para. 18 of the Commentary on Article 5 UN Model 2021 with reference to paras 58 and 61 of the Commentary on Article 5 OECD Model 2017.
1045. *See* para. 18 of the Commentary on Article 5 UN Model 2021 with reference to para. 71 of the Commentary on Article 5 OECD Model 2017.
1046. *See, e.g.*, Freitas de Moraes e Castro & Moraes do Rego Monteiro, *supra* n. 13, at 55; Barrios Correa, *supra* n. 470, at 152 et seq.
1047. *See* Article 12A(4) UN Model 2021.
1048. *See* Article 24(3) UN Model 2021: 'The taxation on a permanent establishment which an enterprise of a Contracting State has in the other Contracting State shall not be less favourably levied in that other State than the taxation levied on enterprises of that other State carrying on the same activities. ….'

ii Overlap with Article 14 UN Model

1 Preliminary Remarks on Potential Overlaps

Independent personal services that fulfil the definition of Article 12A(3) UN Model shall be deemed to arise in the state in which the payee of the fees provides independent personal services through a fixed base and such fees are effectively connected with the fixed base.[1049] In such a case, Article 14(1)(a) UN Model takes precedence over the application of Article 12A UN Model. If, however, the payee does not have a fixed base regularly available to him in the other contracting state and technical services are not provided through it, the fees for these services will be taxed on the basis of Article 12A(2) UN Model. As a result, the source state has – irrespective of the application of either Article 12A or 14 UN Model – a taxing right on fees for technical services. The main difference in the application of Articles 12A and 14 UN Model, however, is the tax base upon which a tax is levied. While Article 12A(2) UN Model clearly provides for gross taxation of technical service fees, the application of Article 14 UN Model is – according to several scholars[1050] – based on net taxation.

2 General Remarks on Article 14 UN Model

Article 14 UN Model allocates the taxing rights on income derived from professional services and other activities of an independent character.[1051] It generally grants a taxing right to the residence state of the income recipient. However, the source state will be allocated a taxing right if the income recipient 1) has a fixed base regularly available to him in the source state for the purposes of performing his activities, or 2) his stay in the source state amounts or exceeds 183 days within a twelve-month period.[1052] Article 14(1) UN Model 1980 also included a third criterion establishing source taxing rights for independent personal activities. As mentioned in *Chapter 3.C.iii.2.*, this criterion was based on the base-erosion principle as it referred to a remuneration threshold paid by a resident of the source state.[1053] This third criterion was ultimately removed from the UN Model as part of its 2001 update.

While Article 14 has been included in the UN Model since its first version of 1980, it was deleted from the OECD Model on 29 April 2000 on the basis of the report 'Issues Related to Article 14 of the OECD Model Tax Convention' that was adopted by the Committee on Fiscal Affairs on 27 January 2000.[1054] The decision to delete Article 14 stems from the fact that the committee concluded that no practical differences between

1049. *See, e.g.*, para. 12 of the Commentary on Article 14 UN Model 2021.
1050. *See, e.g.*, Arnold, *supra* n. 6, at 62 and Alexander Rust & Benjamin Walker, *Independent and Dependent Personal Services*, in: Michael Lang et al. (eds), *The UN Model Convention and Its Relevance for the Global Tax Treaty Network* vol. 7, 71, 85 (IBFD 2017).
1051. *See* Article 14(1) UN Model 2021.
1052. *See* Article 14(1)(a) and (b) UN Model 2021.
1053. *See* Article 14(1)(c) UN Model 1980.
1054. *See* OECD, *Issues Related to Article 14 of the OECD Model Tax Convention* vol. 7, 3 (OECD Publications 2000).

Articles 7 and 14, *in concreto,* between the application and profit attribution of a PE and fixed base were apparent.[1055] In this regard, however, it also needs to be mentioned that Article 14 of the OECD Model 1998 did not include Article 14(1)(b) UN Model which also allows taxation at source if the income recipient is present in that state for more than 183 days in any twelve-month period.[1056] This is due to the fact that Article 14(1)(b) UN Model deviates from the fixed place of business concept which is not supported by OECD Member States as reflected in the OECD Model.[1057]

3 *Technical Services Covered by Article 14 UN Model*

a Independent Professional Services

(i) Scope of Services Covered

Article 14 UN Model covers the allocation of taxing rights of income derived from professional services and other activities of an independent character,[1058] but the term 'professional services' is not defined in Article 14 UN Model. Article 14(2) UN Model, however, provides a list of activities that are specifically regarded as professional services. It includes examples of typical liberal professions such as independent activities of physicians, lawyers, engineers, architects, dentists, and accountants as well as independent scientific, literary, artistic, educational, or teaching activities. In addition, Article 14(1) UN Model mentions that other activities of an independent character are also included in the scope of this provision. Such 'independent' personal services need to be differentiated from those falling under Article 15 UN Model on 'dependent' personal services. Such a distinction is also of utmost importance in relation to the application of Article 12A UN Model as dependent personal services are explicitly excluded from the scope of Article 12A according to Article 12A(3)(a) UN Model. Therefore, if, e.g., a physician, lawyer, or engineer performs professional services under an employment contract, such services would not be in the scope of Article 14 but subject to Article 15 UN Model and as a result excluded from the scope of Article 12A UN Model. Besides activities of a dependent character, Article 14 UN Model also excludes industrial and commercial activities[1059] as well as services provided by artists and sportspersons[1060] from its scope.

As the terms 'dependent' and 'independent' are not defined in the UN Model, several states hold recourse to definitions provided by their domestic law based on

1055. *See ibid.*, at 12 et seq.
1056. *See* Article 14 OECD Model 2018.
1057. *See* with respect to tax treaties concluded between OECD and non-OECD members including a provision on independent personal services: Wijnen, de Goede & Alessi, *supra* n. 3, at 34: '...as expected in tax treaties between UN and OECD countries more tax treaties (212) follow the OECD provision....'
1058. *See* Article 14(1) UN Model 2021.
1059. *See* para. 10 of the Commentary on Article 14 UN Model 2021.
1060. Jonathan Velo, *Taxation of Independent Personal Services*, in: Anna Binder & Viktoria Wöhrer (eds), *Special Features of the UN Model Convention* vol. 117, 371, 380 (Linde Verlag 2019).

Article 3(2) UN Model. Although, as expressed by *Rust/Walker*, it is not obvious that 'the context otherwise requires',[1061] several authors[1062] assume that the general criteria to distinguish 'dependent' and 'independent' services can be derived from a treaty autonomous interpretation. Based on the context in which the aforementioned terms are embedded, these authors assume that 'entrepreneurial risk' and a certain degree of 'subordination' are relevant criteria for establishing whether independent or dependent personal services are furnished.[1063] In this regard, *Lang* also points out that these two criteria may indicatively be derived from the OECD Model and its corresponding commentaries in its English and French versions.[1064]

Several tax administrations base their interpretation on the scope of 'activities of an independent character'[1065] in their domestic law due to the application of a treaty provision corresponding to Article 3(2) OECD and UN Models.[1066] However, they often disregard the prevalence of the concept 'unless the context otherwise requires' referring to the primacy of treaty autonomous interpretation. As *Lang* pointed out, the automatic recourse to domestic law might lead to undesirable results from a treaty standpoint as it potentially leads to double taxation[1067] and ultimately to an increasing number of mutual agreement procedures. Such a result, however, might likely be avoided if both contracting states would apply a treaty autonomous interpretation with regards to the interpretation of '(in)dependent' services.

(ii) Services Rendered by an Individual?

Article 14(1) UN Model refers to income derived by a resident of a contracting state. The term 'resident of a contracting state' is defined in Article 4(1) UN Model as any person who, under the laws of a contracting state, is liable to tax therein based on the connecting factors mentioned in Article 4(1) UN Model. The term 'resident of a contracting state' therefore refers to any individual, company, or other body of persons.[1068]

1061. *See* Article 3(2) UN Model and Rust & Walker, *supra* n. 1050, at 74.
1062. *See, e.g.*, Rene Kreisl, *Characterization of artistic income without public performance*, in: Walter Loukota & Markus Stefaner (eds), *Taxation of Artistes and Sportsmen in International Tax Law* vol. 51, 137, 152 (Linde Verlag 2007); Kasper Dziurdź, *Kurzfristige Arbeitnehmerüberlassung im internationalen Steuerrecht* vol. 75, 113 et seq. (Linde Verlag 2013); Alexander Hemmelrath, *Artikel 14 Selbständige Arbeit*, in: Roland Ismer (ed.), *Doppelbesteuerungsabkommen*, m.no. 12 (7th ed., Beck 2021) and Michael Lang, *Introduction to the Law of Double Taxation Conventions*, 18 (3rd ed., Linde Verlag 2021).
1063. *See* Hemmelrath, *supra* n. 1062, at m.no. 12 and Lang, *supra* n. 1062, at 71.
1064. Michael Lang, *Off-Track Interpretation of Double Taxation Treaties as Exemplified by the Taxation of Lecturers*, SWI 508, 510 (1998); *see also* Hemmelrath, *supra* n. 1062, at m.no. 13.
1065. *See* Article 14(1) UN Model 2021.
1066. *See* Frank P. G. Pötgens, *Income from Inactivity under Article 15 of the OECD Model Tax Convention – Part 1*, 63 BIT 428, 428 (2009) DOI: 10.59403/j8mtmk.
1067. Lang, *supra* n. 1064, at 508 et seq.
1068. *See* Article 3(1)(a) UN Model 2021.

Whether Article 14 UN Model applies to enterprises or only to individuals has been a subject of debate in the past.[1069] This is due to the presence of the word 'his' in Article 14 OECD Model 1998 and Article 14(1)(a) and (b) UN Model.[1070] Especially with regards to Article 14(1)(b) UN Model, the question arises whether any person other than an individual might be able to fulfil the requirement of being physically present in a state ('his stay').

In this regard, the OECD noted that the argument raised by certain states that Article 14 only applies to individuals is not convincing as Article 4(1) OECD Model also uses the term 'his' when referring to a 'resident of a contracting state'.[1071] It is therefore the view of the OECD that Article 14 OECD Model 1998 also covers the rendering of services by persons other than individuals. This was also one of the reasons why the OECD decided to delete Article 14 from the OECD Model and cover service taxation generally under Article 7 icw Article 5 OECD Model.[1072]

The UN Tax Committee, however, takes a different approach. As displayed by the Commentary on Article 14 UN Model, a distinction on the scope needs to be made with respect to the application of the service PE provision of Article 5(3)(b) UN Model in relation to Article 14(1)(b) UN Model.[1073] Both rules essentially apply the same time test, i.e., the 183-day threshold, however, both aforementioned rules intend to cover a different scope. Article 5(3)(b) UN Model covers the furnishing of services by 'an enterprise through employees or other personnel engaged by the enterprise'. Article 14(1)(b) UN Model, on the other hand, refers to a resident of a contracting state and 'his stay' in the other contracting state 'in the aggregate 183 days'. By its very nature, such a stay can only be fulfilled by individuals and not an enterprise.[1074] Therefore, the Commentary on Article 14 UN Model argues that Article 14 UN Model may, in contrast to Article 5(3)(b) UN Model, only cover services provided by individuals.[1075] The intended differing scope of application is also reflected in the Commentary on Article 5 UN Model in relation to the inclusion of alternative wording to the service PE provision of Article 5(3)(b) UN Model if states decide to not include Article 14 UN Model to their tax treaty. In this regard, the Commentary on Article 5 UN Model suggests including an

1069. *See, e.g.*, Edwin van der Bruggen, *Developing Countries and the Removal of Article 14 from the OECD Model*, 55 BIT 601, 602 (2001); Sriram P. Govind, *The International Tax Treatment of Cross-Border Services*, 66 BIT 1, at footnote 33 (2012) DOI: 10.59403/3ejy4kx and Rust & Walker, *supra* n. 1050, at 80.

1070. *See* Article 14(1)(a) and (b) UN Model 2021: '(a) if he has a fixed base regularly available to him in the other Contracting State for the purpose of performing *his activities*; in that case, only so much of the income as is attributable to that fixed base may be taxed in that other Contracting State; or (b) if *his stay* in the other Contracting State is for a period or periods amounting to or exceeding in the aggregate 183 days in any twelve-month period commencing or ending in the fiscal year concerned, in that case, only so much of the income as is derived from his activities performed in that other State may be taxed in that other State.' (the relevant wording has been italicized by the author).

1071. OECD, *supra* n. 1054, at 10.

1072. OECD, *supra* n. 1054, at 10 and 11.

1073. *See* para. 9 of the Commentary on Article 14 UN Model 2021.

1074. *See, e.g.*, Claudine Devillet & Xavier van Vlem, *Belgium*, in: *Cahiers de droit fiscal international IFA Cahiers* vol. 97a, 133, 151 (Sdu 2012).

1075. *See* paras 41 et seq. of the Commentary on Article 5 and para. 9 of the Commentary on Article 14 UN Model 2021.

additional subparagraph c to Article 5(3) UN Model explicitly covering the performance of services by individuals. The suggestion to add subparagraph c therefore reflects the general understanding of the Commentary to the UN Model that 'Article 14 deals only with individuals.'[1076]

If an individual therefore receives payments for the provision of services in his independent capacity, such services shall – subject to the fulfilment of the other requirements – be within the scope of Article 14 UN Model. On the other hand, if a payment is made to an enterprise for services provided by its employees or other personnel, such services shall be within the scope of Article 7 icw Article 5 UN Model. The subsequent remuneration paid by the enterprise to the employee would then be subject to Article 15 UN Model[1077] or, if the enterprise concluded a contract with an independent individual service provider, subject to Article 14 UN Model.[1078]

Article 12A(1) UN Model applies to payments received by a resident of a contracting state. Based on Article 4(1) UN Model, this may be any person. The term 'person' is defined in Article 3(1)(a) UN Model as 'an individual, a company and any other body of persons'. Therefore, based on the understanding of the UN Model and its commentaries, any service provider covered by Article 14 UN Model, may also qualify as a recipient of fees for technical services. This is especially true for independent personal services provided by a service provider without a fixed base in the other contracting state but fulfilling the 183-day requirement of Article 14(1)(b) UN Model. The relationship between Articles 12A and 14(1)(b) UN Model, however, is not explicitly covered by Article 12A(4) UN Model as the latter-mentioned provision only refers to the precedence of the concept of a fixed base, i.e., the application of Article 14(1)(a) UN Model. As will be shown in *Chapter 4.D.ii.3.b.*, the author therefore argues that the application of Article 12A shall take precedence over Article 14(1)(b) UN Model.

(iii) Performance of Activities

Both (a) and (b) of Article 14(1) UN Model refer to the performance of activities. In this regard, however, Article 14(1)(b) UN Model clearly refers to 'activities performed in that other state'. Therefore, according to the Commentary on Article 14 UN Model, the performance of activities is dependent upon the physical exercise of services in the source state.[1079] In contrast hereto, if a service provider has a fixed base in the source state available to him to perform his activities, neither the wording of Article 14(1)(a)

1076. *See* para. 43 of the Commentary on Article 5 UN Model 2021 and Rust & Walker, *supra* n. 1050, at 80; *See also* the reservation of the United States with respect to Article 14 UN Model 1980: United Nations, *supra* n. 359, at 144: 'The United States reserves the right to tax services performed by individuals who are present in the United States for more than 183 days during the taxable year. The United States *also believes that this Article should be limited to individuals* and to income from the performance of personal services.' (word order italicized by the author).
1077. *See* van der Bruggen, *supra* n. 1069, at 602.
1078. *See* para. 9 of the Commentary on Article 14 UN Model 2021.
1079. *See* para. 6 of the Commentary on Article 14 UN Model 2021: '...from activities exercised in that country....'

UN Model nor its commentary clarify whether activities need to be performed in the source state or if the mentioned provision also covers activities performed in a third state ('performing his activities').

In this regard, with respect to the provision of Article 14 OECD Model 1998 that is reflected in Article 14(1)(a) UN Model, *Wassermeyer* opines that the independent activity does not necessarily need to be performed in the source state. This is because this provision only requires the fulfilment of a fixed base that is regularly available in the source state 'for the purpose of performing his activities'. As the wording of Article 14(1)(a) UN Model does not provide a requirement of where independent activities need to be performed, it would be sufficient that the services provider only partially performs his activities in the source state through a fixed base therein.[1080]

Although *Arnold* partly takes a similar view as he states that income attributable to a fixed base (Article 14(1)(a) UN Model) 'could' also include that derived from activities performed outside that state but connected to the fixed base, he acknowledges that the UN Model generally establishes that only income from services performed in the source state is subject to tax therein.[1081] The latter mentioned 'general principle'[1082] is, in the author's opinion, based on the fact that the allocation of profits to a fixed base is based on the same principles that would apply to a PE. This is acknowledged by the fact that the Commentary on Article 14 UN Model makes reference to Article 14 of the OECD Model 1997, stating that the Commentary on Article 7 shall be used as a guidance to interpret and apply Article 14 UN Model.[1083] In this respect, this author already mentioned in *Chapter 4.D.i.4.e.* that only such income shall be attributable to a PE that is derived from services performed in the PE-state. In the author's opinion, this principle shall – due to the similarities of the concepts of PE and fixed base – also apply to Article 14(1)(a) UN Model and the concept of fixed base.

As mentioned in *Chapter 4.A.i.3.*, in contrast to Article 14 UN Model, the source rules of Article 12A UN Model are based on the base-erosion principle. According to it the mere possibility to deduct payments for fees for technical services sufficiently justifies the allocation of source taxing rights to the state where such fees might be deductible as business expenses, irrespective of the place of performance of technical services. It therefore follows from the extraterritorial application of this source rule that the deductible payment may also include payments for technical services 'physically' rendered in a third state.

1080. Franz Wassermeyer, *OECD-MA 2017 Art. 14,* in: Franz Wassermeyer, Christian Kaeser, Michael Schwenke & Klaus-Dieter Drüen (eds), *DBA*, m.no. 81 (158th ed., C.H. Beck 2022).

1081. Brian J. Arnold, *The Taxation of Income from Services under Tax Treaties: Cleaning Up the Mess – Expanded Version*, 65 BIT, at 2.2.7. (2011, published online 22 December 2010: DOI: 10.59403/22g7sar).

1082. *Ibid.*, at 2.2.7.

1083. *See* para. 10 of the Commentary on Article 14 UN Model 2021 with reference to para. 3 of the Commentary on Article 7 OECD Model 1997.

(iv) 183-Day Period

Article 14(1)(b) UN Model establishes source taxing rights for independent personal services if the stay of a non-resident service provider amounts to or exceeds an aggregate period of 183 days in any twelve-month period commencing or ending in the fiscal year concerned. The 183-day requirement was not included in Article 14 OECD Model 1998 which is also consistent with the view taken by the Commentaries to the OECD Model that source taxing rights for service taxation shall only arise in the existence of a fixed place of business.[1084] The threshold of Article 14(1)(b) UN Model is based on tax treaty provisions concluded before the UN Model 1980 was published. These provisions have their origin in the models drafted by the former League of Nations which did not differentiate between independent and dependent income from services.[1085] Therefore, with respect to the underlying principles and the calculation of the 183-day period,[1086] recourse can be made to the Commentary on Article 15(2)(a) UN Model.[1087] Just as the aforementioned provision requires the physical presence of the individual in the source state so does Article 14(1)(b) UN Model. With respect to the calculation of the 183-day period of Article 14(1)(b) UN Model, the Commentary to the UN Model suggests applying the 'days of physical presence' test.[1088] Under it, only one out of two outcomes would be possible, i.e., the individual is either present in a state or not.[1089] Therefore, also the date of arrival or departure or only days partly spent in a state would count as one day of presence according to the aforementioned test as already only a brief time spent in a state would generally fulfil the requirements set by the Commentaries to the OECD and UN Models.[1090] As a result, the 183-day threshold may also be met if the individual mostly spends days in the state of performance for private purposes. Nevertheless, Article 14(1)(b) UN Model establishes that only such part of income from activities actually performed in the state of performance will be subject to source taxation. Therefore, if no activities of an independent nature are performed in the source state, the fulfilment of the 183-day threshold is irrelevant.[1091]

b *Overlap with Article 12A UN Model*

From a historical perspective, technical and professional services are closely linked to each other as several tax treaties include professional services as mentioned in Article 14(2) UN Model in a separate article jointly with technical services.[1092] In this respect,

1084. *See* paras 3 et seq. of the Commentary on Article 14 OECD Model 1998.
1085. *See* Velo, *supra* n. 1060, at 373.
1086. As regards the interpretation and application of the 183-day period in Article 5(3)(b) UN Model 2021, *see* Chapter 4.D.i.4.g.(iii).
1087. *See* Hemmelrath, *supra* n. 1062, at m.no. 36.
1088. *See* para. 42 of the Commentary on Article 5 UN Model 2021.
1089. *See* para. 5 of the Commentary on Article 15 OECD Model 2017.
1090. *See* Giorgio Beretta, *'Work on the Move': Rethinking Taxation of Labour Income under Tax Treaties*, 5 ITAXS 2, 12 (2022) DOI: 10.59403/3mgn45y.
1091. Similarly, with respect to Article 15(2) OECD Model: *Ibid.*, at 12.
1092. *See* Chapter 4.A.ii.1.b. and Appendices 1, 2, 3 and 5 of this publication.

the definition of the term 'management fees' as found in Article 12(4) DTC Germany-Kenya (1977) includes services of a technical or consultancy nature as well as independent activities of physicians, lawyers, engineers, architects, dentists, and accountants within its scope.[1093]

As mentioned in *Chapter 4.A.ii.2.*, the term 'technical' as included in the header of Article 12A UN Model on 'fees for technical services' refers to services of a specialized nature within a particular art or profession. Although the Commentary on Article 14 UN Model does not include a reference regarding the specialized nature of professional services and other services of an independent character, the Commentary on Article 12A UN Model explicitly regards services provided by 'regulated professions' as described in Article 14(2) UN Model as services that require specialized knowledge, skill, or expertise. It additionally concludes that services provided by other occupations such as pharmacists or generally academics may also constitute technical services if they apply specialized knowledge, skill, or expertise.[1094] The inclusion of professional services in the scope of Article 12A UN Model is based on the ordinary meaning of the term 'technical' that is used by the Commentary on Article 12A UN Model, i.e., 'the application of specialized knowledge, skill or expertise with respect to a particular art, science, profession or occupation'.[1095] The Commentary on Article 12A UN Model therefore assumes that it is inherent to services provided by professionals as referred to in Article 14(2) UN Model that specialized knowledge, skill, or expertise is applied. In this regard, also *Rust/Walker* opine that the provision of professional services without the application of specialized knowledge, skill, or expertise is 'difficult to imagine'.[1096] This is due to the fact that such specialized services provided by professionals are derived from specific education or creative abilities.[1097] The requirement of specialized knowledge or skills is partially even required by law, such as for the professions of a lawyer or notary.[1098]

The aforementioned considerations are also reflected in the Protocol to the DTC Eswatini-Lesotho (2019) as the contracting states clarified that the term 'technical services' generally includes services 'that require special knowledge and skills acquired through learning the established principles of a defined discipline' and as such means 'accounting, auditing, economic, financial, legal, medical, management, engineering, architectural, surveying and information technology or other similar professional services'.[1099]

1093. *See*, however, Article 22(3) of the DTC Egypt-Italy (1979) explicitly excluding payments for independent personal services from the scope of 'management fees'.
1094. *See* para. 65 of the Commentary on Article 12A UN Model 2021: 'Technical services are not limited to the professional services referred to in Article 14, paragraph 2.'
1095. *See* para. 64 of the Commentary on Article 12A UN Model 2021.
1096. *See* Rust & Walker, *supra* n. 1050, at 85.
1097. *See, e.g.*, Stefan Bendlinger & Karl Waser, *Art 14 Einkünfte aus selbständiger Arbeit*, in: Dietmar Aigner, Georg Kofler & Michael Tumpel (eds), *DBA-Kommentar*, at m.no. 116 (Linde Verlag 2017).
1098. *See, e.g.*, in Austria for lawyers and notaries: RGBl, 96/1868 (Rechtsanwaltsordnung) and RGBl, 75/1871 (Notariatsordnung).
1099. *See* no. 2 of the Protocol to the DTC Eswatini-Lesotho (2019).

The most common activities rendered by professionals are consultancy services. These services generally refer 'to services constituting in the provision of advice by someone, such as a professional, who has special qualifications allowing him to do so'.[1100] Similarly, the High Court of Delhi contemplates that consultancy services involve 'offering advice, or extending advisory services by a professional'.[1101] In this regard, professional services would certainly fall within the definition of Article 12A(3) UN Model as consultancy services are explicitly included in the scope of Article 12A UN Model. In general, however, professional services may also fall within the definition of managerial or technical services in a narrow context.[1102] If, for example, professional services in the form of handling maintenance, testing, and customer support services are rendered in a state, such services might – due to their technical nature in the field of engineering[1103] – be within the scope of Article 12A and Article 14 UN Model.

The Commentary on Article 14 OECD Model 1963 mentions that Article 14 is intended to cover professional services and other independent activities 'of a similar character'.[1104] The reference 'of a similar character' with regards to professional services has not been included to the Commentary on Article 14 OECD Model 1977 and the following commentary versions. However, it is still assumed in literature that 'other activities of an independent character'[1105] shall cover such services from occupations applying specialized knowledge and skills derived from specific education or creative capabilities.[1106] As such, they need to be comparable to the liberal professions.[1107] Nevertheless, neither Article 14 UN Model itself nor its commentary establishes a criterion for the application of its services to be of a specialized nature. In general, the objective of Article 14 UN Model is to apply to all types of services that might also be rendered in the context of an employment relationship (Article 15 UN Model) except for industrial and commercial activities.[1108] Article 14 UN Model therefore also applies to standardized, routinely provided services rendered by professionals or other independent service providers. Such routine services, however, are mostly of an auxiliary nature and do not constitute the core activities of a professional or another independent service provider. They are also generally not customized to the needs of a specific client, such as the provision of legal document templates.[1109]

Although the ITAT Ahmedabad concluded that the 'scope of...independent personal service completely covers the fees for technical services as well', this author

1100. OECD Technical Advisory Group on Treaty Characterization of Electronic Commerce Payments, *supra* n. 636, at para. 45.
1101. *See* High Court of Delhi, *supra* n. 698, at para. 13.4.
1102. *See* para. 66 of the Commentary on Article 12A UN Model 2021.
1103. *See* ITAT Bangalore, *Wifi Networks P. Ltd. v. Deputy Commissioner of Income Tax*, ITA No. 943/Bang/2017, para. 7 (5 April 2019).
1104. *See* para. 1 of the Commentary on Article 14 OECD Model 1963.
1105. *See* Article 14(1) UN Model 2021.
1106. *See, e.g.*, Bendlinger & Waser, *supra* n. 1097, at m.nos 2 and 7.
1107. *See* Lang, *supra* n. 1062, at 78.
1108. *See, e.g.*, para. 10 of the Commentary on Article 14 UN Model 2021 with reference to para. 1 of the Commentary on Article 14 OECD Model 1997.
1109. *See, e.g.*, LawBite, *Legal Document Templates*, https://www.lawbite.co.uk/legal-and-business-documents (accessed 15 November 2022): These documents include Shareholders' Agreement, Agency Agreement, Unsecured Loan Agreement and so forth.

shares the view of the Supreme Court of India as cited by the AAR New Delhi in the case *Intertek Testing Services India (P.) Ltd.* that 'not any or every professional service...amounts to technical service. Professionalism and an element of expertise should be at the back of such services'.[1110] Therefore, the scope of activities covered by Article 14 UN Model is generally broader than that of Article 12A UN Model due to the application of former mentioned article on standardized, non-customized services.[1111] However, as referenced, it may be concluded that Article 12A UN Model covers the core activities most commonly provided by independent service providers, i.e., services requiring the application of specialized knowledge, skill, or expertise based on education in a specific discipline. As, according to Article 12A(2) UN Model, Article 12A applies 'notwithstanding the provisions of Article 14', it will generally take precedence over the application of Article 14 UN Model. This applies unless, as will be shown in the following chapters, independent personal services are provided by the beneficial owner of a contracting state through a fixed base in the other contracting state and fees for these services are effectively connected with such fixed base. This rule of precedence of the concept of fixed base is enshrined in Article 12A(4) UN Model.

4 *Precedence of Fixed Base Concept of Article 14 UN Model*

a Fixed Base as a PE?

While Article 14 on independent personal services is still present in the current UN Model, it was removed from the OECD Model as part of its revision in the year 2000.[1112] The reason is that the OECD did not encounter any substantial differences between the PE concept of Article 5 and the fixed base concept of Article 14, therefore, they were practically identical.[1113] In this respect, also several scholars[1114] emphasize that the requirements to establish a PE according to Article 5 OECD Model[1115] can generally be applied to interpret the term 'fixed base'. This is necessarily also true for Article 14(1)(a) UN Model as the commentary on the mentioned provision refers to the relevant paragraphs of the Commentary on Article 14 OECD Model 1998 mentioning

1110. AAR New Delhi, *supra* n. 641, at para. 10.6.
1111. *See also* the remarks made with regards to independent personal services in the field of ADS: Chapter 4.C. of this publication.
1112. *See* van der Bruggen, *supra* n. 1069, at 601: 'The removal of Art. 14 is the result of the OECD's Report entitled "Issues Related to Article 14 of the OECD Model Tax Convention" (Report), released in 2000. The Report concludes that a tax treatment for income from independent personal services which is separate from the tax treatment for business profits is no longer justified.'
1113. Based on the view taken by the Commentary on Article 14 OECD Model 1963, the concept of 'fixed base' intends to cover types of income that are different from those covered by the term 'permanent establishment'. In this regard, the commentary mentions that income from industrial or commercial activities shall be covered by the PE concept: para. 3 of the Commentary on Article 14 OECD Model 1963.
1114. *See, e.g.*, Bendlinger & Waser, *supra* n. 1097, at m.no. 16 and Wassermeyer, *supra* n. 1080, at m.no. 66.
1115. *See* Chapter 4.D.i.4. of this publication.

that Article 14 is based on the same principles as Article 7.[1116] This view is also shared by the Supreme Court of the Netherlands (Hoge Raad) as it noted that, based on the Commentaries on Article 5 OECD and UN Model, the establishment of a fixed base requires a certain degree of permanency and excludes activities of only a temporary nature from its scope.[1117] The Hoge Raad held that the requirements to determine the existence of a PE under the Commentaries to the OECD and UN Models may also be applied to the concept of a 'fixed base' due to the latter's similar functions as a connecting factor for source taxing rights.[1118]

However, it still needs to be mentioned that – although the concepts of 'fixed base' and 'permanent establishment' are substantially the same – interpretative guidance with respect to the provisions of Article 5 outside of paragraph 1 shall not be applicable regarding the interpretation of Article 14 UN Model, e.g., the principles upon which the construction PE of Article 5(3) OECD and Article 5(3)(a) UN Model rely.[1119]

b Service Fee in Connection with a Fixed Base

Similarly, as already mentioned in *Chapter 4.D.i.* with respect to Article 7 and the establishment of a PE, Article 14 UN Model only takes precedence over the application of Article 12A UN Model if fees for technical services are 'effectively connected' with a fixed base in the source state.[1120] Whether this is the case must be determined on a case-by-case basis and relies upon the degree to which technical services are closely related or connected with a fixed base.[1121] In this regard, it has to be mentioned that the force-of-attraction rule as established in Article 7(1)(b) and (c) UN Model is not included in Article 14 UN Model. Therefore, the 'effective' connection of technical service fees with respect to a fixed base is already – by its wording – narrower in Article 14(1)(a) than the one in Article 7 UN Model.[1122]

As mentioned in *Chapter 4.D.i.4.e.*, it is generally understood that the wording 'effectively connected' has the same meaning as 'attributable to'. In this regard, the Commentary on Article 14 UN Model does not contain detailed rules on the attribution of profits to a fixed base. However, based on the parallels of classification between a 'fixed base' and a PE,[1123] it can be assumed that the rules on the attribution of profits before the AOA was introduced as part of the 2008 revision of the OECD Model[1124]

1116. *See* para. 10 of the Commentary on Article 14 UN Model 2021.
1117. *See* Hoge Raad der Nederlanden, ECLI:NL:HR:2016:44 (15 January 2016).
1118. *Ibid.*, at paras 4 et seq.
1119. *See, e.g.*, with respect to the activities of architects: Austrian Ministry of Finance, *Express Antwort Service 2981*, BMF-010221/1571-IV/4/2008 (11 June 2008).
1120. *See* Article 12A(4) UN Model 2021.
1121. *See* para. 106 of the Commentary on Article 12A UN Model 2017.
1122. *See* Article 7(1)(b) and (c) UN Model 2021.
1123. *See, e.g.*, Arnold, *supra* n. 6, at 63; the OECD Model (1977), while it retained the article, had referred to Article 7 rules regarding the attribution of profits to a fixed base in respect of independent personal services.
1124. *See* para. 1 of the Commentary on Article 7 UN Model 2021: The UN Tax Committee decided to not adopt the AOA as part of the UN Model.

would also apply to interpret the term 'effectively connected' in the context of Article 12A(4) UN Model.

5 *Room for Applicability of Article 12A UN Model*

By virtue of Article 12A(4)(a) UN Model, Article 14 UN Model takes precedence over the application of Article 12A if technical services that are within the scope of Article 14 UN Model are performed in the contracting state from a fixed base therein and fees for such services are effectively connected with that fixed base. The wording of Article 12A(4) UN Model only refers to the concept of fixed base enshrined in Article 14(1)(a) UN Model. It does not refer to the prevalence of Article 14(1)(b) UN Model in relation to Article 12A UN Model. This, however, was not always the case as the draft commentary of Article 12A UN Model referred to the prevalence of application of the 183-day threshold of Article 14(1)(b) UN Model.[1125] Such reference was nevertheless not included in the final version of the Commentary on Article 12A UN Model 2017.

Therefore, as neither the wording of nor the Commentary on Articles 12A and 14 UN Model refers to the precedence of the 183-day rule as established in Article 14(1)(b) UN Model, Article 12A UN Model takes precedence over the application of Article 14(1)(b) UN Model. Such precedence is also established in the wording of Article 12A(2) UN Model, as latter mentioned provision provides that Article 12A shall apply 'notwithstanding the provision of Article 14'.

Although, in the author's opinion, such priority was already sufficiently clear, the UN Tax Committee still decided – as part of the latest update of the UN Model – to clarify that Article 12A UN Model is only preceded by Article 14 in case of the existence of a fixed base in the source state, therefore, only if Article 14(1)(a) UN Model applies:

> However, if a resident of one Contracting State provides independent personal services (that are technical services) that arise in the other Contracting State, but those services are not provided through a fixed base in that other State, the fees for those services are taxable by that other State under paragraph 2 of Article 12A.[1126]

Nevertheless, it must still be borne in mind that Article 12A UN Model only applies to B2B services. Therefore, Article 14(1)(b) UN Model would still be applicable instead of Article 12A UN Model if the requirements of the former mentioned provision are fulfilled in the B2C context. What is more, Article 14(1)(b) UN Model would also apply to teaching services as excluded by Article 12A(3)(b) UN Model.

Although Article 14(1)(a) UN Model takes precedence over Article 12A UN Model, the latter-mentioned provision will – just as in relation to Article 7 and 5 UN Model[1127] – be applicable from the first payment made in consideration for fees for technical services rendered in a B2B context. While Article 12A(2) UN Model clearly provides for gross taxation of technical service fees, the application of Article 14 UN

1125. *See* Rust & Walker, *supra* n. 1050, at 84 et seq.
1126. *See* para. 12 of the Commentary on Article 14 UN Models 2017 and 2021.
1127. *See* Chapter 4.D.i. of this publication.

Model is based on net taxation.[1128] Therefore, from the moment that a fixed base is established and the other criteria of Article 14(1)(a) UN Model are fulfilled, gross taxation will switch to net taxation. This may possibly result in a refund of excessive tax withheld at source due to the deduction of costs incurred. This issue, however, is a matter of the source state's domestic law.

E ARTICLE 12A UN MODEL 2017: OVERLAP WITH ARTICLES 8, 16, 17 AND 21 UN MODEL

i Overlap with Article 8 UN Model

1 Preliminary Remarks on Potential Overlaps

Article 12A(2) UN Model establishes the precedence of application of Article 8 UN Model if shipping or air transport services fall within the definition of technical services as defined in Article 12A(3) UN Model. In this regard, the Commentary on Article 12A UN Model recognizes that certain payments for international shipping and air transportation services could be encapsulated within the definition of 'fees for technical services'.[1129] To avoid uncertainty with regard to the qualification of such services, the UN Tax Committee established in Article 12A(2) UN Model that Article 8 shall take precedence over Article 12A if services are covered by the scope of both allocation rules. Therefore, taxing rights for fees for technical services (12A(3) UN Model) received from the operation of ships or aircraft in international traffic shall exclusively be allocated on the basis of Article 8 UN Model.[1130]

2 General Remarks on Article 8 UN Model

Article 8 UN Model deals with the allocation of taxing rights of profits of an enterprise from the operation of ships and aircraft in international traffic. In contrast to Article 8 OECD Model, Article 8 UN Model includes two alternative versions: Alternative A and Alternative B. In this respect, the former reproduces Article 8 OECD Model while the latter, on the other hand, has been included – in different wording – since the UN Model 1980. Alternative A of Article 8 UN Model grants an exclusive taxing right to the residence state of the enterprise that derives profits from the operation of ships or aircraft in international traffic. Alternative B provides a shared taxing right for 'more than casual' shipping activities, i.e., 'a scheduled or planned visit of a ship to a

1128. Note, however, that the wording of Article 24(3) UN Model only covers a permanent establishment and not a fixed base. Therefore, according to *Rust/Walker*, it does not seem too obvious that a fixed base is entitled to the same treatment as an enterprise of the source state: Rust & Walker, *supra* n. 1050, at 80.
1129. *See* para. 49 of the Commentary on Article 12A UN Model 2021.
1130. *See* para. 8 of the Commentary on Article 8 UN Model 2021.

particular country to pick up freight or passengers', otherwise also referring to exclusive residence taxation in its paragraph 1.[1131]

Article 8 UN Model generally takes precedence over Article 7 and the PE concept.[1132] However, it does not generally cover the allocation of taxing rights of profits from the operation of ships or aircraft but only those from international traffic. The term 'international traffic' is defined in Article 3(1)(d) UN Model 2021, as 'any transport by a ship or aircraft, except when the ship or aircraft is operated solely between places in a Contracting State and the enterprise that operates the ship or aircraft is not an enterprise of that State'.[1133] Therefore, if an Austrian enterprise conducts flights between Mallorca and Madrid (both in Spain), profits from the transport by aeroplane would not be covered by Article 8 as the definition of 'international traffic' would not be fulfilled.

The special treatment of profits from international shipping and air transport originated already in the 1920s due to the 'very particular nature of their activities and of the difficulty of apportioning the profits, particularly in the case of companies operation in a number of countries'.[1134] The very particular nature of these activities is reflected by the fact that – to a large extent – these are conducted outside of territorial waters or space of a state.[1135] Therefore, such profits shall, in general, be solely taxed in the residence state of the enterprise engaged in the operation of ships or aircraft.[1136] In this respect, Article 8 UN Model is an exception to the general rule on business profits that allows for shared taxing rights. However, the deviation from the general rule is justified due to the inherent difficulty of allocating income from the operation of ships and aircraft in international traffic based on the specific nature of activities conducted through these.[1137]

3 *Technical Services Covered by Article 8 UN Model*

a *Services in International Shipping and Air Transport*

Article 8 UN Model focuses on transportation services of persons and freight. It therefore also intends to encompass services directly connected with such transportation. However, activities that are not directly connected to such transportation

1131. *See* para. 16 of the Commentary on Article 8 UN Model 2021.
1132. *See* Article 7(6) UN Model 2021 and para. 8 of the Commentary on Article 8 UN Model 2021.
1133. *See also* para. 18 of the Commentary on Article 8 UN Model 2021: Inland waterways transport is covered by Article 8 (Alternatives A and B) only if such transport constitutes international traffic.
1134. *See* League of Nations, *Double Taxation and Tax Evasion Report and Resolutions – Report and Resolutions submitted by the Technical Experts to the Financial Committee*, F.212 (7 February 1925).
1135. *See* Guglielmo Maisto, *Shipping, Inland Waterways Transport and Air Transport (Article 8 OECD Model Convention)*, in: Michael Lang, Pasquale Pistone, Josef Schuch & Claus Staringer (eds), *Source Versus Residence – Problems Arising from the Allocation of Taxing Rights in Tax Treaty Law and Possible Alternatives* vol. 20, 21, 27 et seq. (Wolters Kluwer 2008).
1136. *See* para. 10 of the Commentary on Article 8 UN Model 2021: Alternatively, states could decide to specifically refer to the place of effective management of the enterprise.
1137. *See* Maisto, *supra* n. 1135, at 33 et seq.

activities shall also be covered by Article 8 if they are ancillary to the operation of ships or aircraft in international traffic.[1138] Activities, such as engineering or consultancy services, are ancillary to such an operation if they only make a minor contribution in relation to an enterprise's own operation of ships or aircraft and are so closely related to such operation that they cannot be regarded as a separate source of income for that enterprise.[1139]

Activities covered by Article 8 UN Model include, *inter alia*, the following:

- the direct or indirect (online) selling of tickets for international transportation services;[1140]
- leasing a ship or aircraft on charter as it is treated like the carriage of passengers or cargo;[1141]
- transportation activities directly connected with the business of transportation by ship or aircraft (by that enterprise) or similar ancillary activities such as transportation of an enterprise's passengers by bus to the airport for its international flights;[1142]
- arranging transportation of passengers or cargo from the international airport of destination;[1143]
- advertising offered aboard a ship or aircraft or at its other business locations (ancillary activity);[1144]
- short-term storage of containers that are used for the operation of activities on ships or aircraft (ancillary activity);[1145]
- provision of engineering or customer services by maintenance staff to another company (as part of a pooling arrangement) if a company has such personnel available in a state for the purposes of the operation of ships or aircraft.[1146]

Some UN Tax Committee members, however, opine that activities of an ancillary nature shall not be covered by Article 8 UN Model as these are not mentioned in the wording 'profits from the operation of ships or aircraft in international traffic'.[1147]

1138. *See* para. 12 of the Commentary on Article 8 UN Model 2021 with reference to para. 4 of the Commentary on Article 8 OECD Model 2017.
1139. *See* para. 12 of the Commentary on Article 8 UN Model 2021 with reference to para. 4.2 of the Commentary on Article 8 OECD Model 2017.
1140. *See* para. 60 subpara. (iv) of the Commentary on Article 12B UN Model 2021 and para. 13 of the Commentary on Article 8 UN Model 2021 with reference to para. 8 of Commentary of OECD Model 2017.
1141. *See* para. 13 of the Commentary on Article 8 UN Model 2021 with reference to para. 5 of the Commentary on Article 8 OECD Model 2017.
1142. *See* para. 13 of the Commentary on Article 8 UN Model 2021 with reference to para. 6 of the Commentary on Article 8 OECD Model 2017.
1143. *See* para. 13 of the Commentary on Article 8 UN Model 2021 with reference to para. 7 of the Commentary on Article 8 OECD Model 2017.
1144. *See* para. 13 of the Commentary on Article 8 UN Model 2021 with reference to para. 8.1 of the Commentary on Article 8 OECD Model 2017.
1145. *See* para. 13 of the Commentary on Article 8 UN Model 2021 with reference to para. 8.1 of the Commentary on Article 8 OECD Model 2017.
1146. *See* para. 13 of the Commentary on Article 8 UN Model 2021 with reference to paras 10 and 10.1 of the Commentary on Article 8 OECD Model 2017.
1147. *See* para. 14 of the Commentary on Article 8 UN Model 2021.

b Overlap with and Room for Applicability of Article 12A UN Model

Remuneration for services covered by Article 8 UN Model are typically not of a technical services nature. However, the Commentaries on Article 8 OECD and UN Models acknowledge that ancillary services in connection to the operation of ships or aircraft, such as engineering or customer services, might be provided[1148] and be considered such services.

In this respect, the decision of the High Court of Delhi in *Lufthansa Cargo India Pvt. Ltd. v. Director of Income Tax* might be notable.[1149] As stated in *Chapter 4.A.ii.3.*, it had to decide on the question of the technical nature of repair and overhaul services.[1150] In this respect, it pointed out that repair and maintenance services for aircraft require a significant level of technical expertise and therefore need to be differentiated from general repair and overhaul work. Therefore, the former-mentioned services shall be qualified as being in the nature of technical services.[1151] Similarly, in *Sahara Airlines Ltd. v. Deputy Commissioner of Income Tax*, the ITAT Delhi held that the repair of aeroplane engines and other aeroplane equipment amounts to fees for technical services.[1152]

In contrast hereto, as also mentioned in *Chapter 4.A.ii.3.*, fees for the use of a standard facility are not regarded as technical services due to their non-customized nature. In this respect, in *Merchant Shipping Services Pvt. Ltd. v. Assistant Commissioner of Income Tax*, the question arose whether fees paid in consideration for container handling services are of a technical services nature or that of a 'contracts of work'.[1153] In this regard, the ITAT Mumbai concluded that the use of cranes to move containers is not regarded as a technical service but the mere use of a standard facility[1154] that is available to anyone who is interested in moving containers.[1155]

A few tax treaties also specifically include income from training schemes in the scope of their article on international shipping and air transport.[1156] In this respect, training of personnel has been regarded as technical in nature by the ITAT Delhi in the case of *Sahara Airlines Ltd. v. Deputy Commissioner of Income Tax*.[1157] In it, the ITAT Delhi decided that instructions on the use of a flight simulator to train pilots are of a technical services nature. These services were and could only be provided by trained flight personnel who had knowledge of the use of these highly sophisticated flight simulators.[1158] Therefore, the training was considered a technical service.

1148. *See* para. 13 of the Commentary on Article 8 UN Model 2021 with reference to paras 10 and 10.1 of the Commentary on Article 8 OECD Model 2017.
1149. High Court of Delhi, *supra* n. 694.
1150. *Ibid.*, at paras 2 et seq.
1151. *Ibid.*, at para. 20.
1152. ITAT Delhi, *Sahara Airlines Ltd. v. Deputy Commissioner of Income Tax*, 2002 83 ITD 11 Delhi (2003) 79 TTJ Delhi 268, para. 31 (12 February 2002).
1153. *See* ITAT Mumbai, *supra* n. 688.
1154. *See* Chapter 4.A.iii.2.a.(ii) of this publication for a discussion on standard facilities.
1155. *See* ITAT Mumbai, *supra* n. 688, at para. 15.
1156. *See, e.g.*, Article 9(3) no. 3 DTC Gambia-UAE (2015) and Article 9(4) no. 3 DTC Senegal-UAE (2015): '...profits derived from:...3) income from training schemes'.
1157. *See* ITAT Delhi, *supra* n. 1152.
1158. *Ibid.*, at para. 23.

However, even if activities were to be considered technical, as long as they are ancillary to the operation of ships or aircraft, Article 8 UN Model will apply based on the rule of precedence included in Article 12A(2) UN Model ('subject to').[1159] In this regard, the ITAT Mumbai had to decide whether the services in connection with the use of an IT-system that handles the tracking of containers, accounting of freight receipts, etc., are technical services that are connected to shipping operations in a way that they cannot be separated from the business of shipping.[1160] Concerning this question, the ITAT Mumbai decided that the use of such software cannot be segregated from shipping operations in order to qualify them as technical services that are separate from the operation of shipping services.[1161]

As mentioned previously, certain types of technical services as defined in Article 12A(3) UN may be provided in the context of Article 8 UN Model. These services may – amongst others – include engineering services in the form of repair works of aeroplanes as part of a pooling arrangement or training services provided by highly skilled personnel to train pilots. Services provided through a standard facility, such as container handling services, however, are routine services without requiring the application of specialized knowledge, skill or expertise to specifically adapt the service to the needs of a certain customer. Nevertheless, it may be repeatedly noted that technical services covered by Article 8 UN Model will take precedence over the application of Article 12A UN Model if these services are ancillary to the operation of ships or aircraft in international traffic.

ii Overlap with Article 16 UN Model

1 Preliminary Remarks on Potential Overlaps

Article 12A(2) UN Model expressly establishes the precedence of Article 16 UN Model if services covered by Article 16 UN Model are also within the definition of Article 12A(3) UN Model. Technical services potentially being within the scope of Article 16 UN Model especially concern managerial services rendered by directors or top-level managerial officials. When fees for such services are within the scope of Articles 12A and 16 UN Model, the application of the latter-mentioned provision shall take precedence over Article 12A according to Article 12A(2) UN Model. Therefore, fees for technical services paid to individuals for managerial services provided in a capacity as a member of the board of directors or as a top-level managerial official would be outside the scope of Article 12A UN Model due to the rule of precedence of Article 12A(2) UN Model.

1159. *See also* the exclusion in Article 12(5)(b) DTC India-United States (1989): 'for services that are ancillary and subsidiary to the rental of ships, aircraft, containers or other equipment used in connection with the operation of ships or aircraft in international traffic'.

1160. *See* ITAT Mumbai, *Deputy Commissioner of Income Tax v. A.P. Moller Maersk A/S*, ITA no.1798/Mum./2015 (15 February 2017).

1161. *Ibid.*, at para. 4.

2 *General Remarks on Article 16 UN Model*

Article 16(1) UN Model reproduces Article 16 OECD Model. It covers the allocation of taxing rights of remuneration received by a resident of a contracting state for services performed in the capacity of a member of the board of directors of a company. According to Article 16(1) UN Model, the company's residence state (source state) and the director's residence state share a taxing right for his remuneration. The inclusion of the residence state as the deemed source state is due to the inherent difficulty 'to ascertain where the services [of a director] are performed'.[1162] The approach of such a deemed source rule originates from the work conducted by the OEEC in the second half of the 1950s and has basically remained unchanged since then.[1163]

The UN Model also includes a second paragraph in Article 16 that is absent in Article 16 OECD Model. Article 16(2) UN Model deals with the allocation of taxing rights of top-level managerial officials. In this regard, the same principles of allocation of taxing rights for remuneration paid to such persons shall apply as that for directors in the context of Article 16(1) UN Model.[1164]

Article 16(2) UN Model specifically aims at persons who - apart from the directors - are responsible for high-level affairs of an enterprise.[1165] It therefore extends source taxation to remuneration received by persons who are not formally, i.e., according to the national company laws of contracting states, members of the board of directors. In contrast to Article 16(1) UN Model, the second paragraph uses the wording 'salaries, wages and other similar remuneration' which is derived from Article 15(1) UN Model on dependent personal services. It can therefore be deducted from the wording that Article 16(2) UN Model only intends to cover payments derived from an employment relationship.[1166] In contrast hereto, Article 16(1) UN Model does not make such a distinction. To the contrary, the wording is intentionally designed in a broad manner to cover payments that, under the domestic laws of the contracting states, might either fall under employment or other types of income. The latter is specifically applicable to non-executive directors who are commonly not in an employment relationship with the enterprise.[1167]

1162. *See* para. 2 of the Commentary on Article 16 UN Model 2021 with reference to para. 1 of the Commentary on Article 16 OECD Model 2017.
1163. *See* OEEC Fiscal Committee, *supra* n. 368, Article IX; *see also* Chapter 3.C.ii.2. of this publication for more information.
1164. *See* para. 4 of the Commentary on Article 16 UN Model.
1165. *See* para. 5 of the Commentary on Article 5 UN Model.
1166. *See* Axel Cordewener, *Article 16. Directors' Fees/Directors' Fees and Remuneration of Top-Managerial Officials*, in: Ekkehart Reimer & Alexander Rust (eds), *Klaus Vogel on Double Taxation Conventions* vol. 2, m.no. 98 (4th ed., Wolters Kluwer 2015).
1167. *See* Rainer Prokisch, *Directors' Fees (Article 16 OECD Model Convention)*, in: Michael Lang, Pasquale Pistone, Josef Schuch & Claus Staringer (eds), *Source Versus Residence – Problems Arising from the Allocation of Taxing Rights in Tax Treaty Law and Possible Alternatives* vol. 20, 197, 206 (Wolters Kluwer 2008).

3 *Technical Services Covered by Article 16 UN Model*

a *Services as a Director or Top-Level Managerial Official*

The interpretation and application of Article 16 OECD and UN Models have led to difficulties in the past. This is due to differing company laws worldwide. In this regard, especially the question arises of whether a 'board of directors' as mentioned in Article 16 OECD and Article 16(1) UN Models may exercise both supervisory and managerial functions. In this regard, the functions of a member of the board of directors differ substantially based on the underlying board structure. While civil-law countries usually base their board structure on a two-tier system including a management and a supervisory board, common-law countries generally adhere to a one-tier system and include managerial and supervisory activities within one board.[1168]

According to the BMF[1169] and several German authors,[1170] Article 16 OECD Model shall only apply to the remuneration of directors acting in their capacity within a supervisory board. This view is primarily based on a combination of the narrow wording of the unofficial German translation of Article 16 OECD Model ('Aufsichts- oder Verwaltungsrat') and the application of provisions of domestic law.[1171] As the German version of the OECD Model is often used by Austria, Germany, and Switzerland as the basis for its authentic German tax treaty text when concluding tax treaty negotiations with another state, conflicts of interpretation may occur that must be solved on the basis of Articles 31 to 33 VCLT.[1172] This is due to the fact that authentic tax treaty texts that are based on the English or French version of the OECD Model do not *per se* preclude managerial activities of directors from the scope of Article 16 OECD or Article 16(1) UN Models. In this respect, the English term 'board of directors' is broader than 'Aufsichts- oder Verwaltungsrat' and also includes executive and non-executive members of the board. What is more, the French text of the OECD Model[1173] refers to the 'conseil d'administration ou de surveillance' which was a body able to exercise supervisory and managerial functions with respect to former joint-stock companies in France.[1174] Therefore, also the authentic French text of the OECD Model does not per se exclude managerial activities from the scope of Article 16 OECD Model.

As noted in *Chapter 2.B.ii.3.c.*, there will be more emphasis on the English or French version of the OECD Model as these two languages are also the authentic

1168. *See* Cordewener, *supra* n. 1166, at m.no. 34.
1169. *See* Austrian Ministry of Finance, *Express Antwort Service 3431*, 2021-0.061.324 (12 April 2021) with reference to EAS 168, EAS 655, EAS 1015, EAS 1633, EAS 2032, EAS 3355 and the decision of the Austrian Federal Administrative Court (VwGH) of 31 July 1996, 92/13/0172.
1170. *See* Franz Wassermeyer & Klaus-Dieter Drüen *OECD-MA 2017 Art.* 16, in: Franz Wassermeyer, Christian Kaeser, Michael Schwenke & Klaus-Dieter Drüen (eds), *DBA*, m.no. 13 (158th ed., C.H. Beck 2022) and Rainer Prokisch, *Art. 16 Aufsichtsrats- und Verwaltungsratsvergütungen*, in: Roland Ismer (ed.), *Doppelbesteuerungsabkommen*, m.nos 7 et seq. (7th ed., C.H. Beck 2021).
1171. *See* Prokisch, *supra* n. 1170, at m.no. 10.
1172. *See* with respect to different language versions: Chapter 2.B.ii.3.c. of this publication.
1173. *See* with respect to issues of interpretation regarding the OECD and UN Models: Chapter 2.B.ii. of this publication.
1174. *See* Prokisch, *supra* n. 1167, at 197.

languages of the convention establishing the OECD as an organization and are also used as a basis for any other official – but not authentic – languages of the OECD Model and its corresponding commentaries. In addition, as Article 16(1) UN Model is based on the OECD Model, also the English and French versions of the text of the OECD Model and its commentaries shall be taken into account when interpreting Article 16(1) UN Model. Therefore, considering the English and French versions of the OECD Model, it cannot per se be excluded that managerial activities shall not be covered by Article 16 OECD and Article 16(1) UN Model. However, as *Cordewener* opines, Article 16 OECD Model and Article 16(1) UN Model shall not apply to the day-to-day activities of managers but only those activities of top-level functions setting the general, strategic direction of an enterprise.[1175]

In the author's opinion, this is also true with respect to Article 16(2) UN Model with the main difference being that paragraph 2 does not require a formal membership to a board of directors. According to the Commentary on Article 16 UN Model, the position of a top-level managerial official refers only to a limited group of persons who are primarily responsible for the general decisions of an enterprise.[1176] Therefore, the Commentary on Article 16 UN Model does not intend to cover all types of managers of a company. According to *Orlet/Schuch*, one of the reasons why Article 16(2) UN Model does not apply to lower-management officials is based on the fact that Article 16 OECD and Article 16(1) UN Models are drafted with the assumption that it is difficult to ascertain where the services are performed. As lower-management officials are usually based in the same workplace and are not as mobile as top-level management officials, the assumption upon which the aforementioned articles are drafted is certainly not applicable to lower-management officials.[1177] In the context that Article 16(2) UN Model merely intends to extend the scope of Article 16(1) UN Model, in the author's opinion, the provision shall cover those managers who are not formally on the board of directors but are exercising similar tasks of 'primary responsibility'[1178] of formally appointed directors. Therefore, certain managers such as a chief risk officer (CRO) or a chief information officer (CIO) would be regarded as top-level managerial officials in the context of Article 16(2) UN Model.[1179]

b Overlap with and Room for Applicability of Article 12A UN Model

The term 'management' generally refers to services of a managerial nature, i.e., 'services in performing management functions'.[1180] The Commentary on Article 12A UN Model defines the term 'management' more narrowly as 'the application of

1175. *See* Cordewener, *supra* n. 1166, at m.no. 37.
1176. *See* para. 5 of the Commentary on Article 16 UN Model 2021.
1177. *See* Patrick Orlet & Josef Schuch, *Director's Fees and Remuneration of Top-Level Managerial Officials*, in: Michael Lang et al. (eds), *The UN Model Convention and Its Relevance for the Global Tax Treaty Network* vol. 7, 159, 175 (IBFD 2017).
1178. *See* para. 5 of the Commentary on Article 16 UN Model 2021.
1179. *See* Orlet & Schuch, *supra* n. 1177, at 176.
1180. *See* OECD Technical Advisory Group on Treaty Characterization of Electronic Commerce Payments, *supra* n. 636, at para. 43.

knowledge, skill or expertise in the control or administration of the conduct of a commercial enterprise or organization'.[1181] The term 'management' would therefore include functions on the question of how a business is operated and not on the functions to carry on that business.[1182] Therefore, a company working as an agent on a commission basis does not provide managerial services if it only arranges timely payments from customers.[1183] The High Court of Delhi contemplated that a service provider 'must partake the character and role of a manager'.[1184]

In *Dalmia v. Commissioner of Income-Tax New Delhi*, the Supreme Court of India established that the term 'manage' in the context of business has the meaning of controlling, guiding, administering, or conducting the direct affairs of a business.[1185] Based on the aforementioned decision, the AAR New Delhi concluded that assistance in relation to global policies and framework on environmental health and safety support, overall operations assistance, human resource (HR) support, learning and development initiatives, assistance on key projects, and assistance in relation to financial reporting and monitoring would – although overlapping with technical and consultancy services – be covered by the term 'managerial'.[1186] This assumption is based on the purpose of the activities undertaken which is to provide direction or guidance to the company as a whole.[1187]

The ITAT Kolkata shared a broad understanding of the term 'managerial' as referred to by the AAR. According to the court, management support services provided under a management support services agreement (MSSA) are also included within the definition of managerial services[1188] even if such services broadly refer to the assistance of financial, accounting, auditing, fiscal, and legal matters as well as personnel matters and insurances.[1189]

As mentioned in *Chapter 4.A.ii.1.*, managerial services are commonly included in the definition of fees for technical or other similar services. From a historical perspective, the allocation of taxing rights for managerial services in the context of technical services has already been included either jointly with royalties[1190] or in a separate article[1191] since the 1970s. In this regard, the term 'management fees' not only included managerial services but also such services of a technical or consultancy character.[1192]

1181. *See* para. 63 of the Commentary on Article 12A UN Model 2021.
1182. *See* OECD Technical Advisory Group on Treaty Characterization of Electronic Commerce Payments, *supra* n. 636, at para. 43.
1183. *See* ITAT Mumbai, *supra* n. 865, at paras 17 et seq.
1184. High Court of Delhi, *supra* n. 698, at para. 13.
1185. *See* Supreme Court of India, *Dalmia v. Commissioner of Income Tax*, 1977 AIR 988, 1977 SCR (2) 654 (19 January 1977).
1186. AAR New Delhi, *Invensys Systems Inc. v. Director Income Tax (International Taxation)*, A.A.R. No.796 of 2009, para. 8.2 (6 August 2009).
1187. *Ibid.*, at para. 8.1.
1188. *See* the definition of 'fees for technical services' in section 9(1)(vii) of the Indian Income Tax Act.
1189. *See* ITAT Kolkota, *Koninklijke Philips Electronics N.V. v. Deputy Commissioner of Income Tax*, ITA No. 1889/Kol/2012 (25 October 2018).
1190. *See, e.g.*, Article 12 DTC Germany-Kenya (1977): 'Royalties and management fees'.
1191. *See, e.g.*, Article 14 DTC Kenya-UK (1973), and Article 13 DTC Ivory Coast-UK (1985): 'Management fees'.
1192. *See* Article 12(4) DTC Germany-Kenya (1977).

Similarly, Article 22(3) DTC Egypt-Italy (1979) defines 'management fees' as payments in consideration for '...the provision of industrial or commercial advice, or management or technical services, or similar services or facilities, or hire of plant or equipment....'

Management services in the context of fees for technical services may concern both, those rendered by third parties as well as those conducted by directors from an enterprise's own board of directors or by top-management officials employed by the enterprise. In this regard, the Commentary on Article 12A UN Model mentions that, if an enterprise's management is contracted out to persons other than directors, management-officials, or employees,[1193] then the payments for such managerial services would be subject to source taxing rights on the basis of Article 12A(2) UN Model, as these services are generally excluded from the scope of Article 16 UN Model.[1194] As managerial services are not precisely defined in the Commentary on Article 12A UN Model, these services may also constitute consultancy services. Such a case would occur if a management consultant provides guidance to an enterprise on corporate governance[1195] or on the operation and business objectives of such an enterprise.[1196]

In the author's opinion, the definition of managerial services as found in the Commentary on Article 12A UN Model also covers activities rendered by directors and top-management officials as referred to in Article 16 UN Model as the application of specialized knowledge, skill, or expertise is inherent to the position of a director or top-level managerial official. Nevertheless, Article 12A(2) UN Model clearly provides that fees for technical services, such as managerial services, are subject to Article 16 UN Model if the services are performed by directors or top-level managerial officials in their capacity as a member of the board of directors or of top-level management respectively. If, however, such members or officials take on other functions within the company, such as a consultant, Article 12A UN Model would be applicable as the member or official does not act in the capacity of a member of the board of directors or member of the top-level management. This has also been clarified through explanations in the Commentary to Article 16 UN Model. In addition, Article 12A UN Model will also cover such managerial services that are contracted out to third parties. These services might even broadly include assistance services to the board of directors or top-level managerial officials based on an MSSA.[1197]

1193. *See* Article 12A(3)(a) UN Model 2021: Payments to employees are explicitly excluded from the scope of Article 12A UN Model.
1194. *See* para. 63 of the Commentary on Article 12A and para. 2 of the Commentary on Article 16 UN Model 2021 with reference to para. 2 of the Commentary on Article 16 OECD Model 2017.
1195. *See* para. 80 of the Commentary on Article 12A UN Model 2021.
1196. *See, e.g.*, no. 3 of the Protocol of the DTC Cambodia-Thailand (2017).
1197. ITAT Kolkota, *supra* n. 1189.

iii Overlap with Article 17 UN Model

1 Preliminary Remarks on Potential Overlaps

Fees or salaries paid to artistes or sportspersons are subject to the allocation of taxing rights based on Article 17 UN Model 2017. Article 12A(2) UN Model explicitly mentions that the application of Article 12A is subject to Article 17 UN Model. Therefore, if technical services are regarded as activities performed by an entertainer or sportsperson, these payments would be subject to the allocation of taxing rights on the basis of Article 17 UN Model. To clarify the relationship between Article 12A and Article 17 UN Model, the Commentary on Article 17 UN Model mentions that personal activities of artists and sportspersons performed in the source state may – on the basis of Article 17 UN Model – be taxed there whether these are in the nature of business (in)dependent or technical services.[1198]

2 General Remarks on Article 17 UN Model

Article 17 UN Model applies to income derived by artistes or sportspersons from personal activities 'as such' exercised in a contracting state.[1199] Both the residence state of the artiste or sportsperson as well as the state in which the activities are performed (source state) have a taxing right on the income received for the performance. In this regard, Article 17 UN Model is a general exception from the limitations of source taxation established in Articles 7 (icw 5), 14, and 15 UN Model as there is no minimum threshold of days spent or performed in a contracting state.[1200] This is due to the fact that Article 17 UN Model aims to 'avoid practical [enforcement] difficulties' arising from the taxation of highly mobile and highly paid individuals from performances in a contracting state.[1201] This view has been criticized by several authors.[1202] In this respect, it has been noted that enforcement difficulties also arise with regard to high-value services provided on a short-term basis. If these difficulties are the reason to justify source taxation, then also short-term activities of high-value service providers, such as technical services, may be taxed on such a basis. In this regard, 'one must wonder why the provision is limited to the world of entertainment and sports'.[1203]

Article 17 UN Model covers payments directly made to the artiste or sportsperson but also payments made to another third person if such payments concern the

1198. *See* para. 2 of the Commentary on Article 17 UN Model 2021 with reference to a modified version of para. 1 of the Commentary on Article 17 OECD Model 2008.
1199. *See* Article 17(1) UN Model 2021.
1200. *See* Arnold, *supra* n. 1081, at 2.3.9.
1201. *See* para. 2 of the Commentary on Article 17 UN Model 2021 with reference to a modified version of para. 3 of the Commentary on Article 17 OECD Model 2008.
1202. *See, e.g.*, Daniel Sandler, *Artistes and Sportsmen (Article 17 OECD Model Convention)*, in: Michael Lang, Pasquale Pistone, Josef Schuch & Claus Staringer (eds), *Source Versus Residence – Problems Arising from the Allocation of Taxing Rights in Tax Treaty Law and Possible Alternatives* vol. 20, 215, 220 with further references (Wolters Kluwer 2008) and Arnold, *supra* n. 1081, at 2.3.9.
1203. *See* Sandler, *supra* n. 1202, at 225.

performance of an entertainer or sportsperson. This is due to the explicit rule of Article 17(2) UN Model that was included to counter abusive situations due to the establishment of what is known as a 'star-company'.[1204]

The terms 'entertainer' and 'sportsperson' are not defined in the UN Model. However, with respect to the former, Article 17(1) UN Model provides a non-exhaustive list[1205] of persons qualifying as such. This list includes musicians and theatre, motion picture, as well as radio and television artistes.[1206] Regarding sportspersons, the article itself does not provide examples. The Commentary on Article 17 UN Model, however, mentions that traditional athletes such as runners, jumpers, or swimmers as well as persons exercising mental activities such as chess players are regarded as 'sportspersons'.[1207]

3 *Technical Services Covered by Article 17 UN Model*

a *Services of Entertainers, Sportspersons, or Independent Contractors*

The application of Article 17 UN Model requires that artistes and sportspersons receive income from their personal activities 'as such', i.e., a performance with entertaining character[1208] in front of an audience.[1209] This is predominantly present in activities of a performing nature such as taking part in a show, film, on stage, or participating in a sporting event.[1210] Activities without an entertainment character such as acting as a speaker at a conference or administrative or support staff (e.g., technical staff) are outside the scope of Article 17 UN Model.[1211] If an entertainer or sportsperson undertakes activities with an entertainment character and other activities, an apportionment of the income received might be necessary, however, this will be omitted if the performing character is only a 'negligible' part of the entire amount of income received.[1212]

1204. *See* para. 11.1 of the Commentary on Article 17 UN Model 2021.
1205. *See* para. 2 of the Commentary on Article 17 UN Model 2021 with reference to a modified version of para. 3 of the Commentary on Article 17 OECD Model 2008.
1206. *See* Article 17(1) UN Model 2021.
1207. *See* para. 2 of the Commentary on Article 17 UN Model 2021 with reference to para. 6 of the Commentary on Article 17 OECD Model 2008.
1208. Kevin Holmes, *International Tax Policy and Double Tax Treaties*, 330 et seq. (2nd ed., IBFD 2014) and para. 2 of the Commentary on Article 17 UN Model 2021 with reference to para. 6 of the Commentary on Article 17 OECD Model 2008.
1209. *See* Luis A. Romero Topete, *Analysis of the Case Law on the Scope of Article 17 of the OECD Model: Issues Resolved and Yet to Be Resolved*, 71 BIT 3/4 (2017) at 1.2. with further references, DOI: 10.59403/11ehxje.
1210. *See* para. 2 of the Commentary on Article 17 UN Model 2021 with reference to a modified version of paras 4 et seq. of the Commentary on Article 17 OECD Model 2008.
1211. *See* para. 2 of the Commentary on Article 17 UN Model 2021 with reference to a modified version of para. 3 of the Commentary on Article 17 OECD Model 2008.
1212. *See* para. 2 of the Commentary on Article 17 UN Model 2021 with reference to para. 4 of the Commentary on Article 17 OECD Model 2008.

An artiste or sportsperson may assign a management company with the tasks of organizing, arranging, or managing activities related to appearances. Payments received by a management company for such activities are outside the scope of Article 17 UN Model. However, if this occurs for one or more performances on behalf of the artiste or sportsperson, such payments would be covered by Article 17 UN Model.[1213] Similarly, the state of performance would be entitled to tax the proportion of employment income accrued by the entertainer or sportsperson from the performance of activities in a contracting state. This is based on the fact that Article 17 UN Model takes precedence over the application of Article 15 UN Model.[1214]

b Overlap with and Room for Applicability of Article 12A UN Model

According to the Commentary on Article 12A UN Model, fees paid for sports and entertainment activities that are subject to the allocation of taxing rights under Article 17 will unlikely be within the scope of the definition of 'fees for technical services' (Article 12A(3) UN Model).[1215] This is due to the very specific scope of Articles 12A and 17 UN Model.

As mentioned in *Chapter 4.A.ii.2.*, Article 12A(3) UN Model basically includes three categories of services: 'technical services of managerial nature', 'technical services of technical nature', and 'technical services of consultancy nature'. The definition of 'technical' as found in the super category of Article 12A UN Model 'involves the application of specialized knowledge, skill or expertise with respect to a particular art, science, profession or occupation'.[1216] This definition has to be read in connection with the subcategory terms of 'technical', 'consultancy', and 'managerial' as found in the definition of 'fees for technical services' in Article 12A(3) UN Model. Thus, it must be borne in mind that – although possibly being provided in front of an audience,[1217] such as a presentation or lecture by an in-house consultant – the provision of the aforementioned services is not predominantly of a performing nature, as would be required by Article 17 UN Model.[1218] In addition, technicians, consultants, and managers would also not qualify as 'artistes' or 'sportspersons'.[1219]

Artistes and sportspersons may – in addition to the income for their actual performance – also receive fees from royalties, sponsorship, or advertising. Such

---

1213. *See* para. 2 of the Commentary on Article 17 UN Model 2021 with reference to para. 7 of the Commentary on Article 17 OECD Model 2008.
1214. *See* para. 2 of the Commentary on Article 17 UN Model 2021 with reference to a modified version of para. 8 of the Commentary on Article 17 OECD Model 2008.
1215. *See* para. 51 of the Commentary on Article 12A UN Model 2021.
1216. *See* para. 62 of the Commentary on Article 12A UN Model 2021.
1217. *See, e.g.*, Michael Lang, Selina Siller & Stephanie Zolles, *Austria: Entertainers under Article 17*, in Eric C.C.M. Kemmeren et al. (eds), *Tax Treaty Case Law Around the Globe 2016* vol. 102, 245, 245 (Linde Verlag 2017): Article 17 only applies to performances carried out in front of an audience.
1218. *See* para. 2 of the Commentary on Article 17 UN Model 2021 with reference to para. 4 of the Commentary on Article 17 OECD Model 2010.
1219. *See* Romero Topete, *supra* n. 1209, at 1.4.: Although having a minor entertaining character in front of an audience, even broadcasters, reporters, or referees are not regarded as 'entertainers' in the context of Article 17 OECD and UN Models.

royalties and other fees that have to be directly connected to the performance of an artiste or sportsperson, however, do not include any technical assistance or other technical services. This fact is also recognized by the Commentary on Article 17 UN Model 2021 as it does not mention the possible applicability of Article 12A UN Model on such fees if they are not directly connected with the performance of an artiste or sportsperson but rather the fall-back to Articles 7, 14, and 15 UN Model.[1220]

In the author's opinion, fees for technical services as defined in Article 12A(3) UN Model are generally not covered by Article 17 UN Model. The UN Tax Committee also did not intend to cover payments to artistes and sportspersons in the scope of Article 12A. This is because payments falling under Article 17 UN Model are generally not subject to concerns of tax base erosion.[1221] Ultimately, the inclusion of a rule of precedence with regards to the relationship of Articles 12A and 17 UN Model in Article 12A(2) UN Model might merely be seen as a measure to provide certainty to taxpayers and tax authorities in the event of doubts in the application or interpretation of Article 12A UN Model.[1222]

iv Overlap with Article 21 UN Model

1 Preliminary Remarks on Potential Overlaps

Neither Article 12A UN Model nor its commentary include a rule on their relationship with Article 21 UN Model. This might be explained by the fact that Article 21 UN Model is a mere backfall clause for those types of income that are not covered by another allocation rule of the UN Model, i.e., Articles 6 to 20. Therefore, if Article 12A UN Model applies, it takes precedence over the application of Article 21 UN Model. However, as the scope of Article 12A UN Model is restricted to fees for technical services arising in the other contracting state,[1223] not all situations are covered by the source rules of Article 12A UN Model. Article 21 UN Model, on the other hand, does not restrict its scope to such Income. It covers income arising in the residence state, the source state, and any third state. The scope of Article 21 UN Model is therefore similar to those of Articles 7, 13(5), and 15 UN Model.[1224]

2 General Remarks on Article 21 UN Model

Article 21 UN Model reproduces Article 21 OECD Model to a great extent. Deviations in comparison to the latter are found in paragraphs 2 and 3 with the latter being a specific provision that is only found in the UN Model.

1220. *See* para. 9 of the Commentary on Article 17 UN Model 2021.
1221. Arnold, *supra* n. 1081, at 2.3.9.
1222. *See* para. 51 of the Commentary on Article 12A UN Model 2021.
1223. *See* Article 12A(5) and (6) UN Model.
1224. *See* Alexander Rust, *Art. 21. Other Income*, in: Ekkehart Reimer & Alexander Rust (eds), *Klaus Vogel on Double Taxation Conventions* vol. 2, 1745, m.no. 26 (5th ed., Wolters Kluwer 2015).

Article 21 UN Model on 'other income' specifically aims at covering those types of income that are not covered by another allocation rule of the UN Model as well as income that has its source in a jurisdiction that is different than the one specifically mentioned by the specific allocation rule. Therefore, Article 21 UN Model also applies to income arising in a third state.[1225]

Article 21(1) UN Model is a reproduction of Article 21(1) OECD Model. Based on the characterizations made by *Rust* for Article 21(1) OECD Model, Article 21(1) UN Model aims to cover the following situations:[1226]

(1) The item of income is arising in the other contracting state but does not fall within the scope of Articles 6 to 20 UN Model.
(2) The item of income is arising either in the residence state or a third state and is not covered by one of the Articles of 6 to 20 UN Model.
(3) The item of income is arising in either the residence state or a third state and is covered by one of the Articles of 6 to 20 UN Model, however, it does not fulfil the source rule of the specific article as the type of income arises in the residence state or a third state.

If either of these situations is fulfilled, Article 21(1) UN Model allocates an exclusive taxing right to the residence state of the income recipient.

The scope of Article 21(1) UN Model is limited by Article 21(2) and (3) UN Model. In this regard, Article 21(2) UN Model shall apply if the income recipient has a PE or fixed base in the other contracting state through which business is carried out and the right or property upon which the payment of the income is based, is effectively connected the PE or fixed base. In these cases, Article 7 or 14 UN Model shall apply granting the state of the PE or fixed base the primary taxing right. These considerations, however, do not apply to income from immovable property as defined in Article 6(2) UN Model even if income from it is effectively connected with a PE or fixed base.[1227]

As mentioned, Article 21(1) UN Model is also limited by Article 21(3) UN Model. The latter grants an unlimited source taxing right to the other contracting state if the income arises therein (see aforementioned situation 1 with respect to Article 21(1) UN Model).[1228] In contrast to Articles 10, 11, 12, 12A, and 12B UN Model, however, Article 21(3) UN Model does not include a specific rule to determine where the income 'arises'. Although Article 21(3) generally supports the goal of the UN Model to expand source taxing rights, the term 'arising in' should not be interpreted differently from the source rules of Articles 10 to 12B UN Model for those types of income that are already mentioned in these articles. However, if the item of income is not even mentioned, *Rust* contends that the source of income will be determined by reference to the domestic law

1225. *See* para. 2 of the Commentary on Article 21 UN Model 2021.
1226. *See* Alexander Rust, *Other Income (Article 21 OECD Model Convention)*, in: Michael Lang, Pasquale Pistone, Josef Schuch & Claus Staringer (eds), *Source Versus Residence – Problems Arising from the Allocation of Taxing Rights in Tax Treaty Law and Possible Alternatives* vol. 20, 327, 328 (Wolters Kluwer 2008).
1227. *See* Article 21(2) UN Model 2021.
1228. *See* para. 3 of the Commentary on Article 21 UN Model 2021.

of each contracting state in accordance with Article 3(2) UN Model.[1229] The Commentary on Article 21 UN Model therefore suggests including a source rule similar to those found in Articles 10 to 12B UN Model.[1230] Its inclusion might especially be beneficial in those situations in which the domestic laws of the contracting states differ with a possible result of either double taxation or double non-taxation.

3 *Overlap with and Room for Applicability of Article 12A UN Model*

The relationship between Articles 12A and 21 UN Model is not expressly dealt with in Article 12A UN Model nor its corresponding commentary. In this respect, however, Article 21(1) UN Model establishes that only those items of income that are 'not dealt with in the foregoing Articles' of the UN Model shall be covered by the scope of this provision therefore also expressly including Article 12A UN Model. As a result, it can be concluded that the application of Article 12A UN Model takes precedence over Article 21(1) UN Model if service fees are within the scope of the former.[1231] Whether an item of income is within its scope, however, must be ascertained with a treaty autonomous interpretation.[1232] What is more, even if service fees do not meet the definition of fees for technical services in the context of Article 12A(3) UN Model, Article 21(1) UN Model is not automatically applicable as the service fees in question might still be within the scope of another allocation rule that takes precedence over Article 21(1) UN Model, e.g., Article 7 UN Model.[1233] It therefore can be deduced from these explanations that Article 21(1) UN Model has a rather limited scope.[1234]

However, according to Article 12A(1) UN Model, only income arising in a contracting state is subject to the rules of this article. In this regard, Article 12A(5) and (6) UN Model establish where fees for technical services are deemed or are not deemed to arise. As elaborated in *Chapter 4.A.i.3.*, fees for technical services are considered to originate in the residence state of the payer or in the contracting state in which the payer has a PE or fixed base and the fees are borne by one of them.[1235] Article 12A UN Model is not applicable, however, if the payer and the payee are residents of the same contracting state or the payer is a resident of a third state without a PE or fixed base in

---

1229. *See* Rust, *supra* n. 1224, at m.no. 37.
1230. *See* para. 9 of the Commentary on Article 21 UN Model 2021.
1231. *See also* Article 22(1) DTC Egypt-Italy (1979) expressly excluding management fees (including technical services) from the scope of the article on 'other income'.
1232. *See* Chapter 2.B.iii.3.
1233. *See*, however, the remarks on the interpretation of Brazil's tax authorities on the allocation of taxing rights for fees for technical services and technical assistance without the transfer of technology: Chapter 5.C.iv.2.a., *see also* the critique by *Arnold* to tax fees for technical services on the basis of the article on other income (in the absence of a treaty provision on fees for technical services) as – based on the fundamental structure of the OECD and UN Models – it is difficult to justify that services provided by a non-resident who conducts business in the source state are not taxed on the basis of either Article 7 or 14 UN Model: Arnold, *supra* n. 1081, at 2.3.11 and 2.3.12.
1234. *See* Rust, *supra* n. 1224, at m.no. 29 and Gustav Wurm, *Art 21 Andere Einkünfte*, in: Dietmar Aigner, Georg Kofler & Michael Tumpel (eds), DBA-Kommentar, m.no. 28 (2nd ed., Linde Verlag 2019).
1235. *See* Article 12A(5) UN Model 2021.

a contracting state. The same is true if one of these is located in the residence state of the payee[1236] or a third state.[1237] In contrast hereto, Article 21(1) UN Model applies to items of income 'wherever arising' which means that Article 21(1) UN Model also covers income arising in the residence state and any third state. Therefore, in the latter-mentioned situations, Article 21(1) UN Model would apply with the result being that the taxing right for fees for technical services will exclusively be allocated to the residence state of the payee. This is justified by the fact that a sufficient nexus for source taxation as determined in Article 12A(5) UN Model is not met. The other contracting state is impeded from taxing such fees for technical services as Article 21(1) UN Model does not grant a shared taxing right. In this regard, that contracting state would also not be able to successfully claim that Article 21(3) UN Model is applicable as it requires that fees for technical services arise in that contracting state. Whether these originate there, however, has already been 'negatively' determined by applying the source rules of Article 12A(5) and (6) UN Model. As Article 21(3) UN Model does not broaden the scope of source taxation by establishing a different source rule in these cases,[1238] Article 21(1) UN Model remains applicable.

As already mentioned, Article 21(2) UN Model establishes the precedence of the PE and fixed base concept if the right or property upon which the payment of the income is based, is effectively connected with the PE or fixed base. This rule is, in principle, similar to that established in Article 12A(4) UN Model with the exception that Article 12A(4) UN Model explicitly refers to services and also refers to fees for technical services that are effectively connected with other business activities of the same or similar types as those effected through the PE.[1239]

The application of Article 21(2) UN Model requires (in a first step) that the item of income is within the scope of Article 21(1) UN Model. It is therefore required that fees for technical services are not covered by Article 12A UN Model as they are not arising in conformity with the source rule of Article 12A(5) UN Model. If this is the case, Article 12A(4) UN Model would also not be applicable.[1240] Therefore, the aforementioned services would not be in the scope of Articles 7 or 14 UN Model either. This leads to the application of Article 21(1) UN Model, even in the existence of a PE or fixed base

1236. Article 12A(6) UN Model expressly mentions such a situation if the payer is a resident of the other contracting state and conducts business in the residence state of the payee via a PE or fixed base therein.

1237. *See, e.g.*, para. 41 of the Commentary on Article 12A UN Model 2021: 'Article 12A deals only with fees for technical services arising in a Contracting State and paid to a resident of the other Contracting State. It does not, therefore, apply to fees for technical services arising in a third State.'

1238. *See* Rust, *supra* n. 1224, at m.no. 36: 'It would be against the object and purpose…to allow the other Contracting State to tax the income through the backdoor of Article 21(3) UN MC….'

1239. *See also* Chapter 4.C.i.4.f.

1240. Note that Articles 11(4) and 12(4) UN Model include a comma after 'arise'. *See, e.g.*, Article 12(4) UN Model: '… carries on business in the other Contracting State in which the royalties arise, through ….' Such a comma, however, is missing in the text of Article 12A(4) UN Model: '… carries on business in the other Contracting State in which the fees for technical services arise through …'. Whether the omission of the comma was intentionally made, cannot be ultimately determined. Nevertheless, if the omission was unintentional, a comma should be included in the next update of the UN Model to avoid interpretative difficulties.

of the payee (likely the service provider) in the other contracting state. Article 21(2) UN Model and its throwback to Articles 7 and 14 UN Model, however, would not apply to fees for technical services as the former mentioned provision only applies to a right or property upon which the payment of the income is based. As Article 21(2) UN Model does not refer to fees for technical services effectively connected with a PE or fixed base of the payee but only to passive income in the meaning of Articles 10 to 12 UN Model,[1241] Article 21(1) UN Model applies instead of Articles 7 or 14 UN Model. This constellation leads to the paradoxical situation that the current version of the UN Model restricts source taxing rights for fees for technical services, even if these are effectively connected with a PE or fixed base of the payee in the other contracting state. This is due to the fact that without a provision corresponding to Article 12A UN Model, a source state would have a taxing right in the aforementioned situation due to the applicability of either Article 7 or 14 UN Model. In the author's opinion, this result is contrary to the ultimate aim of the inclusion of Article 12A to the UN Model 2017, i.e., the extension of source taxing rights for fees for technical services. Hence, it might be advisable to change Article 21(2) UN Model to also include a reference with regard to fees for technical services effectively connected with a PE or fixed base, to prevent such – in the author's opinion – undesirable result.

1241. *See* Rust, *supra* n. 1226, at 331 et seq.

CHAPTER 5

Conclusion

The UN Tax Committee introduced Article 12A on the taxation of fees for technical services as part of the 2017 update of the UN Model in May 2018 in New York. The introduction of such a provision was the result of long-enduring discussions beginning in the third session of the UN Tax Committee in 2007. During this session, possible revisions to Article 5 UN Model on permanent establishments were proposed by the Subcommittee on Definition of Permanent Establishment (*Chapter 3.B.i.*).

In its eighth session in 2012, the UN Tax Committee declared discussions on the taxation of fees for technical services as the most pressing issue as substantial amounts of revenue may be generated from technical services provided in a state without being physically present therein. This could lead to tax base erosion. In this regard, the consultant of the UN Subcommittee on the Taxation of Services, Prof. *Arnold*, noted early that the term 'technical services' is inherently difficult to define as states use it to describe several different types of services such as managerial, consultancy, or administrative services. The introduction of a separate article on the taxation of fees for technical services was subsequently repeatedly subject to criticism by *Arnold* and several members of the UN Tax Committee as tax base erosion is not specific to technical but to all types of services. However, after presenting several different options for consideration to the UN Tax Committee in the eighth session of the UN Tax Committee, it was finally decided to include a separate provision on the taxation of fees for technical services to the UN Model. In this regard, it seems that the UN Tax Committee chose one of the least favourite options presented by *Arnold* as he mentioned that drafting a new provision will face several serious challenges, especially the one of drafting a definition of technical services that would provide sufficient legal certainty for taxpayers and tax administrations. Furthermore, several members of the UN Tax Committee were rather in favour of adapting Article 5 UN Model on permanent establishments to face the challenges of being substantially involved in a state without being physically present therein (*Chapter 3.B.ii.*).

Some members of the UN Tax Committee who were appointed by OECD members were – due to its deviation from the PE principle – naturally against the inclusion of Article 12A to the UN Model. However, several non-OECD Member States already established a common practice of taxing fees for technical services at the level of the resident payer if services are provided by a non-resident. Non-OECD Member States usually base the allocation of taxing rights for fees for technical services on royalties or an autonomous article of the respective DTC in order to expand source taxing rights. This established practice already began in the early 1970s. In this regard, *Chapter 4.A.ii.1.* has shown that provisions on the taxation of fees for technical and other similar services take a vast variety of forms that are challenging to cluster. The emergence of a wide variety of different provisions on the taxation of fees for technical and other similar services in tax treaties might be explained by the non-existence of explicit treaty provisions on the taxation of fees for technical services in the OECD and UN Models before the introduction of Article 12A to the UN Model 2017. The non-existence of such a model provision that might serve as a basis for tax treaty negotiations in conjunction with a corresponding means of interpretation as found in the Commentaries to the OECD and UN Models led – in the author's opinion – to an increasing level of uncertainty for tax authorities and taxpayers.

The UN Tax Committee based the definition of fees for technical services as defined in Article 12A(3) UN Model on the autonomous articles concluded by non-OECD Member States in the past. In this respect, as also the historical analysis by the author showed, certain types of services are commonly found in the definition of fees for technical services irrespective of the labelling as 'Royalties and Fees for Technical Services', 'Technical Fees', 'Management Fees', 'Management and Technical Fees', or others alike. These services include technical, managerial, and consultancy services. They are also those that the UN Tax Committee decided to include in the definition of fees for technical services of Article 12A(3) UN Model. The inclusion of an exhaustive definition of 'fees for technical services' without reference to domestic law has the purpose of providing legal certainty to taxpayers and tax administrations in the future (*Chapter 4.A.ii.*).

In the author's opinion, however, it is actually due to the ordinary meaning of the term 'technical' and its circular use as a definition for the super category and the subcategory of Article 12A UN Model that the scope of this article cannot easily be established (*Chapter 4.A.ii.2.*). Subsequently, technical services also cannot be easily differentiated from other non-technical services which lead to legal uncertainty for taxpayers and tax administrations.

The term 'technical' as found in the Commentary on Article 12A UN Model is defined as involving 'the application of specialized knowledge, skill or expertise with respect to a particular art, science, profession or occupation'.[1242] Ascribing a universal meaning to the term 'technical' in the context of Article 12A UN Model based on its ordinary meaning, however, would be exuberant and redundant. As opined in *Chapter 4.A.ii.2.*, the term 'technical' as found in Article 12A(3) UN Model necessarily needs to be ascribed a different meaning than the one in the super category of Article 12A UN Model. In the author's opinion, the definition of Article 12A(3) UN Model covers three

1242. *See* para. 64 of the Commentary on Article 12A UN Model 2021.

categories of services: (1) fees for 'technical services of technical nature', (2) 'technical services of managerial nature', and (3) 'technical services of consultancy nature'. All three categories of services have in common that specialized knowledge, skill, or expertise is used to provide these services either in the field of engineering (1), through application of managerial services (2), or consultancy services, most likely by professionals or other independent persons covered by Article 14(2) UN Model (3). These different types of services might also overlap. Examples would include consulting on issues of corporate governance of an enterprise on issues referring to the field of engineering.

The term 'technical' as used in the context of Article 12A UN Model has to be distinguished from the one used in the alternative version of Article 12 UN Model on fees for included services. This is because technical and consultancy services related to the latter-mentioned provision have a narrower meaning than that under Article 12A UN Model. Fees for included services provisions usually only include such technical or consultancy services within their scope if they are ancillary and subsidiary to the application or enjoyment of the right, property, or information for which a royalty is received. These provisions are, from a historical perspective, closely connected to the concept of the transfer of IP rights or, more concretely, know-how. The transfer of know-how often required additional auxiliary services from the grantor to the grantee so that the grantee would be able to make use of them. As concluded in *Chapter 4.B.ii.3.*, the term 'technical' therefore has a narrower meaning in the context of the aforementioned situation as it solely relates to services requiring an expertise in technology. In addition, also consultancy services need to be interpreted in light of such context, i.e., consulting on technological issues. Some non-OECD members, such as India, also additionally include make-available provisions in the article on 'Royalties and fees for technical services' to further expand the concept of the transfer of know-how to services that are not only of auxiliary character to the transfer of know-how. Therefore, also technical services forming the principal part of the contract would be covered by the make-available provision if the service enables the grantee the use of technical knowledge, experience, skill, know-how, or processes.

Such 'technical assistance', however, is already covered by Article 12 UN Model. This is clarified through the explanations in the Commentary on Article 12 UN Model on mixed contracts.

As aforementioned, Article 12A UN Model intends to cover specialized services of a technical, managerial, or consultancy nature. These services are covered by the mentioned article only if they are rendered in a B2B context. This is due to the fact that only B2B services have a base-eroding character. Article 12A UN Model, however, does not fully implement the base erosion principle as it does not cover all types of service payments in a B2B context. Nevertheless, the partial implementation of the base-erosion principle serves the object and purpose of the inclusion of Article 12A UN Model. The UN Tax Committee did not intend to include a provision covering all types of services within the UN Model but only those that are of a specialized nature that are rendered in a B2B context for a short period of time. It therefore also deviates from the general PE principle that services need to be physically rendered in a state through a specific period of time. This is based on the fact that non-resident service providers earn substantial amounts of income from the provision of specialized services that often cannot be provided by service providers from developing countries. The advancements in modern communication technologies also fostered the possibility of rendering specialized services such as consulting and management services through digital means without the requirement of being physically present in a state (*Chapter 3.C.ii.*).

Although Article 12A UN Model applies to services that are not physically rendered in a state, the article does not apply to services that build the essential core of the digital economy, i.e., digital advertising or intermediation services. This is, on the one hand, based on the fact that Article 12A UN Model does not apply to B2C services and, on the other hand, due to the fact that Article 12A UN Model only applies in the existence of a human element in the provision of services. This requirement is not explicitly mentioned in the Commentary on Article 12A UN Model. However, it has been used by Indian courts in several cases to distinguish technical services in a broad context from other non-technical services on the basis of the rule of *noscitur a sociis* (*Chapter 4.A.ii.3.*) The element of human involvement has also been adopted by the UN Tax Committee in the drafting process of Article 12B UN Model. It now serves as a further element to distinguish fees for technical services and income from automated services; the latter is covered by Article 12B UN Model.

However, the human element mainly refers to the customization of the services to the needs of a specific customer. It is also an element used by Articles 12A and 12B UN Model to distinguish specialized from routine services to determine the scope of these articles. In the author's opinion, however, customization is not an appropriate element to determine whether services are of a specialized or routine nature. This is generally due to the fact that the Commentary on Article 12B UN Model connects the concepts of human involvement and customization to each other using several vague and undefined terms such as 'minimal', 'ancillary', 'limited', 'high', 'significant', or 'additional', but not clearly defining the concepts of human involvement and customization (*Chapter 4.C.*).

In the author's opinion, the use of the concept of 'standard facility' as defined by Indian jurisprudence might serve as a more appropriate means to distinguish specialized from routine services either within the definition of Article 12A itself or between the aforementioned article and Article 12B UN Model. The mentioned concept refers to the possibility of the use of standardized, routine services by an undefined number of persons without the requirement to specifically adapt services to the needs of a specific customer (*Chapter 4.A.ii.3.*). This might include the use of transportation services by a bus, renting a crane to load cargo for shipping, the access to a database, or the use of a digital interface that is available to an undefined number of persons. The distinction between specialized and routine services is crucial for the application of Article 12A as it only intends to cover specialized services. However, the Commentary on Article 12A does not provide sufficient guidance in this regard. Therefore, there is a high risk that several tax administrations of non-OECD Member States will presumably apply a withholding tax on any type of service payment received by a non-resident service provider from a resident of that state. This is due to reasons of generating profits and administrative simplicity. In this regard, the refund of excessive tax withheld will be challenging for taxpayers as it will be inherently difficult for taxpayers to prove that specialized knowledge, skill, or expertise was not applied in the rendering of a specific service leading to the application of a withholding tax.

Except for Articles 12A and 12B UN Model, other allocation rules of the UN Model do not differentiate between specialized and routine services. In this regard, the scope of Article 12A UN Model is more specific in relation to Articles 7 and 14 UN Model. The scope of the latter-mentioned articles is generally broader than that of Article 12A UN Model as they also include routine services and B2C services within their scope. Within the scope of Articles 7 and 14 UN Model, the PE principle and the concept of fixed base – but not the 183-day rule of Article 14(1)(b) – take precedence over Article 12A UN Model if technical services are also within the scope of the formerly mentioned articles (*Chapter 4.D.*). In this respect, technical services as defined in Article 12A(3) UN Model 2021 will generally be within the scope of Article 7 UN Model as a subcategory of business profits. In this regard, especially the deletion of the wording 'for the same or connected project' in Article 5(3)(b) as part of the 2017 revision of the UN Model broadens the scope of the service PE provision. The result is the narrowing down of the scope of Article 12A UN Model in certain circumstances such as technical services provided by an enterprise for several unrelated projects during a time span of more than 183 days in the source state.

Concerning the application of Article 14 UN Model, it may be concluded that Article 12A UN Model covers the core activities most commonly provided by independent service providers, such as professionals. These services generally require the application of specialized knowledge, skill, or expertise based on education in a specific discipline. Although Article 14 UN Model also covers routine services provided by professionals or other independent service providers, such services are usually only of an auxiliary nature and are not part of the core activities covered by Article 14 UN Model (*Chapter 4.D.ii.*). According to Article 12A(4)(a) UN Model, Article 14 UN Model shall take precedence over Article 12A if technical services that are within the scope of Article 14 UN Model are performed in the contracting state from a fixed base therein and fees for such services are effectively connected with such fixed base. In the absence of a fixed base, however, Article 12A UN Model applies – on the basis of the wording of Article 12A(2) UN Model – notwithstanding the provisions of Article 14 UN Model.

The application of Article 12A UN Model is subject to the provisions of Articles 8, 16, and 17 UN Model. Therefore, if technical services are covered by the aforementioned articles, their application takes precedence over Article 12A UN Model (*Chapter 4.E.*) These might include engineering or consultancy services that are ancillary to the operation of ships or aircraft (Article 8) or managerial services provided by directors or top-level managerial officials (Article 16). Regarding Article 17 UN Model, in the author's opinion, it is difficult to imagine that technical services as defined in Article 12A(3) UN Model would fall under Article 17 UN Model. This is generally due to a lack of a predominantly entertaining character of technical, consultancy, and managerial services.

Regarding the application of Article 21 UN Model on fees for technical services, it can be concluded that Article 21(1) UN Model applies to these 'wherever arising'. Therefore, Article 21(1) UN Model would apply to these fees when they arise in the residence state of the payee or any third state. In the author's opinion, states cannot successfully claim that Article 21(3) UN Model is applicable, as its application has already been 'negatively' determined by the source rules of Article 12A(5) and (6) UN Model and, in the author's opinion, Article 21(3) UN Model does not aim to expand source taxing right by establishing a broader source rule. The situation as specified in Article 21(2) UN Model does not cover fees for technical services effectively connected with a PE or fixed base. This results in the non-applicability of Article 21(2) UN Model as well as the precedence of the PE principle and the concept of a fixed base.

The introduction of Article 12A to the UN Model 2017 may be seen as a significant step forward in the discussion on broadening source taxing rights for specialized services that are conducted without or with only a small degree of physical presence in a state. In this regard, especially developing countries in their function as importers of specialized services may benefit from the inclusion of a provision equivalent to Article 12A UN Model in their tax treaties. Indeed, the source rules of Article 12A UN Model are relatively easy to apply as they mainly focus on the payer-payee relationship with the application of gross taxation on the payment made. In addition, tax administrations of developing countries may justify the broadening of the scope of Article 12A UN Model on all types of services since there is insufficient guidance of the Commentary on Article 12A UN Model with regards to the interpretation of the term 'fees for technical services'.

However, the view of OECD members is that it is required in the current landscape of international tax policy that a certain degree of physical presence of the service provider exists in a state in order to justify source taxation. However, it may still be challenging for a non-OECD member to agree with an OECD Member State to include a provision equivalent to Article 12A UN Model in a tax treaty. In this respect, OECD Member States may – due to their function as an exporter of technical services – be less interested in including Article 12A UN Model in a tax treaty under negotiations with a non-OECD member. In addition, even if such an inclusion might be considered beneficial by an OECD member to a bilateral relationship with a particular non-OECD member due to special features of such a bilateral relationship, it remains challenging to set a tax rate that not only is sufficiently low so as to not discourage inbound investments but is also high enough to effectively address tax base erosion.

Appendices

APPENDIX I

Table of Examined Tax Treaties of Selected African States Including Provisions on Fees for Technical Services

	No. of Examined Tax Treaties[1243]	*Autonomous Fees for Technical Services Provision*	*Fees for Technical Services and Other Similar Services in the Article on Royalties*	*Other Provisions Including Fees for Technical Services*	*Exclusions of Fees for Technical Services from Source Taxation Without a PE*
Angola	1	1			
Benin	4		1		
Botswana	20	19	1		
Cape Verde	3		1		
Congo	8	1			
Egypt	52	1	9	1	2
Gabon	10				
Gambia	7	2		1	
Ghana	16	11	5		
Kenya	18	7	1		1
Lesotho	4	2			
Mauritius	40	2	2		2
Nigeria	18	1			2
Rwanda	7	6	1		

1243. Note: If a tax treaty between two examined states exists, such treaty was counted only once for purposes of this study. The study takes into account tax treaties that were signed before the UN Model 2017 was published (May 2018). It also considers tax treaties that are not yet in force or that were already terminated.

	No. of Examined Tax Treaties[1243]	*Autonomous Fees for Technical Services Provision*	*Fees for Technical Services and Other Similar Services in the Article on Royalties*	*Other Provisions Including Fees for Technical Services*	*Exclusions of Fees for Technical Services from Source Taxation Without a PE*
Senegal	17	3	2	1	
South Africa	69	4	4		2
Tunisia	51	2	17	3	1
Uganda	9	5	1		1
Zimbabwe	15	9	1		
Total	**369**	**76**	**46**	**6**	**11**

APPENDIX II

List of Examined Tax Treaties of Selected African States

State	*Treaty Partners*	*Autonomous Fees for Technical Services Provision*	*Fees for Technical Services and Other Similar Services in the Article on Royalties*	*Other Provisions Including Fees for Technical Services*	*Exclusion of Fees for Technical Services from Source Taxation Without a PE*
Angola	United Arab Emirates (2018)	United Arab Emirates (2018): Article 14 (Fees for technical and other services)			
Benin	France (1975), Kuwait (2009), Norway (1979), United Arab Emirates (2013)		United Arab Emirates (2013): Article 13 (Royalties)		
Botswana	Barbados (2005), Belgium (2017), China (2020), France (1999) India (2006), Ireland (2014), Lesotho (2010), Malawi (2016), Malta (2017), Mauritius (1995, 2015), Mozambique (2009), Namibia (2004), Russia (2003), Seychelles (2004), South Africa (2003, 2013), Swaziland (2010), Sweden (1992, 2013), United Kingdom (2005), Zambia (2013), Zimbabwe (2004)	Barbados (2005): Article 21 (Technical Fees), Belgium (2017): Article 20 (Technical Fees), France (1999): Article 21 (Management, consultancy and technical fees), India (2006): Article 13 (Technical Fees), Ireland (2014):	China (2012): Article 12 (Technical and consultancy fees)		

		Article 20 (Technical Fees), Lesotho (2010): Article 13 (Technical Fees), Malawi (2016): Article 20 (Technical Fees), Malta (2017): Article 20 (Technical Fees), Mauritius (1995, 2015): Article 22 (Management, consultancy and technical fees), Mozambique (2009): Article 21 (Technical Fees), Namibia (2004): Article 21 (Technical Fees), Russia (2003): Article 21 (Management, consultancy and technical fees), Seychelles (2004): Article 21 (Technical fees), South Africa (2003, 2013): Article 20 (Technical fees), Swaziland (2010): Article 13 (Technical Fees), Sweden (1992, 2013):			

State	*Treaty Partners*	*Autonomous Fees for Technical Services Provision*	*Fees for Technical Services and Other Similar Services in the Article on Royalties*	*Other Provisions Including Fees for Technical Services*	*Exclusion of Fees for Technical Services from Source Taxation Without a PE*
		Article 21 (Management, consultancy and technical fees), United Kingdom (2005): Article 13 (Technical Fees), Zambia (2013): Article 13 (Technical Fees), Zimbabwe (2004): Article 13 (Technical Fees)			
Cape Verde	Mauritius (2017), Portugal (1999), Spain (2017)		Protocol to the DTC Mauritius (2017) on Article 12 (Royalties)		
Congo	Belgium (2007), China (2018), France (1987), Italy (2003), Mauritius (2010), South Africa (2005), Tunisia (2005), Zimbabwe (2002)	Zimbabwe (2002): Article 13 (Technical Fees)			

Egypt	Albania (2005), Algeria (2001), Armenia (2005), Austria (1962), Bahrain (2016), Belarus (1998), Belgium (1991), Bulgaria (2003), Canada (1983), China (1997), Croatia (2005), Czech Republic (1995), Denmark (1989), Ethiopia (2011), Finland (1965, 1974), France (1980, 1999), Georgia (2010), Germany (1987), Greece (2004), Hungary (1991), India (1969), Indonesia (1998), Iraq (1968), Ireland (2012), Italy (1979), Japan (1968), Jordan (1996), Korea (1992), Macedonia (1993), Malaysia (1997), Malta (1999), Morocco (1989), Netherlands (1999), Norway (1964), Pakistan (1995), Poland (1996), Romania (1979), Russia (1997), Saudi-Arabia (2016), Serbia and Montenegro (2005), Singapore (1996), Slovak Republic (2004),	Pakistan (1995): Article 12 (Fees for technical services)	Bahrain (2016): Article 12 (Royalties), Croatia (2005): Article 12 (Royalties), Georgia (2010): Article 12 (Royalties), Greece (2004): Article 12 (Royalties), Indonesia (1998): Article 12 (Royalties), Morocco (1989): Article 12 (Royalties), Saudi-Arabia (2016): Article 12 (Royalties), Serbia and Montenegro (2005): Article 12 (Royalties), Spain (2005): Article 12 (Royalties)	Italy (1979): Article 22 (Other Income)	Protocol to the DTC Korea (1992) on Article 7 (Business profits), Protocol to the DTC Netherlands (1999) on Articles 7 (Business profits) and 14 (Independent personal services)

State	*Treaty Partners*	*Autonomous Fees for Technical Services Provision*	*Fees for Technical Services and Other Similar Services in the Article on Royalties*	*Other Provisions Including Fees for Technical Services*	*Exclusion of Fees for Technical Services from Source Taxation Without a PE*
	Spain (2005), Sweden (1994), Switzerland (1987), Syria (1991), Thailand (2006), Turkey (1993), Ukraine (1997), United Arab Emirates (1994), United Kingdom (1977), Vietnam (2006)				
Gabon	Belgium (1993), Canada (2002), France (1995), Italy (1999), Korea (2010), Lebanon (2001), Mauritius (2013), Morocco (1999), South Africa (2005), Tunisia (1986)				
Gambia	Norway (1994), Qatar (2014), Switzerland (1963), Taiwan (1998), Turkey (2014), United Arab Emirates (2015), United Kingdom (1980)	Norway (1994): Article 14 (Management fees), United Kingdom (1980): Article 14 (Fees for technical services)		United Arab Emirates (2015): Article 9 (Shipping and Air Transport)	

Ghana	Barbados (2008), Belgium (2005), Czech Republic (2017), Denmark (2014), France (1993), Germany (2004), Ireland (2018), Mauritius (2017), Morocco (2017), Netherlands (2008, 2017), Serbia and Montenegro (2000), Seychelles (2014), Singapore (2017), South Africa (2004), Switzerland (2008 2014), United Kingdom (1993)	Barbados (2008): Article 13 (Management fees), Belgium (2005): Article 18 (Management fees), France (1993): Article 13 (Management fees), Ireland (2018): Article 13 (Technical services fees), Mauritius (2017): Article 13 (Technical services fees), Morocco (2017): Article 13 (Fees for technical services), Serbia and Montenegro (2000): Article 13 (Management fees), Seychelles (2014): Article 13 (Technical fees), Singapore (2017): Article 13 (Services Fees), South Africa (2004): Article 20 (Management Fees), United Kingdom (1993): Article 17 (Management and technical fees)	Czech Republic (2017): Article 12 (Royalties and services fees), Denmark (2014): Article 12 (Royalties and Services Fees), Germany (2004): Article 12 (Royalties and Services fees), Netherlands (2008, 2017): Article 12 (Royalties and technical service fees), Switzerland (2008, 2014): Article 12 (Royalties and services fees)		

State	*Treaty Partners*	*Autonomous Fees for Technical Services Provision*	*Fees for Technical Services and Other Similar Services in the Article on Royalties*	*Other Provisions Including Fees for Technical Services*	*Exclusion of Fees for Technical Services from Source Taxation Without a PE*
Kenya	Canada (1983), China (2017), Denmark (1972), France (2007), Germany (1977), India (2016), Iran (2012), Italy (1979), Korea (2014), Kuwait (2013), Netherlands (2015), Norway (1972), Qatar (2014), Seychelles (2014, 2015), Singapore (2018), Sweden (1973), United Kingdom (1976), Zambia (1968)	Canada (1983): Article 14 (Management and professional fees), China (2017): Article 13 (Technical Fees), Denmark (1972): Article 14 (Management or professional fees), India (2016): Article 13 (Fees for Management, Professional and Technical Services), Norway (1972): Article 14 (Management or professional fees), Seychelles (2014, 2015): Article 13 (Management, Professional or Technical Fees), United Kingdom (1976): Article 14 (Management fees)	Germany (1977): Article 12 (Royalties and management fees)		Protocol to the DTC Netherlands (2015) on Article 7 (Business profits) and 14 (Independent personal services)

Lesotho	Mauritius (1997), Seychelles (2011), South Africa (2014), United Kingdom (2016)	Seychelles (2011): Article 13 (Technical Fees), South Africa (2014): Article 13 (Technical Fees)			
Mauritius	Australia (2010), Bangladesh (2009), Barbados (2004, 2017), Belgium (1995), China (1994, 2006), Croatia (2002), Cyprus (2000, 2017), Egypt (2012), France (1980), Germany (2011), Guernsey (2013), Italy (1990, 2010), Kuwait (1997), Luxembourg (1995), Madagascar (1994), Malaysia (1992), Malta (2014), Monaco (2013), Morocco (2015), Mozambique (1997), Namibia (1995), Nepal (1999), Nigeria (2012), Oman (1998), Pakistan (1994), Qatar (2008), Russia (1995), Rwanda (2013), Seychelles (2005),	Rwanda (2013): Article 13 (Management or Professional Fees), Uganda (2003): Article 13 (Technical Fees)	Egypt (2012): Article 12 (Royalties), Kuwait (1997): Article 12 (Royalties)		Protocol to the DTC France (1980) on Article 7 (Business profits), Protocol to the DTC Germany (2011) on Article 7 (Business Profits)

State	*Treaty Partners*	*Autonomous Fees for Technical Services Provision*	*Fees for Technical Services and Other Similar Services in the Article on Royalties*	*Other Provisions Including Fees for Technical Services*	*Exclusion of Fees for Technical Services from Source Taxation Without a PE*
	Singapore (1995), South Africa (2013), Sri Lanka (1996), Swaziland (1994), Sweden (2011), Thailand (1997), Uganda (2003), United Arab Emirates (2006), United Kingdom (1981, 2018), Zambia (2011), Zimbabwe (1992)				
Nigeria	Belgium (1989), Canada (1992), China (2002), Czech Republic (1989), France (1990), Korea (2006), Kuwait (2011), Netherlands (1991), Pakistan (1989), Philippines (1997), Qatar (2016), Romania (1992), Singapore (2017), Slovak Republic (1989), Spain (2009), Sweden (2004), United Arab Emirates (2016), United Kingdom (1987)	United Arab Emirates (2016): Article 14 (Technical Service Fees)			Protocol to the DTC France (1990) on Article 12 (Royalties), Protocol to the DTC Netherlands (1991) on Article 7 (Business profits)

Rwanda	Barbados (2014), Belgium (2007), Jersey (2015), Morocco (2016), Singapore (2014), South Africa (2002), United Arab Emirates (2017)	Barbados (2014): Article 13 (Management or Professional Fees), Belgium (2007): Article 13 (Technical fees), Jersey (2015): Article 13 (Management or Professional Fees), Singapore (2014): Article 13 (Management or Professional Fees), South Africa (2002): Article 14 (Technical Fees), United Arab Emirates (2017): Article 14 (Management or professional fees)	Morocco (2016): Article 12 (Royalties and fees for technical services)		
Senegal	Belgium (1987), Canada (2001), France (1974, 1991), Iran (2010), Italy (1998), Lebanon (2002), Luxembourg (2016), Malaysia (2010), Mauritania (1971), Morocco (2002), Norway (1994), Portugal (2014), Qatar (1998),	Iran (2010): Article 13 (Fees for Technical Services), Malaysia (2010): Article 13 (Fees for Technical Services), Portugal (2014): Article 13 (Remuneration for technical services)	France (1974, 1991): Article 20 (Royalties), Morocco (2002): Article 12 (Royalties)	United Arab Emirates (2015): Article 9 (Shipping and Air Transport)	

State	*Treaty Partners*	*Autonomous Fees for Technical Services Provision*	*Fees for Technical Services and Other Similar Services in the Article on Royalties*	*Other Provisions Including Fees for Technical Services*	*Exclusion of Fees for Technical Services from Source Taxation Without a PE*
	Spain (2006), Tunisia (1984), United Arab Emirates (2015), United Kingdom (2015)				
South Africa	Algeria (1998), Australia (1999, 2008), Austria (1996, 2011), Belarus (2002), Belgium (1995), Brazil (2003, 2015), Bulgaria (2004), Cameroon (2015), Canada (1995), Chile (2012), China (2000), Croatia (1996), Cyprus (1997, 2015), Czech Republic (1996), Denmark (1995), Egypt (1997), Ethiopia (2004), Finland (1995), France (1993), Germany (1973), Greece (1998), Grenada (1960), Hungary (1994), Indonesia (1997), Iran (1997), Ireland (1997, 2010), Israel (1978), Italy (1995),	Cameroon (2015): Article 14 (Fees for technical services), Malaysia (2005, 2011): Article 13 (Fees for Technical Services), Swaziland (2004): Article 13 (Technical Fees), Zimbabwe (2015): Article 13 (Technical Fees)	Australia (1999, 2008): Article 12 (Royalties), Brazil (2003, 2015): Protocol to the DTC on Article 12 (Royalties), Indonesia (1997): Article 12 (Royalties), Pakistan (1998): Article 12 (Royalties and fees for technical services)		Protocol to the DTC United States (1997) on Article 12 (Royalties), Protocol to the DTC Netherlands (2005, 2008) on Article 7 (Business Profits)

	Japan (1997), Kenya (2010), Korea (1995), Kuwait (2004), Luxembourg (1998), Malawi (1971), Malaysia (2005, 2011), Malta (1997, 2012), Mexico (2009), Mozambique (2007), Namibia (1998), Netherlands (2005, 2008), New Zealand (2002), Nigeria (2000), Norway (1996, 2012), Oman (2002, 2011), Pakistan (1998), Poland (1993), Portugal (2006), Qatar (2015), Romania (1993), Russia (1995), Saudi Arabia (2007), Seychelles (1998, 2011), Sierra Leone (1960), Singapore (2015), Slovak Republic (1998), Spain (2006), Sudan (2007), Swaziland (2004), Sweden (1995, 2010), Switzerland (2007), Tanzania (2005), Thailand (1996), Turkey (2005, 2013), Ukraine (2003), United Arab Emirates (2015),				

State	*Treaty Partners*	*Autonomous Fees for Technical Services Provision*	*Fees for Technical Services and Other Similar Services in the Article on Royalties*	*Other Provisions Including Fees for Technical Services*	*Exclusion of Fees for Technical Services from Source Taxation Without a PE*
	United Kingdom (2002, 2010), United States (1997), Zambia (1956), Zimbabwe (2015)				
Tunisia	Algeria (1985), Austria (1977), Belgium (2004), Burkina Faso (2003), Cameroon (1999), Canada (1982), Chad (2012), China (2002), Czech Republic (1990), Denmark (1981), Egypt (1989), Ethiopia (2003), France (1973), Germany (2018), Greece (1992, 2007), Guinea (1993), Hungary (1992), Indonesia (1992), Iran (2001), Italy (1979), Ivory Coast (1999), Korea (1988), Kuwait (2000), Luxembourg (1996, 2014), Mali (2000), Malta (2000), Morocco (1974), Netherlands (1995), Norway (1978), Oman (1997),	Serbia (2012): Article 13 (Technical Fees), South Africa (1999): Article 12A (Technical Fees)	Belgium (2004): Article 12 (Royalties), Cameroon (1999): Article 12 (Royalties), Canada (1982): Article XII (Royalties), China (2002): Article 12 (Royalties), Czech Republic (1990): Article 12 (Royalties), Hungary (1992): Article 12 (Royalties), Indonesia (1992): Article 12 (Royalties), Korea (1988): Article 12 (Royalties), Luxembourg (1996, 2014): Article 12 (Royalties), Malta (2000): Article 12 (Royalties), Netherlands (1995): Article 12 (Royalties), Pakistan (1996):	France (1973): Article 7 (Business profits), Norway (1978): Article 7 (Business profits), Togo (1987): Article 7 (Business profits)	Protocol to the DTC Germany (2018) with respect to Article 7 (Business profits)

	Pakistan (1996), Poland (1993), Portugal (1999), Qatar (1997), Romania (1987), Saudi Arabia (2010), Serbia (2012), Singapore (2018), Slovak Republic (1990), South Africa (1999), Spain (1982), Sweden (1981), Switzerland (1994), Syria (1998), Togo (1987), Turkey (1986), United Arab Emirates (1996), United Kingdom (1982), United States (1985, 1989), Vietnam (2010), Yemen (1998)		Article 12 (Royalties), Poland (1993): Article 12 (Royalties), Portugal (1999): Article 12 (Royalties), Romania (1987): Article 13 (Royalties), Singapore (2018): Article 12 (Royalties), United States (1985, 1989): Article 12 (Royalties)		
Uganda	Belgium (2007), China (2012), Denmark (2000), India (2004), Italy (2000), Norway (1999), South Africa (1997), United Kingdom (1992), Zambia (1968)	Denmark (2000): Article 13 (Administration and management fees), Italy (2000): Article 13 (Technical fees), Norway (1999): Article 13 (Administration and management fees), South Africa (1997): Article 13 (Technical fees), United Kingdom (1992): Article 13 (Technical fees)	India (2004): Article 12 (Royalties and fees for technical services)		Protocol to the DTC Belgium (2007) on Article 12 (Royalties)

State	*Treaty Partners*	*Autonomous Fees for Technical Services Provision*	*Fees for Technical Services and Other Similar Services in the Article on Royalties*	*Other Provisions Including Fees for Technical Services*	*Exclusion of Fees for Technical Services from Source Taxation Without a PE*
Zimbabwe	Bulgaria (1988), Canada (1992), China (2015), France (1993), Germany (1988), Indonesia (2001), Kuwait (2006), Malaysia (1994), Netherlands (1989), Norway (1989), Poland (1993), Serbia and Montenegro (1996), Seychelles (2002), Sweden (1989), United Kingdom (1982)	Bulgaria (1988): Article 11 (Technical fees), Canada (1992): Article 13 (Technical fees), Indonesia (2001): Article 13 (Technical fees), Malaysia (1994): Article 13 (Technical fees), Norway (1989): Article 13 (Technical fees), Serbia and Montenegro (1996): Article 13 (Technical fees), Seychelles (2002): Article 12B (Technical and management fees), Sweden (1989):	Germany (1988): Article 12 (Royalties and fees for technical services)		

		Article 13 (Technical fees), United Kingdom (1982): Article 13 (Technical fees)			
Total	**369**	**76**	**46**	**6**	**11**

APPENDIX III

Table of Autonomous Fees for Technical Services Provisions in Examined Tax Treaties of Selected African States

	Number of Provisions	Fees for Technical Services	Technical Fees	Remuneration for Technical Services	Fees for Technical and Other Services	Management, Consultancy and Technical Fees	Management Fees
Angola	1				1		
Botswana	19		15			4	
Congo	1		1				
Egypt	1	1					
Gambia	2	1					1
Ghana	11	1	1				5
Kenya	7		1				1
Lesotho	2		2				
Mauritius	2		1				
Nigeria	1						
Rwanda	6		2				
Senegal	3	2		1			
South Africa	4	2	2				
Tunisia	2		2				
Uganda	5		3				
Zimbabwe	9		8				
Total	**76**	**7**	**38**	**1**	**1**	**4**	**7**

Management and Technical Fees	*Services Fees*	*Technical Services Fees*	*Management or Professional Fees*	*Management, Professional or Technical Fees*	*Fees for Management, Professional and Technical Services*	*Administration and Management Fees*	*Technical and Management Fees*
1	1	2					
			3	1	1		
			1				
		1					
			4				
						2	
							1
1	**1**	**3**	**8**	**1**	**1**	**2**	**1**

APPENDIX IV

Table of Fees for Technical and Other Similar Services in the Article on Royalties in Examined Tax Treaties of Selected African States

	Number of Provisions	*Royalties*	*Royalties and Fees for Technical Services*	*Royalties and Technical Services Fees*	*Royalties and Services Fees*	*Royalties and Management Fees*
Benin	1	1				
Botswana	1	1				
Cape Verde	1	1				
Egypt	9	9				
Ghana	5			1	4	
Kenya	1					1
Mauritius	2	2				
Rwanda	1		1			
Senegal	2	2				
South Africa	4	3	1			
Tunisia	17	17				
Uganda	1		1			
Zimbabwe	1	1				
Total	**46**	**37**	**3**	**1**	**4**	**1**

APPENDIX V

Table of Definitions in the Autonomous Fees for Technical Services Provisions in Examined Tax Treaties of Selected African States

Part 1[1244]

	Number of provisions	*Any service of a technical, managerial or consultancy nature*[1245]	*Any service of a managerial, professional, technical or consultancy nature or such similar service, performed by a resident of a Contracting State for a resident of the other Contracting State.*	*Any service of a technical, managerial, professional or consultancy nature, unless the payment is the reimbursement of actual expenses incurred by that person with respect to the service*
Fees for technical services	7	6		
Technical fees	38	10		1
Remuneration for technical services	1	1		
Fees for technical and other services	1	1		
Management, consultancy and technical fees	4			
Management fees	7	6		
Management and technical fees	1	1		
Services Fees	1	1		
Technical services fees	3	2	1	
Management or professional fees	8			1
Management, professional or technical fees	1			
Fees for management, professional and technical services	1			

1244. Due to the huge variety of different definitions, the author decided to display these by providing two tables.

1245. This category also includes 'any services of a managerial, technical or consultancy nature', 'managerial or technical or consultancy services' and 'any managerial, technical or consultancy service'.

Any services of an administrative, technical, managerial or consultancy nature performed outside that State	*Any services of a managerial, technical, professional or consultancy nature*	*Any services of an administrative, technical, managerial or consultancy nature*	*Any service of a technical or consultancy nature*	*Any service of an administrative, technical, managerial or consultancy nature, unless the payment is the reimbursement of actual expenses incurred by that person with respect to the service*
			1	
4	1	15		1
4				
	7			
	1			
	1			

	Number of provisions	*Any service of a technical, managerial or consultancy nature*	*Any service of a managerial, professional, technical or consultancy nature or such similar service, performed by a resident of a Contracting State for a resident of the other Contracting State.*	*Any service of a technical, managerial, professional or consultancy nature, unless the payment is the reimbursement of actual expenses incurred by that person with respect to the service*
Administration and management fees	2			
Technical and management fees	1			1
Total	**76**	**28**	**1**	**3**

Any service of an administrative, technical, managerial or consultancy nature, unless the payment is the reimbursement of actual expenses incurred by that person with respect to the service			**1**
Any service of a technical or consultancy nature			**1**
Any services of an administrative, technical, managerial or consultancy nature			**15**
Any services of a managerial, technical, professional or consultancy nature			**10**
Any services of an administrative, technical, managerial or consultancy nature performed outside that State			**8**

Part 2

	Number of provisions	*Any service of an administrative, technical, managerial or consultancy nature. rendered in the Contracting State of which the payer is resident.*	*Any services of an administrative, technical, managerial or consultancy nature other than services which under paragraph 3 of Article 5 are considered a permanent establishment (i.e., construction and services PE)*	*Provision of industrial or commercial advice, or management or technical services, or similar services or facilities*
Fees for technical services	7			
Technical fees	38	1	1	
Remuneration for technical services	1			
Fees for technical and other services	1			
Management, consultancy and technical fees	4			
Management fees	7			1
Management and technical fees	1			
Services Fees	1			
Technical services fees	3			
Management or professional fees	8			
Management, professional or technical fees	1			

											Any services of an administrative or managerial nature, if such services make available administrative or managerial knowledge, experience, skills or know-how, but only to the extent that the services are performed on a regular basis or for a period of more than six months.
									1		*Any services of a technical, managerial or consultancy nature, performed by a resident of a Contracting State in the other Contracting State for a period or periods exceeding in the aggregate 6 months in any twelve-month period commencing or ending in the fiscal year concerned.*
									1		*For any services such as technical and economic studies and technical assistance and other services of a technical or consultancy nature.*
									1		*Any services of a managerial, technical or consultancy nature, including technical and economic studies or technical assistance carried out in the State in which the technical fees arise.*
									1		*(i) rendering any managerial, technical or consultancy services including the services of technical or other personnel; (ii) the supply of any technical, industrial, commercial or scientific knowledge, experience or skill; (iii) the supply of services which are ancillary and subsidiary for which technical fees are received.*

	Number of provisions	*Any service of an administrative, technical, managerial or consultancy nature. rendered in the Contracting State of which the payer is resident.*	*Any services of an administrative, technical, managerial or consultancy nature other than services which under paragraph 3 of Article 5 are considered a permanent establishment (i.e., construction and services PE)*	*Provision of industrial or commercial advice, or management or technical services, or similar services or facilities*
Fees for management, professional and technical services	1			
Administration and management fees	2			
Technical and management fees	1			
Total	**76**	**1**	**1**	**1**

2		2[1246]		*Any services of an administrative or managerial nature, if such services make available administrative or managerial knowledge, experience, skills or know-how, but only to the extent that the services are performed on a regular basis or for a period of more than six months.*
1				*Any services of a technical, managerial or consultancy nature, performed by a resident of a Contracting State in the other Contracting State for a period or periods exceeding in the aggregate 6 months in any twelve-month period commencing or ending in the fiscal year concerned.*
1				*For any services such as technical and economic studies and technical assistance and other services of a technical or consultancy nature.*
1				*Any services of a managerial, technical or consultancy nature, including technical and economic studies or technical assistance carried out in the State in which the technical fees arise.*
1				*(i) rendering any managerial, technical or consultancy services including the services of technical or other personnel; (ii) the supply of any technical, industrial, commercial or scientific knowledge, experience or skill; (iii) the supply of services which are ancillary and subsidiary for which technical fees are received.*

1246. This number also includes one tax treaty that does not incorporate a make-available provision with regards to any services of an administrative or managerial nature: Article 13 DTC Norway-Uganda (1999).

APPENDIX VI

Table of Definitions in the Article on Royalties with Respect to Fees for Technical and Other Services in Examined Tax Treaties of Selected African States

Title of provision	*Number of provisions*	*Payments in consideration for any services of a managerial, technical or consultancy nature*[1247]	*Payments in consideration of any services of a managerial, technical or consultancy nature as well as payments made in consideration of the independent activities of physicians, lawyers, engineers, architects, dentists and accountants*	*Any services of a managerial, technical or consultancy nature rendered in a contracting State*	*Technical services*	*Technical and consultancy services*	*Consideration for any services of a technical, managerial, administrative or consultancy nature rendered in the State of which the payer is a resident*	*Technical assistance and the services delivery and staff services*	*Payments for studies of a scientific, geological or technical nature and for engineering projects with plans pertaining thereto*	*Payments for technical or economical studies*	*Payments for studies or technical assistance*
Royalties	37				1	1	1	1	1	2	1
Royalties and fees for technical services	3	3									
Royalties and technical services fees	1	1									
Royalties and services fees	4	1		3							
Royalties and management fees	1		1								
Total	**46**	**5**	**1**	**3**	**1**	**1**	**1**	**1**	**1**	**2**	**1**

1247. Including 'payment of any kind in consideration for the rendering of any managerial, technical or consultancy services' (Article 12(2)(b) DTC India-Uganda (2004)) and 'for the provision or rendering of any managerial, technical or consultancy services' (Article 12(4) DTC Pakistan-South Africa (1998)).

8					8	*Payments for technical or economical studies or for technical assistance*
2					2	*Payments for technical or economical studies or for technical assistance provided in the source state*
2					2	*Payments for technical or economical studies or for technical services provided in the source state*
1					1	*Payments for technical assistance or technical or economic studies in connection with the transfer of IP rights*
1					1	*Technical services and technical assistance*
1					1	*Technical assistance and furnishing of services*
1					1	*Accessory technical assistance for the use of IP rights if assistance is performed in source state of payment*
1					1	*Inclusion of consultancy and technical assistance as part of 'know-how'*
1					1	*Supply of ancillary and subsidiary technical assistance performed in a contracting state in relation to transfer of IP rights*
8					8	*Technical assistance performed in a contracting state in relation to transfer of IP rights (without the requirement of being ancillary)*
1					1	*Technical assistance in relation to transfer or IP rights irrespective of the place of performance*
2					2	*Supply of ancillary and subsidiary assistance enabling the application or enjoyment of IP rights*

Bibliography

Mansi Agrawal, *India at the Forefront in Implementing BEPS-Related Measures: Equalization Levy in Line with Action 1*, 23 ITPJ 323-326 (2016).

Agreement Among the Governments of the Member States of the Caribbean Community for the Avoidance of Double Taxation and the Prevention of Fiscal Evasion with Respect to Taxes on Income, Profits or Gains and Capital Gains and for the Encouragement of Regional Trade and Investment (1994).

Evert Alkema, *The Commentaries on the OECD Model Tax Convention on Income and on Capital: Effective in Domestic Law or in Need of Alternatives?*, in: Sjoerd Douma & Frank Engelen (eds), *The Legal Status of the OECD Commentaries*, 163-194 (IBFD 2008).

Christiane Anger & Thorsten Wagemann, *Zweifelsfragen bei der Auslegung von Doppelbesteuerungsabkommen*, 17 IStR 611-616 (2014).

Brian J. Arnold, *The Taxation of Income from Services under Tax Treaties: Cleaning Up the Mess – Expanded Version*, 65 BIT (2011, published online 22 December 2010: https://doi.org/10.59403/22g7sar).

Brian J. Arnold, *The Taxation of Income from Services under Tax Treaties: Cleaning Up the Mess*, 65 BIT 59-68 (2011).

Brian J. Arnold, *Tax Treaty News*, 65 BIT 118-122 (2011).

Brian J. Arnold, *The Taxation of Income from Services, Papers on Selected Topics in Protecting the Tax Base of Developing Countries*, https://www.un.org/esa/ffd/wp-content/uploads/2014/10/20140604_Paper2_Arnold.pdf (accessed 2 January 2024).

Brian J. Arnold, *Tax Treaty Case Law News*, 69 BIT 53-57 (2015).

Brian J. Arnold, *The UN Committee of Experts and the UN Model: Recent Developments*, 71 BIT 131-136 (2017).

Brian J. Arnold, *The Interpretation of Tax Treaties: Looking to the Future*, 75 BIT 665-672 (2021).

Vanessa Arruda Ferreira, *Outbound Payment for Training Services – Clarified*, IBFD Report of 9 March 2018, https://research.ibfd.org/#/doc?url=/data/tns/docs/html/tns_2018-03-09_br_2.html (accessed 28 August 2022).

Anthony Aust, *Modern Treaty Law and Practice* (3rd ed., Cambridge University Press 2013).

Austrian Ministry of Finance, *Express Antwort Service 2981*, BMF-010221/1571-IV/4/2008 (11 June 2008).

Austrian Ministry of Finance, *Express Antwort Service 3136*, BMF-010221/0627-IV/4/2010 (15 March 2010).

Austrian Ministry of Finance, *Express Antwort Service 3224*, BMF-010221/1104-IV/4/2011 (17 June 2011).

Austrian Ministry of Finance, *Express Antwort Service 3431*, 2021-0.061.324 (12 April 2021).

John F. Avery Jones, *A Fresh Look at Article 3(2) of the OECD Model*, 74 BIT 654-659 (2020).

John F. Avery Jones et al., *The Interpretation of Tax Treaties with Particular Reference to Article 3(2) of the OECD Model-II*, BTR 90-128 (1984).

John F. Avery Jones et al., *The Origins of Concepts and Expressions Used in the OECD Model and their Adoption by States*, 60 BIT 220-254 (2006).

Andrés Báez Moreno, *The Taxation of Technical Services under the United Nations Model Double Taxation Convention: A Rushed – Yet Appropriate – Proposal for (Developing) Countries?*, 7 WTJ 267-328 (2015).

Andrés Báez Moreno, *Because not Always B Comes after A: Critical Reflections on the New Article 12B of the UN Model on Automated Digital Services*, 13 WTJ 501-532 (2021).

Andrés Báez Moreno & Yariv Brauner, *Withholding Taxes in the Service of BEPS Action 1: Address the Tax Challenges of the Digital Economy* (IBFD White Paper 2015).

Philip Baker, *The Meaning of 'Beneficial Ownership' as Applied to Dividends under the OECD Model Tax Convention*, in: Guglielmo Maisto (ed.), *Taxation of Intercompany Dividends under Tax Treaties and EU Law* vol. 8, 87-106 (IBFD 2012).

Aleksandra Bal, *The Sky's the Limit – Cloud-Based Services in an International Perspective*, 68 BIT 515-521 (2014).

Aleksandra Bal & Carlos Gutiérrez, *Taxation of the Digital Economy*, in: Madalina Cotrut (ed.), *International Tax Structures in the BEPS Era: An Analysis of Anti-Abuse Measures* vol. 2, 249-280 (IBFD 2015).

Rodrigo Barrios Correa, *Uruguay's Treaty Policy*, 71 BIT 137 (2017).

Nazreen Begg, *A Technical Analysis of the Difference in Treatment of Technical Fees in Relation to the Receipt of Management Fees by a Resident of South Africa Sourced from Botswana and Zambia Including the Impact of Domestic and Treaty Relief* (University of Cape Town 2019).

Lorenzo Bellavite, Davide Morabito & Riccardo Tognettini, *The Digital Service Tax in Italy: Main Characteristics and Practical Issues*, 60 ET 351-356 (2020).

Stefan Bendlinger, *Art 5 Betriebstätte*, in: Dietmar Aigner, Georg Kofler & Michael Tumpel (eds), *DBA-Kommentar* (Linde Verlag 2017).

Stefan Bendlinger & Karl Waser, *Art 14 Einkünfte aus selbständiger Arbeit*, in: Dietmar Aigner, Georg Kofler & Michael Tumpel (eds), *DBA-Kommentar* (Linde Verlag 2017).

Sandra Benedetto & Liselott Kana, *Chile*, in: *Cahiers de droit fiscal international* vol. 97a, 191-208 (Sdu 2012).

Giorgio Beretta, *'Work on the Move': Rethinking Taxation of Labour Income under Tax Treaties*, 5 ITAXS 2-28 (2022).

Nathalie Bravo, *Interpreting Tax Treaties in the Light of Reservations and Opt-Ins under the Multilateral Instrument*, 74 BIT 231-241 (2020).

Cambridge University Press & Assessment, *Cambridge Dictionary*, https://dictionary.cambridge.org/dictionary/english/perform (accessed 7 October 2022).

Cambridge University Press & Assessment, *Cambridge Dictionary*, https://dictionary.cambridge.org/de/worterbuch/englisch-deutsch/technical (accessed 5 September 2022).

Vikram Chand & Andrés Báez Moreno, *Solving the Allocation of Taxing Rights Debate for the Digitalized Economy: Shortcomings of the Digital PE Proposal and Reconsideration of the Base-Eroding Payments Proposal*, in: Pasquale Pistone & Dennis Weber (eds), *Taxing the Digital Economy: The EU Proposals and Other Insights*, 119-160 (IBFD 2019).

Mohammed M. Chishty & Sumangala A. Chakalabbi, *Royalties and Fees for Technical Services in International Trade*, 18 APTB 40-49 (2009).

Richard Collier, Michael P. Devereux & John Vella, *Comparing Proposals to Tax Some Profit in the Market Country*, 13 WTJ 405-439 (2021).

Committee of Experts on International Cooperation in Tax Matters, *Report on the third session*, E/C.18/2007/19, https://financing.desa.un.org/sites/default/files/2023-03/N0820731%20%281%29.pdf (accessed 6 January 2024).

Committee of Experts on International Cooperation in Tax Matters, *Revision of the Commentaries of the UN Model Convention – Note by the coordinator of the working group on Commentaries of the UN Model Convention*, E/C.18/2008/CRP.1, https://www.un.org/esa/ffd/wp-content/uploads/2014/10/4STM_EC18_2008_CRP1.pdf (accessed 6 January 2024).

Committee of Experts on International Cooperation in Tax Matters, *Report on the fourth session*, E/C.18/2008/6, https://financing.desa.un.org/sites/default/files/2023-03/N0921065%20%282%29.pdf (accessed 6 January 2024).

Committee of Experts on International Cooperation in Tax Matters, *Note Provided by the Coordinator of the Subcommittee on Article 14 and the Tax Treatment of Services*, E/C.18/2009/CRP.4, https://www.un.org/esa/ffd/wp-content/uploads/2014/10/5STM_E-C18-2009-CRP4.pdf (accessed 6 January 2024).

Committee of Experts on International Cooperation in Tax Matters, *Report on the fifth session*, E/C.18/2009/6 (SUPP), https://financing.desa.un.org/sites/default/files/2023-03/N1021312_0.pdf (accessed 6 January 2024).

Committee of Experts on International Cooperation in Tax Matters, *Note on the Taxation of Services under the United Nations Model Tax Convention*, E/C.18/2010/CRP.7, https://www.un.org/esa/ffd/wp-content/uploads/2014/10/6STM_NoteTaxationOfServices.pdf (accessed 6 January 2024).

Committee of Experts on International Cooperation in Tax Matters, *Note by the Secretariat: Additional Note by Mr. Brian Arnold on the Tax Treatment of Services*,

E/C.18/2010/CRP.7/Add.1, https://www.un.org/esa/ffd/wp-content/uploads/2014/10/6STM_CRP7_Add1.pdf (accessed 6 January 2024).

Committee of Experts on International Cooperation in Tax Matters, *Report on the sixth session*, E/C.18/2010/7, https://financing.desa.un.org/sites/default/files/2023-03/N1120859_0.pdf (accessed 6 January 2024).

Committee of Experts on International Cooperation in Tax Matters, *Note by the Secretariat on 'Country Observations, Reservations and Positions: Relevance to the United Nations Model Tax Convention'*, E/C.18/2011/4, https://digitallibrary.un.org/record/709968?ln=en (accessed 6 January 2024).

Committee of Experts on International Cooperation in Tax Matters, *Subcommittee on Tax Treatment of Services*, E/C.18/2011/CRP.7, https://www.un.org/esa/ffd/wp-content/uploads/2014/10/7STM_CRP7.pdf (accessed 6 January 2024).

Committee of Experts on International Cooperation in Tax Matters, *Report on the seventh session*, E/2011/45-E/C.18/2011/6, https://financing.desa.un.org/sites/default/files/2023-03/N1222955_0.pdf (accessed January 2024).

Committee of Experts on International Cooperation in Tax Matters, *Taxation of fees for technical and other services under the United Nations Model Convention – Note by the Secretariat*, E/C.18/2012/4, https://financing.desa.un.org/events/eighth-session-committee-experts-international-cooperation-tax-matters (accessed 6 January 2024).

Committee of Experts on International Cooperation in Tax Matters, *Follow Up Note on Taxation of Fees for Technical Services and Comments on that Note*, E/C.18/2012/CRP.4, https://www.un.org/esa/ffd/wp-content/uploads/2014/09/8STM_CRP4-Fees-for-Technical-Services-Follow-Up-Note021012.pdf (accessed 6 January 2024).

Committee of Experts on International Cooperation in Tax Matters, *Additional Comments on Follow-Up Note on Taxation of Fees for Technical Services*, E/C.18/2012/CRP.4/Add. 1, https://www.un.org/esa/ffd/wp-content/uploads/2014/09/8STM_CRP4_Add1.pdf (accessed 6 January 2024).

Committee of Experts on International Cooperation in Tax Matters, *Report on the eighth session*, E/2012/45-E/C.18/2012/6, https://financing.desa.un.org/sites/default/files/2023-03/N1323910_1.pdf (accessed 6 January 2024).

Committee of Experts on International Cooperation in Tax Matters, *Note on a new Article of the UN Model Convention dealing with the Taxation of Fees for Technical and Other Services*, E/C.18/2013/CRP.5, https://www.un.org/esa/ffd/wp-content/uploads/2014/09/9STM_CRP5_Services.pdf (accessed 6 January 2024).

Committee of Experts on International Cooperation in Tax Matters, *Secretariat Note – Recent Work of the Committee on Tax Treatment of Services*, E/C.18/2013/CRP.17, https://www.un.org/esa/ffd/wp-content/uploads/2014/09/9STM_CRP17_Services.pdf (accessed 14 January 2024).

Committee of Experts on International Cooperation in Tax Matters, *Report on the ninth session*, E/2013/45-E/C.18/2013/6, https://financing.desa.un.org/sites/default/files/2023-03/N1422114.pdf (accessed 6 January 2024).

Committee of Experts on International Cooperation in Tax Matters, *Note from the Coordinator of the Subcommittee on Tax Treatment of Services: Draft Article and*

Commentary on Technical Services, E/C.18/2014/CRP.8, https://www.un.org/esa/ffd/wp-content/uploads/2014/10/10STM_CRP8_TechnicalServices1.pdf (accessed 6 January 2024).

Committee of Experts on International Cooperation in Tax Matters, *Report on the tenth session*, E/2014/45-E/C.18/2014/6, https://financing.desa.un.org/sites/default/files/2023-03/N1469313.pdf (accessed 6 January 2024).

Committee of Experts on International Cooperation in Tax Matters, *Revised Draft Article and Commentary UN Model Tax Convention – Fees for Technical and Other Services*, E/C.18/2015/CRP.5, https://www.un.org/esa/ffd/wp-content/uploads/2015/10/11STM_CRP.5_Services.pdf (accessed 6 January 2024).

Committee of Experts on International Cooperation in Tax Matters, *Report on the eleventh session*, E/2015/45-E/C.18/2015/6, https://financing.desa.un.org/sites/default/files/2023-03/N1546004.pdf (accessed 6 January 2024).

Committee of Experts on International Cooperation in Tax Matters, *Taxation of Services – Report of the Coordinator (Ms. Liselott Kana)*, E/C.18/2016/CRP.1, https://www.un.org/esa/ffd/wp-content/uploads/2016/10/12STM_CRP1_Services.pdf (accessed 6 January 2024).

Committee of Experts on International Cooperation in Tax Matters, *Proposed addition to the Commentary on Article 12: Fees for Included Services*, E/C.18/2016/CRP.1 Annex 3, https://www.un.org/esa/ffd/wp-content/uploads/2016/10/12STM_CRP1_Services.pdf (accessed 6 January 2024).

Committee of Experts on International Cooperation in Tax Matters, *Report on the twelfth and thirteenth sessions*, E/2016/45-E/C.18/2016/7, https://financing.desa.un.org/sites/default/files/2023-03/English_31.pdf (accessed 6 January 2024).

Committee of Experts on International Cooperation in Tax Matters, *Revised Commentary on Article 12A: Fees for Technical services*, E/C.18/2017/CRP.1, https://financing.desa.un.org/sites/default/files/2023-03/14STM_CRP1_Article12A_technical-services.pdf (accessed 6 January 2024).

Committee of Experts on International Cooperation in Tax Matters, *Report on the fourteenth session*, E/2017/45-E/C.18/2017/3, https://financing.desa.un.org/sites/default/files/2023-03/N1715746.pdf (accessed 6 January 2024).

Committee of Experts on International Cooperation in Tax Matters, *The taxation of fees for technical, managerial and consultancy services in the digital economy with respect to Art 12A of the 2017 UN Model*, E/C.18/2017/CRP.23, https://financing.desa.un.org/sites/default/files/2023-03/15STM_CRP23_Technical-Services.pdf (accessed 6 January 2024).

Committee of Experts on International Cooperation in Tax Matters, *Report on the fifteenth session*, E/2018/45-E/C.18/2018/1, https://financing.desa.un.org/sites/default/files/2023-03/N1746399.pdf (accessed 6 January 2024).

Committee of Experts on International Cooperation in Tax Matters, *Report on the sixteenth session*, E/2018/45/Add.1-E/C.18/2018/7, https://financing.desa.un.org/sites/default/files/2023-03/N1818654.pdf (accessed 6 January 2024).

Committee of Experts on International Cooperation in Tax Matters, *Summary of the United Nations Practical Portfolio on Protecting the Tax Base of Developing*

Countries against Base Erosion: Income from Services, E/C.18/2018/9, https://financing.desa.un.org/sites/default/files/2023-03/N1824764.pdf (accessed 6 January 2024).

Committee of Experts on International Cooperation in Tax Matters, *Tax Issues related to the Digitalization of the Economy: Report*, E/C.18/2019/CRP.12, https://financing.desa.un.org/sites/default/files/2023-03/18STM_CRP12-Work-on-taxation-issues-digitalization.pdf (accessed 6 January 2024).

Committee of Experts on International Cooperation in Tax Matters, *Co-coordinators' Paper on Tax Issues related to the Digitalization of the Economy for the 20th Session of the UN Committee of Experts on Cooperation in Tax Matters*, E/C.18/2020/CRP.25, https://financing.desa.un.org/sites/default/files/2023-03/CICTM%2020th_CRP.25%20_%20Digitalized%20Economy.pdf (accessed 6 January 2024).

Committee of Experts on International Cooperation in Tax Matters, *Co-coordinators' Paper on Tax Issues related to the Digitalization of the Economy for the 20th Session of the UN Committee of Experts on Cooperation in Tax Matters*, E/C.18/2020/CRP.41, https://financing.desa.un.org/events/21st-session-committee-experts-international-cooperation-tax-matters (accessed 6 January 2024).

Committee of Experts on International Cooperation in Tax Matters, *Proposed Changes to the UN Model including the Commentaries thereon as a consequence of the proposed inclusion of Article 12B on automated digital services*, E/C.18/2021/CRP.15 Rev.1, https://financing.desa.un.org/sites/default/files/2023-03/CRP15_Rev.1%20_Article%2012B%20Consequential%20Changes%20final.pdf (accessed 15 January 2024).

Committee of Experts on International Cooperation in Tax Matters, *Report on the twentieth session*, E/2021/45-E/C.18/2020/3, https://financing.desa.un.org/sites/default/files/2023-03/Report%20on%2020th%20Session_EN.pdf (accessed 6 January 2024).

Committee of Experts on International Cooperation in Tax Matters, *Report on the twenty-first session*, E/2021/45/Add.1-E/C.18/2020/4, https://digitallibrary.un.org/record/3898885?ln=en (accessed 6 January 2024).

Committee of Experts on International Cooperation in Tax Matters, *Report on the twenty-second session*, E/2021/45/Add.2-E/C.18/2021/2, https://digitallibrary.un.org/record/3930124?ln=en (accessed 6 January 2024).

Committee of Experts on International Cooperation in Tax Matters, *Taxation issues related to the digitalized and globalized economy: Co-Coordinators' Report*, E/C.18/2022/CRP.6, https://financing.desa.un.org/sites/default/files/2023-03/CRP.6%20Digitalized%20and%20Globalized%20Economy.pdf (accessed 13 January 2024).

Committee of Experts on International Cooperation in Tax Matters, *Taxation issues related to the digitalized and globalized economy: Co-Coordinators' Report*, E/C.18/2023/CRP.1, https://financing.desa.un.org/sites/default/files/2023-04/CRP.1%20Co-Coordinator%20report%20on%20Taxation%20of%20the%20Digitalized%20Economy%20CICTM%2026%20120323%20pdf%20merged.pdf (accessed 13 January 2024).

Committee of Experts on International Cooperation in Tax Matters, *Taxation issues related to the digitalized and globalized economy: Co-Coordinators' Report*, E/C.18/2023/CRP.40, https://financing.desa.un.org/sites/default/files/2023-11/CRP.40%20Combined%20Final%20with%20all%20annexes-Copy.pdf (accessed 13 January 2024).

Committee on Fiscal Affairs, *Eighth Report of the U.N. Group of Experts on Tax Treaties between Developed and Developing Countries*, DAF/CFA/80.5 (19 March 1980).

Andy Cools, *Article 16 of the OECD Model: A Plea to Extend the Scope of the Ratione Personae*, 70 BIT 558-575 (2016).

Andy Cools, *What Is the Scope of the Concept of 'Income' in Article 16 of the OECD Model?*, 71 BIT 3/4 (2017).

Graeme S. Cooper, *Building on the Rubble of Pillar One*, 75 BIT 533-542 (2021).

Axel Cordewener, *Article 16. Directors' Fees/Directors' Fees and Remuneration of Top-Managerial Officials*, in: Ekkehart Reimer & Alexander Rust (eds), *Klaus Vogel on Double Taxation Conventions* vol. 2, 1223-1286 (4th ed., Wolters Kluwer 2015).

Council of the European Union, *Council Directive (EU) 2022/2523 of 14 December 2022 on ensuring a global minimum level of taxation for multinational groups and large-scale domestic groups in the Union*, L 328/1, https://eur-lex.europa.eu/legal-content/EN/TXT/?uri=CELEX%3A32022L2523 (accessed 6 January 2024).

Álvaro de la Cueva González-Cotera & Adrián Arroyo Ataz, *Tax Treaty Interpretation: A New Beginning?*, 61 ET 60-67 (2021).

Charlotte De Jaegher, *International Taxation of Directors' Fees: Article 16 of the OECD Model or How to Reconcile Disagreement among Neighbours*, 5 WTJ 215-268 (2013).

Pieter de Ridder, *Indonesia – Taxation of Cross-Border Dividends, Interest, Royalties and Service Fees*, 19 APTB 323-327 (2013).

Department of Economic and Social Affairs, *Subcommittees*, https://financing.desa.un.org/subcommittees (accessed 29 December 2023).

Claudine Devillet & Xavier van Vlem, *Belgium*, in: *Cahiers de droit fiscal international IFA Cahiers* vol. 97a, 133-153 (Sdu 2012).

Direktorat Jenderal Pajak, *Surat Edaran Direktur Jenderal Pajak*, SE03/PJ.101/1996 (29 March 1996).

Richard L. Doernberg, *Electronic Commerce and International Tax Sharing*, 16 TNI 1013-1022 (1998).

Richard L. Doernberg & Luc Hinnekens, *Electronic Commerce and International Taxation* (Wolters Kluwer 1999).

Oliver Dörr & Kirsten Schmalenbach, *Vienna Convention on the Law of Treaties – A Commentary* (Springer 2012).

Patrícia Duarte da Conceição Machado, *Evolution of the Concept of Technical Services and the Policy Considerations Driving Their Development*, 4 ITAXS 2-20 (2021).

Thomas Dubut, *The International Tax Policy of the Least Developed Countries: The Case of the Partner States of the East African Community – Burundi, Kenya, Rwanda,*

Tanzania and Uganda, in: Yariv Brauner & Pasquale Pistone (eds), *BRICS and the Emergence of International Tax Coordination*, 327-352 (IBFD 2015).

Kasper Dziurdź, *Kurzfristige Arbeitnehmerüberlassung im internationalen Steuerrecht* vol. 75 (Linde Verlag 2013).

Economic and Social Council, *Tax treaties between developed and developing countries*, Resolution 1273 (XLIII), E/4429 (4 August 1967).

Economic and Social Council, *Tax treaties between developed and developing countries*, Resolution 1541 (XLIX), E/4904 (30 July 1970).

Economic and Social Council, *Committee of Experts on International Cooperation in Tax Matters*, Resolution 2004/69, E/2004/L.60 (11 November 2004).

Frank Engelen, *Interpretation of Tax Treaties under International Law* vol. 7 (IBFD 2004).

Frank Engelen, *Some Observations on the Legal Status of the Commentaries on the OECD Model*, 60 BIT 105-109 (2016).

Monica Erasmus-Koen & Sjoerd Douma, *Legal Status of the OECD Commentaries – In Search of the Holy Grail of International Tax Law*, 61 BIT 339-352 (2007).

European Commission, *Proposal for a Council Directive laying down rules relating to the corporate taxation of a significant digital presence*, COM(2018) 147 final, https://eur-lex.europa.eu/legal-content/DE/TXT/?uri=CELEX%3A52018PC0147 (accessed 6 January 2024).

European Commission, *Proposal for a Council Directive on the common system of a digital services tax on revenues resulting from the provision of certain digital services*, COM(2018) 148 final, https://eur-lex.europa.eu/legal-content/EN/TXT/?uri=COM%3A2018%3A148%3AFIN (accessed 6 January 2024).

European Commission, *Proposal for a Council Directive on ensuring a global minimum level of taxation for multinational groups in the Union*, COM(2021) 823 final, https://eur-lex.europa.eu/legal-content/EN/ALL/?uri=COM:2021:0823:FIN (accessed 6 January 2024).

Tatiana Falcão & Bob Michel, *Scope and Interpretation of Article 12A: Assessing the Impact of the New Fees for Technical Services Article*, BTR 422-440 (2018).

Tatiana Falcão & Bob Michel, *Tax Consequences of the Digitalised Economy – Input to the United Nations Committee of Experts on International Cooperation in Tax Matters*, https://www.un.org/development/desa/financing/document/comment-tatiana-falcao-and-bob-michel-20th-session-tax-committee-crp-25 (accessed 4 August 2022).

Belisa Ferreira Liotti, *Limits of International Cooperation: The Concept of 'Jurisdiction Not to Tax' from the BEPS Project to GloBE*, 76 BIT 63-81 (2022).

Financial Action Task Force on International Standards on Combating Money Laundering and the Financing of Terrorism & Proliferation, *International Standards on Combating Money Laundering and the Financing of Terrorism & Proliferation* (2012-2022).

Fiscal Committee, *Minutes of the 4th Session*, FC/M(57)2 (3 July 1957).

Fiscal Committee, *Minutes of the 8th Session*, FC/M(58)3 (16 June 1958).

Fiscal Committee, *Minutes of the 9th Session*, FC/M(58)4 (31 October 1958).

Fiscal Committee, *Minutes of the 10th Session*, FC/M(58)5 (16 December 1958).

Fiscal Committee, *Minutes of the 22nd Session*, FC/M(61)1 (17 February 1961).

Wolfgang W. Fischer, Christian Klein & Matthias Eilers, *Quellensteuerproblematik bei produktbegleitenden technischen Dienstleistungen in DBA-Outbound-Fällen*, IStR 483-488 (2012).

Leonardo Freitas de Moraes e Castro & Alexandre Luiz Moraes do Rêgo Monteiro, *Qualification of Services Under Double Tax Treaties in Brazil: Open Issues After Iberdrola case*, 45 Intertax 54-66 (2017).

Maria F. Furtado, Henny Verboom & Cedrik Lütter, *No Brazilian Withholding Tax on Payments for Technical Services?*, 69 BIT 558-562 (2015).

Stjepan Gadžo, *Nexus Requirements for Taxation of Non-Residents' Business Income – A Normative Evaluation in the Context of the Global Economy* vol. 41 (IBFD 2018).

Alejandro Garcia Heredia, *Who Knows the Riddle of Know-How? Spain Becomes Entangled in the Web of Intangibles*, 45 European Taxation 103-112 (2005).

Vladimir A. Gidirim, *Taxation of Foreign Multinational Enterprises Conducting Business in and with Saudi Arabia*, 70 BIT 230-235 (2016).

Maximilian Görl & Christoph Gradl, *Artikel 5 Betriebstätte*, in: Roland Ismer (ed.), *Doppelbesteuerungsabkommen*, 718-895 (7th ed., C.H. Beck 2021).

Dietmar Gosch, *Bedeutung des OECD-Kommentars für die Auslegung des DBA Österreich-Deutschland*, SWI 505-514 (2015).

Sriram P. Govind, *The International Tax Treatment of Cross-Border Services*, 66 BIT 1 (2012).

Karin Heger, *The Relationship Between Tax Treaty Law and National Tax Law*, SWI 95-104 (2011).

Alexander Hemmelrath, *Artikel 14 Selbständige Arbeit*, in: Roland Ismer (ed.), *Doppelbesteuerungsabkommen*, 1599-1623 (7th ed., Beck 2021).

Matthias Herdegen, *Völkerrecht* (17th ed., Beck 2018).

Kevin Holmes, *International Tax Policy and Double Tax Treaties* (2nd ed., IBFD 2014).

International Chamber of Commerce, *ICC's perspectives on the taxation of technical services*, https://www.un.org/esa/ffd/wp-content/uploads/2014/10/10STM_LetterICC_perspectivesTTS.pdf (accessed 6 January 2024).

Sholpan Issakova, *Taxing Automated Digital Services: Targeted Online Advertising*, 61 ET 174-178 (2021).

Adolfo M. Jiménez, *Article 12 OECD/UN Models: Definition of Royalties and 'Overlapping' Between Articles 7, 12 and 13*, in: Guglielmo Maisto (ed.), *Taxation of Intellectual Property under Domestic Law, EU Law and Tax Treaties* vol. 16, 117-146 (IBFD 2018).

Joint Committee on Taxation, *Explanation of proposed Income Tax Treaty (and proposed Protocol) between The United States of America and The Republic of India*, JCS-20-90 (14 June 1990).

Christian Kaeser, *Besteuerung technischer Dienstleistungen: Tendenzen*, in: *Festgabe Wassermeyer, Doppelbesteuerung*, 335-340 (C.H. Beck 2015)

Louise F. Kjærsgaard, *Allocation of the Taxing Right to Payments for Cloud Computing-as-a-Service*, 11 WTJ 379-423 (2019).

Michael Kobetsky, *International Taxation of Permanent Establishments* (Cambridge University Press 2011).

Georg Kofler, Gunter Mayr & Christoph Schlager, *Digitalisierung und Betriebsstättenkonzept*, RdW 369-387 (2017).

Rene Kreisl, *Characterization of artistic income without public performance*, in: Walter Loukota & Markus Stefaner (eds), *Taxation of Artistes and Sportsmen in International Tax Law* vol. 51, 137-158 (Linde Verlag 2007).

Henrietta Kristanto, *Indonesia – Corporate Taxation – Country Tax Guides* (accessed online on the IBFD-Tax Research Platform on 6 January 2024).

Steffen Lampert, *Germany*, in: Michael Lang, Pasquale Pistone, Josef Schuch & Claus Staringer (eds), The impact of the OECD and UN Model Conventions on bilateral tax treaties, 466-531 (Cambridge University Press 2012).

Shimeng Lan, *A Comparative Study of the 'Royalties' Provisions in the Tax Treaties Concluded by China*, 72 BIT 142-158 (2018).

Michael Lang, *Off-Track Interpretation of Double Taxation Treaties as Exemplified by the Taxation of Lecturers*, SWI 508-513 (1998).

Michael Lang, *Art. 3 Abs. 2 OECD-MA und die Auslegung von Doppelbesteuerungsabkommen*, IWB 281-294 (2011).

Michael Lang, *Auslegung von Doppelbesteuerungsabkommen und authentische Vertragssprachen*, IStR 403-410 (2011).

Michael Lang, *Die Auslegung von Doppelbesteuerungsabkommen als Problem der Planungssicherheit bei grenzüberschreitenden Sachverhalten*, in: Siegfried Grotherr (ed.), *Handbuch der internationalen Steuerplanung*, 1865-1880 (3rd ed., NWB 2011).

Michael Lang, *Schweizer Grundsatzurteil zum Beneficial Owner nach DBA-Recht*, SWI 226-230 (2012).

Michael Lang, *Die Bedeutung des OECD-Kommentars und der Reservations, Observations und Positions für die DBA-Auslegung*, in: Jürgen Lüdicke, Rudolf Mellinghoff & Thomas Rödder (eds), *Nationale und internationale Unternehmensbesteuerung in der Rechtsordnung – Festschrift für Dietmar Gosch*, 235-248 (C.H. Beck 2016).

Michael Lang, *Introduction to the Law of Double Taxation Conventions* (3rd ed., Linde Verlag 2021).

Michael Lang & Florian Brugger, *The Role of the OECD Commentary in Tax Treaty Interpretation*, 23 Australian Tax Forum 95-108 (2008).

Michael Lang, Selina Siller & Stephanie Zolles, *Austria: Entertainers under Article 17*, in Eric C.C.M. Kemmeren et al. (eds), *Tax Treaty Case Law Around the Globe 2016* vol. 102, 245-256 (Linde Verlag 2017).

Shee Boon Law, *Withholding Taxes on Services Income – A 21st Century Outlaw or a Necessary Evil?*, in: Carlos Gutiérrez & Andreas Perdelwitz (eds), *Taxation of Business Profits in the 21st Century: Selected Issues under Tax Treaties –Essays in Commemoration of IBFD's 75th Anniversary Written by Tax Research Staff of IBFD*, 79-102 (IBFD 2013).

LawBite, *Legal Document Templates*, https://www.lawbite.co.uk/legal-and-business-documents (accessed 15 November 2022).

League of Nations, *Double Taxation and Tax Evasion Report and Resolutions – Report and Resolutions submitted by the Technical Experts to the Financial Committee*, F.212 (7 February 1925).

League of Nations, *Double Taxation and Tax Evasion: Report presented by the Committee of Technical Experts on Double Taxation and Tax Evasion*, C.216.M.85 (12 April 1927).

League of Nations Fiscal Committee, *Report to the Council on the Work of the Second Session of the Committee*, C.340.M.140.1930.II. (31 May 1930).

League of Nations Fiscal Committee, *Report to the Council on the Fourth Session of the Committee*, C.399.M.204 1933.II.A. (June 1933).

League of Nations Fiscal Committee, *Second Regional Conference in Mexico – Report on the work of the Conference*, F/Fiscal/131 (29 July 1943).

League of Nations Fiscal Committee, *London and Mexico Model Tax Conventions – Commentary and Text*, C.88.M.88.1946.II.A. (November 1946).

Anna Leisner-Egensperger, *DBA-Auslegung unter Rückgriff auf nationales Recht*, IStR 10-15 (2014).

Michael Lennard, *The UN Model Tax Convention as Compared with the OECD Model Tax Convention – Current Points of Difference and Recent Developments*, 15 APTB 4-11 (2009).

Michael Lennard, *Base Erosion and Profit Shifting and Developing Country Tax Administrations*, 44 Intertax 740-745 (2016).

Jinyan Li, *Protecting the Tax Base in the Digital Economy, Papers on Selected Topics in Protecting the Tax Base of Developing Countries*, https://www.un.org/esa/ffd/wp-content/uploads/2014/10/20140604_Paper9_Li.pdf (accessed 4 January 2024).

Tizhong Liao, *Taxation of Cross-border Trade in Service: A Review of the Current International Tax Landscape and the Possible Future Policy Options*, E/C.18/2013/CRP.16, https://www.un.org/esa/ffd/wp-content/uploads/2014/09/9STM_CRP16_CrossBorderTrade.pdf (accessed 4 January 2024).

Ulf Linderfalk & Maria Hilling, *The Use of OECD Commentaries as Interpretative Aids – The Static/Ambulatory–Approaches Debate Considered from the Perspective of International Law*, NTJ 34-59 (2015).

Doreen Liu, Jaap Reyneveld & Charlotte Straatman, *OECD's Work on the Digital Economy: Impact Far Beyond the Digital Economy*, 26 ITPJ 295-304 (2019).

Tiago Machado Graça, *Portuguese-Speaking African Countries: Same Background, Different Solutions*, 70 BIT 717-723 (2016).

Guglielmo Maisto, *Shipping, Inland Waterways Transport and Air Transport (Article 8 OECD Model Convention)*, in: Michael Lang, Pasquale Pistone, Josef Schuch & Claus Staringer (eds), *Source Versus Residence – Problems Arising from the Allocation of Taxing Rights in Tax Treaty Law and Possible Alternatives* vol. 20, 21-57 (Wolters Kluwer 2008).

Monique T. Malan, *New Article 12A of the UN Model Regarding Fees for Technical Services: Ahead of Its Time or a Step Too Far?*, 73 BIT 58-68 (2019).

Arnold D. McNair, *The Law of Treaties* (Clarendon Press 1961).

Amar Mehta, *'Equalization Levy' Proposal in Indian Finance Bill 2016: Is It Legitimate Tax Policy or an Attempt of Treaty Dodging?*, 22 APTB 2 (2016).

Amar Mehta, *Importance of Human Involvement for Income Characterization as Fees for Technical Services*, 22 APTB 2 (2016).

Merriam-Webster, *Dictionary*, https://www.merriam-webster.com/dictionary/technical (accessed 5 September 2022).

Bob Michel, *Developing Countries Put Their Cards on the Table in the Digital Economy Tax Debate – But Is the UN Committee of Experts Playing a Winning Hand?* (published online on the IBFD – Tax Research Platform on 15 June 2021).

Angharad Miller, *Taxing Cross-Border Services: Current Worldwide Practices and the Need for Change* vol. 37 (IBFD 2015).

Martti Nieminen, *OECD Commentaries under the Vienna Rules* (Tampereen Yliopisto 2014).

Martti Nieminen, *Dual Role of the OECD Commentaries – Part 1*, 43 Intertax 636-659 (2015).

OECD, *Model Tax Convention on Income and on Capital: Condensed Versions of 1994, 1995, 1997, 1998, 2000, 2003, 2005, 2008, 2010, 2014, and 2017* (OECD Publishing).

OECD, *Recommendation of the OECD Council concerning the Model Tax Convention on Income and on Capital, C (97)195/Final*, https://one.oecd.org/document/C(97)195/FINAL/en/pdf (accessed 5 January 2024).

OECD, *Issues Related to Article 14 of the OECD Model Tax Convention* vol. 7 (OECD Publications 2000).

OECD, *Behind the Corporate Veil: Using Corporate Entities for Illicit Purposes* (OECD Publications 2001).

OECD, *Addressing the Tax Challenges of the Digital Economy – Action 1: 2015 Final Report* (OECD Publishing 2015).

OECD, *Tax Challenges Arising from Digitalisation – Interim Report 2018: Inclusive Framework on BEPS* (OECD Publishing 2018).

OECD, *Addressing the Tax Challenges of the Digitalisation of the Economy – Policy Note – 23 January 2019*, https://www.oecd.org/tax/beps/policy-note-beps-inclusive-framework-addressing-tax-challenges-digitalisation.pdf (accessed 1 January 2024).

OECD, *Statement by the OECD/G20 Inclusive Framework on BEPS on the Two-Pillar Approach to Address the Tax Challenges Arising from the Digitalisation of the Economy – January 2020*, http://www.oecd.org/tax/beps/statement-by-the-oecd-g20-inclusive-framework-on-beps-january-2020.pdf (accessed 25 July 2022).

OECD, *Tax Challenges Arising from Digitalisation – Report on Pillar One Blueprint: Inclusive Framework on BEPS* (OECD Publishing 2020).

OECD, *Statement on a Two-Pillar Solution to Address the Tax Challenges Arising from the Digitalisation of the Economy – 8 October 2021*, https://www.oecd.org/tax/beps/statement-on-a-two-pillar-solution-to-address-the-tax-challenges-arising-from-the-digitalisation-of-the-economy-october-2021.pdf (accessed 1 January 2024).

OECD, *OECD Secretary-General Tax Report to G20 Finance Ministers and Central Bank Governors – July 2022*, www.oecd.org/g20/topics/international-taxation/oecd-secretary-general-tax-report-g20-finance-ministers-indonesia-july-2022.pdf (accessed 7 August 2022).

OECD, *Outcome Statement on the Two-Pillar Solution to Address the Tax Challenges Arising from the Digitalisation of the Economy*, https://www.oecd.org/tax/beps/outcome-statement-on-the-two-pillar-solution-to-address-the-tax-challenges-arising-from-the-digitalisation-of-the-economy-july-2023.pdf (accessed 30 December 2023).

OECD Technical Advisory Group on Treaty Characterization of Electronic Commerce Payments, *Tax Treaty Characterisation Issues Arising from E-Commerce: Report to Working Party No. 1 of the OECD Committee on Fiscal Affairs*, https://web-archive.oecd.org/2012-06-15/167336-1923396.pdf (accessed 5 January 2024).

OEEC Fiscal Committee, *The Elimination of Double Taxation: 2nd Report*, FC(59)2 (18 June 1959).

Annet W. Oguttu, *A Critique from a Developing Country Perspective of the Proposals to Tax the Digital Economy*, 12 WTJ 799-828 (2020).

Annet W. Oguttu, *Addressing the Tax Challenges Arising from the Digitalization of the Economy – Action 1 and Subsequent Work*, in: Emily Muyaa et al. (eds), *Base Erosion and Profit Shifting: A Blueprint for Africa's Response*, 563-616 (IBFD 2021).

Marcel Olbert & Christoph Spengel, *International Taxation in the Digital Economy: Challenge Accepted?*, 9 WTJ 3-46 (2017).

Marcel Olbert & Christoph Spengel, *Taxation in the Digital Economy – Recent Policy Developments and the Question of Value Creation*, 2 ITAXS 3 (2019).

Eduardo Orellana Polo, *The 'Other Income' Article in Tax Treaties as Interpreted by the Courts: A Case Law Analysis*, 71 BIT 3/4 (2017).

Patrick Orlet & Josef Schuch, *Director's Fees and Remuneration of Top-Level Managerial Officials*, in: Michael Lang et al. (eds), *The UN Model Convention and Its Relevance for the Global Tax Treaty Network* vol. 7, 159-180 (IBFD 2017).

David Orzechowski, *The Relevance of the Commentaries on the OECD and UN Models for the Interpretation of the UN Model*, in: Michael Lang et al. (eds), *The UN Model Convention and Its Relevance for the Global Tax Treaty Network* vol. 7, 1-24 (IBFD 2017).

David Orzechowski, *Die abkommensrechtliche Relevanz von Art 12A UN-MA 2017*, ÖStZ 638-644 (2019).

Oxford University Press, *Oxford Learner's Dictionaries*, https://www.oxfordlearnersdictionaries.com/definition/american_english/assist_1 (accessed 10 September 2022).

Oxford University Press, *Oxford Learner's Dictionaries*, https://www.oxfordlearnersdictionaries.com/definition/english/furnish?q=furnish (accessed 7 October 2022).

Jyoti Pal, *Taxation of Fees for Technical Services: An Analysis of Indian Tax Treaties and Their Journey Through the Courts*, 23 APTB 1 (2017).

PGFN & CAT, *Nota No. 2363/2013*, https://www.ibet.com.br/wp-content/uploads/2019/06/Parecer_2363-2013.pdf (accessed 5 January 2024).

Leonardo T. Pignatari, *Article 15(2) of the OECD Model and the International Hiring-Out of Labour: New Criteria Required?*, 74 BIT 487-496 (2020).

Hans Pijl, *Capital Gains: The History of the Principle of Symmetry, the Internal Order of Article 13 and the Dynamic Interpretation of the Changes in the 2010 Commentary on 'Forming Part' and 'Effectively Connected'*, 5 WTJ 3-98 (2013).

Dale Pinto, *The Need to Reconceptualize the Permanent Establishment Threshold*, 60 BIT 266-279 (2006).

João F. Pinto Nogueira, *GloBE and EU Law: Assessing the Compatibility of the OECD's Pillar II Initiative on a Minimum Effective Tax Rate with EU Law and Implementing It within the Internal Market*, 12 WTJ 465-498 (2020).

Reinhard Pöllath, *Art. 12 Lizenzgebühren*, in: Moris Lehner (ed.), *Doppelbesteuerungsabkommen*, 1143-1199 (4th ed., Beck 2003).

Frank P. G. Pötgens, *Income from Inactivity under Article 15 of the OECD Model Tax Convention – Part 1*, 63 BIT 428-440 (2009).

Priestley, *Australia*, in: *Cahiers de droit fiscal international* vol. 97a, 87-106 (Sdu 2012).

Rainer Prokisch, *Directors' Fees (Article 16 OECD Model Convention)*, in: Michael Lang, Pasquale Pistone, Josef Schuch & Claus Staringer (eds), *Source Versus Residence – Problems Arising from the Allocation of Taxing Rights in Tax Treaty Law and Possible Alternatives* vol. 20, 197-213 (Wolters Kluwer 2008).

Rainer Prokisch, *Art. 16 Aufsichtsrats- und Verwaltungsratsvergütungen*, in: Roland Ismer (ed.), Doppelbesteuerungsabkommen, 1771-1788 (7th ed., C.H. Beck 2021).

Receita Federal, *Instrução Normativa (Normative Instruction) 1,455/2014*, http://normas.receita.fazenda.gov.br/sijut2consulta/link.action?idAto = 50414&visao = anotado (accessed 5 January 2024).

Receita Federal, *Instrução Normativa (Normative Instruction) 1,645/2016*, http://normas.receita.fazenda.gov.br/sijut2consulta/link.action?visao = anotado&idAto = 74319 (accessed 5 January 2024).

Receita Federal, *Solução de Consulta (Private ruling) 155/2016*, http://normas.receita.fazenda.gov.br/sijut2consulta/link.action?visao = anotado&idAto = 78944 (accessed 5 January 2024).

Receita Federal, *Solução de Consulta (Private ruling) 5/2017*, http://normas.receita.fazenda.gov.br/sijut2consulta/link.action?idAto = 79701&visao = anotado (accessed 6 January 2024).

Receita Federal, *Solução de Consulta (Private ruling) 99006/2020*, http://normas.receita.fazenda.gov.br/sijut2consulta/link.action?visao = anotado&idAto = 111584 (accessed 6 January 2024).

Receita Federal, *Solução de Consulta (Private ruling) 99001/2021*, http://normas.receita.fazenda.gov.br/sijut2consulta/link.action?visao = anotado&idAto = 116528 (accessed 6 January 2024).

Sergio A. Rocha, *Brazil's Treaty Policy*, 71 BIT 333-339 (2017).

Luis A. Romero Topete, *Analysis of the Case Law on the Scope of Article 17 of the OECD Model: Issues Resolved and Yet to Be Resolved*, 71 BIT 3/4 (2017).

Florian Rosenberger, Marco Vitali & Ulrich Ziehr, *Die Dienstleistungsbetriebsstätte: Internationale Entwicklungen und ihre Rezeption im Internationalen Steuerrecht Deutschlands, Österreichs und der Schweiz*, IStR-Beiheft 1-35 (2010).

Alexander Rust, *Other Income (Article 21 OECD Model Convention)*, in: Michael Lang, Pasquale Pistone, Josef Schuch & Claus Staringer (eds), *Source Versus Residence – Problems Arising from the Allocation of Taxing Rights in Tax Treaty Law and Possible Alternatives* vol. 20, 327-345 (Wolters Kluwer 2008).

Alexander Rust, *'Business' and 'Business Profits'*, in: *Maisto* (ed.), *The Meaning of 'Enterprise', 'Business' and 'Business Profits' under Tax Treaties and EU Tax Law* vol. 7, 85-106 (IBFD 2011).

Alexander Rust, *Article 3(2) OECD and UN MC*, in: Ekkehart Reimer & Alexander Rust (eds), *Klaus Vogel on Double Taxation Conventions* vol. 1, 206-216 (4th ed., Wolters Kluwer 2015).

Alexander Rust, *Art. 21. Other Income*, in: Ekkehart Reimer & Alexander Rust (eds), *Klaus Vogel on Double Taxation Conventions* vol. 2, 1745-1778 (5th ed., Wolters Kluwer 2021).

Alexander Rust & Benjamin Walker, *Independent and Dependent Personal Services*, in: Michael Lang et al. (eds), *The UN Model Convention and Its Relevance for the Global Tax Treaty Network* vol. 7, 71-88 (IBFD 2017).

Alessandro Samari, *The OECD Public Consultation Document on Addressing the Tax Challenges of the Digitalization of the Economy: Strengths and Weaknesses of the Three Proposals for Revising Profit Allocation and Nexus Rules*, 26 ITPJ 265-271 (2019).

Daniel Sandler, *Artistes and Sportsmen (Article 17 OECD Model Convention)*, in: Michael Lang, Pasquale Pistone, Josef Schuch & Claus Staringer (eds), *Source Versus Residence – Problems Arising from the Allocation of Taxing Rights in Tax Treaty Law and Possible Alternatives* vol. 20, 215-245 (Wolters Kluwer 2008).

Dhruv Sanghavi, *Report IFA 68th Congress in Mumbai – Seminar F: UN Matters – UN and OECD Differences in Model, TP, etc.* (accessed online on the IBFD-Tax Research Platform on 16 July 2022).

Sanjay Sanghvi & Ritu Shaktawat, *Taxation of Fees for Technical Services and Royalties*, 18 APTB 452-459 (2012).

Jacques Sasseville, *The OECD Model Convention and Commentaries*, in: Guglielmo Maisto (ed.), *Multilingual Texts and Interpretation of Tax Treaties and EC Tax Law*, 129-136 (IBFD 2005).

Jacques Sasseville, *'Enterprise', 'Business' and 'Business Profits': From the League of Nations to the Current OECD Model Tax Convention*, in: *Maisto* (ed.), *The Meaning of 'Enterprise', 'Business' and 'Business Profits' under Tax Treaties and EU Tax Law* vol. 7, 85-106 (IBFD 2011).

Jacques Sasseville, *Source vs Residence Taxation of Royalties: A Historical Perspective*, in: Guglielmo Maisto (ed.), *Taxation of Intellectual Property under Domestic Law, EU Law and Tax Treaties* vol. 16, 97-115 (IBFD 2018).

Luis E. Schoueri & Mateus C. Barbosa, *Brazil: Technical Services and the Application of Article 7 under Brazilian Treaty Practice – A Case Study*, in Michael Lang et al.

(eds), *Tax Treaty Case Law Around the Globe 2013* vol. 81, 103-116 (Linde Verlag 2013).

Jonathan Schwarz, *Permanent Establishment: Geographic and Temporal Issues*, in: Guglielmo Maisto (ed.), *New Trends in the Definition of Permanent Establishment* vol. 17, 45-58 (IBFD 2019).

Dina Scornos, *Cloud Computing: Difficulties in Applying Current and Proposed Nexus and Profit Allocation Rules in a Cross-Border Scenario*, 74 BIT 88-97 (2020).

D. P. Sengupta, *India: Siemens Ltd – To Be Taxed as Fees for Technical Services Some Human Intervention Is a Must*, in: Eric C.C.M. Kemmeren et al. (eds), *Tax Treaty Case Law Around the Globe 2014* vol. 89, 211-220 (Linde Verlag 2015).

Sir Ian McTaggart Sinclair, *The Vienna Convention on the Law of Treaties* (2nd ed., Manchester University Press 1984).

Manoj K. Singh, *Conflict of Source versus Residence-Based Taxation in India with Reference to Fees for Technical Service*, 44 Intertax 525-537 (2016).

Franziska Sixdorf & Sebastian Leitsch, *Taxation of Technical Services under the New Article 12A of the UN Model – Improved Taxation or a Step in the Wrong Direction*, 57 ET 234-242 (2017).

Arvid A. Skaar, *Permanent Establishment: Erosion of a Tax Treaty Principle* vol. 13 (Kluwer Law and Taxation 1991).

Fernando Souza de Man, *Taxation of Services in Treaties between Developed and Developing Countries: A Proposal for New Guidelines* vol. 39 (IBFD 2017).

Guillermo O. Teijeiro & Juan Manuel Vázquez, *Taxation of the Ride-Sharing Economy: Source Taxation Through Service Permanent Establishment Provisions Revisited – The Case under the Argentine Treaty Network*, 73 BIT 667-682 (2019).

The Commission of the Cartagena Agreement, *Standard Agreement to avoid double taxation between Member Countries and other States outside the Subregion*, http://www.sice.oas.org/trade/junac/decisiones/dec040e.asp (accessed 19 January 2024).

The eCom Taxpert Group, *Taxation of Electronic Commerce in India*, 8 APTB 241-243 (2002).

Laura Turcan, *The OECD Update 2014 and Its Impact on the UN Model Convention*, in: Michael Lang et al. (eds), *The OECD-Model-Convention and its Update 2014* vol. 90, 207-240 (Linde Verlag 2015).

U.S. Department of the Treasury, *United States Model Technical Explanation accompanying the United States Model Income Tax Convention of November 15, 2006)*, https://home.treasury.gov/system/files/131/Treaty-US-Model-TE-2006.pdf (accessed 18 November 2022).

United Nations, *United Nations Conference on the Law of Treaties: Documents of the Conference*, A/CONF.39/11/Add.2, https://treaties.un.org/doc/source/docs/A_CONF.39_11_Add.2-E.pdf (accessed 19 January 2024).

United Nations, *United Nations Model Double Taxation Convention between Developed and Developing Countries*, ST/ESA/102 (United Nations Publication 1980).

United Nations, *United Nations Model Double Taxation Convention between Developed and Developing Countries*, ST/ESA/PAD/SER.E/21 (United Nations Publication 2001).

United Nations, *United Nations Model Double Taxation Convention between Developed and Developing Countries*, https://www.un.org/esa/ffd/wp-content/uploads/2014/09/UN_Model_2011_Update.pdf (accessed 2 January 2024)

United Nations, *United Nations Model Double Taxation Convention between Developed and Developing Countries 2017*, ST/ESA/PAD/SER.E/213 (United Nations Publication 2017).

United Nations, *United Nations Model Double Taxation Convention between Developed and Developing Countries 2021*, ST/ESA/378 (United Nations Publication 2021).

United Nations General Assembly, *Revised Draft of the Outcome Documents*, https://www.un.org/esa/ffd/wp-content/uploads/2015/05/revised-draft-outcome.pdf (accessed 17 November 2022).

United Nations General Assembly, *Addis Ababa Action Agenda of the Third International Conference on Financing for Development (Addis Ababa Action Agenda)*, A/RES/69/313, https://www.un.org/en/development/desa/population/migration/generalassembly/docs/globalcompact/A_RES_69_313.pdf (accessed 5 January 2024).

United Nations General Assembly, *Promotion of inclusive and effective international tax cooperation at the United Nations: Report of the Secretary-General*, A/78/235, https://digitallibrary.un.org/record/4019360?v=pdf (accessed 20 March 2024).

United Nations General Assembly, *Macroeconomic policy questions: promotion of inclusive and effective international cooperation on tax matters at the United Nations*, A/78/459/Add.8, https://digitallibrary.un.org/record/4030104?v=pdf (accessed 20 March 2024).

United Nations General Assembly, *Macroeconomic policy questions: promotion of inclusive and effective international cooperation on tax matters at the United Nations: Resolution adopted by the General Assembly on 22 December 2023*, A/RES/78/230, https://financing.desa.un.org/sites/default/files/2024-01/A.RES_.78.230_English.pdf (accessed 5 January 2024)

Matthias Valta, *Article 12: Income from Royalties*, in: Ekkehart Reimer & Alexander Rust (eds), *Klaus Vogel on Double Taxation Conventions* vol. 1, 955-1032 (4th ed., Wolters Kluwer 2015).

Matthias Valta & Stella Langner, *Article 12: Income from Royalties*, in: Ekkehart Reimer & Alexander Rust (eds), *Klaus Vogel on Double Taxation Conventions* vol. 1, 1097-1198 (5th ed., Wolters Kluwer 2021).

Edwin van der Bruggen, *Source Taxation of Consideration for Technical Services and Know-How*, 7 APTB 42-60 (2001).

Edwin van der Bruggen, *Developing Countries and the Removal of Article 14 from the OECD Model*, 55 BIT 601-607 (2001).

Jonathan Velo, *Taxation of Independent Personal Services*, in: Anna Binder & Viktoria Wöhrer (eds), *Special Features of the UN Model Convention* vol. 117, 371-390 (Linde Verlag 2019).

Sagar Wagh, *The Taxation of Digital Transactions in India: The New Equalization Levy*, 70 BIT 538-552 (2016).

David A. Ward QC, *Is There an Obligation in International Law of OECD Member Countries to Follow the Commentaries on the Model?*, in: Sjoerd Douma & Frank Engelen (eds), *The Legal Status of the OECD Commentaries*, 73-94 (IBFD 2008).

Franz Wassermeyer, *OECD-MA 2017 Art. 14,* in: Franz Wassermeyer, Christian Kaeser, Michael Schwenke & Klaus-Dieter Drüen (eds), *DBA* (158th ed., C.H. Beck 2022).

Franz Wassermeyer & Klaus-Dieter Drüen *OECD-MA 2017 Art.* 16, in: Franz Wassermeyer, Christian Kaeser, Michael Schwenke & Klaus-Dieter Drüen (eds), *DBA* (158th ed., C.H. Beck 2022).

Wim Wijnen & Jan de Goede, *The UN Model in Practice 1997–2013*, 68 BIT 118-146 (2014).

Wim Wijnen, Jan de Goede & Andrea Alessi, *The Treatment of Services in Tax Treaties*, 66 BIT 27-38 (2012).

Working Party No. 6 of the Fiscal Committee, *Transfer Pricing: Rights and Services*, DAF/CFA/74.13 (12 September 1974).

Working Party No. 8 of the Fiscal Committee, *Report on the Direct Taxation of Patent Royalties and Similar Payments*, FC/WP8(58)1 (12 February 1958), https://www.taxtreatieshistory.org/data/html/FC-WP8(58)1E.html (accessed 6 November 2022).

Working Party No. 8 of the Fiscal Committee, *Second Report on the Direct Taxation of Patent Royalties and Similar Payments*, FC/WP8(58)2, (3 September 1958), https://www.taxtreatieshistory.org/data/html/FC-WP8(58)2E.html (accessed 6 November 2022).

Gustav Wurm, *Art 21 Andere Einkünfte*, in: Dietmar Aigner, Georg Kofler & Michael Tumpel (eds), *DBA-Kommentar* (2nd ed., Linde Verlag 2019).

Armando L. Yaffar & Michael Lennard, *An Introduction to the Updated UN Model (2011)*, 66 BIT 590-597 (2012).

Xeniya Yeroshenko, *Introducing a Digital Services Tax in the Czech Republic*, 27 ITPJ 199-204 (2020).

Yansheng Zhu, *Proposed changes to the UN Model Tax Convention dealing with the Cyber-based Services*, E/C.18/2014/CRP.9, https://www.un.org/esa/ffd/wp-content/uploads/2014/10/10STM_CRP9_CyberServices.pdf (accessed 2 January 2024).

Table of Cases

Index

K

L

M

O

P

R

S

T

U

SERIES ON INTERNATIONAL TAXATION

1. Alberto Xavier, *The Taxation of Foreign Investment in Brazil,* 1980 (ISBN 90-200-0582-0).
2. Hugh J. Ault & Albert J. Rädler, *The German Corporation Tax Law with 1980 Amendments,* 1981 (ISBN 90-200-0642-8).
3. Paul R. McDaniel & Hugh J. Ault, *Introduction to United States International Taxation,* 1981 (ISBN 90-6544-004-6).
4. Albert J. Rädler, *German Transfer Pricing/Prix de Transfer en Allemagne,* 1984 (ISBN 90-6544-143-3).
5. Paul R. McDaniel & Stanley S. Surrey, *International Aspects of Tax Expenditures:* A *Comparative Study,* 1985 (ISBN 90-654-4163-8).
6. Kees van Raad, *Nondiscrimination in International Tax Law,* 1986 (ISBN 90-6544-266-9).
7. Sijbren Cnossen (ed.), *Tax Coordination in the European Community,* 1987 (ISBN 90-6544-272-3).
8. Ben Terra, *Sales Taxation. The Case of Value Added Tax in the European Community,* 1989 (ISBN 90-6544-381-9).
9. Rutsel S.J. Martha, *The Jurisdiction to Tax in International Law: Theory and Practice of Legislative Fiscal Jurisdiction,* 1989 (ISBN 90-654-4416-5).
10. Paul R. McDaniel & Hugh J. Ault, *Introduction to United States International Taxation* (3rd revised edition), 1989 (ISBN 90-6544-423-8).
11. Manuel Pires, *International Juridicial Double Taxation of Income,* 1989 (ISBN 90-6544-426-2).
12. A.H.M. Daniels, *Issues in International Partnership Taxation,* 1991 (ISBN 90-654-4577-3).
13. Arvid A. Skaar, *Permanent Establishment: Erosion of a Tax Treaty Principle,* 1992 (ISBN 90-6544-594-3).
14. Cyrille David & Geerten M.M. Michielse (eds), *Tax Treatment of Financial Instruments,* 1996 (ISBN 90-654-4666-4).
15. Herbert H. Alpert & Kees van Raad (eds), *Essays on International Taxation,* 1993 (ISBN 90-654-4781-4).
16. Wolfgang Gassner, Michael Lang & Eduard Lechner (eds), *Tax Treaties and EC Law,* 1997 (ISBN 90-411-0680-4).
17. Glória Teixeira, *Taxing Corporate Profits in the EU,* 1997 (ISBN 90-411-0703-7).
18. Michael Lang et al. (eds), *Multilateral Tax Treaties,* 1998 (ISBN 90-411-0704-5).
19. Stef van Weeghel, *The Improper Use of Tax Treaties,* 1998 (ISBN 90-411-0737-1).

20. Klaus Vogel (ed.), *Interpretation of Tax Law and Treaties and Transfer Pricing in Japan and Germany*, 1998 (ISBN 90-411-9655-2).
21. Bertil Wiman (ed.), *International Studies in Taxation: Law and Economics; Liber Amicorum Leif Mutén*, 1999 (ISBN 90-411-9692-7).
22. Alfonso J. Martín Jiménez, *Towards Corporate Tax Harmonization in the European Community*, 1999 (ISBN 90-411-9690-0).
23. Ramon J. Jeffery, *The Impact of State Sovereignty on Global Trade and International Taxation*, 1999 (ISBN 90-411-9703-6).
24. A.J. Easson, *Taxation of Foreign Direct Investment*, 1999 (ISBN 90-411-9741-9).
25. Marjaana Helminen, *The Dividend Concept in International Tax Law: Dividend Payments Between Corporate Entities*, 1999 (ISBN 90-411-9765-6).
26. Paul Kirchhof, Moris Lehner, Kees van Raad, Arndt Raupach & Michael-Rodi (eds), *International and Comparative Taxation: Essays in Honour of Klaus Vogel*, 2002 (ISBN 90-411-9841-5).
27. Krister Andersson, Peter Melz & Christer Silfverberg (eds), *Liber Amicorum Sven-Olof Lodin*, 2001 (ISBN 90-411-9850-4).
28. Juan Martín Jovanovich, *Customs Valuation and Transfer Pricing: Is It Possible to Harmonize Customs and Tax Rules?*, Second Edition, 2018 (ISBN 978-90-411-6134-5).
29. Stefano Simontacchi, *Taxation of Capital Gains under the OECD Model Convention: With Special Regard to Immovable Property*, 2007 (ISBN 978-90-411-2549-1).
30. Michael Lang, Josef Schuch, & Claus Staringer (eds), *Tax Treaty Law and EC Law*, 2007 (ISBN 978-90-411-2629-0).
31. Duncan Bentley, *Taxpayers' Rights: Theory Origin and Implementation*, 2007 (ISBN 978-90-411-2650-4).
32. Sergio André Rocha, *Interpretation of Double Taxation Conventions: General Theory and Brazilian Perspective*, 2008 (ISBN 978-90-411-2822-5).
33. Robert F. van Brederode, *Systems of General Sales Taxation: Theory, Policy and Practice*, 2009 (ISBN 978-90-411-2832-4).
34. John G. Head & Richard Krever (eds), *Tax Reform in the 21st Century: A Volume in Memory of Richard Musgrave*, 2009 (ISBN 978-90-411-2829-4).
35. Jens Wittendorff, *Transfer Pricing and the Arm's Length Principle in International Tax Law*, 2010 (ISBN 978-90-411-3270-3).
36. Marjaana Helminen, *The International Tax Law Concept of Dividend*, Second Edition, 2017 (ISBN 978-90-411-8394-1).
37. Robert F. van Brederode (ed.), *Immovable Property under VAT: A Comparative Global Analysis*, 2011 (ISBN 978-90-411-3126-3).
38. Dennis Weber & Stef van Weeghel, *The 2010 OECD Updates: Model Tax Convention & Transfer Pricing Guidelines - A Critical Review*, 2011 (ISBN 978-90-411-3812-5).
39. Yariv Brauner & Martin James McMahon, Jr. (eds), *The Proper Tax Base: Structural Fairness from an International and Comparative Perspective— Essays in Honour of Paul McDaniel*, 2012 (ISBN 978-90-411-3286-4).
40. Robert F. van Brederode (ed.), *Science, Technology and Taxation*, 2012 (ISBN 978-90-411-3125-6).

41. Oskar Henkow, *The VAT/GST Treatment of Public Bodies*, 2013 (ISBN 978-90-411-4663-2).
42. Jean Schaffner, *How Fixed Is a Permanent Establishment?*, 2013 (ISBN 978-90-411-4662-5).
43. Miguel Correia, *Taxation of Corporate Groups*, 2013 (ISBN 978-90-411-4841-4).
44. Veronika Daurer, *Tax Treaties and Developing Countries*, 2014 (ISBN 978-90-411-4982-4).
45. Claire Micheau, *State Aid, Subsidy and Tax Incentives under EU and WTO Law*, 2014 (ISBN 978-90-411-4555-0).
46. Robert F. van Brederode & Richard Krever (eds), *Legal Interpretation of Tax Law*, 2014 (ISBN 978-90-411-4945-9).
47. Radhakishan Rawal, *Taxation of Cross-border Services*, 2014 (ISBN 978-90-411-4947-3).
48. João Dácio Rolim, *Proportionality and Fair Taxation*, 2014 (ISBN 978-90-411-5838-3).
49. Paulo Rosenblatt, *General Anti-avoidance Rules for Major Developing Countries*, 2015 (ISBN 978-90-411-5839-0).
50. Gaspar Lopes Dias V.S., *Tax Arbitrage through Cross-Border Financial Engineering*, 2015 (ISBN 978-90-411-5875-8).
51. Geerten M.M. Michielse & Victor Thuronyi (eds), *Tax Design Issues Worldwide*, 2015 (ISBN 978-90-411-5610-5).
52. Oktavia Weidmann, *Taxation of Derivatives and Cryptoassets*, Second Edition, 2024 (ISBN 978-94-035-2383-5).
53. Chris Evans, Richard Krever & Peter Mellor (eds), *Tax Simplification*, 2015 (ISBN 978-90-411-5976-2).
54. Reuven Avi-Yonah & Joel Slemrod (eds), *Taxation and Migration*, 2015 (ISBN 978-90-411-6136-9).
55. Alexander Bosman, *Other Income under Tax Treaties: An Analysis of Article 21 of the OECD Model Convention*, 2015 (ISBN 978-90-411-6610-4).
56. John Abrahamson, *International Taxation of Manufacturing and Distribution*, 2016 (ISBN 978-90-411-6664-7).
57. Frederik Boulogne, *Shortcomings in the EU Merger Directive*, 2016 (ISBN 978-90-411-6713-2).
58. Angelika Meindl-Ringler, *Beneficial Ownership in International Tax Law*, 2016 (ISBN 978-90-411-6833-7).
59. Andreas Waltrich, *Cross-Border Taxation of Permanent Establishments: An International Comparison*, 2016 (ISBN 978-90-411-6832-0).
60. Sergio André Rocha & Allison Christians (eds), *Tax Sovereignty in the BEPS Era*, 2017 (ISBN 978-90-411-6707-1).
61. Peter Antony Wilson, *BRICS and International Tax Law*, 2018 (ISBN 978-90-411-9435-0).
62. Louise Otis, Brigitte Alepin & Blanca Moreno-Dodson (eds), *Winning the Tax Wars: Tax Competition and Cooperation*, 2018 (ISBN 978-90-411-9460-2).

63. Marta Castelon, *International Taxation of Income from Services under Double Taxation Conventions: Development, Practice and Policy*, 2018 (ISBN 978-90-411-9594-4).
64. D.M. Broekhuijsen, *A Multilateral Tax Treaty: Designing an Instrument to Modernise International Tax Law*, 2018 (ISBN 978-90-411-9872-3).
65. John Abrahamson, *International Taxation of Energy Production and Distribution*, 2018 (ISBN 978-90-411-9101-4).
66. Leopoldo Parada, *Double Non-taxation and the Use of Hybrid Entities*, Second Edition, 2024 (ISBN 978-94-035-4666-7).
67. Richard Snoeij, *International Tax Aspects of Sovereign Wealth Investors: A Source State Perspective*, 2018 (ISBN 978-90-411-9431-2).
68. Aleksandra Bal, *Taxation, Virtual Currency and Blockchain*, 2019 (ISBN 978-94-035-0103-1).
69. Werner Haslehner, Georg Kofler, Katerina Pantazatou & Alexander Rust (eds), *Tax and the Digital Economy: Challenges and Proposals for Reform*, 2019 (ISBN 978-94-035-0361-5).
70. Eva Escribano, *Jurisdiction to Tax Corporate Income Pursuant to the Presumptive Benefit Principle: A Critical Analysis of Structural Paradigms Underlying Corporate Income Taxation and Proposals for Reform*, 2019 (ISBN 978-94-035-0640-1).
71. Jérôme Monsenego & Jan Bjuvberg (eds), *International Taxation in a Changing Landscape: Liber Amicorum in Honour of Bertil Wiman*, 2019 (ISBN 978-90-411-9234-9).
72. Kasper Dziurdź, *Non-discrimination in Tax Treaty Law and World Trade Law: The Impact of Formal, Substantive and Subjective Approaches*, 2019 (ISBN 978-94-035-0904-4).
73. Félix Daniel Martínez Laguna, *Hybrid Financial Instruments, Double Nontaxation and Linking Rules*, 2019 (ISBN 978-94-035-1074-3).
74. Jan Gooijer, *Tax Treaty Residence of Entities*, 2019 (ISBN 978-94-035-1301-0).
75. John Abrahamson, *International Taxation of Banking*, 2020 (ISBN 978-94-035-1094-1).
76. Richard Krever & François Vaillancourt (eds), *The Allocation of Multinational Business Income: Reassessing the Formulary Apportionment Option*, 2020 (ISBN 978-94-035-0614-2).
77. Ajit Kumar Singh, *Exploring the Nexus Doctrine in International Tax Law*, 2021 (ISBN 978-94-035-3363-6).
78. Galya Savir, *Regulation and Tax in Space*, 2021 (ISBN 978-94-035-3393-3).
79. Rita Julien, *Credit Method Compatibility and Constraints under EU Law: An Analysis of the Case Law of the CJEU*, 2022 (ISBN 978-94-035-2363-7).
80. Sergio André Rocha & Allison Christians (eds), *A Multilateral Convention for Tax: From Theory to Implementation*, 2022 (ISBN 978-90-411-9428-2).
81. Brigitte Alepin, Lyne Latulippe & Louise Otis (eds), *Coordination and Cooperation: Tax Policy in the 21st Century*, 2022 (ISBN 978-94-035-3740-5).
82. Chunyang Zhang, *The Role of Tax Law in Mergers and Acquisitions: A Chinese Perspective*, 2022 (ISBN 978-94-035-3741-2).

83. Florian Navisotschnigg, *Substance in International Tax Law: DEMPE Approach, Substantial Activity Requirement and Beneficial Ownership*, 2022 (ISBN 978-94-035-4895-1).
84. Mees Vergouwen, *The Effect of Directives Within the Area of Direct Taxation on the Interpretation and Application of Tax Treaties*, 2023 (ISBN 978-94-035-0907-5).
85. Rachna Matabudul, *Tax Treaty Dispute Resolution: Lessons from the Law of the Sea*, 2023 (ISBN 978-94-035-3407-7).
86. David Orzechowski-Zölzer, *The Taxation of Fees for Technical Services on the Basis of Article 12A UN Model Convention*, 2024 (ISBN 978-94-035-4297-3).

www.ingramcontent.com/pod-product-compliance
Lightning Source LLC
Chambersburg PA
CBHW071241230926
51849CB00001B/190
9789403542973